Financial Macroeconomics

Financial Macroeconomics

Jan Kregel

ANTHEM PRESS

Anthem Press
An imprint of Wimbledon Publishing Company
www.anthempress.com

This edition first published in UK and USA 2024
by ANTHEM PRESS
75–76 Blackfriars Road, London SE1 8HA, UK
or PO Box 9779, London SW19 7ZG, UK
and
244 Madison Ave #116, New York, NY 10016, USA

British Library Cataloguing-in-Publication Data
A catalogue record for this book is available from the British Library.

Library of Congress Cataloging-in-Publication Data: 2023943638
A catalog record for this book has been requested.

ISBN-13: 978-1-83999-033-5 (Hbk)
ISBN-10: 1-83999-033-3 (Hbk)

This title is also available as an e-book.

CONTENTS

INTRODUCTION

When I arrived as a research student under Joan Robinson's supervision in the University of Cambridge Faculty of Economics and Politics in the late 1960s the capital theory controversies were still dominating students and faculty discussions. These debates had only arrived on the periphery of graduate education in the US, but I had the benefit of what was then considered an alternative training in Keynes from Paul Davidson's tutelage which required detailed knowledge of Keynes' *Treatise on Money* and *General Theory* supplemented by Sidney Weintraub's influence on Davidson and Smolensky's Aggregate Supply and Demand textbook presentation of Keynes. How Joan Robinson's "big book", as the *Accumulation of Capital* was known, fit into this framework was far from clear to Davidson and his students. In the US economists were more concerned with the impact of the "classical dichotomy" on Keynes's monetary theory.

In England the focus was on the derivation of an alternative to the marginal theory of distribution implicit in the capital aggregate in the production function represented by Keynesian aggregate theories of growth and distribution formulated by Kaldor, Robinson and Kalecki. By the time I arrived in Cambridge criticism of capital theory had evolved to accommodate the more direct attack based on Sraffa's *Production of Commodities,* reinforced by Pierangelo Garegnani's own developments and presence to highlight the lacunae in marginal price theory. The state of the debate was presented in Geoff Harcourt's popular representation in *Some Cambridge Controversies in the Theory of Capital.*

At the time it was common to refer to all this as the "Anglo-Italian" theory, but there was little that was common to the two approaches. Joan Robinson sat in the centre of this combination, having credited Sraffa with the hint that produced her classic book on imperfect competition, while adopting a Marshallian framework, which the same work by Sraffa had criticized, as the framework for understanding the generalization of the *General Theory* to the long period reflecting Harrodian dynamics. My arrival in Cambridge was to understand where money and uncertainty fit into all this, but instead my attention was refocused on answering the question of "what determines the rate of profit" – which implicitly bridged the differences between the attack on one-commodity models with aggregate capital and the alternative Italian criticism since the response required an understanding of the denominator. Joan Robinson eventually found it difficult to renounce a Marshallian reading of Keynes and opted for History to replace equilibrium. I rather opted for the theory of money as the centre of the problem, rather than the theory of capital, finding Sandro Roncaglia's reading of Sraffa as representing a snapshot of the historical movement in which one could insert a Keynesian theory of interest and demand.

The Cambridge version of these debates, in opposition to the Harvard MIT defense of the marginal approach, eventually came to be known as "post Keynesian", largely because of a review summary published in the *Journal of Economic Literature* written with Al Eichner. The term was not very informative (and generated a debate about hyphenation) since the term had been common in post-war analysis and extension of Keynes and Kenneth Kurihara (whose macro lectures I had also attended before Davidson's seminars) had already produced a collection with that title. My subsequent attempt to provide an Introduction to this approach in the early 1970s carried the title "Reconstruction of Political Economy" in an effort to stretch the Keynesian roots to cover the neo-Ricardian classical aspects.

The essays reprinted in Part One of this collection provide further elaboration on the attempt to avoid what I believed to be a misunderstanding of Keynes's theory as 'short period', in contrast to its extension to the Marshalling long period to deal with issues of growth and distribution. The first paper, which appeared as the lead article in the *Economic Journal* in 1976 is really only a suggestion that chapter 18 of the *General Theory* allows an alternative to surpass the Marshallian methodology which was still present in Cambridge despite Sraffa's critique. The second and third chapter are more pedagogical attempts to explain how the approach differs from what was then the mainstream neoclassical synthesis with emphasis on static equilibrium. The fourth recognizes the role of French circuit economists, in particular Alain Parguez, in launching a critique of marginal theory through the elaboration of the *Treatise on Money* concept of the monetary circuit, which built on criticism of Hicks via Clower's dual decision hypothesis and disequilibrium price adjustments. It was subsequently recast by Augusto Graziani under Keynes's term of "monetary production" economics. The aim was to preserve the centrality of liquidity preference in Keynes's approach linking effective demand and price relations. The last piece tries to undermine Samuelson's definition of economics as "science" which provided the framework for the mainstream approach which post-Keynesian theory meant to displace.

The papers in Part Two are representative of the duality in the capital theory criticisms noted above. Extensions of the Sraffian approach adopted the short-long period dichotomy and sought to promote a long-period theory of effective demand buried in Classical theory. In particular the first paper seeks to counter the neoRicardian claim that Keynes's concept of the marginal efficiency of capital allowed the marginal theory of distribution in through the back door so to speak and the appropriate solution was a Classical long period theory represented as a centre of gravity. It also represents the beginning of the attempt to provide a location for discussion of the two approaches in what came to be known as the Trieste Summer School organized by Sergio Parrinello, Pierangelo Garegnani and myself.

The next two essays are again pedagogical pieces seeking to explicate the genesis of effective demand as distinguished from aggregate demand as a national income accounting concept. The next paper in this section, initially presented in Paris at an anniversary celebration of the publication of the *General Theory* organized by Doyen

Alain Barrère of the Sorbonne, was one of the first attempts to emphasise that Keynes did have a micro theory of prices, and that there was a market price adjustment process underlying the operation of the income multiplier. In short, there was something more to Keynesian policy than government fiscal policy: that effective demand to expand output and employment required policies to influence expectations of future prices that correspond to what Keynes had described in the *Treatise* as "normal backwardation." This approach, recognizing the interpretation of Keynes provided by Hugh Townshend, was eventually transformed into the slogan that "liquidity preference is a theory of prices". This is the point where my work left the realm of growth and distribution of the "big book" and joined that of Hy Minsky whom at the time was promoting his explanation of financial fragility with the slogan "liquidity preference is a theory of asset prices." The last essay in this section is an early attempt to generalise the importance of the price theory underlying the Keynesian system.

The elaboration of this approach is reflected in the papers collected in Part Three. There are two central themes represented here. The first is the relation between Keynes and Fisher, which Keynes himself had highlighted, calling Fisher his "great grandparent" and crediting Fisher as the precursor of his marginal efficiency of capital, and the difference reflected in Fisher's time preference representing the intertemporal allocation of economic activity and Keynes liquidity preference as the final critique of the quantity theory of the value of money. The second is the fact that both were active participants in financial markets and were familiar with and developed or used financial instruments in the development of their theories of interest. Both entered economic policy with the discussion of the late 19th century proposals for reform of the gold standard system and the proposal for bimetallism. For Fisher the analysis produced the famous "Fisher Relation" of "Appreciation and Interest" while for Keynes it was the proposal to replace India's silver standard with a gold standard. Both adopted the definition of interest rates as the arithmetical relation of spot and forward prices, both recognized commodity or own rates of interest, and Fisher produced the ideas of forward interest rates and forward rates initiating at future dates to provide every possible way to redistribute income over time. Keynes on the other hand developed the interest rate parity theorem, the theory for the determination of forward and future and options contracts as well as the concept of duration, which became the crux of liquidity preference. Summaries of these similarities and difference are set out in Chapters 11 and 12. The formal similarities between these concepts and the importance of duration are set out in two class notes (Chapters 13 and 14) that I have long used in a course on Financial Macroeconomic. The essay on aspects of a post Keynesian theory of finance (Chapter 15) integrates some of the ideas that are set out more explicitly in the essay on Keynes's contribution to modern economics (Chapter 16). The essay (Chapter 17) on "Instability, Volatility and the Process of Capital Accumulation' uses options contracts to explicate the way Keynes envisaged options theory to explain user costs representing expectations on the supply side and provides the possibility of a measure of the liquidity premium. This section also contains an essay (Chapter 18) on uncertainty and expectations. I have never been invested in the criticism of probability and ergodicity, rather looking more to Keynes's prior work on probability; instead of arguing that money and money contracts were a response to economic uncertainty, as distinguished from risk, and preferring to argue that it was the existence of money that produced uncertainty and instability. To prevent the idea of animal spirits from being classified as irrational or some sort of behavioral imperfection, I coined the term "rational spirits" as promoting decisions taken when there is no possible comparison with past events and the weight of the argument becomes sufficient to justify committing money to finance production activity.

The penultimate entry in this section provides a "tongue in cheek" essay produced in response to Geoff Harcourt's request for an essay on "what Keynes would have thought" of his theory some half century later. It is written from Keynes's point of view. It draws attention to the existence of two alternative methodologies in the book: one Marshallian and the other based on financial instruments represented in Chapter 17 which formed the basis of virtually all the responses Keynes penned in response to critics after the *General Theory* was published. The last essay seeks to point out how the "new" Keynesian explanation of impediments to price adjustments producing market failures has nothing to do with the kind of supply and demand theory that Keynes thought he was developing.

Section four provides some examples of how this alternative interpretation of Keynes's theory of liquidity preference as a theory of prices in policy proposals. Again with emphasis on policy action taken on the influence on expectations of future prices represented in the relation of spot and forward prices that define the rate of interest. The first deals with the place of fiscal policy, and the other two deal with the introduction of zero or negative real interest rates in response to financial crisis in Japan and in the United States, usually buttressed on the basis of Hiscksian ISLL analysis which Keynes rejected. Currently the discussion of the impact of a sustained period of zero or negative rates has reengendered interest in the concept of duration as rising interest rates have had little impact of inflation but the negative impact on bank reserves has led to bank failures.

This book is dedicated to Maurice Townsend, friend and collaborator first of Hyman Minsky and then myself, whose contributions and memory I would like to honour.

References

Robert Clower "The Keynesian Counter-Revolution: A Theoretical Appraisal," in F.H. Hahn and F.P.R. Brechling, ed., *The Theory of Interest Rates*. Macmillan, 1965

Paul Davidson and Eugene Smolensky, *Aggregate Supply and Demand Analysis*, New York, Harper and Row, 1964

Pierangelo Garegnani, *Il Capitale nelle Teorie della Distribuzione*, Roma, 1960

Augusto Graziani, *The Monetary Theory of Production*, Cambridge University Press, 2003

G. C. Harcourt, *Some Cambridge Controversies in the Theory of Capital*. Cambridge: Cambridge University Press, 1972

J A Kregel, *The Reconstruction of Political Economy*, London, Macmillan, 1973

Alain Parguez, *Monnaie et Macroéconomie: Théorie de la monnaie en déséquilibre*, Paris, Económica,1975

Joan Robinson, *The Accumulation of Capital*, London, Macmillan, 1956

______, "Spring Cleaning,"1982

Alessandro Roncaglia, *Sraffa and the Theory of Prices*, Wiley, 1978

Piero Sraffa, *Production of Commodities by Means of Commodities*, Cambridge, 1960.

Sidney Weintraub, *An Approach to the Theory of Income Distribution*, Philadelphia, Chilton, 1958

Part One

METHODOLOGY

Chapter 1

ECONOMIC METHODOLOGY IN THE FACE OF UNCERTAINTY: THE MODELLING METHODS OF KEYNES AND THE POST-KEYNESIANS

Keynes's major contribution to economic theory is often characterised as an emphasis on the possible difference between *ex-ante* decisions and *ex-post* results or on the recognition that, in an uncertain world, expectations may be disappointed. On such an appreciation of Keynes's contribution to economic theory numerous writers have, reasonably, questioned the frequently avowed Keynesian parentage of what has come to be called post-Keynesian (or Cambridge) economic theory. Professor Lachmann[1] maintains that the practitioners of the "Cambridge School" are "ill-equipped to deal with autonomous changes in demand or in the range of divergence of expectations, to which Keynes attributed importance and drew our attention, and on which the pattern of specifying investment decisions depends", and that the approach thus lacks essential factors associated with Keynes's work. Professor Lachmann further maintains that this deficiency is especially visible in the complete reliance of the Cambridge school on static macro equilibrium; a concept that he believes to be non-existent in, and certainly inconsistent with, any economic theory claiming Keynes as parent.

Professor Blaug has recently echoed this particular theme,[2] asserting that post-Keynesian theory has "been no more successful than the orthodox theory in throwing off the straitjacket of equilibrium analysis in conditions of perfect certainty and full information".[3]

Such arguments lead to two conclusions. First, that the post-Keynesian generalisation of the *General Theory* is a sham and neglects the most important aspects of Keynes's work, especially through reliance on steady-state equilibrium models; and secondly, that the use of such an equilibrium approach makes the theory a poor substitute for, if not identical with, the orthodox theory of static equilibrium (cf. Blaug, *op. cit.*, pp. 83–6).

It is the purpose of what follows to show the dubious nature of such conclusions and to demonstrate both how post-Keynesian theory can be seen as a legitimate extension of the basic methodology employed by Keynes in the *General Theory* and that the nature and use of the concept of equilibrium in post-Keynesian theory is unmistakably different from the orthodox nature and use of the concept. The implicit conclusion is, of course, that most critics have seriously misinterpreted Keynes's methodological position in the *General Theory*.

THE PLACE OF EXPECTATIONS

In Keynes's surviving written work there is no indication that he considered expectations as *the* distinguishing feature of his approach. Pride of place was instead reserved for the principle of "effective demand or, more precisely, of the demand schedule for output as a whole". Indeed, expectations and disappointment are consciously made to take second place in relation to the exposition of this principle. "To me, the most extraordinary thing regarded historically, is the disappearance of the theory of demand and supply for output as a whole, i.e. the theory of employment, *after* it had been for a quarter of century the most discussed thing in economics. One of the most important transitions for me, after my *Treatise on Money* had been published, was suddenly realising this."[4] It was this realisation that shifted his work from revision and extension of the theory of money to the development of an original and *general* theory of prices, employment and output as a whole in which there could be no distinction between "monetary" and "real" relations. Keynes moved on to deal with the "monetary production (or entrepreneur) economy", where "money plays a part of its own and affects motives and decisions and is, in short, one of the operative factors in the situation, so that the course of events cannot be predicted, either in the long period or in the short, without a knowledge of the behaviour of money between the first state and the last" (*C.W.* xiii, pp. 408–9) in distinction to a neutral or "real-exchange economy" which recognises money but uses it merely as a neutral link between transactions in real things and real assets and does not allow it to enter into motives or decisions (*ibid.* p. 408). It was in a monetary production economy that effective demand took on importance because of the existence of uncertainty, disappointment and expectations. Thus, underlying the shift of emphasis were two important changes.

(1) *A Shift from Actual to Expected Magnitudes.* In the *Treatise* Keynes felt he had given "insufficient attention to the distinction between actual and anticipated demand" (*C.W.* xiii, p. 434). "I did not in that book distinguish clearly between expected and realised results" (*ibid.* p. 437). Thus the *General Theory* emphasises that the correct magnitude is the expected or anticipated value of a variable, e.g. the expected proceeds of a given volume of employment. Even in an early draft Keynes says explicitly that the dependent variables in his functional relations are "to be interpreted in this context in terms of expectations, i.e. as the expected rates of consumption and investment" (*C.W.* xiii, pp. 441–42).

(2) *A Distinction between Particular Individual (short-period) Expectations and the Effect of the State of "General" (Long-period) Expectations.* In an early draft of the *General Theory* the consumption and investment functions contained an explicit variable, E, to represent the state of long-term expectations which were independent of the system, such that a stochastic change in E could shift the entire functional relation. Only with E assumed given and constant at some particular level could the functions be assumed constant.

It was the express introduction of these two points that underlined the fact that the world that was under analysis was one in which, "the organisations change and develop, information arrives and decisions are taken sequentially. No present moment is like any past moment and organisations and units adapt and re-adapt."[5] But such a picture with unpredictable shifting functions and unforeseen change was ill suited to the exposition of what Keynes felt to be his most fundamental contribution, the principle of effective demand. The problem that had to be faced was "how [the real world] can usefully be tamed to serve the analyst and the practitioner" (*ibid.*), to serve the simple exposition of effective demand in determining the level of employment.

There was one obvious way to resolve the dilemma. Keynes could have assumed away ill-informed expectations and uncertainty; as Blaug says, assume "conditions of perfect certainty and full information". Having worked out the analysis the assumptions could then have been relaxed one by one until reality was approximated: but Keynes realised that this could not easily be done. Moreover, such a course would have been patently inconsistent, for this is the solution that he had accused the proponents of "neutral economy" of adopting: and which was then, and is now, the basis of the current orthodoxy, and which effectively obliterated the problems that Keynes was trying to bring into the scope of analysis. Indeed, such a method would have implied rejecting those very features which he considered crucial in a monetary production economy, and without which there would be no need for a theory of effective demand, since under such neutral conditions all money income would be fully spent on current output.[6]

Keynes thus had to find another way to "tame" the real world. The method that he adopted represents one of the most essential and most often overlooked differences between post-Keynesian and neoclassical methodology.

ASSUMPTIONS ABOUT EXPECTATIONS

Keynes chose to make assumptions, not about the absence of false expectations and uncertainty in the economy under consideration, thus creating an economy with perfect information and certainty, but rather to assume that although expectations and uncertainty are always present, yet different assumptions could be made about the constancy of expectations and their effect on the system. It is not the assumptions made about the economy under analysis that are different, but the assumptions made about expectations in an economy in which these play an integral part.

The simplest solution seemed to be to assume that the general long-period state of expectations was given and constant. This assumption of constant long-period expectations allowed the specification of simple, continuous functional relationships which constantly shifting long-period expectations would have made impossible. Keynes could thus "lock-up" this effect of general expectations and uncertainty without assuming that they did not exist. He could then proceed to analyse the results of alternative differing given and constant states of expectations, rather than first analysing an economy assuming perfect information and certainty, and then trying to adapt this analysis to study a "realistic" model of the real world.

Keynes made this assumption of constant long-period expectations. "Having, however, made clear the part played by *expectations* in the economic nexus and the reaction of realised results on future expectations, it will then be safe for us in what follows often to discard express reference to expectations. It is important to make the logical point clear and to define the terminology precisely so that it will apply without ambiguity in all cases" (*C.W.* xiv, p. 397). The assumption thus meant remembering at the back of our minds that "we shall not in any way be precluded from regarding the propensity itself as subject to change" (*C.W.* xiii, p. 440) due to a change in general expectations when faced with analysing the real world. The assumption of constant expectations is obviously something quite different from the assumptions of perfect foresight and certainty.

At the same time, such an assumption leaves open the possibility that particular individual expectations are free to be disappointed, but that such possible disappointment will not react on the general state of expectations which is, under this assumption, independent of the disappointment of particular expectations.

Thus, while considering the importance of expectations and the difference between expected and actual results in influencing expectations, Keynes felt that these parts of the economic nexus could be held in abeyance in order to give full scope to the demonstration of the role played by effective demand in the determination of employment, thus allowing a clear demonstration that the system could produce an equilibrium position with less than full employment. The relative importance of long- and short-period expectations are thus given varying weight in the *General Theory* and at certain points in the book Keynes does not make it clear what he is assuming about each. The most usual tactic was to hold the state of long-term expectations (the state of the news) constant when talking of functional relationships (hoping, with "the introduction of user cost and the marginal efficiency of capital" to give a role to expectation "whilst reducing to a minimum the necessary degree of adaptation" of the orthodox theory (*G.T.* p. 146), but occasionally introducing the effects of disappointment of particular expectations into the discussion of the position of equilibrium of the stable functions (i.e. assuming independence between disappointment and shifts in long-term expectations)). This rather confusing mix, in which particular expectations could be disappointed, but could not affect long-term expectations which by assumption were held constant, Keynes found to be unsatisfactory, since readers of his book still seemed to credit to expectations what they should have credited to the theory of effective demand. This led Keynes to comment in his 1937 lectures that, "if I were writing the book again I should begin by setting forth my theory on the assumption that short-period expectations were always fulfilled; and then have a subsequent chapter showing what differences it makes when short-period expectations are disappointed. For other economists, I find, lay the whole emphasis, and find the whole explanation in the *differences* between effective demand and income; and they are so convinced that this is the right course that they do not notice that in my treatment this is *not* so." Such an assumption, Keynes felt, would pinpoint the essential "operative factor" as "effective demand" for "the theory of effective demand is substantially the same if we assume that short-period expectations are always fulfilled" (*C.W.* xiv, p. 181). Thus, "The main point is to distinguish the forces determining the position of equilibrium [point of effective demand] from the technique of trial and error by means of which the entrepreneur discovers where the position is" (i.e. the revision of expectations in the face of realised results) (*ibid.* p. 182). Such a division would allow greater emphasis on the basic point that "the economic system may find itself in stable equilibrium with N at a level below full employment, namely at the level given by the intersection of the aggregate demand function on the aggregate supply function" (*G.T.* p. 30). Keynes's theory could thus be stated without reference to the Swedish approach for "*ex ante* decisions in their influence on effective demand relate solely to *entrepreneurs*' decisions", the disappointment of expectations influences the next *ex-ante* decisions, but even on the assumption, "of the identity of *ex post* and *ex ante* my theory remains . . . I should have distinguished more sharply between a theory based on *ex ante* effective demand, however arrived at, and a psychological chapter indicating *how* the business world reaches its *ex ante* decisions" (*C.W.* xiv, pp. 182–3).

Thus in the *General Theory* Keynes presents a world in which long-period expectations may shift quite independently of strictly economic results; where short-period expectations about particular results may be disappointed (and may affect long-period expectations). His "tamed" model assumes that long-period expectations are constant and disappointed; short-period expectations do not reflect on long-period expectations. In the lecture notes he suggests a third possibility of assuming that long-period expectations are constant and that short-period expectations are *always* realised in order to put expectations into the back seat, giving all the emphasis to effective demand. It was this purely static model, divorced from disappointment and shifts in expectations, that Keynes finally preferred to use for demonstrating that unemployment was not a short-run disequilibrium phenomenon, that it was not the result of the booms and slumps that might result from inexact entrepreneurial expectations,[7] and that in theory the system could settle in equilibrium at almost any level of employment between zero and full employment. The emphasis that is commonly placed on the possible divergence of *ex-ante* and *ex-post* values and on the possible disappointment of expectations as *the* crucial factors in Keynes contribution seems both misplaced and historically inaccurate.

KEYNES'S THREE MODELS

The foregoing account suggests that Keynes may have had in mind three distinct classes of models of the economy: two which he used explicitly in the *General Theory,* and the third which he suggested in the 1937 Lectures. These three models differ, not in the existence or absence of expectations, disappointment and uncertainty, but in terms of the various assumptions made about the effect of these phenomena on the system. Let us recall the expectational factors that Keynes considered important:

(a) The state of general or long-period expectations is independent of the system and may shift autonomously in reaction to economic or non-economic factors and will be a major determinant of the marginal efficiency of capital, liquidity preference and the propensity to consume.
(b) Individual, particular short-period expectations may be disappointed.
(c) Disappointment of expectations in (*b*) may affect (*a*) and vice versa.

The three models can be distinguished by the different assumptions made about these three properties of a monetary production system.

1. The Model of Static Equilibrium – 1937

The state of general expectations is given and constant at a particular level. They do not respond to individual realised short-period expectations which are, by assumption, always realised. Thus the aggregate demand and supply functions once drawn up for a given state of general expectations are fixed and cannot shift; the system moves instantly to the point of effective demand. This, Keynes felt, was the most suitable way to show that the point of effective demand could occur at less than full employment for a given state of expectation, and this was *irrespective* of the process by which the system reacted to disappointed expectations. The theory of effective demand could thus be set out without the concepts of *ex-ante* and *ex-post,* and with expectations always realised; but without having to assume that there was perfect certainty or that the whole future was perfectly known.[8]

2. The Model of Stationary Equilibrium

Here the state of general expectations is still held constant so that functional relations can be specified, since present disappointment, which can now exist, is assumed to have no effect on long-period expectations. It is this model that Keynes relies upon, for the first 18 chapters of the *General Theory,* as the basic expository device for the demonstration of the principle of effective demand as the main determinant of the level of employment. The method of operation of this model was to compare different given and constant long-period levels of expectations (cf. *G.T.* p. 48, and note 1) while at the same time allowing for the fact that short-period expectations were subject to disappointment. Disappointed entrepreneurs could then revise their expectations of the point of effective demand and their employment decisions until, by trial and error, they hit on the point of effective demand, i.e. they could shift position on the aggregate supply curve without the curve itself actually shifting.[9]

It is obvious, however, that this was the only solution if Keynes was to emphasise uncertainty and expectations as a prerequisite for the theory of effective demand and allow shifts along functions without bringing shifts in the functions themselves. It was the only way both could be kept in the spotlight as mutual co-determinants. Unfortunately, Keynes often changed what he was assuming about expectations to suit a particular purpose and, in general, when making statements about general policy he often slipped into adopting the assumptions of the third model.

3. The Model of Shifting Equilibrium

This is Keynes's complete dynamic model where current disappointment may affect the state of general expectations and thus the independent expectational functions are free to shift over time; where expectations normally are disappointed. Here failure to hit on the point of effective demand may mean not only that the system has missed the intersection of the aggregate demand and supply curves, but that this will cause the curves themselves to shift, since their underlying determinants (propensity to consume, liquidity preference, marginal efficiency of capital) will be readjusting to disappointment (and this is in addition to any shift which is independent of these factors).

By taking as the objective the real world in which uncertainty is an integral part, the different models are made to refer, not to differences in what is to be described, but to what conditions the observers foresee in the real world; for "it is not the economy under observation which is moving in the one case and stationary in the other, but our expectations of the future environment which are shifting in one case and stationary in the other" (*C.W.* xiv, p. 511). This distinction is also noted in the *General Theory* (*G.T.* p. 293) in terms of a "line of division between the theory of stationary equilibrium and the theory of shifting equilibrium – meaning by the latter the theory of a system in which changing views about the future are capable of influencing the present situation".[10] In such a world expectations are not always realised and actual proceeds may not be what had been expected. Entrepreneurs observe their errors through changes in desired inventories, or changes in order books, and responses are made as the general state of expectations interacts with present realisations. The system will be shifting along the aggregate supply and demand curves at the same time as these curves will themselves be shifting their positions as the system reacts to disappointment of the two types of expectations. The extreme complexity of such a situation explains why Keynes was willing to "tame" this system, first making assumptions that allowed the definition of functions that he knew did not exist through their entire range, expressly in order to give force to the theory of effective demand. Here the Swedish concepts of *ex-ante* and *ex-post* were of little use, for the impact of any specific set of expectations could not be accurately calculated in a real-world situation since the assumptions of the stationary equilibrium model were insufficient for obtaining a full explanation of the interactions of the economic nexus.

In the shifting equilibrium model entrepreneurs may carry out plans that lead to realised effective demand (with its associated actual rate of growth) which differs from the level of effective demand that would result if plans were realised (as Keynes stressed in a letter to Harrod (*C.W.* xiv, p. 322), "*ex-ante* is what entrepreneurs plan to do, not what they ought to do to assure the equality *of ex-ante* and *ex-post*"). Keynes thus suggested that the growth rate associated with realisation of expectations be called the "warranted" rate of growth (*ibid.*), adding that if the actual rate is different from the warranted rate and expectations are not given, the reaction of economic agents might be to rethink their overall expectations which might lead to further divergence between the actual and warranted rate as the warranted rate itself shifts to what Keynes christened a "temporarily warranted rate" (*ibid.*) (explaining his reluctance to accept Harrod's definition of warranted growth).

On this view entrepreneurs take actions based on expectations regarding an uncertain future. If, by chance, the actions of entrepreneurs are compatible in the aggregate, the economy will be on the warranted or equilibrium path (but this need not imply full employment). If, on the other hand, initial plans are disappointed then equilibrium can be obtained, after a period of historical time, *only* if it is assumed that despite entrepreneurial realisation of mistakes, the state of short-period expectations is independent of general expectations, so that entrepreneurs persist in their beliefs until equilibrium is established by trial and error. This was a process which Keynes did not expect to occur naturally in any real economy, but which his stationary model allowed to occur for pedagogical purposes.

If, however, realisation of error alters the state of expectations and shifts the independent behavioural functions, Keynes's model of shifting equilibrium will describe an actual path of an economy over time chasing an ever-changing equilibrium – it need never catch it.

We can characterise the three models in terms of the three expectational factors given above.

	(*a*) Long-period expectations	(*b*) Short-period expectations	(*c*) Interaction of long- and short-period expectations
Static model	Constant at a given level	Realised	Independent
Stationary model	Constant at a given level	May be disappointed	Independent
Shifting model	Shifting over time	Disappointed	Interdependent

This approach to modelling is, however, conceptually distinct from the manner of use of equilibrium to tame the system adopted in most other approaches from the monetarist to general equilibrium. It is, however, consistent with the methodology used by the post-Keynesian writers who employ models of tranquillity, which are identical with the model of stationary equilibrium or with models of warranted growth which require a mix of the static and stationary models. Whereas Joan Robinson prefers to put the example in terms of two economies with different rates of investment, Keynes would have used the stationary model with two different levels of expectations to trace out the long-period path compatible with each set of expectations (*G.T.* p. 48). The underlying methodology is exactly the same.[11] The differences that do exist lie in the problems chosen for analysis.

THE FORMATION OF A MODEL: CHOOSING DEPENDENT, GIVEN AND INDEPENDENT VARIABLES

Although Keynes believed his model to be general[12] he used it to analyse a specific problem, the determination of the level of money income and employment. The choice of the problem to be analysed to a large extent determines what variables are to be classed as independent, given and dependent in Keynes's methodology.

"The division of the determinants of the economic system into the two groups of given factors and independent variables is, of course, quite arbitrary from any absolute standpoint. The division must be made entirely on the basis of experience, so as to correspond on the one hand to the factors in which the changes seem to be slow or so little relevant as to have only a small and comparatively negligible short-term influence on our *quaesitum;* and on the other hand to those factors in which the changes are found in practice to exercise a dominant influence on our *quaesitum*. Our present object is to discover what determines at any time the national income of a given economic system and (which is almost the same thing) the amount of its employment; which means in a study so complex as economics, in which we cannot hope to make completely accurate generalisations, the factors whose changes *mainly* determine our *quaesitum*. Our final task might be to select those variables which can be deliberately controlled or managed by central authority in the kind of system in which we actually live" (*G.T.* p. 247, cf. *C.W.* xiii, pp. 481–3). Keynes's particular *quaesitum* was the determination of the volume of employment and money national income. In this context he believed that the following factors could be considered as given:

(1) The existing skill and quantity of labour.
(2) The existing quality and quantity of productive equipment.
(3) The existing techniques of production.
(4) The degree of competition.[13]
(5) The tastes and habits of consumers.
(6) The disutility of different intensities of labour and activities of supervision and organisation.

These factors are considered as given but not necessarily constant, by which Keynes meant that the effect and consequences of changes in them were not under consideration. The given factors then "influence our independent variables, but do not completely determine them" (*G.T.* p. 246). Keynes's basic independent variables are the three psychological relations: the propensity to consume, the marginal efficiency of capital, and liquidity preference; along with the wage unit and the quantity of money as determined by the Central Bank.[14] It is in the formulation of the three independent "psychological" variables that expectations play the crucial role in the system. In the stationary model a given level of expectation gives constant values for the independent variables in the system. In the shifting model the independent variables are free to move independently of the performance of the system itself.

This is then the division that Keynes believed to be the most useful for the analysis of his dependent variables, but the framework is general in the sense that it can be rearranged like a puzzle to investigate other dependent variables, requiring, naturally, a different division of the determinants of the economic system as between given factors and independent variables[15] (or, used to analyse, one at a time, different *quaesita*).

It seems obvious that the study of growth and capital accumulation, for example, requires productive capacity to become a dependent variable instead of being given: liquidity preference may become a datum as well as the propensity to consume. Population must be assumed to be constant or growing in a specified manner. The independent variable is then the marginal efficiency of capital or "animal spirits". One can then analyse the system with a stationary equilibrium approach, by looking at the effect of two different given constant levels of expectations on the rate of change of the quantity of productive equipment. Or one might prefer to look at the development of two different economies, say alpha and beta, where the entrepreneurs in alpha have higher "animal spirits" than those in beta (as in, for example, Joan Robinson, *op. cit.*).

Likewise the direct analyses of distribution, technical progress, the determination of prices and markups would require their own particular divisions of the determinants of the economic system. Such an extension of Keynes's model to analyse these various problems has been the goal of post-Keynesian theory. The post-Keynesian approach is simply to use the general model of the *General Theory* to expand the analysis to cover different questions by taking the determinants of the Theory in different combinations. It is thus in no sense "ill-equipped", and has simply chosen to analyse additional problems because all the problems of interest cannot be analysed under Keynesian methodology at the same time nor with the same division of the economic determinants.[16]

This view provides an explanation of Professor Robinson's often repeated *caveat* that the analysis of steady growth has to be fully worked out and understood before moves can be made to the analysis of dynamic change over time (as well as of her occasional excursions into the analysis of change over time). She is simply saying that the analysis must first be fully worked out on the level of Keynes's stationary model before we can hope to try a hand at the analysis of the shifting model, for it is indeed that model which she, like Keynes, has in the back of the mind when passing occasional *obiter dicta* about actual change in the system. Thus, as Keynes reminds us, the examination of any actual problem can be eased by putting it first in the form of the stationary model and then passing to the shifting position where, "not one of the factors is not liable to change without much warning, and sometimes substantially. Hence the extreme complexity of the actual course of events" (*G.T.* p. 249).

THE SPECIFICATION OF MODEL EQUILIBRIUM

Professor Blaug would thus seem to have mistaken the "strait jacket", since the particular one to which he refers was never worn and thus need not be thrown off. Further developments of the theory are then not to be found, as Blaug (*op. cit.* pp. 82–3) and Brown (*op. cit.* p. 487) suggest, in the writings of Clower and Grossman, nor of Phelps nor of Arrow. For post-Keynesian theory the next step is not disequilibrium, but the model of shifting equilibrium in a monetary-production economy. But before that, to echo a familiar theme, the full analysis of the stationary monetary-production economy must be carried out and understood, for it is on this basis that the full model of shifting equilibrium will be seen and understood. It is doubtful whether the disequilibrium exchange mechanics of a "neutral" system will be of crucial importance for this task, for the simple reason that it takes a non-Keynesian specification of equilibrium as its starting point.[17]

The basic question that remains is the one well-posed by Hahn: how best to "tame" the real world to make it amenable to analysis and understanding. The early neoclassical economists thought that the best way to tame the world was to start with the analysis of the economy of Robinson Crusoe, extending it to a world of perfect competition and perfect foresight. The most recent development of this line of thought is to assume a given number of goods distinguished one from the other by their physical property, by their location in space and in time and by the state of the world, with "a price defined for each good".[18] One can then demonstrate the conditions that would be required for the decisions of households and firms to be mutually consistent such that for no good does demand exceed supply at the assumed prices. Information about all possible present and future prices and the costs and availability of contingent actions is perfect and costless. All actions take place at a point in time and contain contingent elements (*ibid.* p. 15).

Such a position has been described as one in which, "every feature of an actual economy which Keynes regarded as important is missing" (*ibid.* p. 34). For if actions are sequential and "states depend on the actions of agents, some contingent markets could not logically exist" (*ibid.* p. 15). The theory as currently expounded is not yet in a position to involve sequence or "the description of the terminal state of economic processes" (*ibid.* p. 15). In short it cannot meaningfully relax the "taming" assumption of certainty and foresight (this is the main preoccupation of chapter 14 of Arrow and Hahn, *op. cit.*). It was the appropriateness of the assumption of perfect foresight within the analysis of a monetary-production economy that Keynes called into question in the *General Theory* for it depicted behaviour only likely to be found in a "lunatic asylum" – money and uncertainty could find no meaningful place in such a world where money was by definition "neutral". Instead Keynes chose to take the world as it was and to make an objective choice of the variables to be analysed (employment and money income) dividing the determining variables into those which could be considered given for the purpose of the analysis and those which were to be taken as independent – primarily the state of long-period expectations.

Instead of assuming that the future was known (or that there were sufficient future markets and that all future prices could be taken as known) he maintained the assumption that it was in the nature of a monetary economy that the future could not be known. He chose instead to work out the effects of different states of expectations on employment and income under the provisional assumption that differences between expectations and realisations would not affect general expectations – that is, to work with a model of stationary equilibrium. This is precisely the position and assumption that underlies the use of tranquility in the method of comparative dynamics in the post-Keynesian models, but with a different choice of given and dependent variables.[19]

The full model for analysing a monetary economy can be achieved by allowing disappointment of expectations to interact with the general state of expectations which is free to shift autonomously as well in what Keynes called his model of shifting equilibrium (*G.T.* p. 293). In such an approach one does not "tame" the problems of the real world by creating and analysing a world in which they are absent, and then searching for the minimum conditions for the existence of such a world. Rather one attempts to make an ordering of the categories of the real world that are the object of analysis. One need not assume that the world is different from what it actually is and then try to find the conditions required for that other world to actually exist, but rather one may simply look at the actual world in a number of stages with different orderings of that actual world, so as to analyse particular effects within it. This distinction could indeed be seen as nothing more than that between the Marshallian and Walrasian method.

CONCLUDING REMARKS

It has been argued above that the methodology that Keynes chose in confronting the analysis of an uncertain world was in terms of alternative specifications about the effects of uncertainty and disappointment and not in terms of their existence or absence. His procedure can be characterised in terms of three models of equilibrium, a static, a stationary, and a shifting equilibrium model, each depicting different assumptions about the effect of uncertainty and disappointment. This procedure produces an alternative approach to the concept of equilibrium which is, in addition, incompatible with the concepts *ex-ante* and *ex-post*. In fact, Keynes argued that his approach could not assume perfect foresight and full information, for under such an assumption his main theoretical contribution, the theory of effective demand, had no meaning.

Further, the paper argues that Keynes's own view of his general theoretical approach was that it could be used to analyse a range of problems in addition to that which he found most pressing, i.e. the determination of the level of output and employment. Different problems would, however, require different basic assumptions about the dependent, given, and independent variables in the system.

Finally, it is argued that what has come to be called "Cambridge" or " post-Keynesian" theory can be viewed as an attempt to analyse various different economic problems, e.g. capital accumulation, income distribution, etc., through the methodology of Keynes's "stationary model".

It would then appear to be a disservice to both Keynes's methodology and that of the post-Keynesian writers to accuse them of some other parentage, or as some recent critics have done to bracket their writings with orthodox approaches in terms of their use of equilibrium. Their basic methodology is distinctly different as also is the concept of equilibrium which results therefrom. One may believe that further exploration of the orthodox approach may be useful. This does not alter the fact that it has not yet succeeded in relaxing its taming assumption concerning perfect foresight and uncertainty, nor that this is a drawback (strait jacket) that cannot be attributed to Keynes nor the post-Keynesians. Those who do see such similarities have seriously misunderstood the methodology of the economics of uncertainty and the specification of equilibrium that corresponds to this methodology.

APPENDIX

For those who consider *ex-ante* and *ex-post* as ideas crucial to the exposition of the Keynesian system, Keynes's reasons for rejecting the concepts may be instructive as well as shedding light on why he chose the particular treatment of uncertainty that he did. The explanation is bound up with the conception of time. Keynes recognised that the essence of the problems of uncertainty and expectations is that time elapses between the taking of a decision and the ultimate outcome of the decision and further that the outcome itself may occur through a passage of time. Drawing the distinction between *ex-ante* and *ex-post* concepts is one way of making this point, none the less Keynes rejected this method because the passage of time between the decision and the outcome "was incapable of being made precise" (*C.W.* xiv, p. 179). If this passage of time could not be made precise, then there could be no definite way to link a particular decision to a particular outcome or to prove that there was a "definite relationship between aggregate effective demand at one time and aggregate income at some later time". This impossibility led Keynes to reject the Swedish approach "owing to my failure to establish any definite unit of time". In this context Keynes says "I used to speak of the period between expectation and result as 'funnels of process', but the fact that the funnels are all of different lengths and overlap one another meant that at any given time there was no aggregate realised result capable of being compared with some aggregate expectation at some earlier date" (*C.W.* xiv, pp. 184–5).[20] Given that one could identify an *ex-ante* expectation one could never be sure of identifying a particular *ex-post* result to be linked with that expectation.

Keynes thus substituted his stationary model which allows, although in a very arbitrary but exact way, the tracing through of the influence of any given state of aggregate expectations to the "long-period level of employment" associated with it. Accordingly he chose to define the short-run in terms of "the shortest interval after which a firm is free to revise its decisions as to how much employment to offer. It is, so to speak, the minimum effective unit of economic time" (*G.T.* p. 47, n. 1). Cf. also *C.W.* xiv, p. 333: "The relevant unit of time is presumably the interval which has to elapse before previous decisions can be effectively revised in the light of current facts." In setting up the stationary model he then assumed "a state of expectation to continue for a sufficient length of time for the effect on employment to have worked itself out so completely . . . The steady level of employment thus obtained may be called the long-period level of employment corresponding to that state of expectation" (*G.T.* p. 48). And even though "expectation may change so frequently that the actual level of employment has never had time to reach the long-period employment corresponding to the existing state of expectation, nevertheless every state of expectation has its definite corresponding level of long-period employment" (*ibid.* p. 48). In this way the relation between expectation and result could be made precise.[21]

In addition Keynes seemed to believe that it was not too far removed from reality to assume that short- and long-period expectations were more or less independent (i.e. that the system could shift along the aggregate supply and demand curves groping for the point of effective demand without the curves bodily shifting due to a change in expectations). If we think of the problem as follows the reasoning may become clear. Consider the producer of electrical power. Short-period expectation determines how many kilowatts he expects to produce and how much labour he wants to hire to produce them, given capacity. Long-period expectations determine how much capacity he should have at various future dates and determine overall investment decisions and plans. If in one quarter demand for electricity falls by 5%, is this likely to cause a revision of long-period expectations of required future capacity? Keynes answers no; thus an unrealised short-period expectation is independent of long-period expectation, "for it is of the nature of long-term expectations that they cannot be checked at short intervals in the light of realised results" (*G.T.* p. 51).

As a matter of everyday occurrence Keynes believed that entrepreneurs "do not, as a rule, make wildly wrong forecasts of the equilibrium position" (*C.W.* xiv, p. 182). But because of the difficulty of ascertaining the position "in practice there is a large overlap between the effects on employment of the realised sale-proceeds of recent output and those of the sale-proceeds expected from current output; and producers' forecasts are more often gradually modified in the light of results than in anticipation of prospective changes", so that, "expected and realised results run into and overlap one another in their influence" (*G.T.* pp. 50–1). On this view Keynes could merge the expected and realised demand functions as being nearly identical. Entrepreneurs had a reasonable idea of the *shape* of the aggregate demand curve and Keynes felt that the existence of this knowledge was quite independent of both their ability to predict and their actions to determine the *position* of the curve on the aggregate supply functions. This, of course, does not imply that long-period expectations are fixed, just that they may be more directly affected by factors other than disappointment of short-period expectations, and thus that long-period expectations must be explicitly taken into account.

Notes

1 *Macro-economic Thinking and the Market Economy,* Hobart Paper No. 56 (London, Institute of Economic Affairs, 1973), p. 51.
2 *The Cambridge Revolution,* Hobart Paperback No. 6 (London, IEA, 1974), p. 82.
3 Professor Brown takes the argument one step further intimating that post-Keynesian theory *stops* at "Comparative dynamics which is little more than comparative statics in a steady growth world" and thus does not even allow "truly dynamic considerations" (*Journal of Economic Literature,* vol. xiii, June 1975, p. 487).
4 *The Collected Writings of John Maynard Keynes,* vol. xiv (London: Macmillan, 1973), p. 85. Further references to this edition will be indicated as *C.W.* followed by the volume number, except for the *General Theory* which will be indicated as *G. T.*
5 F. H. Hahn, "The Winter of Our Discontent", *Economica,* vol. xl (August 1973), p. 326.
6 R. B. Bryce, Notes of Keynes's Lectures, 23 October 1933 (mimeo, Cambridge).
7 The traditional explanation of unemployment linked the mistaken expectations of entrepreneurs (too optimistic in the boom and too pessimistic in the slump) to fluctuations in output and employment. See, for example, F. Lavington, *The Trade Cycle* (London: P. S. King, 1922), who gives the view that "these cyclical changes of business activity are probably the most important single cause of unemployment" (p. 16) and that these cyclical changes in "the current activity of business depends on the estimates made by business men of future market conditions, and that these estimates in their turn are affected materially by the general state of confidence in the business outlook" (p. 29) while "the principal influence lies in the tendency of confidence to rise or fall cumulatively". In his Preface Lavington indicates this to be a summary of views held by Marshall, Pigou, Robertson, W. C. Mitchell and Aftalion. Keynes could thus hardly claim anything novel in his emphasis on expectations (the passage quoted from Lavington covers the two points listed on page 8 above!), nor is it surprising that many of Keynes's contemporaries, thus mistaking his message, could find little new in his explanation of unemployment except a lot of new names for old concepts.
8 This seems to be similar to what Professor Hahn has called a "notional system" where "Current demand for inputs is thus a function of expected future sales", and "routine behaviour" (constancy of the form of the expectation function) is possible. It should be noted, however, that the form of the problem differs. Keynes derives those positions of equilibrium that would result from various assumptions about expectations while Professor Hahn enquires into what assumptions about expectations will be compatible with various equilibria, or more generally what sets of individual plans are mutually consistent over time. Keynes is more preoccupied with the analysis of the process by which the economic system makes inconsistent plans consistent. Cf. F. H. Hahn, "Expectations and Equilibrium", *Economic Journal,* vol. lxii, December 1952, p. 806.
9 Which obviously implies that factor (*c*) outlined above does not hold – a state of affairs that led to much confusion and Keynes's eventual rejection of this model in favour of the static model for the exposition of the principle of effective demand. Keynes seems, however, to

have thought the assumption reasonably realistic (cf. Appendix, below). Hahn's analysis (*ibid.*) would seem to imply that such inconsistent short-period expectations would "exclude the possibility of equilibrium" (p. 808) unless there was an appropriate adjustment in the form of the expectations function (cf. p. 813). In this context it is interesting to note the assumption employed by Joan Robinson in *The Accumulation of Capital* (London: Macmillan, 1956, p. 67): "when something occurs which causes change, we assume that expectations are immediately adjusted, and that no further change is expected".

10 Thus such a position is neither short- nor long-period equilibrium in Hahn's sense (*ibid.* p. 806), but it is compatible with the statement that "short-run instability does not necessarily imply long-run instability" (*ibid.* p. 818). Here a "new model" is set up for every shift in expectation, and although Keynes believed expectations to be volatile he also believed the system to be "not violently unstable" (*G.T.* p. 249).

11 This method is simply the third of Marshall's "three familiar scientific methods", i.e. "to find two cases which resemble one another in every respect except that one cause is present in one of them but not in the other. Then by holding the cases up to the light, as it were, against one another the effect of that cause is made to stand out." Marshall's Inaugural lecture: "The Present Position of Economics" reprinted in A. C. Pigou (ed.), *Memorials of Alfred Marshall* (London: F. Cass, 1956), p. 168.

12 Keynes's model is not general in the same sense as the model of general equilibrium which claims to encompass all basic economic interrelations at the same time. Keynes's claim to generality comes rather from the explanation of the one magnitude that the orthodox theory took as given; the level of output and employment which in Keynes's theory can be anything from zero to full employment; whereas he accused the orthodox theory of only operating under the *assumption* of full employment (*C.W.* xiv, p. 106). His position is indeed closer to Marshall's partial or one at a time method, although his system is interdependent in a sense that Marshall's is not. This also implies that Keynes's view of the "generality" of his theory is incompatible with the "Generalized General Theory" that Hicks suggests when, for reasons of "Mathematical elegance", he turns the theory into a simultaneous equation system in three variables; income, the rate of interest, and the value of investment (in "Mr Keynes and the Classics", pp. 134–5, reprinted in *Critical Essays in Monetary Theory* (Oxford University Press, 1967)). Such "Generalisation" wipes out the theory of effective demand "at a stroke" (cf. L. L. Pasinetti, "The Economics of Effective Demand", p. 47, in *Growth and Income Distribution* (Cambridge University Press, 1974)) and eliminates causality.

13 The discussion about what kind of market Keynes was assuming is thus nugatory – any would do, for Keynes felt it would make no difference to the exposition of effective demand. Many economists find it easier to understand Keynes's model by assuming imperfect competition or monopoly. Kalecki provided an equivalent to Keynes's model working from just this standpoint, but it is not crucial to Keynes's own position as long as the degree of competition, whatever it is, can be taken as given (cf., however, "Relative Movements of Real Wages and Output", *Economic Journal*, vol. xlix, March 1939). For other problems, however, it is of interest to consider what effects differences in market structure will have, and this has led several writers to enquire into a model where pricing becomes the dependent and/or independent variable (cf. D. J. Harris, "The Price Policy of Firms, the Level of Employment and Distribution in the Short-run", *Australian Economic Papers*, vol. xiii, June 1974, for a useful survey).

14 Keynes seemed undecided about the proper placing of the propensity to consume which in one draft was given, thus leaving his independent variables as "(1) the state of long-term expectation, (2) the state of liquidity preference and (3) the quantity of money measured in terms of wage-units" (*C.W.* xiii, pp. 481–2).

15 Valuable insight into the use that should be made of this framework is found in Keynes's discussions on methodology with Harrod (cf. *C. W.* xiv, pp. 295–306); but similar points are also made in *G. T.* p. 297.

16 It is in this sense that the approach is "one at a time" (Marshallian) rather than general (Walrasian) in the sense of being capable of handling all problems at once. This also suggests that such criticisms are misplaced methodologically, e.g. Samuelson's criticism of "Jean Baptiste Kaldor" resulting from Kaldor's perfectly legitimate decision to make the level of employment "given" in an analysis of the growth of productive capacity (cf. R. Lekachman, *Keynes' General Theory* (London: Macmillan, 1964), p. 345).

17 Nor is it possible from this point of view to agree that "Keynes was concerned with what we have called temporary equilibrium" (K. J. Arrow and F. H. Hahn, *General Competitive Analysis* (Edinburgh: Oliver and Boyd, 1971), p. 347), for this equilibrium is specified by zero market excess demands in all markets. To such a position Hahn's ("Expectations and Equilibrium", *op. cit.*) analysis can associate the required form of the expectational functions. In this view involuntary unemployment represents unsatisfied expectation and thus "disequilibrium". Keynes, however, posited equilibrium as the result of given expectations and could thus look upon involuntary unemployment as an equilibrium phenomenon for with short-period expectations of producers realised there was nothing to move the system from its state of rest, this despite the fact that some markets did not clear.

18 F. H. Hahn, *On the Notion of Equilibrium in Economics* (Cambridge University Press, 1973), p. 7.

19 It is interesting to note that Hahn has returned to a concept similar to that which he suggested in "Expectations and Equilibrium" (*op. cit.*, p. 819) in an attempt to redefine the concept of equilibrium used in the theory of general equilibrium (cf. *On the Notion* . . ., p. 25). It is also interesting to note that this approach allows for constant expectations behaviour despite actual disappointment of expectation which allows a broader definition of expectational equilibrium than previously (cf. note 1, p. 215 above) and is thus closer to Keynes's stationary position. But without treatment of long-period expectations which positions Keynes's equilibrium one must suppose that Hahn's equilibrium is positioned by a not "too large" excess demand in any market so that disappointment is not "too great" to justify changing behaviour. It should, however, be emphasised that the distinction remains between (1) the specification of an equilibrium in terms of excess market demand and (2) the subsequent derivation of the expectational functions that are compatible with there being no force to change the situation (in the simplest general equilibrium model zero excess demand is the expectation, so market clearing and realised expectations are one and the same thing and thus Keynes's equilibrium must really be "disequilibrium"), and (3) Keynes's method of setting a given and constant level of general expectations, and finding the level of employment, compatible with those expectations, which allows for positions of less than full employment and for satisfied expectations such that there is no force making for change. See the similar point concerning Patinkin's analysis in P. Davidson, "A Keynesian view of Patinkin's Theory of Employment", *Economic Journal*, vol. lxxvii, September 1967, pp. 562–3.

20 "The point is that the real entrepreneur is never in a position to *measure* the realised cost of a single decision. This imports an element of vagueness into the revisions of past expectations on which his current expectations are in great part founded" (H. Townshend, review of Shackle, *Expectations Investment and Income, Economic Journal*, vol. xlviii, March 1938, p. 523).

21 This view contradicts Shackle's (*Keynesian Kalaidics* (Edinburgh University Press, 1974), p. 14) that the distinction between *ex ante* and *ex post* is "essential and indispensable" to an understanding of Keynes's work. Indeed, Keynes found the distinction misleading in that it prevented the analysis of factors he considered important. As pointed out in note 1, p. 213 above, the distinction represented little advance over earlier "expectations" theories. For example, cf. Brinley Thomas's review of the Swedish theories where Pigou is put on a par with the Swedes in recognising "the fact that entrepreneurs' anticipations of future changes lie at the core of the problem of fluctuations" (*Monetary Policy and Crises, A Study of the Swedish Experience* (London: Routledge, 1936), p. 75).

Chapter 2

POST-KEYNESIAN THEORY: AN OVERVIEW

Alternate Interpretations of Keynes's Theory

Foreign language experts are well aware of words and expressions in every language that defy precise translation. Yet the necessity of communication requires efforts, even if imperfect, to make such translations. The problem is very similar to the idea of the "Gestalt" shift used by Kuhn (1962) to explain differences in theoretical paradigms. Essential components of one theory may not even find expression in another. But such difficulty has not stopped efforts to translate one theoretical perspective into another.

Keynes believed that his 1936 *General Theory* represented a radically new method of economic analysis. He intimated to G. B. Shaw in a letter dated 1 January 1935, "I believe myself to be writing a book on economic theory which will largely revolutionize . . . the way the world thinks about economic problems." His inclination was to accentuate his divergence from existing theory. But he was counseled to maximize communication with "orthodox" economists by preserving as much as possible of the existing "language."

Harrod warned Keynes, "What I fear is that readers may not understand; and that the dust you want to raise will obscure the view of your central points. If the economists who read your book don't take the essential points, the outlook is bad. There is a limit to what the human mind can assimilate" (Keynes XIII, pp. 555–56). "I am thinking of the effectiveness of your work. Its effectiveness is diminished if you try to eradicate very deep-rooted habits of thought *unnecessarily*. One of these is the supply and demand analysis . . . don't impugn that analysis itself" (Keynes XIII, pp. 533–34).

Despite Keynes's belief that his task was to work out "A Monetary Theory of Production" (Ibid., p. 408ff) "in which changing views about the future are capable of influencing the quantity of employment and not merely its direction" (Keynes VIII, p. xxii), economists quickly set to work to try to translate the new theory into more familiar language to compare its "generality" relative to the traditional (Keynes called it "classical") theory. Keynes's theory thus came to be represented as the aggregation of specific groupings or "bundles" of traditional micro supply and demand equations into "market" relations for money, bonds, and goods to determine the level of *real* national income. Hicks's (1937) "Mr. Keynes and the Classics" was the first of a number of attempts to translate Keynes's "revolutionary" approach into traditional language (e.g., Harrod, 1937; Hansen, 1953; Samuelson, 1948; and Modigliani, 1944; among others).

All, not surprisingly, concluded that Keynes's theory did not differ from existing theory, except for the new terminology and the degree of aggregation.

This general line of interpretation, which eventually produced what is known as the "neo-classical synthesis" (to indicate the endurance of the classical position) can be opposed to what has come to be known as "post-Keynesian" theory. This latter approach has attempted to take seriously, first, Keynes's belief that his approach was radically different from traditional theory, and second, that the theory should be developed on the basis of Keynes's exposition of effective demand in a monetary production economy determining the level of employment, rather than through supply and demand in the "real" and "monetary" sectors determining the level of *real output.*

Post-Keynesian Economics: A Generalization of the General Theory

The first attempt to move beyond Keynes's theory can be found in Joan Robinson's 1937 *Essays in the Theory of Employment.* One of the essays extends Keynes's theory to take into account the effect of capital accumulation and changes in technique on the long-period level of employment. This work set off a series of investigations with the aim of "generalizing the 'General Theory.'"

Mrs. Robinson's approach was based on her earlier work in *Imperfect Competition* (1933) and placed great emphasis on the "elasticity of substitution" and the marginal theory of value. It was soon recognized, however, that Keynes's theory was incompatible with traditional marginal analysis. If the level of employment as determined by effective demand was in equilibrium at less than full employment, then marginal productivity and marginal disutility were redundant as determinants of the demand and supply of labor (cf. Weintraub, 1956). If supply and demand based on marginal disutility and productivity of labor no longer determined the quantity of labor hired, neither could it determine labor's real reward. Acceptance of Keynes's theory implied rejection of the marginal productivity theory of distribution as well as the redundancy of the labor market in determining real wages and employment. Kalecki, whose work became known to English readers shortly after Keynes's, had already integrated a theory of distribution based on prices determined by a markup over costs and an explanation of the level of output and its fluctuation (cf. Kalecki, 1971, part II).

Before publication of the *General Theory,* Harrod was working on a theory of the cycle (Harrod, 1936) in reaction to that proposed by Hayek (1933). Harrod's subsequent (1948) development of Keynes's ideas in this direction joined those of Joan Robinson to point the way to an extension of the theory to the analysis of capital accumulation. The theories of Robinson (1956), Harrod (1948), Kaldor (1956, 1960), Kalecki (1971) and Pasinetti (1974, 1981) are the best-known attempts to develop Keynes's work to produce a macro theory of growth and distribution, but Weintraub (1958) and Boulding (1950) independently followed similar lines. The theories of these writers have come to be known as the Cambridge or post-Keynesian theories of capital, growth, and distribution. Useful summaries are available in Harcourt (1972), Harris (1978), and Kregel (1975).

In the process of her work in this area, Joan Robinson came to criticize the concept of aggregate capital used in the aggregate production function (Robinson, 1953–54). The problem was to determine the effect of changes in the technique of production represented by the quantity of capital per man, on the distribution of income between capital and labor. Sraffa's (1960) *Production of Commodities* and Garegnani's (1960) book on the implications of this approach for the role of capital in the theory of distribution criticized the traditional Theory of Capital from another angle (cf. also Garegnani, 1970). The two approaches joined forces to confront the traditional theory in the so-called "Cambridge Controversies in the Theory of Capital" (cf. Harcourt, 1972) as a direct outgrowth of the post-Keynesian extensions of Keynes's theory to growth and distribution. The debates also suggested the possibility of a theoretical integration of Sraffa's rehabilitation of the classical economists and the post-Keynesian approach. Suggestions along these lines can be found in Kregel (1975, 1983), Roncaglia (1978), Garegnani (1983), and Nell (1983).

These developments, which touched the very foundation of traditional theory, reawakened interest in Keynes's original work and the work of those such as Weintraub who had been early critics of the "neo-classical synthesis" interpretation of Keynes. This developed into a renewal of interest in the particularly monetary and financial aspects of Keynes's theory in the work of Davidson (1972), Minsky (1975), Vicarelli (1983), and others. By the 1970s, the assessment of Keynes's theoretical contribution had come full circle and was again presented as a "Gestalt" shift providing a new paradigmatic structure in economics (cf. Eichner and Kregel, 1975). Paradoxically, it was the extension of Keynes's theory to the areas of capital, growth, and distribution that eventually convinced many economists now called post-Keynesian that the *General Theory* did differ radically from the orthodox presentations.

Post-Keynesian theory can thus be represented as a rejection of the possibility of expressing Keynes's theory in the "language" of conventional theory. Rather, it pursues the "study of the forces which determine changes in the scale of output and employment" and its growth and distribution, recognizing "that money enters into the economic scheme in an essential and peculiar manner" in "a monetary economy" that "is essentially one in which changing views about the future are capable of influencing the quantity of employment" (Keynes VII, p. xxii).

The "language" of the Post-Keynesian Interpretations of the *General Theory*

Instead of following Hicks's (1937) IS-LM representation or Samuelson's (1939) 45°-line diagram, the post-Keynesian approach took seriously Keynes's strictures concerning the failure of traditional economics to provide a "theory" of the level of output as a whole. In both the Marshallian "partial" and Walrasian "general" equilibrium theories, output or the demand for particular outputs is exogenously given. In partial analysis, demand curves are independent of the level of individual outputs. In general equilibrium theories, individual endowments that constrain demand are exogenously given. If micro demand curves can only be expressed for exogenous levels of demand, they cannot be aggregated to produce an expression capable of determining the economy-wide demand for output. This recognition led to the study of the "principle of effective demand," which Keynes summarized in Chapter 3 of the *General Theory* as a more correct analytical apparatus than those proposed by Hicks or Samuelson.

Keynes's original formulation of effective demand has the advantage of preserving his unique position concerning the "units" of measure, in particular the role of the wage-unit as the standard for prices. In Chapter 4 of the *General Theory,* Keynes explained the impossibility of reasoning in terms of "real" output, which "is a non-homogeneous complex which cannot be measured. . . . The problem of comparing one real output with another . . . presents conundrums which permit . . . no solution" (Keynes VII, pp. 38–39). Keynes notes, but rejects, the "special case" widely adopted by the neoclassical synthesis where these problems may be overcome: a one commodity world. Instead, "I propose . . . two fundamental units . . . quantities of money-value and quantities of employment" (Ibid., p. 41). Keynes classes the real "quantity of output as a whole" as a "vague concept" of interest for "unprecise and approximate" "historical comparison" (Ibid., p. 43). Oddly enough, neither prices, wages, nor the level of employment appears in either the IS-LM or the 45°-line analysis, both of which, despite Keynes's arguments to the contrary, determine the level of real output in a one commodity world.

The analysis of effective demand in Keynes's framework allows a major role in the influence of changing views about the future. Keynes believed that his greatest contribution was in providing the explanation of the demand for output as a whole that was absent from traditional theory. Once translated into a relation between the expected money receipts that would be necessary to induce entrepreneurs to hire different quantities of labor, supply could be modeled on Marshall's analysis. Weintraub (1958, 1966), Davidson and Smolensky (1964), and Davidson (1972) provide analyses of effective demand in units of employment and money. The importance of the aggregate supply function is given in Tarshis (1977).

The analysis of demand was more difficult. A little thought will suggest that the economist's entire conception of demand must change if employment and output are endogenous variables, for then income cannot be considered a constraint on expenditure. Instead, expenditure decisions will determine income, output, and employment. It is thus appropriate to give the concept a different name, such as "effective demand." Keynes sought to identify the effective constraint on aggregate expenditure, distinguishing between consumption and investment expenditure. The former was closely related to wage incomes, and the total of wage incomes was itself determined by the level of employment. The propensity to consume determined the precise relation between an increase in employment and total consumption given the money-wage rate. Thus, consumption expenditure was itself determined by the level of employment and output, while the "psychological law," which governed the propensity to consume, implied that higher levels of employment would lead to a lower proportion of consumption demand in total output. If this "gap" between consumption and output were not taken up, producers would incur losses and the level of employment would be cut back. Consumption expenditures could not be considered an exogenous variable to determine income.

Investment expenditures were the factor that would fill the "gap." In traditional theory, investment was limited by the amount individuals were willing to save at any given rate of interest. But, Keynes observed, since saving will be the difference between income and consumption expenditure, which itself depends on income, saving could not be the constraint on investment spending, for this would reintroduce income as a constraint.

The income multiplier showed how changes in the level of investment would lead to a multiple expansion in the level of income, the size of the multiple depending on the propensity to consume, the tax system, the openness of the economy, and so forth. But the multiplier cannot provide the constraint on investment decisions that should replace saving and the rate of interest in the traditional approach.

Some have suggested that Keynes resolved this problem by making investment an autonomous variable in his system, but this is not correct. Investment, rather, reflects Keynes's concern about changes in expectations of the future having importance in a monetary production economy. Keynes makes his position clear in the opening passage of Chapter 5 of the *General Theory:*

> All production is for the purpose of ultimately satisfying a consumer. Time usually elapses, however—and sometimes much time—between the incurring of costs by the producer (with the consumer in view) and the purchase of the output by the ultimate consumer. Meanwhile the entrepreneur *(including both the producer and the investor* in this description) has to form the best expectations he can as to what the consumers will be prepared to pay when he is ready to supply them (directly or indirectly) after the elapse of what may be a lengthy period; and he has no choice but to be guided by these expectations, if he is to produce at all by processes which occupy time. (Keynes VII, p. 46, italics added)

This passage, in capsule, demonstrates why time, expectations, uncertainty, the setting of prices, and financial institutions all play a major role in post-Keynesian theory. As Keynes himself noted, economists were prone to reduce the analysis of the effects of investment to a single period (Keynes VII, p. 138). But if all activity in the economy takes place within a single period, then such problems will not arise. In a Walrasian system, or equilibrium in a Hicksian week, or even an Arrow-Debreu intertemporal system with complete futures markets, all decisions concerning the future are taken in a single period—the present; once decided, they do not change; only foreseen contingencies can be met. The recognition that the return to an investment includes "the series of increments which it is expected to obtain *over the whole life* of the additional capital asset" leads to the recognition that "this involves the whole question of the place of expectation in economic theory" (Ibid.). "It is important to understand the dependence of the marginal efficiency of a given stock of capital on changes in expectation because it is chiefly this dependence that renders the marginal efficiency of capital subject to the somewhat violent fluctuations" that lead to fluctuations in investment and trade cycles (Keynes VII, pp. 143–44). The explanation Keynes gives of the constraint on investment expenditure is thus linked to his ideas about monetary production.

Monetary Production Economics

Since the decisions of both the "producer and the investor" depend on time, expectations, uncertainty, and so on about the future prices at which goods or assets may be sold, it would not be an exaggeration to say that Keynes's conception of a monetary production economy is grounded in ubiquitous "speculation" (cf. Minsky, 1975). The producer must take a position in labor and raw materials (buy in the expectation of later sale with profit), inventories of his product, and so forth in the hopes of being able to sell these goods at some unknown future date. Further, since these decisions must be taken and capital expenditures made far in advance of the "market experiment" in which the outputs are offered to buyers, producers will have to form expectations about the quantities and prices at which they will offer their outputs. Labor, when it accepts a wage that it hopes to exchange at some future date and time for the goods desired, also takes a "position." Of course, financial markets are the classic case of speculation.

Successful speculation depends on buying cheap and selling dear, or simply knowing better than the market. Since everyone is trying to outguess the market, it is not surprising that opinion about the future course of prices may be divided—the famous "Bulls" and "Bears." It also means that shifts in the *division* of opinion influences current prices and the expected profitability of investment: "By 'uncertain' knowledge, let me explain, I do not mean merely to distinguish what is known for certain from what is only probable. The sense in which I am using the term is that in which the prospect of a European war is uncertain, or the price of copper and the rate of interest twenty years hence. . . . About these matters there is no scientific basis on which to form any calculable probability whatever. We simply do not know" (Keynes XIV, pp. 113–14). Shackle (e.g., 1972, 1973) has been instrumental in elaborating the consequences of uncertainty for the traditional concept of economics as rational choice among known alternatives subject to a constraint.

But if the knowledge of future choices postulated by the traditional theory cannot exist, what could people do to quell their uncertainty? It is here that money enters Keynes's system. The absence of future markets for every possible future event means that "open" or speculative positions must be held over time if investments that produce output and require employment are to be undertaken. But open positions may produce losses. The price of money, by definition, does not change, so that among all possible open positions "investment" in money provides the most certain way to link today and tomorrow. Changes in the division of opinion about future conditions will change the price of "security," the certainty about the future value of wealth gained by taking a position in money. The "price" that measured the markets' preference for this "security" against the unknown future Keynes called "liquidity" preference. Thus, the "liquidity preference theory of the rate of interest" allowed Keynes to identify the constraints on investment expenditure. Certain "essential properties" for the asset chosen as money are also required. Compare Davidson (1972, 1980b), Kregel (1980), Minsky (1975), and Nell (1983).

Since Keynes is referring to speculative decisions in the sense that "producers and investors" may be expected to take positions according to their best expectations concerning future movements in prices and demand, "the significance of such changes in expectations lies in their effect on the readiness to produce *new* assets through their reaction on the marginal efficiency of capital" (Keynes VII, p. 142). The production of new assets is net investment expenditure. Investors will be concerned to obtain the highest rate of return by purchasing either existing or newly produced capital goods. Thus, net investment will depend on expectations of prospective gains and the ability to take advantage of such opportunities. The limit on investment expenditure is given by the ability and cost of procuring and creating debt to control the balance sheet. We often speak of buying shares on "margin." In the same way, business firms produce and invest on "margin." Thus, finance is crucial to the ability to take advantage of expected future profit opportunities through new investment expenditure. The cost of finance is determined by the liquidity preferences of the public *and* the commercial banks, relative to the balance sheet position of the central bank (which is presumed not to be influenced by the profit motive). The determinants of new investment expenditures are then expected future prices, sales of output, and costs of inputs relative to current equipment and finance costs. Eichner (1976), among others, has also emphasized the role of the decision over current prices in providing cash flow and thus *internal* finance for new investment.

New investment, however, must compete with existing durable goods, including financial assets and money; it will be pursued only if it clearly gives a higher rate of return than any other type of investment expenditure. If expenditure is directed to previously existing capital assets or to assets that can be produced without application of labor, then underemployment equilibrium may be established either because of a depressed general state of expectations or an excessive state of liquidity preference. Keynes expressed these two factors in his first analysis of such problems (the 1914 financial crisis), as the "state of consumption" (in which he included expectations of all types of expenditure) and the "state of finance" (Keynes XI, p. 269). Thus, we can see that those aspects of Keynes's theory considered of major importance to the post-Keynesians (cf. Davidson, 1980a) clearly emerge in any attempt to specify demand independently of the income constraint, that is, to formulate the principle of effective demand in a monetary production economy.

Monetary Production and Unemployment Equilibrium

The recognition of the importance of expectations and finance for the constraint on investment expenditure was rooted in Keynes's views on money and monetary production. Already in his *Treatise on Money* (Keynes V, VI), Keynes had defined money as "that by delivery of which debt-contracts and price-contracts are *discharged,* and in the shape of which a store of General Purchasing Power is held." Its importance derived from its being the unit in which "debts and prices must first have been expressed" (Keynes V, p. 3).

These ideas were later expressed in Keynes's distinction between his own theory of an "entrepreneur" or monetary production economy, a co-operative (or real wage economy), and a "neutral" economy. As seen above, Keynes insisted on the use of money or labor units. Neither "real" nor "nominal" values, which corresponded to "real wage" and "neutral" analysis, were acceptable. Only prices in terms of money and quantities in wage units could express the new theory of effective demand. Keynes put it this way:

> An entrepreneur is interested, not in the amount of product, but in the amount of *money* which will fall to his share. He will increase his output if by so doing he expects to increase his money profit, *even though this profit represents a smaller quantity of product than before.* The explanation of this is evident. The employment of factors of production to increase output involves the entrepreneur in the disbursement, not of product, but of money. The choice before him in deciding whether or not to offer employment is a choice between using money in this way or in some other way or not using it at all. . . . The only question before him is to choose, out of the various ways of employing £100,—that way which will yield the largest profit in terms of money. . . . For the entrepreneur is guided, not by the amount of product he will gain, but by the alternative opportunities for using money having regard to the spot and forward price structure taken as a whole. (Keynes XXIX, pp. 82–83, italics added)

For Keynes, "forward" prices were a representation of expected future market conditions (cf. Davidson [1972] for an analysis in these terms). The difference between the spot and forward price as a proportion of the spot price represents the expected return from taking a position (investing) in the asset in question. Following the principle of maximization of money profit, investors will allocate their resources to yield the highest return. Neither the amount of output produced nor employment created by these decisions is of any direct importance to the decision. Thus, Keynes retains the assumption of profit maximization but rejects the use of a "real" income constraint, showing that the forces of competition may lead to an equilibrium in which investors earn maximum money returns without this implying either maximum output or employment. The automatic tendencies supposed by the classical theory operate in guiding investment decisions *in money terms*; they need not operate to produce full employment of either labor or capital.

Keynes represented the complex of expected rates of return on investments in capital assets by the marginal efficiency of capital, the expected returns on money by the liquidity premium. The rate of return on financial assets would, by definition, equal the liquidity premium; otherwise, agents would prefer to hold money. Equilibrium thus implied that the liquidity premium as determined by liquidity preference would be equal to the rate of interest on financial assets, which in turn was equal to the marginal efficiency of capital. Thus, Keynes could argue (Keynes XIV, pp. 202–203) that money was a *real* phenomenon because preferences to hold money set the rate of interest with which capital assets had to compete if they were to be newly produced (and thus create additional employment opportunities). He continued this paradoxical argument by then stating that the *rate of interest* was a *"monetary"* phenomenon (Ibid., p. 80) because it was independent of the real (marginal/physical) productivity of capital; rather, it was given by the relation between the spot and future price of money. ("The money-rate of interest—we remind the reader—is nothing more than the percentage excess of a sum of money contracted for forward delivery—for example, a year hence—over what we may call the 'spot' or cash price of the sum thus contracted for forward delivery" [Keynes

VII, p. 222].) Keynes thus denied the importance of either productivity or thrift in the determination of the rate of interest.

This view of underemployment equilibrium does not rely on a "breakdown" of the forces of the competitive market—which continue to operate, but with respect to "money" variables, not on output or employment. This is the essence of *monetary* production. The real constraint on investment is thus competition from money assets.

Economic Policy

Keynes was hesitant to recommend unique policies to eliminate depression. He was clearer on what would be required to prevent them: a high and stable state-supported rate of investment with a balanced full employment budget. The current federal government budget deficit is of much less significance to current conditions than the sharp reduction in nonmilitary investment that it has caused. Deficit expenditure creates cash flow and profits for private enterprise that will be drawn to the most profitable activities. But this does not guarantee that these activities will also increase output or create employment. From this point of view, the problem with the deficit is that it does not encourage employment-creating investment on the expenditure side, and its effect in the money market leads investors to financial rather than employment-creating investment.

The post-Keynesian position thus reflects Keynes's belief that laissez-faire capitalism might be made to work, while rejecting that it will automatically produce results which are socially compatible with its survival. It is not that the self-adjusting mechanisms do not work, just that they work on money values, not real variables. Thus, the system may be in equilibrium in the sense that no rearrangement of individual investments could increase expected rates of return. There is no reason to assume, however, that such an equilibrium provides the number of jobs that people desire at current wage rates or the amount of output that people would like to consume at prevailing prices. The traditional monetarist and "Keynesian" theory assumes that only impediments to the free functioning of the price mechanism might produce this result. Their policy recommendations thus concern improvements of the operation of the market mechanism and elimination of positions of market power.

The post-Keynesian position is rather that the market works well enough, but not necessarily on those real variables that may be the goals of government policy. This position leaves no place for policies that attempt control of *real* values, such as real wages to increase profitability and investment. In a monetary production economy, it is, in any case, only the "money" wage for a given number of jobs that is determined in the labor market. Real wages are determined by the prices that eventually result from the output and pricing decisions of firms. This does not imply that labor suffers from money illusion, only that unions can be no more successful in determining their real wage than governments are in affecting real product or employment by means of operating on the fiscal deficit in a money-wage economy. Since unions cannot affect either investment or prices, they cannot affect their real wages. Since money-wages have no direct effect on real wages or employment, but may have direct effects on price levels and thus on the relation between spot and future prices, post-Keynesians have been led to suggest that money-wages may better be determined by some other mechanisms than by free collective bargaining. Incomes policies (cf. Weintraub, 1978, pp. 121 ff) have been designed to produce stable money-wages while preserving the function of money-wages of indicating wage relativities. Thus, allocation of labor should remain efficient, eliminating the futile attempt to influence wages through a variable that has only an indirect relation to them. The role of policy must thus be to create conditions such that stable prices, full employment, and capacity utilization are compatible with maximum profit. This was the case in the 1950s and 1960s. It cannot be achieved in the 1980s unless economists recognize that they live in a monetary production economy and formulate policy on that basis.

References

Boulding, K., *A Reconstruction of Economics*, New York: Wiley, 1950.

Davidson, P., *Money and the Real World*, 2nd ed., London: Macmillan, 1972, 197.

———, "Post Keynesian Economics," *The Public Interest*, Special Issue, 1980a, 151–173.

———, "The Dual-Faceted Nature of the Keynesian Revolution," *Journal of Post-Keynesian Economics*, Spring 1980b, *3*.

Eichner, A. S., *The Mega-Corp and Oligopoly*, New York: Cambridge University Press, 1976.

Eichner, A. S., and Kregel, J. A., "An Essay on Post-Keynesian Theory: A New Paradigm in Economics," *Journal of Economic Literature*, December 1975, *13*, 1293–1314.

Garegnani, P., II *Capitale nelle Teorie della Distribuzione*, Milan: Giuffre, 1960.

———, "Heterogeneous Capital, the Production Function and the Theory of Distribution," *Review of Economic Studies*, 1970, *37*.

———, "Two Routes to Effective Demand: Comment on Kregel," in *Distribution, Effective Demand and International Economic Relations*, London: Macmillan, 1983.

Hansen, A. H., *A Guide to Keynes*, New York: McGraw-Hill, 1953.

Harcourt, G. C. *Some Cambridge Controversies in the Theory of Capital*, Cambridge: Cambridge University Press, 1972.

Harris, D. J., *Capital Accumulation and Income Distribution*, Stanford: Stanford University Press, 1978.

Harrod, R. F., *The Trade Cycle*, Oxford: Clarendon Press, 1936.

———, *Towards a Dynamic Economics*, London: Macmillan, 1948.

———, "Keynes and Traditional Theory," reprinted in Harrod, R. F., *Economic Essays*, 2nd ed., London: Macmillan, 1972, 237–253.

Hayek, F. A., *Monetary Theory and the Trade Cycle*, London: Cape, 1933.

Hicks, J. R., "Mr. Keynes and the Classics," reprinted in Hicks, J., *Collected Essays on Economic Theory*, Vol. II, Oxford: Blackwell, 1982, 100–115.

Kaldor, N., "Alternative Theories of Distribution," *Review of Economic Studies*, 1956, *23*.

———, *Essays on Economic Stability and Growth*, London: Duckworth, 1960.

Kalecki, M., *Selected Essays on the Dynamics of the Capitalist Economy, 1933–70*, Cambridge: Cambridge University Press, 1971.

Keynes, J. M., *The Collected Writings of John Maynard Keynes*, New York: Cambridge University Press, V, VI, *A Treatise on Money*, 1971; VII, *The General Theory of Employment, Interest and Money*, 1973; XI, *Economic Articles and Correspondence: Academic*, 1973; XIII, *The General Theory and After: Part I*, 1973; XIV, *The General Theory and After: Part II*, 1973; XXIX, *The General Theory and After: A Supplement*, 1979.

Kregel, J. A., *The Reconstruction of Political Economy*, An Introduction to Post-Keynesian Economics, 2nd ed., 1975, London: Macmillan, 1973.

———, "Markets and Institutions as Features of a Capitalistic Production System," *Journal of Post-Keynesian Economics*, Fall 1980, *3*, 32–48.

———, "Effective Demand, Origin and Development of the Notion," in *Distribution, Effective Demand and International Relations*, London: Macmillan, 1983.

Kuhn, T. S., *The Structure of Scientific Revolutions*, Chicago: University of Chicago Press, 1962.

Minsky, H. P., *John Maynard Keynes*, New York: Columbia University Press, 1975.

Modigliani, F., "Liquidity Preference and the Theory of Interest and Money," *Econometrica*, January 1944, *12*, reprinted in *Readings in Monetary Theory*, Homewood, Illinois: Richard D. Irwin, 1951, 186–240.

Nell, E. J., "Keynes after Sraffa: The Essential Properties of Keynes's Theory of Interest and Money: Comment on Kregel," in *Distribution, Effective Demand and International Relations*, London: Macmillan, 1983.

Pasinetti, L. L., *Growth and Income Distribution*, Cambridge: Cambridge University Press, 1974.

———, *Structural Change and Economic Growth*, Cambridge: Cambridge University Press, 1981.

Robinson, J., *The Economics of Imperfect Competition*, London: Macmillian, 1933.

———, *Essays in the Theory of Employment*, London: Macmillian, 1937.

———, "The Production Function and the Theory of Capital," *Review of Economic Studies*, 1953–54, *21*.

———, *The Accumulation of Capital*, London: Macmillian, 1956.

Roncaglia, A. *Sraffa and the Theory of Prices*, Chichester: J. Wiley, 1978.

Samuelson, P. A., "A Synthesis of the Principle of Acceleration and the Multiplier," *Journal of Political Economy*, December 1939, *47*.

———, "The Simple Mathematics of Income Determination," *Income, Employment and Public Policy*, Essays in Honor of Alvin H. Hansen, New York: Norton, 1948, 133–155.

Shackle, G. L. S., *Epistemics and Economics*, Cambridge: Cambridge University Press, 1972.

———, "Keynes and Today's Establishment in Economic Theory: A View," *Journal of Economic Literature*, June 1973, *11*.

Sraffa, P., *Production of Commodities by Means of Commodities*, Cambridge: Cambridge University Press, 1960.

Tarshis, L., "Keynes as Seen by His Students" in D. Patinkin and J. C. Leith, *Keynes, Cambridge and the General Theory*, London: Macmillan, 1977, 48–63.

Vicarelli, F., *Keynes: On the Instability of Capitalism*, Philadelphia: University of Pennsylvania Press, 1984.

Weintraub, S., "A Macroeconomic Approach to the Theory of Wages," *American Economic Review*, December 1956, *46*, 835–856.

———, *An Approach to the Theory of Income Distribution*, Philadelphia: Chilton, 1958.

———, *A Keynesian Theory of Employment, Growth and Income Distribution*, Philadelphia: Chilton, 1966.

———, *Capitalism's Inflation and Unemployment Crisis*, Boston: Addison-Wesley, 1978.

Chapter 3

EVOLUTION VERSUS EQUILIBRIUM: REMARKS UPON RECEIPT OF THE VEBLEN-COMMONS AWARD

Joan Robinson used the aphorism "[t]ime is a device to keep everything from happening at once" to distinguish history from an economy in equilibrium with complete markets for all states, times and places and allows all decisions about the future to be taken in the present. In such conditions there can be no default, since its occurrence would evidence a market failure. Alan Greenspan supported financial innovation to provide more complete markets and more efficient distribution of risk. However, in reality the complete markets were provided by AIG's Financial Products unit. The rest is history.

Explanations of the crisis blame the unexpected appearance of Black Swans with fat tails in one hundred year floods. This is recognition of the difficulties in reducing history to moments of a probability distribution. Economists have not been ignorant of these difficulties. Knight distinguished between risk and uncertainty, Shackle highlighted crucial experiments, Davidson emphasizes the distinction between non-ergodic and ergodic processes, and Benoit Mandelbrot has pictured known fractal chaotic processes that are unpredictable. All suggest that statistical estimates of unknown future events cannot be predicted by past events. Recently, David Hendry has noted that time series data cannot provide the basis for forecasts of the future of the economy, which renders the dynamic general equilibrium model logically inconsistent. Sample statistics are not good estimates of population parameters when the population changes over time. This attempt to use statistical methods to incorporate history has failed. Modern economics thus restricts itself to an unchanging environment in which agents are capable of acquiring full knowledge of system evolution to form "rational" expectations. This is the approach that grounded value at risk (VAR) and the risk assessment of every insolvent structured derivative entity. The rest is history.

Is economics condemned by Santayana's curse to repeat its equilibrium past? There is a call for a "new economic paradigm," but recollection of Keynes's theory and evolutionary economists might better serve this purpose.

In stating that "the whole problem of monetary theory is largely one of deducing changes in anticipations from the changes in objective data that draw them forth," Hicks (1935, 13) was concerned with the problem of how individuals transformed objective data into expectations, viz. his "elasticity of expectations." Hayek's response in "Economics and Knowledge" (1937, 44) stated that the conditions of general equilibrium represent "objective data" and suggested that "the knowledge and intentions of the different members of society are supposed to come more and more into agreement . . .

that the expectations of the people and particularly of entrepreneurs will become more and more correct." Thus, "it is only relative to the knowledge which a person is bound to acquire in the course of the attempt to carry out his original plan that equilibrium is likely to be achieved." In this approach, not only is the set of objective data forming a general equilibrium presumed to exist, it is assumed that this objective data is independent of the process (Smith's "higgling and bargaining of the market?") of acquiring the knowledge necessary to achieve it.

Lachmann (1943, 15-16) noted that Hayek's "[e]quilibrium economics studies the full implications of the set of data, the open conditions of equilibrium"; [but] "it does not study the ways in which these logical implications are translated into human action, which is thus conceived as a quasi-automatic response to an external stimulus." A "determinate solution does not entail that those attempting its solution will actually succeed." For Lachmann the problem is that equilibrium economics does not "study the ways in which these logical implications are translated into human action." What is needed is to "fill in those formal propositions with definite statements about how knowledge is acquired and communicated."

Keynes's *Treatise on Probability* (1921) notes that expectations formation should not be over the frequency of "objects" or realizations, but the complex of factors that produce the events and realizations. Even if there exist stationary realizations from an ergodic stochastic process individuals may nonetheless be uncertain about what specific process has produced them. It is not the probability of the "events" that is of importance, but rather the estimation of the probability that a particular process has produced the events that are being observed. Expectation formation should not concern whether a fair coin will come up heads or tails, but the "theory" explaining the occurrence of the event (e.g., how a particular combination of muscle movements will produce a head or a tail). For Keynes, "[a] proposition is not probable because we think it so. When once the facts are given which determine our knowledge, what is probable or improbable in these circumstances has been fixed objectively, and is independent of our opinion. The theory of probability is logical, therefore, because it is concerned with the degree of belief which is rational to entertain in given conditions" (1921, 4).

While Lachmann suggests the pursuit of equilibrium may influence the objective data; Keynes goes further to suggest that the appropriate expectations are about the process that produces the objective data rather than about the data itself. Indeed, if decisions of individuals taken on the basis of expectations of the process that determine future outcomes, as in the impact of investment on income and sales via the multiplier, then there are no "objective data" to serve as the object of expectations since it will be determined by the expectations determining spending decisions (Kregel 1986).

History is then how the rational belief in the processes that produce realizations creates the evolution of the objective data. The possibility that there are no "objective data" to anchor expectations and produce equilibrium provides the basis for Keynes's query: "Is the economic system self-adjusting?" Keynes developed an alternative explanation of the evolution of the economy, which I have suggested (Kregel 1976) was best characterized as "shifting equilibrium" in which the system is ever-changing. For Keynes, "equilibrium is blither" (Shackle 1972, 233).

But Keynes was part of a long tradition rejecting the vision of the system self-adjusting to general equilibrium. This approach places the emphasis on the way rational individuals' expectations in conditions of uncertainty over the determinants of the objective data generate endogenous forces that produce changes in the objective data that preclude any conception of equilibrium.

Consider Veblen (1898, 388; emphasis added):

> For the purpose of economic science the process of cumulative change that is to be accounted for is the sequence of change in the methods of doing things, – dealing with the material means of life. . . . The physical properties of the materials accessible to man are constants: it is the human agent that changes, – his insight and his appreciation of what these things can be used for is what develops . . . the limitation imposed is on what men can do and on the methods of doing it. *The changes that take place in the mechanical contrivances are an expression of changes in the human factor. Changes in the material facts breed further change only through the human factor.* . . . Economic action must be subject matter of the science if the science is to fall into line as an evolutionary science.

For Schumpeter (1975, 82)

> "Capitalism, then, is by nature a form or method of economic change and not only never is but never can be stationary. And this evolutionary character of the capitalist process is not merely due to the fact that economic life goes on in a social and natural environment which changes and by its change alters the data of economic action; this fact is important and these changes (wars, revolutions and so on) often condition industrial change, but they are not its prime movers. Nor is this evolutionary character due to a quasi-automatic increase in population and capital or to the vagaries of monetary systems, of which exactly the same thing holds true. The fundamental impulse that sets and keeps the capitalist engine in motion comes from the new consumers, goods, the new methods of production or transportation, the new markets, the new forms of industrial organization that capitalist enterprise creates."

Gunnar Myrdal (1955, 11–12) notes:

> "in the normal case there is no such tendency towards automatic self-stabilisation in the economic system, but that the system, if left to itself, will steadily be on the move away from such a state. If left to take its natural course, the economic process will be cumulative instead of equilibrating – in the meaning that secondary changes usually have the same direction as the primary ones and not the opposite one – and it will then most often tend to create inequalities and not equality, and to increase existing inequalities."

In the development field similar ideas can be found in the work of Hirschman and Prebisch.

Nicholas Kaldor building on the work of Allyn Young:

> Once however we allow for increasing returns, the forces making for continuous changes are endogenous – "they are engendered from within the economic system" (Young 1928,

> 530) – and the actual state of the economy during any one "period" cannot be predicted except as a result of the sequence of events in previous periods which led up to it. As Young put it, with increasing returns "change becomes progressive and propagates itself in a cumulative way" (533).
>
> . . . When every change in the use of resources every reorganisation of productive activities – creates the opportunity for a further change which would not have existed otherwise, the notion of an 'optimum' allocation of resources – when every particular resource makes as great or greater contribution to output in its actual use as in any alternative use – becomes a meaningless and contradictory notion . . . The whole view of the economic process as a medium for the "allocation of scarce means between alternative uses" falls apart. (Kaldor 1972, 1244-1245)

Hyman Minsky (1964) asked, "[a]re financial markets self-adjusting?" He argued that equilibrium theory in which financial disruption could not occur was an insurmountable impediment to understanding the persistence of financial crisis. In Minsky's financial instability hypothesis uncertainty is the result of engaging in commitments to make future financial payments with financial receipts that are uncertain because they, too, will occur in future periods and will be determined by the actions taken on the basis of individual expectations. Thus future receipts will not be forthcoming unless at that future time there is a willingness to enter into additional financial commitments (since spending in the future will determine future receipts). Both are self-referential or reflexive endogenous processes. His description of the endogenous process by which stability engenders a cumulative progression toward more risky financial structures is well known and has gained new attention as the result of the recent crisis.

George Soros's theory of reflexivity (1987) is the most recent in this line of analysis. Following Veblen it distinguishes between the taxonomy of material goods or "objective data" achieved through cognition and the actions taken by economic agents to change the type and disposition of those goods. In Soros's theory of reflexivity, evolution of commonly held equilibrium values is the result of the interaction of two means of dealing with human uncertainty: cognition, the attempt to increase knowledge of the objective conditions, and praxis, the attempt to use that knowledge which when successful will change the existing body of knowledge and render cognition more difficult. Soros's theory of disequilibrium is based on the idea that the results of cognition will be erroneous because it fails to consider the impact of praxis on values. This causes a divergence in expected and actual values that modifies them. Positive and negative feedback loops seek to identify the cumulative forces that determine the directions of these price movements.

It is important to note that all of these approaches incorporate what Soros has called the general "human uncertainty principle" and differs from "radical" existential uncertainty or irrational bubbles or behavioral explanations. In this principle uncertainty is the endogenous result of the operation of the purposive actions of individuals facing uncertainty produces cumulative processes which have no preordained point of equilibrium and is thus impossible to predict. It is the very action to determine objective data which determines that data, or the act of innovation that opens up a range of future possibilities, or the endogenous adaptation of margins of safety that provide endogenous determination of "objective data." This is the history that Joan Robinson contrasted to equilibrium.

It would be a mistake to believe the absence of history arose from modern general equilibrium. Both Walras and Marshall attempted to explain the process of equilibrium price formation, and both chose a real-world example: the stock market (details in Kregel 1992). Walras's tâtonnement reflects the process of price formation on the Paris Bourse, while Marshall's description corresponds quite closely to the system of price determination, which is employed in British continuous auction broker-dealer markets. The basic difference between Walras and Marshall is thus between discrete and continuous trading markets.

Walras's tâtonnement is a discrete bid auction with recontracting options in which prices are "fixed" at a daily "call" by an auctioneer of the list of stocks for a fixed period of time. Access to the auction is limited to government licensed agents who execute orders on behalf of their clients. The agents are forbidden from trading for their own account. Thus when the agents assemble for the call they possess all the information that is necessary to derive the supply and demand functions necessary to determine the equilibrium prices of the stocks to be traded. It is "discovered" by an employee of the Bourse – the "auctioneer" who calls out a range of prices for each stock; for each price the agents reveal their clients buy and sell orders that are only executed when a balance between bids and offers has been achieved at what then becomes the official market, or equilibrium price "fix." In this way the auctioneer via the tâtonnement elicits the relevant portions of the supply and demand curves for each stock via a price discovery process, which assures that the equilibrium price is set in conditions of perfect knowledge concerning consumer preferences for the moment of time when the auction takes place. Note that it is the institutional structure of the price discovery process that insures perfect information and that there is no necessary relation between the prices fixed at each successive call.

Marshall (1920) instead describes bilateral "higgling and bargaining" that takes place throughout the day. There will be a series of different prices, each the result of an individual exchange. But this is unacceptable since a competitive market should have a uniform price. Marshall argues that the average of all the prices for bargains made during the day will turn out to be the same as would have resulted if there had been a Walrasian tâtonnement. To explain this Marshall introduces a dealer who has "perfect knowledge of the conditions of the market" and buys below, and sells above the equilibrium. The price thus established "has some claim to be called the true equilibrium price: because if it were fixed at the beginning, and adhered to throughout, it would exactly equate demand and supply . . .; and because every dealer who has perfect knowledge of the circumstances of the market expects that price to be established. If he sees the price differing much from [the equilibrium price] he expects that a change will come before long, and by anticipating it he helps it to come quickly" (1920, 333–334).

But if dealers carry inventories to intervene then they may influence supply thus the equilibrium price. Marshall argues that perfect knowledge for dealers is not necessary even if they hold inventories. As justification Marshall makes a "latent" assumption: the constancy of the marginal utility of money. "This assumption is justifiable with regard to most of the market dealings" because a dealer looks to reselling "and therefore his potential resources are not diminished" so "there is no appreciable change in his willingness to part with money . . . there are sure to be present some dealers with large stocks of money at their command; and their influence steadies the market" (Marshall 1920, 335). This rules out income effects arising from the path of prices diverging from equilibrium, and also rules out cumulative price trends.

Thus even conscious attempts to provide an explanation of the process by which a market, much less the economy, could reach equilibrium rely on institutional or ad hoc assumptions that eliminate the possibility of cumulative causation. Perhaps it is time to give up the attempt to describe equilibrium as an historical process that can provide insight into economic activity.

References

Hayek, F. A. "Equilibrium and Knowledge." *Economica* IV (1937): 33–54.

Hicks, J. R. "Suggestions for Simplifying the Theory of Money." *Economica* II (1935): 1–19.

Kaldor, Nicholas. "Irrelevance of Equilibrium Economics." *Economic Journal* 82, 328 (1972): 1237–1255.

Keynes, J. M. *A Treatise on Probability*. London: Macmillan, 1921.

Kregel, J. A. "Economic Methodology in the Face of Uncertainty: The Modelling Methods of Keynes and the Post-Keynesians." *Economic Journal* 86, 342 (1976): 209–225.

———. "Conceptions of Equilibrium: The Logic of Choice and the Logic of Production." In *Subjectivism, Intelligibility and Economic Understanding*, edited by Israel Kirzner, pp. 155–170. New York: New York University Press, 1986.

———. "Walras' Auctioneer and Marshall's Well-Informed Dealers." *Quaderni di storia dell'economia politica*, 10, 1 (1992): 531–551.

Lachmann, Ludwig. "The Role of Expectations in Economics as a Social Science." *Economica* 14 (1943): 108–119.

Marshall, Alfred. *Principles of Economics*, 8th ed. London: Macmillan, 1920.

Minsky, H. P. "Financial Crisis, Financial Systems, and the Performance of the Economy." In *Private Capital Markets*, pp. 173–380. Englewood Cliffs, NJ: Prentice Hall, 1964.

Myrdal, Gunnar. *Development and Under-Development*. Cairo: National Bank of Egypt Fiftieth Anniversary Commemoration Lectures, 1955.

Schumpeter, J. A. *Capitalism, Socialism and Democracy*. New York: Harper, [1942] 1975.

Shackle, G. L. S. *Epistemics and Economics*, Cambridge: Cambridge University Press, 1972.

Soros, George. *The Alchemy of Finance*. New York: Simon and Schuster, 1987.

Veblen, Thorstein. "Why Is Economics Not an Evolutionary Science." *Quarterly Journal of Economics* 12, 4 (1898): 373–397.

Young, Allyn. "Increasing Returns and Economic Progress." *Economic Journal* December (1928): 527–542.

Chapter 4

SHYLOCK AND HAMLET: ARE THERE BULLS AND BEARS IN THE CIRCUIT?[1]

The circuit approach has done much to reawaken interest in Keynes's monetary theory of production and to extend it in new directions. Yet, it appears to remain confined within the limits of the industrial circulation of Keynes's *Treatise*; it thus does not deal with the determination of investment goods prices nor can it deal with the differential determination of the prices of assets and liabilities introduced in the *General Theory* in terms of the marginal efficiency of capital and liquidity preference. Since the importance of money in Keynes's theory is intimately linked with these concepts, it leads us to conclude that circuit theory needs further development in order to capture Keynes's views on the dominance of money over the real sector in a capitalist economy.

Who Is the Prince of Denmark?

The Cambridge-based Keynesian theories of growth and distribution developed in the 1950s and 1960s were presented as extensions or 'generalizations' of Keynes's *General Theory*. While they were sharply criticized by neoclassical economists, their development was also accompanied by 'internal' criticism which only became externally evident sometime after the 'Cambridge Debates' had come to be classified as a history of economic thought. The first of these internal criticisms was associated with neo-Ricardian economists who emphasized the differences between capital theory based on the generalization of Keynes's *General Theory* and on Sraffa's *Production of Commodities*. The second came from American post Keynesians such as Davidson and Minsky, as well as from Austrian economists such as Ludwig Lachmann, who criticized the emphasis on static or steady-state analysis when it was the process of history that the theory was trying to explain. Both of these criticisms concerned the role of uncertainty and expectations in the theory, the former was critical because it was too great, the latter because it was too small.

A third line of criticism, usually, but not always linked to the second, came from economists who considered Keynes's revolution to have been primarily concerned with monetary theory and considered the long-run models of steady growth in which money played no active role as unacceptable, if not unKeynesian. They argued that Keynes's conception of liquidity should play a crucial role in long-period analysis or else such analysis should be abandoned.

Because of the close relationship that exists between the *Treatise* analysis of the market prices of available and non-available goods and the determination of prices and profits in the post Keynesian long-period growth and distribution models on the one hand, and the modern analysis of the monetary circuit on the other, analysis based on either approach will tend to produce similar results. This presents something of a paradox, for the analysis of the circuit was originally set up to emphasize the role of money and credit, while the first- and second-generation post Keynesian growth and distribution models have been subject to criticism because of their inability to analyse the aspects of money that Keynes considered of importance. As in so many paradoxes, the solution is to be found in a question of definition, in this case in the definition of the essential monetary factors, in who is the Prince of Denmark in the Keynesian Hamlet.

I have recently[2] tried to explain why post Keynesian growth and distribution theory found it difficult to explicitly introduce monetary factors. In simple terms, the story goes something like this. The method of analysis employed in post Keynesian growth theories was to make comparisons of rates of investment presumed to be given exogenously. This eliminated direct discussion of the monetary aspects of the investment decision that Keynes had emphasized in the *General Theory*. Further, the elimination of monetary factors was supported by a widespread interpretation of Keynes's theory as being grounded in the Marshallian short period, which implied that the analysis of growth could be approached only by adapting the theory to long-period conditions by means of the assumption of tranquillity or through comparisons of steady-state expansion paths. In such conditions, the essential components of Keynes's monetary analysis, the interaction of the marginal efficiency of capital and liquidity preference appeared to have little meaning, for their very existence appeared to be grounded in the absence of tranquil or steady-state conditions.

The implications of this interpretation can be seen in the analysis of the determination of the prices of capital goods. While it was assumed that the prices of consumption goods were determined by the supply of output that could be produced by the labour employed by consumption sector entrepreneurs relative to the total demand represented by the expenditures of both consumption and investment sector labourers out of their wages, the prices of capital goods could not be determined in a similar fashion. While the physical supply of investment goods could be considered as determined by the output of the labour employed in the capital goods sectors given technology, the only exogenous market demand for capital goods came from entrepreneurs producing consumption goods. The remaining capital goods were used and purchased within the sector in which they were produced, or even retained for own use by their producers, and therefore netted out within the capital goods sector. It was thus impossible to specify an independent market demand represented by a flow of money expenditures similar to that for the consumption sector output. The most common solution was to consider capital goods prices to be notionally determined; capital goods circulated within the sector and were sold to the consumption goods sector entrepreneurs at equivalent prices unilaterally specified by the capital sector entrepreneurs. To make sense of this explanation, the competitive process applied to the consumption sector was replaced by the assumption of an exogenous mark-up or margin applied to costs of production or that some normal rate of profit was expected in the capital goods sector, equivalent to the rate of profit earned by entrepreneurs in the consumption goods sector, which served to determine margins of prices over costs. But since the rate of profit in the consumption goods sector is itself determined by the level of activity in the investment goods sector, this implied circular reasoning: there was an equilibrium rate of profit associated with the distribution of labour in the two sectors given by the exogenous level of investment, which given wages also determined the absolute and relative price levels in the two sectors. Just as investment was presumed to be exogenous, the rate of profit, or profit margins or mark-ups, supporting the prices of capital goods were also exogenous. Consumption goods prices were only fictitiously competitive, for they were only in equilibrium when they were compatible with these exogenous margins. The only competition which existed in the model was thus the possibility of entrepreneurs to change from one sector to another so as to assure a uniform rate of return on capital.

This is, of course, the very point at which these models departed from Keynes's monetary analysis, for Keynes in the *Treatise* had proposed a rather different explanation of the determination of the prices of capital goods, based on the combined actions of the 'bearishness' of the public and the behaviour of the banking system concerning the 'financial circulation'. These factors produced the prices of capital assets which entered the fundamental equation for the price of output as a whole and which determined the divergence of the value of investment from saving. There was no 'fundamental' price equation for capital assets equivalent to those for consumption goods and output as a whole.

In the *General Theory*, bearishness was replaced by liquidity preference, but now as a determinant of interest rates which, given expectations, implied a given relationship between the spot and forward prices of capital goods. The speculative demand for money replaced the analysis of the financial circulation. The price of investment goods of the *Treatise* was replaced by an interest rate, the marginal efficiency of capital. Despite these differences in presentation, in both the *Treatise* and the *General Theory* the prices of capital goods are integrally related to monetary conditions, and their (spot and future) prices (or their marginal efficiencies) play the central role in determining the investment decisions of entrepreneurs.

Post Keynesian economists who were uneasy with the interpretation of the factors determining capital goods' prices and investment in the long-period steady-state extensions of Keynes's theory thus sought to reintroduce the eliminated monetary factors into the determination of investment goods' prices in attempts to explain the growth process. The work of Minsky stresses the independence of the factors determining the relative prices of capital and consumption goods, emphasizing the influence of money and financial conditions on the former. Davidson offers a stock-flow formulation of spot and forward prices of capital goods, identifying the conditions of backwardation and contango as representing the constellation of prices leading to an expansion and a contraction respectively of the stock of capital. I have myself tried to stress the inherent identity of Keynes's analysis of 'interest rate parity' and his analysis of interest rates and the relation of demand and supply or spot and forward prices of capital goods as represented in Keynes's 'own rate of interest' analysis of investment in chapters XVI and XVII of the *General Theory*. All these interpretations suggest a substantial identity between the *Treatise* analysis of bearishness determining capital goods' *prices* and the theory of liquidity preference determining the marginal efficiencies or *rates of interest* or return of various durable assets. This view of the essential monetary factors stresses an inherent link between the determinants of the money rate of interest, the prices of capital goods and the level of investment.

It is thus the 'bearishness' or 'liquidity preference' theory of the value of capital assets that I referred to as the missing Prince of Denmark in the post Keynesian Hamlet. The circuit approach, while it claims to reflect Keynes's conception of a monetary production economy seems to deny the importance of the link between monetary factors and the prices of capital goods, between the rate of interest and investment; it appears to mistake Shylock for Hamlet.

'All That Glisters Is Not Gold'

One of the characteristic differences of circuit analysis from the earlier post Keynesian growth and distribution models is the explicit discussion of a banking sector alongside the capital and consumption goods sector. The crucial decisions concerning the employment of labour in the consumption and capital goods sectors are thus assumed to require advances from the banking sector for the payment of wages. Following Wicksell, money is assumed to be exogenous credit created *ex nihilo* by the banking sector: a pure credit money. This reflects the so-called 'new approach' to monetary creation in which money creation starts on the asset side of the bank's balance sheet, by the granting of advances which take the form of deposits owned by the borrower on the liability side of the balance sheet.

Let us start by assuming that banks do not charge interest on advances. In this pure credit economy, labour is engaged and paid by means of a transfer of ownership of a bank's deposit liability from entrepreneur to labourer. Total variable factor costs (including the entrepreneur's normal remuneration) are reflected in an equivalent amount of advances to industry on the asset side and an equivalent amount of deposits owned by factors on the liability side of the banking sector's balance sheet. There is a one-to-one correspondence between entrepreneurs' expenditures and the quantity of money represented in this pure credit economy by bank deposits.

The circuit is closed when, as in Keynes's *Treatise* equilibrium, the total of factor costs is used to purchase consumption goods output, and prices are stable. These expenditures are effected by the transfer of ownership of the banks' entire outstanding deposit liabilities to consumption sector entrepreneurs. The difference between their outstanding advances and total deposits is then used to purchase capital goods output from the investment goods sector entrepreneurs. On the assumption that the level of investment and the required margins are given, the ownership of deposits between consumption and investment sector entrepreneurs after the purchase of the capital goods will bear the same proportion as employment, the wage bill and the borrowing from the banks in the two sectors. Each sector thus has ownership of precisely the amount of deposits necessary to discharge their advances from the banks. All labourers' income has been transformed from deposits into consumption output, and all entrepreneurs' income has been transformed into physical capital goods. There is no wealth held in either financial assets or money, nor is there a rate of interest. Clearly, for bearishness to bite in this sort of model something has to allow for the accumulation of wealth in other than real form, or for investment to depart from saving in the *Treatise* sense.

But, first, let us consider this model under the assumption that banks charge interest on advances. The explanation for the existence of interest can only be found in the costs of labour employed in keeping the books of the banking sector in balance, and the normal remuneration of the bank managers. Interest is thus a factor cost just like the payment of labour in the consumption or investment goods sector. Banks now advance to entrepreneurs the amount of their wage bills, and advance to themselves the wages of their own clerks and managers. The creation of deposit liabilities is thus equal to the factor costs in the three sectors taken together. The ownership of these deposits is transferred to the factors in payment for services, who transfer them to consumption sector capitalists in exchange for consumption goods, who in turn transfer a proportion, depending on the ratio of investment to consumption, to the investment sector capitalists, both of whom now possess an amount of deposits which exceeds their outstanding advances by an amount equal to the interest costs on the advances which are paid to the banks. The banks thus receive in interest the ownership of deposits sufficient to extinguish their advances to themselves.

The only difference made by the payment of interest is that the real consumption of labourers is lower due to the consumption of the bank clerks and managers. This is achieved through the higher prices of consumption goods due to the higher ratio of wages in the three sectors to consumption output. The higher receipts are just sufficient to meet the interest costs and the higher prices of capital goods, which reflect the positive interest payments. The payment of interest does not affect the allocation of labour to the production of capital goods, and it is easy to see that the exogenous level of investment may be maintained irrespective of the level of interest, subject to the proviso that real wages do not fall below the subsistence minimum.

Now, as the earlier Cambridge discussions indicate, it is possible to extend this story to allow for savings out of wages and consumption out of profits, the former reducing prices and profits, the latter increasing them. Such an assumption also requires, as Pasinetti pointed out, the existence of a non-commodity store of value which workers may use for savings out of wages, which then implies that their incomes will consist not only of wages but of income received from their stores of value. Pasinetti effectively assumed that physical capital was the only store of value available for workers; they thus received the ruling rate of profit on the value of their capital in addition to their wage incomes. A number of alternative formulations are possible, none of which allows for money as a store of value, and thus they do not change the main results.[3]

Now, as these discussions indicated, the assumption that workers save and capitalists consume is not of particular importance (as the *Treatise* formulation should make clear) except on the level of prices in the consumption sector and thus on real wages and profit rates: a minimum real wage and rate of profit must be stipulated to assure the survival of the system.

The problem of providing financial assets as stores of value for wage earners' savings did, however, open up a number of questions of interest. Consider an economy in which wage-earning households save and buy bonds issued by firms. The mechanism of Kaldor's neo-Pasinetti theorem is that if investment is invariant, changes in the price of bonds (the rate of interest) should adjust households' unearned incomes so as to equate (in the terminology of the *General Theory*) savings by wage earners out of wages and interest plus savings by pure profit recipients to the given level of investment. (In the sense of the *Treatise*, the rate of interest is established at which savings equal the cost of investment.) In equilibrium wage earners' consumption will fall short of their combined earned and unearned income by the same amount that retentions by firms fall short of investment. The saving of households will then be equal to the value of bonds issued with the rate of interest the variable which produces equilibrium by acting on the level of their unearned income, given the propensity to save. If saving at the ruling state of interest were greater than the firms' borrowing requirements, the price of bonds would be higher and the rate of interest would be lower. The return per unit of household wealth would be lower, as would the financing costs to firms.

Whether the financial assets provided to households come directly from the issue of bonds by firms, or whether they choose to hold bank deposits or time deposits with the banks holding the bonds, this result should remain unchanged. The only difference is that the ownership of some of the deposits issued to meet factor costs is not transferred back to the firms to repay the initial advances that brought them into existence. In order to repay advances, the firms simply issue bonds to a value of the shortfall which the banks substitute for the advances on the asset side of their balance sheets. The profits of the banks then also become an adjustment variable to assure that prices are such to justify the prevailing level of investment.

The basic difference between this model and the previous is that the rate of interest is now determined endogenously, just as the price of consumption and capital goods. There are now two aspects to the rate of interest, the first is the margin between borrowing and lending rates which must cover the payment of the banks' factor costs and the second is the banks' profits, which are now also constrained by the economy-wide rate of profit.

It is within this sort of framework that one of the basic propositions of the circuit approach can be clearly seen: the amount of profits in real terms is independent of the rate of interest. But this result is always true within the kind of post Keynesian model discussed here, whether or not the financial analysis considers only bank advances and deposits, or is extended to consider the rate of interest at which households' and firms' savings will balance the given rate of investment. As long as the banking sector is considered on the same basis as the consumption and capital goods sectors the rate of interest will be set, just as the prices of consumption and capital goods, so as to produce the ruling uniform rate of profit required for savings to balance the level of investment. It does not appear to make any difference whether the finance of the deficits of the consumption and capital goods production by the surpluses of households takes place directly or whether it is intermediated by the banking sector. The problem is that once there is private sector savings, the banks' control of liabilities will no longer be directly subject to their lending policy.

This result suggests that the proposition[4] that the level of real profits cannot be independent of the rate of interest in post Keynesian models because they presume that firms sell bonds directly to households, so that higher interest payments create a transfer of wealth from firms to savers, will only hold under two conditions which are not necessarily present in such models: the assets held by banks do not produce wealth transfers similar to those postulated for households, and the rate of interest is either taken to be determined exogenously of conditions prevailing in financial markets or is determined in a different way from the other prices in the model. It would seem that only in the case in which Shylock can extort rates of interest without changing capital values, and bank and household incomes from wealth holding, that the rate of interest is not independent of investment. In either case, however, the objection to such analysis is the fact that it considers changes in the rate of interest without allowing for changes in the rate of investment. When Hamlet plays the Prince, it is impossible to postulate a change in the rate of interest without a change in liquidity preference which will change the prices of capital assets and thus the investment decisions of entrepreneurs.

The proposition that the level of real profits is independent of the rate of interest does not hold rather because a change in the rate of interest is presumed to react instantly on the present and expected profitability of capital goods and thus on their demand prices. Bank assets which pay interest rates provide alternatives to the earning of profit by investment in employing labour in the capital goods sector; entrepreneurs in the capital and consumption sector take advances to purchase financial assets rather than hire labour. The financial circulation expands at the expense of the industrial circulation. Hamlet walks the ramparts, 'to invest or not to invest' is a question that depends on the liquidity preferences of entrepreneurs, workers and the banks. But it is a question that is difficult to discuss if it is presumed that investment is independent of all but the willingness of Shylock to create sufficient credit to allow his clients to pay his exorbitant rates of interest.

Endogenous Money: New View?

There is one further point that concerns the way that money is introduced into the economy which distinguishes the Keynesian Hamlet from Shylock. Since the discovery of the bank multiplier in the 1920s and 1930s and its use to show how a real equilibrium may be disturbed by the creation of money in excess of the money base by Hayek, Mises and others, economists have been taught that an increase in deposit liabilities furnishes the raw material to 'create' money, or that government expenditures financed by borrowing provides the liabilities which create reserves which then lead to money expansion. It was in reaction to this view that the so-called 'new approach' of endogenous money restored the historical approach which considered the process of creation to be built on bank assets rather than liabilities: the banks lend first and look for reserves later, if they don't find them in the interbank market it is up to the central bank to furnish them. That this was once the mainstream view finds testimony in its presence in Dennis Robertson's little book on money in the Cambridge Economic Handbooks series and refers directly to the difficulty faced by the central bank when the borrower happens to be the government, but applies to any borrower with direct access to financial markets.

Thus, in reaction to the view that money creation should be determined by real activity, and in agreement with the 'new view', money in the circuit approach is considered to be an endogenously determined pure credit money. However, this description does not reflect the basic characteristics of the credit money that currently exists in the modern world. Our current cheque and transfer systems did not grow out of the clever goldsmiths lending receipts in an amount greater than their deposits (not that this did not exist, it even existed in the Chicago grain markets at the turn of the century), rather it developed out of the system of inland and overseas bills of exchange. It was the bill on London which was the first pure credit money, and which served to finance the industrial as well as the financial circulation.

In this system, the exporter draws a bill on the importer for goods which will arrive and be sold in the future. The importer accepts the liability to pay the bill at maturity by signing it and returning it to the exporter who discounts it at his bank as payment for the goods exported. When the bill becomes due, it is paid by the importer's bank to the exporter's bank. The importer then has a debt to this bank rather than the exporter (or the exporter's bank) which he is able to discharge when the goods he has imported have arrived and are sold allowing repayment of the importer's debt to his bank. The payments circuit is then closed.

Now, I would suggest that this method of finance allows the more ready introduction of a crucial aspect of the Keynesian conception of money and the introduction of money into the economy. In the circuit approach, it sometimes appears that labour is paid today only in order to spend and allow the bank finance to be repaid by the employer. In the Keynesian (or Marxian) story, labour is paid in order to work. It is the labour contract that is the crux of the monetary system because of the particular nature of the debt contract under which labour works. In the Marxian explanation, the capitalist pays labour its current market value in exchange for an entire day's labour, the positive difference between the latter over the former constitutes surplus value. In the Keynesian system, the labour contract implies the exchange of a day's work against an unknown quantity of future consumption goods because the value of today's wage depends on future consumption goods prices. Labour contracts its wage and is paid in money, the future consumption value of which is a risk borne completely by labour.

In the Keynesian monetary production economy, money is considered to be primarily a transfer of the debt of firms to the banks to labour; a debt which the market or the banks may or may not validate depending on future conditions. Is there a difference between an endogenous credit money and money considered as debt? The difference lies, I think, in the location of the initial debt relationship. The labour contract in Keynes's theory is a debt relationship in which workers exchange present labour for future consumption. In a real wage economy, the amounts of future consumption are specified in terms of the expected future output. In an entrepreneurial economy, labour is contracted for a wage in terms of the money unit of account: present labour is exchanged for an unspecified amount of future consumption which depends on the level of prices and the pattern of consumption. Does this allow us to find the source of interest which is absent in the circuit approach?

One might characterize the Keynesian story as labour drawing an implicit bill on the capitalists when the contract to furnish labour to produce future output for a specified amount of unit of account is agreed. The capitalist's promise to pay future goods allows the labourer to go to his bank and discount the 'bill', that is, the expected receipts of the sale of the output of the hired labour which allows the entrepreneur to agree to hire labour and pay wages is now owed to the bank, transforming the debt of labour to produce future output into a debt of the entrepreneur to pay the proceeds of future output to the bank. The interest due is here clearly seen to be paid by labour rather than by the entrepreneur, for the money value of labour falls short of the expected real value by the amount of the banker's discount in excepting the bill. When the future output is produced labour has extinguished its debt to the entrepreneur; when the output is sold the entrepreneur transfers its deposits to the banker who clears the advance to labour and keeps the discount as his remuneration. Here money is created by discounting future output and it is extinguished when the output is sold in the market. There is no need to assume that interest is produced by the workers employed by the bank: the financing of production is costless, as it should be in a credit economy. And interest is created by the uncertainty of the value of future output which is as it should be. The difference is that the uncertainty is present in the labour contract, as well as in the banker's advances to the capitalist.

Notes

1 Paper presented at the ISMEA Conference on Money and Production, Paris, 14–15 June 1985.

2 "Hamlet Without the Prince: Cambridge Macroeconomics Without Money," *American Economic Review*, 75, May 1985, pp. 133–39.

3 See, for example, J. A. Kregel, *Rate of Profit, Distribution and Growth: Two Views*, Macmillan, 1971; R. Marris, "Why Economics Needs a Theory of the Firm," *Economic Journal*, special issue in honour of Austin Robinson, March 1972. B. J. Moore shows the case where interest payments are less than the ruling rate of profit, "The Pasinetti Paradox Revisited," *Review of Economic Studies*, April, 1974. All of these alternatives make uses in some form or other of Kaldor's "neo-Pasinetti theorem" in "Marginal Productivity and the Macro-Economic Theories of Distribution", *Review of Economic Studies*, Oct. 1966.

4 A. Graziani, "Monnaie, intérêt et dépenses publiques," *Économies et Sociétés*, série *Monnaie et Production*, No. 2, 1985, pp. 209–27.

Chapter 5

THE THEORETICAL CONSEQUENCES OF ECONOMIC METHODOLOGY: SAMUELSON'S FOUNDATIONS

Introduction(*)

The 1930s proved to be one of the most fertile decades of this century from the point of view of the production of original theoretical ideas, the "Years of High Theory" in Shackle's words (Shackle, 1967). The period witnessed the development of the theory of imperfect competition by Harrod, Kahn, Robinson, and Chamberlin; the Keynes-Hayek debates over economic policy with the eventual predominance of Keynes' ideas over those of Hayek and the Austrians; the Swedes' contribution of the concepts of ex-ante and ex-post in a period or sequence analysis to the expectational aspect of Wicksell's theory; Harrod's formulation of his "dynamic" economics; the reworking of demand theory by Hicks and Allen, as well as many other innovations, not least of which the original work on, if not the formal publication of (delayed by the war), Samuelson's *Foundations of Economic Analysis*.

Despite the diverse nature of these theoretical innovations, post-war economic theory exhibited remarkable unity and coherence. The speed with which these widely varied pre-war innovations were incorporated into a commonly accepted framework can, to a large extent, be credited to Samuelson's book which, in contrast to the other innovations of the thirties, did not provide an alternative approach to a particular problem, but rather suggested how particular problems might be handled in a unified, general way. The criticisms of the "equilibrium" theory that have been voiced in recent years (for example by Kaldor, 1972 and Robinson, 1974) would seem to be somewhat wide of the mark unless they were also intended to apply to the unified methodological approach to economic analysis which grew up around the promise of "meaningful theorems" that Samuelson's book offered to the practising economist:

"It is the task of comparative statics to show the determination of the equilibrium values of given variables (unknowns) under postulated conditions (functional relationships) with various data (parameters) being specified." Thus, in the simplest case of a partial-equilibrium market for a single commodity, the two independent relations of supply and demand, each drawn up with other prices and institutional data being taken as given, determine by their intersection the equilibrium quantities of the unknown

---

* The author wishes to thank S. K. Kuipers, A. Roncaglia, and C. Torr for discussions, comments and suggestions without implicating them in the final version.

price and quantity sold. If no more than this could be said, the economist would be truly vulnerable to the gibe that he is only a parrot taught to say "supply and demand". Simply to know that there are efficacious laws "determining equilibrium tells us nothing of the character of these laws. In order for the analysis to be useful it must provide information concerning the way in which our equilibrium quantities will change as a result of changes in the parameters taken as independent data" (Samuelson, 1947, p. 257).

Samuelson's contribution is, indeed, not associated with the concept of equilibrium as such, but with the promise that the construction could be made into an operationally meaningful idea by means of the recognition of two exceedingly simple and general hypotheses: (1) "the conditions of equilibrium are equivalent to the maximisation (minimisation) of some magnitude" (2) "in even the simplest business cycle theories there is lacking symmetry in the conditions of equilibrium so that there is no possibility of directly reducing the problem to that of a maximum or minimum. Instead the dynamical properties of the system are specified, and the hypothesis is made that the system is in 'stable' equilibrium or motion. By means of what I have called the Correspondence Principle between comparative statics and dynamics, definite *operationally meaningful* theorems can be derived from so simple a hypothesis" (*Ibid.*, p. 5).

Armed with these two hypotheses, a set of functional relations and initial conditions the economist was equipped to handle not only the full range of particular problems in economics, but also to give qualitative scientific statements about the behaviour of the system. The transformation of static equilibrium conditions into an operational theory upon which scientific prediction could be made was no small achievement, in particular to the nascent fields of applied economics and econometrics, both of which had achieved a special place in the development of the by then full-blown Keynesian revolution.

Like all innovation, however, this one was not without its drawbacks. It shall be argued that one of these was not only the absorption, but also the elimination of discussion and analysis, of many of the most interesting innovations that had surfaced in the 1930s: The present discussion will introduce two points of criticism in relation to Samuelson's methodological innovation. First, that the limitations that it places on economic analysis have not been adequately recognised, and second, that neither has its full generality been adequately recognised. The limits will be discussed in relation to the inability of the method to accommodate certain other innovations of the period, in particular in monetary theory, without voiding them of meaningful content. The generality argument is advanced with reference to the capital theory debates, by suggesting that the two hypotheses cited by Samuelson may apply to any theoretical system that admits of forces that produce equilibrium as a result of maximisation and need not be limited to the traditional theories of supply and demand. The failure to note these two, seemingly paradoxical, points has allowed Samuelson's innovation to be used as an apology for a particular theoretical approach, often called the "neoclassical synthesis", which has tended to eliminate the consideration of alternative approaches and which produced the coherence and unity of the 'fifties and early 'sixties. It should be noted that these are not criticisms of the method itself, a subject of merit which has been extensively treated elsewhere,[1] but rather of the inappropriate use and interpretation that has been made of the method by economists in general.

I. UNCERTAINTY, EXPECTATIONS AND MONETARY THEORY

A. G. Hart, in his 1951 Preface to the reprint of his 1936 Chicago Ph.D. dissertation (Hart, 1951) notes the excitement generated in the early 1930's in such distant centers as Vienna, London and Chicago by the introduction of an explicit role for expectations in the monetary theories of Hayek, Keynes and the Swedes and the value theories of Knight and Fisher. Early writers cited as being influenced by this approach are Hicks, Lindahl, Abramowitz, Marshak, Shackle, and Tintner, as well as Hart himself. However, he also admits, reviewing this work fifteen years later that the "hopes of developing a formal dynamic theory organised around anticipations do not seem to be panning out". As support for this assessment he notes that "when the American Economic Association assigned P. A. Samuelson to report on the progress of dynamic economics [in the 1948 *Survey of Contemporary Economics,* ed. H. Ellis] the result was an essay on the logic and application of differential equations, with no discussion of anticipations anywhere visible" (op. *cit.,* pp. vii-viii).

The explanation for this lack of success is not hard to find once it is recognised that the dynamic method set out by Samuelson in the *Foundations* left no place for discussion of such matters. In his use of the correspondence principle Samuelson has already claimed for dynamics a special role in the application and interpretation of comparative statics. He had also, however, allowed for the cultivation of "dynamics for its own sake" which was to produce a more powerful "comparative dynamics" (1947, p. 351). Defining a "dynamical system" as "any set of functional equations which together with initial conditions (in the most general sense) determine as solutions certain unknowns in function of time" (*ibid.,* p. 284) "comparative dynamics" ... "consider(s) a much broader class of changes. (a) We may make a change in *initial conditions.* By definition this alters the immediate behavior of the system in a known way. By the assumption of continuity we may infer that the position of the system for some region adjacent to the initial conditions is also altered in the same direction. ... (b) We may make a change in some *force* acting on the system ... [e.g.] cause autonomous investment to vary ... In the case of stable systems the response to a permanent alteration gives us a description of the actual path followed by the system in going from one 'comparative static level' to another. ... (c) Finally, there may be a change in some internal parameter of the system. ... From a short run point of view interest will center on the immediate reaction on the system. The answer to this question can often be secured by a method which is formally like that of comparative statics with the significant difference that some of the variables treated are really dynamic in character". (*Ibid.,* p. 352-3).

Hart himself points out "the difficulty of formalizing the way expectations are formed" noting that if this process is presumed to be endogenous, as it would have to meet the conception of dynamics given in the *Foundations,* and "expectations depend strictly on the previous sequence of economic-quantitative events — and that pattern is stable, then any formal model will show events as a function of expectations, and expectations as a functions of earlier events. In this case events can be reduced to a function of earlier events. The result is a clearcut 'sequence analysis' in which anticipations need not appear explicitly — formally a *mechanical dynamics,* with an *expectational dynamics* between the lines" (*op. cit.*, p. viii). Thus, even if taken into account explicitly, as long as formation is on the basis of endogenous elements expectations themselves need not be expressly referred to, they may remain "between the lines".

On the other hand, "if we assume ... that expectations, on the basis of a past sequence of economic quantities are powerfully influenced by politics, inventions, etc., then without bringing in 'exogenous' variables we cannot get a clearcut process-analysis sequence. We may assume we know expectations and plans at the outset; but after a few 'periods' the influence of revisions accumulates" and "the most we can hope for along this line is to show that some types of starting points will set up 'cumulative processes' — sometimes also that such processes will presently reverse themselves. Even the rather loose generalizations about periodicity and amplitude of fluctuation Hicks offers in his *Trade Cycle* threaten to dissolve into mist. This is a nuisance to theoretical system-builders; also to forecasters" (*Ibid.*, p. ix). In short, unless those other factors influencing expectations can be set out as stable continuous functional relations they must be left outside of the analysis as exogenous, while if they can be so modelled they can be dispensed with altogether. This point has also been stressed repeatedly by Shackle who points out the very process of maximisation can only take place if the elements required for the decisions that lead to a maximum are known. If the most important elements in this process are future values of the variables either they must be reduced to functional relations of known variables or maximisation must be considered as an inappropriate framework of analysis for the economic system. Shackle, following in the tradition of Keynes, Fisher, Myrdal and Hayek, also stresses that the mathematical probabilities of future events cannot provide a suitable proxy since such a method requires that all probable results be known in advance, which violates the definition of an uncertain event as being a unique historical event (Cf. Shackle, e.g. 1968, 1972).

Thus, from the standpoint of Samuelson's methodology, expectations must emerge as either unimportant and unnecessary to the formal model (endogenous formation) or completely outside the scope of the analysis (exogenous formation). As Samuelson himself notes in his application to the analysis of the demand for money, "The most interesting problems arising in connection with money are linked up with the fact of 'uncertainty' in the most general sense, leading into liquidity considerations which cannot be discussed here" (*op. cit.*, p. 117). But, as Hart emphasizes, it is precisely the exogenous aspect of expectations which made uncertainty such an important part of the innovations in monetary theory in the 'thirties. "In monetary theory, *uncertainty* grows more and more crucial. Expectational dynamics is essential in any business cycle theory which is not content to remain purely mechanical" (1951, p. ix).

This point of view is most strongly formulated by Hicks in what became the most influential article of the period on monetary theory, "A Suggestion for Simplifying the Theory of Money" which called for an application of the existing theory of value to the analysis of money: "We have been concerned ... with an analysis ... of the equilibrium of a balance sheet. This analysis has at least shown that the relative size of the different items on this balance-sheet is governed mainly by anticipation of the yield of investments and of risks. It is these anticipations which play a part here corresponding to the part played by prices in value theory. Now the fact that our 'equilibrium' is here determined by subjective factors like anticipations, instead of objective factors like prices, means that this purely theoretical study of money can never hope to reach results so tangible and precise as those which value theory in its more limited field can hope to attain. If I am right, the whole problem of applying monetary theory is largely one of deducing changes in anticipations from the changes in the objective data which call them forth. Obviously, this is not an easy task, and, above all, it is not one which can be performed in a mechanical fashion. It needs judgement and knowledge of business psychology much more than sustained logical reasoning" (Hicks, 1935, pp. 75-6). Hicks thus calls for the continued study of "the connexion between objective facts and anticipations" as well as admonishing economists "to bring out very clearly [their] assumptions ... about the genesis of anticipations" (*ibid.*, p. 76).

Samuelson's method, more suited to the logically precise domain of value theory did not seem to provide a propitious framework for response to either of these points. Thus, the meaningful analysis of the 1930's advances in monetary theory, of whatever variety, remained outside the scope of the 'meaningful propositions' offered by means of the operation of the correspondence principle on comparative static analysis. This is not, of course, meant to indicate that economists who adopted this approach thought such matters unimportant, rather that the framework did not explicitly require their formal consideration. This fact eventually led to the unwarranted belief that anticipations could be considered as unimportant complications: "In fact, any sector of economic theory which cannot be cast into the mold of such a system must be regarded with suspicion as suffering from haziness" (1947, p. 9). Thus expectations which had formed a crucial part of all economic theory, even the most rigorous, before the war, was relegated to an exogenous existence and was eventually banished in the name of precision.

This was particularly true in the case of the representation of the Keynesian system; indeed, it was commonplace only a year after Keynes' book was published for the consumption function, liquidity preference, and the marginal efficiency of capital all to be written as stable, continuous functions of ruling rates of interest and realised levels of income (e.g. Samuelson, 1947, pp. 276 ff.). Ironically, Hicks (1937) also adopted this method despite his 1935 insistence on anticipations in monetary theory and his 1936 *Economic Journal* review of the *General Theory* in which he cited as innovation the explicit use of such.[2] Thus, Keynes insistence on the importance of the future values of variables and the potential instability of expectations about these values, at least in relation to the latter two functions, was conveniently forgotten. It is quite clear that, on Hart's argument, if expectations formation is endogenous this omission can be considered as harmless. If they are exogenous, as Keynes must surely have meant them to be taken (consider his references to the 'State of the News', Shackle's clear statement (Shackle, 1973) and Hicks' subsequent views on Keynes' intentions in Hicks, 1977) they cannot be set out in the formal way that would be required by Samuelson's method and some alternative approach would be necessary.[3] The simple result is that expectations and uncertainty dropped out of the formal Keynesian model that is based on the 'neoclassical synthesis' and Hicks IS-LM representation. The innovations that caused such excitement in the 'thirties have been forced to live on in the economic underground of the post-Keynesian and neo-Austrian challenges to the 'Keynesian' orthodoxy.[4] Certainly, a readier appreciation of the limits of the formal application of the methodology proposed in the *Foundations* might have allowed these innovations to be further developed and discussed instead of being assigned to the realms of 'hazy' economics which might better be avoided by those interested in 'scientific' analysis.[5]

II. CAPITAL THEORY, NON-STEADY-STATE ANALYSIS AND ALTERNATIVE THEORY

The reader should be careful to note that the above criticism is not "the commonplace criticism of comparative statics that it does not do what it is not aimed to do, namely describe the transition paths between equilibria" (Samuelson, 1947, p. 263, n. 8) but rather concerns the failure to recognise explicitly the limits on the generality of the "meaningful statements" that could be made in the face of the recognition of exogenous determinants in expectations formation. The second point to be considered, that of the failure to recognise the full generality or the methodological approach of the *Foundations*, does however touch on confusion over the commonplace criticism of comparative statics, or at least over the meaning to be attached to the comparative dynamics developed from it. This point may be considered with reference to the so-called "reswitching controversy" in the theory of capital.

Recently, Joan Robinson has tried to draw the conclusions of that debate by referring to the "Unimportance of Reswitching" (Robinson 1975 a, 1979 b, 1980). She points out that while the formal results of the debate are derived from comparisons of independent economies in stable equilibrium, each with its own past and its own future (1975 a, p. 38), some economists interested in defending what has come to be called the 'neoclassical parable' often express these arguments as if they were the result of an historical "process of accumulation going on through time" (*Ibid.*, pp. 37-8). She accuses Samuelson of such an error even in his (Samuelson, 1966) admission of the limited generality of the negative monotonic relation between the rate of interest and the capital intensity of production and the falsity of the "non-switching theorem".

There seems to be no question that the early neoclassical theorists (as well as some latter-day exponents) did intend their theory to be interpreted in this way: "In the conventional model, successive sacrifices of consumption and accumulation of capital goods leads to lower interest rates. This conventional neoclassical version of diminishing returns is spelled out at length in my *Economics*" (Samuelson, 1966, p. 241). It also seems clear that the argument posed in this way would be considered in the "parrot" category; its meaningful analysis requiring the application of the correspondence principle. That Samuelson considers the discussion in this way is clearly seen in his response to Joan Robinson's criticism (Robinson, 1975 a).

In the *Foundations* he clearly states "It will be seen that comparative statics involves the special case where a 'permanent' change is made, and only the effects upon final levels of stationary equilibrium are in question" (Samuelson, 1947, p. 352), "of course, if we confine our attention to the behaviour of long period stationary equilibrium positions, the methods of comparative statics come into their own ... the resulting system solved like any statical system" (*Ibid.*, p. 355). Thus, to counter Joan Robinson's accusation that he had inappropriately deduced the movement of a system from one equilibrium to another from equilibrium conditions Samuelson responded: "Suppose that ... I had written ... 'a switchback had *permanently* occurred at a *permanent* low interest rate to the techniques *permanently* viable at a *permanent* high interest rate *subsequent* to successful saving-investment abstaining in the past from then current consumption as envisaged by the neoclassical writers being quoted'" (Samuelson, 1975, pp. 43-4) which clearly marks the analysis as one of comparative statics which, as the warning quoted above makes clear, should not be misconstrued as a description of a transition through time nor as an historical process. Samuelson is clearly responding in a way appropriate to someone who believes that he is being accused of the "commonplace error" noted above. He can thus magnanimously accept Joan Robinson's view that the capital theory debates do not refer to historical process or transition, thereby emphasising his legitimate use of the methodology of the *Foundations* and at the same time leaving open the possibility that such statements might legitimately be made on the basis of a "comparative dynamics" such as discussed above (cf. especially the statement, "In the case of stable systems the response to a permanent alteration gives us a description of the actual path followed by the system ..." (Samuelson, 1947, p. 352)). It would thus appear that Samuelson is quite justified to conclude that Joan Robinson's quarrel is "over whether non-steady-state analysis can be meaningfully formulated and handled" (Samuelson, 1975, p. 45), for she has argued that it cannot when exogenous expectations are considered within an historical process (cf. Robinson, 1974). In particular, her position would seem to challenge the stability and continuity assumptions required for such dynamic analysis on the basis of the *Foundations*.

Samuelson, on the other hand, adopts the position that as long as one considers that "comparative statics is but one special application of the more general practice of scientific deduction in which the behaviour of the system (possibly through time) is defined in terms of a given set of functional equations and initial conditions" (Samuelson, 1947, p. 8) such dynamic analysis "which determines the behaviour through time of all variables from arbitrary initial conditions" (*Ibid.,* p. 266) is not only possible but can be done scientifically, i.e. such as to produce meaningful propositions which may be falsified.

Clearly, this is a rather different idea of dynamics than that of Hart and Robinson. Compare Samuelson: "By a liberal interpretation of the circumlocution 'variable at a different point, in time', we may bring differential equations under the definition, remembering that differential coefficients characterise the behaviour of a function in the neighborhood of a point" (*Ibid.,* p. 314), and "The only sense in which the use of the word causation is admissable is in respect to changes in external data or parameters. As a figure of speech, it may be said that changes in these *cause* changes in the variables of our system" (*Ibid.,* p. 9).

Samuelson's dynamics studies the "responses of equilibrium unknowns to designated changes in paramaters, i.e., we wish to know the properties of the functions" (*Ibid.,* p. 20). It would be impossible to mistake these "limiting rates of change" (*Ibid.,* p. 10) for historical transition or adjustment. But, even though "the problem of stability of equilibrium cannot be discussed without reference to dynamical considerations, however implicit and rudimentary" (*Ibid.,* p. 262) it must be remembered that "from the standpoint of comparative statics equilibrium is not something which is attained; it is something which, if attained, displays certain properties" (*Ibid.*, p. 9). Even in his hints at a "comparative dynamics" in the conclusions to the *Foundations* Samuelson rules out the type of historical process which Joan Robinson accuses him of illegitimately employing and whose proper application she believes capable of demonstrating the errors inherent in neoclassical theory. Samuelson's response is that he is not guilty of the charge, nor is he in agreement on the proper approach to dynamical analysis.

Since Samuelson's reply was perfectly adequate to the criticism as he interpreted it, the reader might well wonder whether the point at issue was nothing more than semantic confusion between mathematical and literary expression (J. Robinson, 1979 b). It would seem clear that Samuelson did not err in applying his methodology. The "changes" to which his analysis refers are precisely those carried out along a Sraffa-type wage-profit relation (or, in Samuelson's terminology, factor-price frontier): virtual changes. Indeed. Joan Robinson herself uses a form of this method when she argues: "Now compare a situation where everything else in the model is the same except that ..." (Robinson, 1975 a, p. 33) which corresponds to Samuelson's "permanent change".

In fact, in the *Foundations* Samuelson does discuss what appears to be the substantive point at issue when he notes "that the restrictions imposed by our hypotheses on our equilibrium equations (stability and maximum conditions, etc.) are not always sufficient to indicate *definite* restrictions as to algebraic sign of the rates of changes of our variables with respect to any parameter" (Samuelson, 1947, p. 19), yet "the usefulness of the formulation of equilibrium conditions ... lies in the fact that by so doing we often gain knowledge concerning possible and necessary responses of our variables to changes in data. ... The properties ordinarily discussed in this connection ... are the kind implied by the law of diminishing returns" (*Ibid.*, p. 12). This particular property (or "law") imposed on the equilibrium equations used in the formulation of the "conventional version" of the neoclassical model is clearly exogenous to the method used to set out its results.[6] It is the "conventional neoclassical version of diminishing returns" introduced as a "definite restriction" into a theoretically agnostic methodological framework which allows the formulation of the "meaningful proposition" that increased saving-accumulation would be associated with lower rates of interest. It was this proposition as expressed in the demand curve for aggregate capital which the capital theory debates showed to be false, irrespective of whether increase is viewed as an "historical" or "permanent" change.

It is here that Joan Robinson's remark that "there is no such phenomenon in real life as accumulation in a given state of technical knowledge" (Robinson, 1975 a, p. 39) applies, indicating that the concept was "created only to give meaning to the marginal productivity of aggregate capital. The assumption is, of course, necessary to give support to the "restriction" of diminishing returns. But, even if a definitive negative response could be given to the question of "whether reswitching is 'likely' to be found in reality" (*Ibid.*) it would not provide justification for the "non-switching theorem" (as Samuelson and Levhari, 1966, p. 247 themselves stress) for the definite restriction of diminishing returns would still not be sufficient to justify the conventional version of the neoclassical relation between saving-accumulation and the rate of interest. In Joan

Robinson's words: "The thought experiment of accumulation in a given state of technical knowledge has not been a success" (Robinson, 1975 b, p. 54).

It is clear that the point at issue is not whether the method used to arrive at this conclusion has application to historical changes or are only logical exercises, but rather concerns the validity of the theoretical system which supplied the restrictions (or "laws") applied to the equilibrium conditions (and which also account for the assumption of a given state of technical knowledge). As Samuelson notes, "without such restrictions our theories would be meaningless" (Samuelson, 1947, p. 12). But, when theory suggests restrictions that produce falsifiable conclusions that are shown to be in error, scientific method suggests that the theory should be revised or abandoned. The point that Joan Robinson presumably wanted answered was why the theory that had produced the errors discovered in the reswitching debates was not also considered to be erroneous. Indeed, it is difficult to accept fully the results of these debates and continue to maintain "the conventional neoclassical version of diminishing returns".

Yet, Samuelson (1975, p. 43, n. 6) states that "From neoclassical considerations alone I should not have been in even momentary doubt on the matter of the falsity [of the non-switching theorem], since how can *one* function, r = r (w), contain the content of independent *two*-sector functions ... I am glad now to reinforce Professor Robinson's warning that, in transient states, the 1962 schedules [of the surrogate production function] will not be observed". It should be clear, however, that spotting such an error has nothing to do with "neoclassical considerations", but with pure logic; neoclassical economics has nothing to say about the proper mathematical specification of an equation system. It was, however, neoclassical considerations that led to the doubts that were expressed about the challenges to the generality of the neoclassical relation between r and w. Neither does the argument turn in any essential way on transient states, for the relation, will be no more general, nor will it be "observed" in equilibrium states, unless diminishing returns to aggregate capital in a given state of technical knowledge is accepted. The problem has little, if anything, to do with the modelling of processes going on over time. Suggesting that it does only allows a perfectly good justification for exonerating "neoclassical considerations" from error.

The confusion that has arisen between these two aspects of the discussion had recently been highlighted by Garegnani (1976, 1979) who objects that Joan Robinson's criticism of the "long-period method" is not germaine to the capital theory debates. He stresses that what is at issue is the theoretical structure to which the method is applied. It is the simple application of neoclassical supply and demand theory to the analysis of capital and distribution that produces the errors, not any limitation of the method that is used to apply the theory. Garegnani proposes that such problems can be better handled within a classical theory based on the work of Ricardo and Marx. Here the question is clearly not the possibility of non-steady-state analysis, but rather the theoretical structure appropriate to such analysis: the discussion should remain a confrontation between alternative approaches to the theory of value.

The *Foundations* has tended to reinforce the idea that the particular version of neoclassical theory to which it was applied was also general and unique. But, the first of the hypotheses proposed in the *Foundations* only presumes maximisation as a condition of equilibrium: it does not specify either constraint nor maximand. It is the content of the equilibrium equations and the restrictions applied to them that depend directly on theoretical vision.

The innovations of the *Foundations* are methodological and as such should be independent of the particular form of theory to which they are applied, or which is used to derive the necessary restrictions. Samuelson clearly recognises this, yet when he discusses alternative equilibrium conditions they are all within the general neoclassical approach (cf. his discussion of the differences between the conditions used by Marshall and Walras in Samuelson, 1947, pp. 260 ff). But, there is no reason why the method cannot be applied to alternative conceptions of equilibrium which also presume maximisation, e.g. competitive forces leading to investment patterns in which the pattern of production yields uniform rates of profit in all lines of production given technology. The method should be general enough to apply to both classical and neoclassical approaches. The failure to recognise this generality has led to a mistaken belief that the theory to which it was applied was also general. But it would certainly be possible to retain the methodological approach of the *Foundations* and accept that the capital theory debates require rejection of neoclassical value theory. This, of course, still leaves the question of the limits of the approach discussed in Part I and implies that that discussion should apply equally to both neoclassical *and* classical theory as generally formulated.[7]

Conclusions

Two criticisms have been made of the impact of the *Foundations*: 1) the failure to recognise explicit limits to the generality of the approach particularly with respect to the place of expectations and the treatment of monetary theory, 2) the failure to recognise the true generality of the method as applying to all approaches in which equilibria are characterised by maxima, irrespective of the theoretical foundation. Both these failures have tended unecessarily and inappropriately to support a particular version of neoclassical theory at the expense of alternative analysis, of both a classical *and* neoclassical lineage. This is most telling in the singular lack of success of the most important innovations of the 'thirties to survive incorporation into the framework of the neoclassical synthesis[8] and the failure to identify formal theoretical differences and draw appropriate scientific conclusions in the capital theory debates.[9]

Notes

1 Criticism of the correspondence principle began early in this journal, cf. Patinkin, 1952. It has been the subject of more intense recent attack (e.g. Arrow and Hahn, 1971, pp. 320-1; Brown and Rogers, 1978; Bryant, 1980; Ott., 1980; Rogers and Torr, 1980, pp. 138 ff.) which suggests that Samuelson's claims for the principle cannot be sustained. These criticisms suggest that the methodology of the *Foundations* is only valid where a proper maximisation problem may be identified. The related question of the identity between the method formulated by Samuelson and neoclassical economics is also excluded. Such identity is implicit in the views of those who equate marginalism, maximisation, equilibrium and neoclassical economics.

2 Hicks (1980-1, p. 140, n. 3) has recently reminded his readers that although, "it is true that when I came to 'Mr Keynes and the Classics' I did propose to make investment depend on current output ... I have never regarded this as an essential part of the IS-LM construction ... it has never been intended ... that investment changes should be entirely explicable by changes in 'output' ... There was always a residual element, depending on expectations, and many other things, which could vary independently". Despite this disclaimer, it should be noted that after his 1935 article Hicks eliminated such effects from his formal models.

3 Keynes himself suggested the explicit introduction of variables to represent the "State of Expectation", a solution also available to Samuelson's method, and which would not require explanation of the process of expectations "formation", a pursuit Keynes believed best lft to psychologists. Cf. the discussion in Kregel, 1976, p. 211.

4 The former has its pole of attraction in the *Journal of Post Keynesian Economics* and the *Cambridge Journal of Economics*, the latter in the programme in Austrian economic theory that has grown up around the seminars that Ludwig Lachmann and other prominent Austrian theorists have conducted at New York University since the mid 'seventies.

5 It is perhaps ironical that Samuelson himself now deplores the implications of the "rational" approach to expectations formation on the basis of closed endogenous models fully consistent with his method. Indeed, these models demonstrate the limits of the methodology in producing "meaningful propositions". Recent work on the use of rational expectations formation in simulating the effects of economic policy instruments (see Bomhoff, 1980, pp. 153 ff.) suggests that only when agents can discriminate between expected and unexpected changes in policy instruments in environments where the past behaviour of these variables can be explicitly described and a "rational" expectation formed, is simulation possible. In an environment where a policy instrument has always been stable and is then increased, or has always been random is increased at a stable rate, even models which include "rational" expectations formation cannot simulate the effects of these changes because they are "exogenous" to the past experience of agents and over the immediate future no rational formation process is yet available. Thus, the cases in which rational expectations formation suggests that government policy is redundant could also have been derived from models developed within the neoclassical synthesis for, as Hart suggests, in such conditions without exogenous changes in variables, it makes no difference if expectations are formally included or not. The rational approach when properly formulated has the benefit of showing how limited these cases are in practice, recognition of which presumably caused the excitement Hart recalls. Thus, both the rational expectations and neoclassical synthesis approaches exclude those factors which make the simple Keynesian policy conclusions a necessity for the management of the economic system.

6 It is interesting to note that a part of Sraffa's early criticism of Marshall was also concerned with the importance of the "law" of diminishing returns to neoclassical theory and that he himself was eventually led to develop a system that was independent of any variation. Cf. Roncaglia, 1978, pp. 9-17.

7 This has been the subject of the recent discussion (1979) between Garegnani and Robinson. The former argues that the discussion of pure value theory should be separated from the questions of the limitations of the method used to exposite the theory. Once the question of the validity of the neoclassical theory of value and in particular the concept of the demand curve for aggregate capital have been resolved the discussion may turn to fruitful discussion of the methodology of long-period theory in general and the role of expectations in particular. When the two are conflated, however, it becomes possible to respond, as did Samuelson, to the methodological question, thereby implying that there is no substantive issue involved. It was thus possible for Samuelson to claim (1975, p. 44) that, as a result of Joan Robinson's criticisms concerning the historical applicability of stability analysis "No substantive contention need be withdrawn or qualified". It would thus appear necessary to attempt, as Garegnani (1976) did, to separate the two issues and discuss them independently. Joan Robinson's position would seem to be (cfr. for example, Robinson, 1980, p. 220) that they cannot be separated. This would imply that the methodology is inextricably bound up with the theory. It need not imply that those who attempt separation also support neo-classical value theory, but rather that they have chosen different lines of criticism.

8 Shackle, in the *Years of High Theory* (1967), which he considers as the period running from around 1921 to the outbreak of the war in 1939, states that "Uncertainty was the new strand placed glowingly in the skein of economic ideas in the 1930's"(p. 6). By the 1950's the gleam had been reduced to a flicker. His book does not discuss Samuelson's contribution.

9 One can only speculate on the relation between the reformulation of Keynes' system within the neoclassical synthesis based on the *Foundations* and the rise in the belief in the possibility of Keynesian "fine-tuning" of the economy, a claim which eventually brought the Keynesian approach into general disrepute amongst economists and politicians. Certainly Keynes cannot be held responsible for the fact that economists considered as "hazy" those factors which caused their models' predictions and policy prescriptions to go awry because they were excluded from scientific consideration.

Bibliography

Arrow K. J. and F. H. Hahn: *General Competitive Analysis*, San Francisco: Holden-Day, 1971.

Bomhoff E. J.: *Inflation, the Quantity Theory, and Rational Expectations*, Amsterdam: North-Holland, 1980.

Brown G. P. and C. Rogers: "Macroeconomics, Comparative Statics and the Correspondence Principle: A Critique," *South African Journal of Economics*, vol. 46, Dec., 1978.

Bryant W. D. A.: "Samuelson's Correspondence Principle: A Comment," *South African Journal of Economics*, Vol. 48, March, 1980.

Ellis H. S. ed.: *Survey of Contemporary Economics*, Philadelphia: Blakiston, 1948.

Garegnani P.: "On a change in the notion of equilibrium in recent work on value and distribution," in *Essays in Modern Capital Theory*, Amsterdam: North-Holland, 1976.

Garegnani P.: "Notes on consumption, investment and effective demand: A reply to Joan Robinson," *Cambridge Journal of Economics*, Vol. 3, 1979.

Hart A. G.: *Anticipations, Uncertainty and Dynamic Planning*, New York, A. Kelley, 1951.

Hicks J. R.: "A Suggestion for Simplifying the Theory of Money," reprinted in Hicks, 1967, 1935.

Hicks J. R.: "Mr Keynes and the Classics," reprinted in Hicks, 1967, 1937.

Hicks J. R.: *Critical Essays in Monetary Theory*, Oxford: Clarendon, 1967.

Hicks J. R.: *Economic Perspectives*, Oxford: Clarendon, 1977.

Hicks J. R.: "IS-LM: An explanation," *Journal of Post Keynesian Economics*, Vol. 3, Winter. 1980.

Kaldor N.: "The Irrelevance of Equilibrium Economics," *Economic Journal*, Vol. 82, Dec., 1972.

Kregel J. A.: "Economic Methodolog y in the Face of Uncertainty," *Economic Journal*, Vol. 86, June, 1976.

Ott M.: "The Incompatibility of Unemployment and the Consistent Neoclassical Model: A Critique of Patinkin," *Economic Inquiry*, Vol. 16, Jan., 1978.

Patinkin D.: "The Limitation of Samuelson's Correspondence Principle, *Metroeconomica*, Vol. 4, 1952.

Robinson Joan: *History versus Equilibrium*, London: Thames Polytechnic, 1974.

Robinson Joan: "The Unimportance of Reswitching," *Quarterly Journal of Economics*, Vol. 89, Feb., 1975 a.

Robinson Joan: "Reswitching: Reply," *Quarterly Journal of Economics*, Vol. 89, Feb., 1975 b.

Robinson Joan: "Garegnani on Effective Demand," *Cambridge Journal of Economics*, Vol. 3, 1979 b.

Robinson Joan: "Misunderstandings in the theory of production," *Greek Economic Review*, Vol. 1. August, 1979 b.

Robinson Joan: "Time in Economic Theory," *Kyklos*, Vol. 33, Fasc. 2.

Rogers C. and C. S. W. "Torr: Intermarket Pressures of the Second Kind," *South African Journal of Economics*, Vol. 48, June, 1980.

Roncaglia A.: *Sraffa and the Theory of Prices*, New York: Wiley, 1978.

Samuelson P. A.: *Foundations of Economic Analysis*, Cambridge: Harvard, 1947.

Samuelson P. A.: "A Summing Up," reprinted in Collected Scientific Papers. Vol. III. Cambridge: MIT. 1972, 1966.

Samuelson P. A.: "Steady-State and Transient Relations: A Reply," *Quarterly Journal of Economics*," Vol. 89, Feb., 1975.

Samuelson A. P. and D. Levhari: "The Nonswitching Theorem is False," reprinted in Samuelson, Collected Scientific Papers, Vol. III, *op. cit.*, 1966.

Shackle G. L. S.: *Years of* High *Theory*, Cambridge: University Press, 1967.

Shackle G. L. S.: *Expectations, Investment and Income*, Second edition. Oxford:
University Press, 1968.

Shackle G. L. S.: *Epistemics and Economics*, Cambridge: University Press. 1972.

Shackle G. L. S.: "Keynes and Today's Establishment in Economic Theory: A View," *Journal of Economic Literature*, Vol. 11, June., 1973.

Part Two

EFFECTIVE DEMAND

Chapter 6

EFFECTIVE DEMAND: ORIGINS AND DEVELOPMENT OF THE NOTION(*)

During the last few days much has been said and written about "long-period" and "short-period" theories of "effective demand". While the original purpose of this paper was to try to clarify, from a Keynesian perspective, what may be meant by the term effective demand, it is obvious that the terms long- and short-period also bear definition. I shall thus commence with a digression on what I shall intend by these terms.

1 DIGRESSION ON LONG- AND SHORT-PERIOD

Marshall is only apparently the source of the problem. Yet, Marshall did not have a short- and a long-period theory of value and distribution (perhaps it would be more correct to say "price"). There is one, and only one, theory of price in Marshall. He did, however, use the market period, the short period and the long period to separate out the analysis of all the various aspects of the relevant forces operating to determine prices. The major operative force was substitution-instigated competition or as Knight was to summarize it, the "law" of one price. The market period concentrates on the operation of competitive forces on prices alone; substitution is only possible among final outputs. In the short period an additional aspect, substitution of existing productive capacity is added. Finally, in the long period substitution operates on all inputs and outputs. The full operation of these forces was thought to produce the tendency towards full employment of all inputs and the sale of all outputs.

In the same way, the Classical economists had only one theory of value and distribution. It emphasized the fundamental forces of competition which lead entrepreneurs to invest in those sectors yielding the highest rates of profit; what is now summarised by the "tendency to a uniform rate of profit". The operation of these forces was analyzed by separating market values from natural values and both from the stationary state. In the case of market values, chance factors could completely offset the fundamental forces; while in the stationary state their work had been brought to the limit set by population growth and technical progress.

Kalecki was always quite clear that he considered his theory to apply to long periods only when viewed as a series of short-period situations. The distinction of Kalecki's approach is that it uses price determination to produce an explanation of the level of output. The theory is again clearly identical in both the short and long run. Keynes also had a single, unified theory of the level of output *viz.* the principle of effective demand.

He separated the analysis of his fundamental forces into what I have elsewhere (Kregel, 1976) called the "Static", "Stationary" and "Shifting" models.

Thus, whether one is discussing value theories or output theories it would seem that the theories themselves are unitary and short- or long-period, or whatever other apparatus may be used to emphasize or exclude the full operation of the forces singled out for analysis serve only as an analytical aid. Such distinction certainly does not serve to differentiate among theories. Rather one might prefer to differentiate by means of the motive forces hypothesized by the theory.

I would then conclude that our objective is not to identify or discover a "long-period" theory of effective demand, but rather to identify, in its most general terms, "effective demand" and then seek to discover whether the motive forces Keynes hypothesized are compatible with those of the Classical economists. If this can be done it then of course becomes possible to analyze the theory under any of a number of analytical conveniences such as runs or periods or whatever. Thus, this paper starts from the position that the determination of effective demand is prior to analyzing limits on its operation and that the short and long-period theories (if one accepts those terms) will have a common basis and must be mutually consistent.

2 EFFECTIVE DEMAND: A KEYNESIAN INVENTION?

"To me, the most extraordinary thing regarded historically, is the disappearance of the theory of demand and supply for output as a whole, i.e. the theory of employment, *after* it had been for a quarter of a century the most discussed thing in economics." (*JMK*, xiv, 1973, p. 85).

This quotation could be interpreted to suggest that Keynes certainly considered the analysis of effective demand to have been an integral part of the Classical discussion of economic problems. It would seem that he had in mind the debate between Ricardo, J. Mill and Malthus. It has also been suggested (e.g. Garegnani, 1976, p. 27) that Smith's conception of "effectual" demand represents, if not a precursor, at least a potential for reconstructing a "Classical" or "long-period" theory of effective demand. In this context it is perhaps important to remember Smith as the first "expositor" of Say's Law, and that Malthus also gave an important place to "effectual" or effective demand. The aim of the present paper is to suggest that the origins of the problem of effective demand were laid much earlier, that effective demand has been a continual preoccupation of economists and, finally, that the search for a Classical or "long-period" theory of effective demand that is independent of Keynes's theory is misconceived.

3 EARLY WRITERS

The economic writings of Hume and Locke were in direct response to the Mercantile position which, properly misconstrued, could be represented as positing precious metals as the sole source of wealth and object of accumulation. In this perversion of the Mercantilists "Only money matters" as long as we recognise that only gold is money. Locke responded to this position by making the very simple point that gold was only as good as the real supply of commodities available to be exchanged for it. Eschewing price illusion (now better known as money illusion) he pointed out that if the King doubled the contents of his exchequer without a change in real supply (either by production or plunder) he could not increase his command over wealth, rather that the purchasing power of gold would be reduced in proportion to its increase. The quantity theory was born as an "Anti-monetarist" position. This proposition is now more commonly presented in terms of the *independence* of the velocity of circulation from the size of the stock or quantity of money.

Smith put the relation in a slightly different way: "In all countries where there is tolerable security, every man of common understanding will endeavour to employ whatever stock he can command in procuring either present enjoyment or future profit. . . . A man must be perfectly crazy who, where there is tolerable security, does not employ all the stock which he commands, whether it be his own or borrowed of other people. . ." (*Wealth of Nations,* Cannan edition, p. 268). This appears to be one of the first, and clearest, statements of Say's Law. Recalling the predominance of commodity money, Smith's position emerges as being identical to that of Locke and Hume: money is always spent, either on present enjoyment or future profit. If money is not held (or, as would become popular 'hoarded') for its own attributes, then Say's Law provides the justification for the independence of the velocity of circulation. If the quantity theory was to hold then Smith's "Law of Spending" had to hold. This independence of money from real phenomena is often characterised as the long-period "neutrality" of money. Considering its classical origin it is perhaps better to say it represents a "natural" relationship, indicating that the "natural" purchasing power of money has a centre of gravity determined by the existing national income, but that the latter is independent of the quantity of money in existence. Smith's effectual demand must then be but a reflection of the "natural" value of money and thus of Say's Law.

It is perhaps unnecessary to point out that the Classical economists did recognise and analyse departures from natural values (indeed some have seen this as the role of "effectual demand") as well as the role such departures played in causing adjustments in the natural values themselves. One does not need to wait for a Cantillon or a Thornton for a description of the process by which changes in the quantity of money do affect the real variables in the economic system! Both Hume and Locke were well aware that quantities will respond to changes in demand, speaking for example of the augmented "spirit of industry" produced by the discovery of additional supplies of the precious metals.[1] But, such discoveries represented no additional production and thus such changes would eventually result in the previous ratio of money to national income being re-established through rising prices (Hume in fact believed that this would occur because of workers being able to bid up wages due to the favourable conditions in the labour markets). Nor was a higher level of output excluded; international application of the quantity theory excluded that it might be permanent.

The Classical position thus has the quantity theory *and* Say's Law as integral parts of the belief that the "natural" values are determined by "real" forces, while during the adjustment process other factors may predominate. Putting the point differently, there is perfect separation of the monetary and real forces in the former and integration in the latter. It is, however, only in the latter that it is possible to speak of a theory of demand for output as a whole for only under conditions of adjustment may Smith's Law of Spending be violated by "rational" (not "crazy") men. In this interpretation the theory of effective demand is born of the attempt to integrate the real and monetary factors at work in the economy, an activity as old as economics itself.

4 THE QUANTITY THEORY AND NATURAL VALUES

It is no secret that Keynes started his career as a professional economist as a believer in the quantity theory and that his basic objection to it was that it only dealt with the determination of natural values (this is, in fact, what is behind the famous long run mortality quotation: "Economists set themselves too easy a task if in tempestuous seasons they can only tell us that when the storm is long past the ocean is flat again."). The basic objection that Keynes made to the quantity theory in the *Treatise* was that it failed in "separating out those factors through which in a modern economic system the causal process actually operates during a period of change". While, "the real task . . . is to treat the problem dynamically, analysing the different elements involved, in such a manner as to exhibit the causal process by which the price level is determined and the method of transition from one position of equilibrium to another" (vol. 1, p. 133). In the *General Theory* this same idea is expressed as "it is in the transition that we actually have our being" (p. 343, n. 3).[2] It would thus not only be misleading to relegate effective demand to the "short period" or to "market" values determined by the random forces of supply and demand or "expectations", but equally so to try to develop a separate or distinct "long-period" theory of effective demand. The prior question would seem to be whether an integration of real and monetary phenomena is possible in the determination of natural values, and the consequences of such an integration for Classical theory.

5 THE INTEGRATION OF REAL AND MONETARY FORCES

Keynes's search for the explanation of the adjustment process *of* (as distinct from *to*) natural values led him back to the circular flow relation underlying Say's Law. Wicksell had already started work on integration of the real and monetary aspects on the basis of a combination of Austrian marginalism and the quantity theory, work which served as the starting point for the analyses of similar problems by, among others, Hayek, Myrdal, Lindahl and Hicks. In Wicksell's theory the integration of money and real phenomena takes place when there is a divergence between the natural and money rates of interest: in conditions of disequilibrium or of cumulative nominal disturbance; monetary neutrality is re-established in the natural position of equilibrium. This type of approach does not then seem to provide a solution to Keynes's question nor the one posed at the end of the last section.

After some consideration of the role of the "natural" rate of interest in the *Treatise*, Keynes also rejected Wicksell's analysis. Keynes's early work was also strongly influenced by D.H. Robertson. Keynes and Robertson sought out an explanation for fluctuations in demand for output (variable velocity of circulation) in blockages in the circular flow: hoarding. Without the introduction of lags, however, this approach was not very promising. In Robertson's famous aphorism, "All money that is anywhere must be somewhere". Money demand could not disappear *permanently* without effect on other factors in addition to total spending.[3]

However, a reasonable theory of adjustment could be worked out by lifting the income constraint on expenditure. A fractional-reserve banking system (which could, however, be gold-based) could allow for variations in spending in excess of current income (a point that also occurred in different contexts to Hayek and Hicks); the motive for doing so was found in the fact that business expenditures on investment in future productive capacity were determined primarily by the demand *expected* at future dates and were thus independent of *current* business receipts.[4] This recognition was sufficient to produce a theory of fluctuations in overall expenditure and to break the link between income and expenditure. But the question remained: fluctuations around what position? It thus became necessary to deal eventually with the determination of the natural or equilibrium or trend position (as both Kalecki and Harrod attempted to do), unless the fluctuations were to be considered as random or around zero trend. "Equilibrium is blither", if it is always changing.

6 FROM PRICE TO OUTPUT EQUILIBRIA

This shift in emphasis is seen in the particular approach of the *General Theory* which rejects the determination of the general level of prices (purchasing power of money) for more direct emphasis on the determination of the level of output and employment. In doing this Keynes adapted Marshall's micro-analysis of the determination of prices to the analysis of aggregate output (cf. Kregel, 1980a).

This created the *formal* possibility of employing Marshall's concepts of market, short- and long-period equilibria to classify adjustment forces: in the market period only prices adjust (and consequently any change in the stock of money produces a proportional and direct adjustment in prices); in the short-period both prices and quantities adjust, there is unused productive capacity which may be transferred to the market in question but with diminishing returns (change in money demand then may be divided between price and quantity changes in the market in question while in the economy as a whole this depends on production elasticities, only with perfect substitution would prices rise proportionally); in the long-period productive capacity adjusts to the pattern of demand (changes in demand increase productive capacity up to full employment and only prices thereafter). In this description Say's Law holds in the long period (and almost by definition in the short) as does the quantity theory.

Keynes, however, did not adopt these classifications, rather his approach to fluctuations required that they be reserved for the factors influencing demand: short- and long-period expectations. The shift in emphasis of the *General Theory* also resulted in greater emphasis being placed on the Say's Law formulation of the real-sector flows, and with it the possibility of multiple equilibria. Within Say's Law any level of employment represents a position in which supply equals demand, although only the full employment position is stable. The neoclassical theory of value and distribution was required to replace the quantity theory explanation of why the fundamental forces of the system would cause the system to adjust to *one* natural position: full employment *equilibrium* (Equilibrium *is* blither).

In Wicksell's theory the real system (productivity theory) produced the forces towards full employment; they were only diverted in disequilibrium when the money rate diverged from the natural value of the interest rate (its marginal productivity given the existing state of technology). But, Keynes argued, why should this natural position predominate? If it did not there would be any number of stable equilibria determined by the combined or integrated real *and* money forces. This would mean that at any point in time there would exist a natural position which could serve as the basis for the explanation of the forces causing the system to preserve *or* to change the natural position. What Keynes rejected was not the concept of a natural position (or equilibrium), but the neoclassical proposition that there is only *one* such position; a proposition which is in contrast with both the Classical use of natural values *and* the quantity theory. It is also instructive to note that Keynes' approach has little, if anything, to do with the specification of analysis into Marshallian periods.

7 POST-WICKSELLIAN INTEGRATION

Keynes was not alone in rejecting Wicksell's method, similar responses can be found in the work of Myrdal, Ohlin, Lindahl and the Swedish school, in the work of Hicks to 1937 and after 1975, and most importantly in the work of Hayek and the expatriate Austrian school. Hayek followed a path of analysis similar to that of Keynes, first working out a theory of fluctuations resulting from the direct impact of monetary factors on real phenomena and then using this theory as the basis for the explanation of the existence of excess productive capacity.[5]

This theory, as first set out in an organised form in *Prices and Production*, was strongly attacked, presumably with Keynes's instigation and agreement, by Sraffa in a review article in the March 1932 *Economic Journal*. In this article we find the two building blocks that were ultimately to distinguish Keynes's theory from the others who were following similar lines. First, Sraffa faults Hayek for failing: "to see at once that the differences between a monetary and a non-monetary economy can only be found in those characteristics which are set forth at the beginning of every text-book on money. That is to say, that money is not only the medium of exchange, but also a store of value, and the standard in terms of which debts, and other legal obligations, habits, opinions, conventions, in short all kinds of relations between men, are more or less rigidly fixed"[6] (p. 43).

The money which [Hayek] contemplates is in effect used purely and simply as a medium of exchange. There are no debts, no money-contracts, no wage agreements, no sticky prices in his suppositions. Thus he is able to neglect altogether the most obvious effects of a general fall, or rise, of prices. This attitude, which amounts to assuming away the very object of the inquiry, appears to originate in a well-founded objection to the vagueness of the conception of "the general price level" understood as anything different from one out of many possible index-numbers of prices, and in the opinion that such a conception can have no place in the theory of money. Such a theory, according to him, "ought simply to consider the influence of money on the relative prices of commodities – which is excellent, provided that money itself is one of the commodities under consideration; but Dr. Hayek goes further and rejects not only the notion of general price-level but every notion of the value of money in any sense whatever. . . . Having thus reduced money to insignificance . . ." (p. 44).

Sraffa accuses Hayek of having failed to produce a convincing distinction between a monetary and non-monetary economy, a point he criticises more directly in his rejection of Hayek's contention that there would be *a unique* natural interest rate which would satisfy conditions of equilibrium:

An essential confusion, which appears clearly from this statement is the belief that the divergence of commodity rates of interest is a characteristic of a money economy: and the confusion is implied in the very terminology adopted, which identifies the "actual" with the "money" rate, and the "equilibrium" with the natural rate. If money did not exist, and loans were made in terms of all sorts of commodities, there would be a single rate which satisfies the conditions of equilibrium but there might be at any one moment as many "natural" rates of interest as there are commodities, though they would not be "equilibrium" rates.

Sraffa then goes on to develop the idea of commodity rates of interest based on prices in commodity spot and forward markets. Sraffa defines these commodity interest rates as "natural" when each commodity rate is measured in terms of itself as standard:

> "In equilibrium the spot and forward price coincide, for cotton as for any other commodity; and all the "natural" or commodity rates are equal to one another, and to the money rate. . . . Suppose there is a change in the distribution of demand between various commodities; immediately some will rise in price, and others will fall; the market will expect that, after a certain time, the supply of the former will increase, and the supply of the latter fall, and accordingly the forward price, for the date on which equilibrium is expected to be restored, will be below the spot price in the case of the former and above it in the case of the latter, in other words, the rate of interest on the former will be higher than on the latter. It is only one step to pass from this to the case of a non-monetary economy, and to see that when equilibrium is disturbed, and during the time of the transition, the "natural" rates of interest on loans in terms of commodities the output of which is increasing must be higher to various extents, than the "natural" rates on the commodities the output of which is falling; and that there may be as many natural rates as there are commodities" (p. 50).

Sraffa then goes on to note that in an expansion "there is no such thing as an equilibrium (or unique natural) rate of interest, so that the money rate can neither be equal to, nor lower than it". While "there is a 'natural' rate of interest which, if adopted as bank-rate, will stabilise a price level (i.e. the price of a composite commodity): it is an average of the 'natural' rates of the commodities entering into the price-level, weighted in the same way as they are in the price-level itself" . . . "such a price-level is not unique, and for *any* composite commodity arbitrarily selected there is a corresponding rate that will equalise the purchasing power, in terms of that composite commodity, of the money saved and of the additional money borrowed for investment" (p. 51). This would seem to be ample justification for abandoning the price-level and the natural rate of interest as objectives for analysis. Further, however, Sraffa's criticism of Hayek provided both an explanation of the "natural" equilibrium position and of the process of transition from one such position to another.[7] It also allowed for monetary influence on real factors. This is very similar to the path that Keynes adopts in his chapter 17 description of the analytical core of his solution to the integration of real and monetary factors in the transition.

8 OWN RATES AND COMMODITY RATES

As I have suggested elsewhere, (Kregel, 1980b, 1980c, 1982) Keynes interest in Sraffa's approach may have been linked to his own similar work on what is now known as the "interest-rate parity theorem". In foreign exchange market equilibrium, the forward premium or discount on a currency measures the "preference" of the market for holding that currency in its national market. This preference is equal to the interest rate differentials between the relevant money market centres. Thus, while interest rates in each centre differ, the return from holding any currency on deposit, measured in terms of a common currency, is driven to uniformity.

Now, if a single economy is considered, and money (or better "liquidity") is one of the commodities under consideration, the market's preference for holding money (or liquidity preference) will be equal to the interest rate differentials between money and other commodities when measured in a common unit (the money commodity). Indeed, what Keynes proposes is a generalised theory of the demand for durable goods, money included. Writing r for the natural rates, and p_s and p_f as the spot and forward prices in terms of this commodity then $r_i = p_s - p_f/p_s = (q_i - c_i) + l_i$ represents the "real" or "own" or "commodity" rate of interest for the ith commodity and is equivalent to Keynes division of the attributes of a position in a durable into its net yield, q its carrying cost, c, and its liquidity premium, l.[8]

In a money economy, however, contracts and debts are written in terms of the money commodity, and thus the general price level in terms of money must also be taken into account. If $-a_i = p_s^m - p_f^m/p_s^m$ is the expected change in the money price of commodity i relative to the money commodity then the market in an "integrated" money-real system will reach equilibrium where $a_i + r_i$ is uniform over all i. For money $a = 0$ by definition, and in equilibrium it will be so for all other commodities, implying that r is uniform over all i, which is Sraffa's specification given above. When there is an overall rise in demand or a shift in the composition of demand these rates will depart from uniformity as quantities adjust. Thus the problem of the transition, and of the natural forces that might lead the system to full employment re-emerge. It is thus clear that in facing this question Keynes was forced to challenge directly the orthodox theory of interest; it is also clear that the approach provides treatment of *both* relative prices and the general level of prices (purchasing power of the money commodity).[9] It would clearly be mistaken to argue that Keynes produced his theory of interest as an afterthought, or that he ignored the theory of relative prices that such a treatment of the theory of interest implied. At the same time, it is clear that Keynes refused to contemplate the independence of money and real factors, producing in difference from Wicksell, an analysis that was fully integrated in *both* its normal and transitional aspects.

9 NATURAL TENDENCY IN AN INTEGRATED SYSTEM

To demonstrate that there was no automatic tendency to full employment Keynes refers to the differing composition of the factors q, l and c in determining the own rates of durable goods. In the case of money, Keynes rejects the position held by the quantity theory elaborators that money has no attribute except as a medium of exchange. Instead money is seen to be on a par with other durables as a means of preserving purchasing power over time. Since it serves as a store of value for future use the quantity held will depend on those factors which determine future action: the liquidity factor l, is thus predominant for money. For other durables the q and c factors will predominate. Thus, while q and c may in general be negatively and positively affected respectively by an increase in demand for durables, i need be little affected. The forces of competition may be expected to cause any increase in demand to be spread over all durables so as to produce a tendency to equalise r. But, if l is little affected by expansion then the own rate on money r, may act as a limit to further supply response in other durables as money offers a more advantageous way of preserving purchasing power. If the equality $r_i = r_m$ occurs before all available real resources are fully utilised then the system has reached a stable, less-than-full employment equilibrium. The natural forces of competition will have completed their work successfully in producing the tendency toward equilibrium of the rates of return; the position, however, need not be full employment.

It is, of course, also necessary to recall the elasticity properties required of the money commodity in order to assure that any increased investment in the money commodity does not "spill over" and create profitable opportunities to employ more labour in the production of money or money substitutes. Both the essential properties of "interest" and of "money" are required to complete the full integration of real and monetary factors in the process which produces a natural position exhibiting natural prices at less than full employment.[10]

10 THE "DIRECTION" OF ADJUSTMENT

This argument has one other highly important characteristic. In Wicksell's theory the system only achieved equilibrium when the money rate of interest adapted to the natural rate. In Keynes's theory, however, the transition process is just the opposite: it is the natural rate which adjusts to equilibrium with the money rate. Thus Keynes's rejection of a single natural rate restricted to full employment and his rejection of the assumption that the natural rate is independent of the process of transition. The latter condition may hold in a real or non-monetary system, it does not in Keynes's integrated system. The full employment rate was thus rechristened as the "neutral" rate (in line with Wicksell and Hayek) leaving open the possibility that any number of rates might be compatible with a position of "natural" equilibrium less than full employment.

Keynes expressed this difference as follows:

> Put shortly, the orthodox theory maintains that the forces which determine the common value of the marginal efficiency of various assets are independent of money, which has,

> so to speak, no autonomous influence, and that prices move until the marginal efficiency of money, i.e. the rate of interest, falls into line with the common value of the marginal efficiency of other assets as determined by other forces. My theory, on the other hand maintains that this is a special case and that over a wide range of possible cases almost the opposite is true, namely, that the marginal efficiency of money is determined by forces partly appropriate to itself, and that prices move until the marginal efficiency of assets fall into line with the rate of interest. (JMK, xiv, 1973, p. 103).

In Keynes's theory the real and monetary sectors are integrated both in and out of equilibrium; his investigation of the transition process led to a redefinition of the determinants of the natural position in terms of both money and real factors. This is Keynes's theory of effective demand. It holds in natural equilibrium by showing that while there are natural forces at work to produce equilibrium there is no necessity for that equilibrium to be a full employment equilibrium; it holds in the transition by showing how changes in the givens of the system (in particular the production technology, the consumption technology, the state of general expectations) will produce a transition to a new set of conditions of equilibrium in which all three of the givens may be affected (we here recognise the ideas of the static and shifting equilibria). Keynes simply rejects that the "real" factors can remain as givens in an integrated-system, which implies that the real factors no longer can determine the "natural" position independent of monetary factors. While it is true that much of the modern explanation of the way real factors produce this independent "real" equilibrium has been based on the neoclassical theory of value and distribution, the criticisms of that theory can do no more than demonstrate that the tendency to full employment was lacking even in the hypothetical conditions of a non-monetary world. If these criticisms are to be used as a basis for the construction of theory or policy, the problem of integrating the real and monetary sectors remains to be faced. Appeal to "natural" positions, when these imply conditions of non-monetary real systems and the results of "real" forces, is not sufficient.

To the extent the Classical theory of natural values preserves the separation of monetary and real factors (a certain requirement of the long-period neoclassical theories) it would seem impossible to conceive of a long-period theory of effective demand based upon them for it seems precluded by definition. Rather it would seem more important to work for such an integration within the Classical theory. On the other hand, as is well known, Keynes assumed that prices were determined under conditions of perfect competition.[11] While Keynes believed this assumption necessary to convince his contemporaries of the radical departure that he had taken from traditional theory, there is no reason now not to pursue investigation of the relations between pricing and demand. This was the subject of Kalecki's early work and has been the subject of recent work by Nell, and earlier investigation by Asimakopulos.[12] But whatever the area of development it will be necessary to be particularly vigilant that the concept of a long-period theory of effective demand does not reinforce the idea that in the long run, real forces determine effective demand and that therefore a non-monetary model is the suitable vehicle for such analysis, a position strongly defended by all brands of neoclassical theory and against which Sraffa argued strongly in his review of Hayek.

11 EXPECTATIONS AND THE THEORY OF EFFECTIVE DEMAND

There are some, however, who believe that direct recognition of monetary factors and/or the process of adjustment to normal positions implies an excessive reliance on subjective factors (meant to connote the "subjective" of the marginalist theories of value), in particular expectations. In this respect it should be noted that while some marginalist theories, especially the Austrian, place great emphasis on expectations this does not imply that the recognition of the role played by expectations in capitalist systems implies adoption of marginalist theories. The pervasiveness of expectations in nearly all varieties of economic theory should provide ample proof.

It is also often argued that recognition of such factors introduces imprecision or indeterminacy into theory. Keynes expressed this idea in a letter to H. Henderson "I should, I think, be prepared to argue that, in a world ruled by uncertainty with an uncertain future linked to an actual present, a final position of equilibrium, such as one deals with in static economics, does not properly exist" (JMK, xxix 1979, p. 222). This is a position not much different from Ricardo, Walras or Clark discussing the relation between their equilibrium constructions and "reality". Yet Keynes, as these authors, is willing to formulate abstract equilibrium of both a short and long (market and normal) term nature. Indeed, as I have argued elsewhere, one of the main aims of the *General Theory* was to show how a particular "long-period" position of employment and output might endure for an unacceptably long period with an unacceptably high level of unemployment. Keynes was first interested to show that there was no "natural tendency" for the system to maintain full employment as its "natural" position. This he achieved by showing that, within Wicksell's terminology, there could be any number of theoretical equilibria. He also argued that the system could settle at a natural position at less than full employment and not be budged from it for long periods. Thus, although he argued that the recognition of uncertainty led him to reject the final position of (full employment) equilibrium posited in static economics, his method of incorporating expectations via static, stationary and shifting equilibria did not prevent him from positing the existence of particular positions of long-period or natural equilibrium at less than full employment.

In so far as Keynes' analysis of such "stationary" or normal positions is concerned, expectations do not enter "directly". As Sraffa noted in his review of Hayek, in the normal position spot and forward prices are equal so that the latter may be dispensed with. The fact that this position may be of less than full employment descends directly from the inclusion of money as one of the commodities in which positions may be taken and in which all debt contracts are expressed. Such a configuration requires no more than a given state of expectations and the recognition of past and future, i.e. that the normal position is not a "long-period equilibrium" in the sense of classical stationary state where accumulation has come to an end, but simply the equilibrium configuration of the forces in action at a particular period in time - in the past they have been of different intensity (and composition) and they shall be so in future.

Keynes' use of a given state of general expectation clearly places expectations among the givens rather than among the variables (but subject to his very special definition:

"This does not mean that we assume these factors to be constant; but merely that, in this place and context, we are not considering or taking into account the effects and consequences of changes in them." (*General Theory*, p. 245).) In the "Static Model" this is especially clear. A number of economists who were involved in the discussion of expectational factors in the 1930s (cf. in particular A.G. Hart (1951) and Paul Sweezy (1937–8) have pointed out that "in strict logic there is no difference between [analysis] in which expectations are *data* and the static [perfect foresight] problem. . . . We arrive in this fashion at the conclusion that it is logically inadmissible to include expectations among the *data* of our problem. Either (1) we do not need them at all, or (2) we must admit that they can be mistaken and, hence, subject to revision in the course of a process of adjustment to what are properly speaking the *data* of the problem" (Sweezy, 1937–8, pp. 234–5).

If the mere inclusion of given expectations does not produce results that differ from those of perfect foresight it seems difficult to accuse Keynes of building his entire theory on subjective elements without voiding it of credibility (a position similar to that taken by Pigou in his famous "recantation"). It should be clear from the above, however, that if Keynes's contribution is interpreted in terms of his particular method of accomplishing the integration of real and monetary analysis, one can also consider it as the basis of his divergence from the orthodox analysis in his treatment of given expectations, rejecting the distinction between Value and Distribution and the Theory of Money and instead suggesting a "line of division between the theory of stationary equilibrium and the theory of shifting equilibrium" (vii, 1936, p. 293). In both cases the economy is one in which the future is unknown and in which expectations must be formulated and acted upon, but "meaning by the latter the theory of a system in which changing views about the future are capable of influencing the present situation" (ibid., p. 293). There is thus no essential role played by expectations in the stationary or normal position, while they come into direct play in the determination of the adjustment process. Some economists have chosen to place particular emphasis on only the later part of Keynes' contribution, yet they are integrally related. When viewed in this way expectations, which are really not very novel in economic analysis, are replaced by the integration of the monetary and real analysis as the crucial factor in Keynes's discussion of both normal positions at less than full employment *and* the analysis of the transition process from one normal position to another.[13] It is here, as Sraffa reminds us (cf. p. 59 above) that "there is no such thing as an equilibrium rate of interest" and none of the values or relations derived from the data of the previous "core" are applicable. It would be unfortunate to continue to mistake expectations for the attempt to integrate monetary and real factors. It is the latter that should be at the centre of any analysis which attempts to resolve the conundrum of a "long-period" theory of effective demand within the Classical context.[14]

Notes

* Some of the ideas used in this paper first appeared in a paper prepared for a CNR research project ("Il problema dell'integrazione fra le teorie del sovrappiù, della domanda effettiva e della moneta attraverso *l*'analisi delle istituzioni e dei conflitti di classe") directed by Sergio Parrinello, and were subsequently presented in seminars directed by Heinz Kurz and Otto

Steiger in the University of Bremen in June 1981. The author should like to thank these individuals and the participants of their projects and seminars without implicating them in the final result.

1 This is perhaps more evident in Hume's writings. Vickers (1959) suggests that such a process implies the existence of excess capacity and thus a previous underemployment equilibrium, cf. also Weintraub (1978) "Some Ancient Reservations", pp. 82–4) who uses the point in criticism of Friedman.

2 The quotation comes in a note to a discussion of Locke in Keynes' "Notes on Mercantilism" (vii, 1936, p. 343): "Hume a little later has a foot and a half in the classical world. For Hume began the practice amongst economists of stressing the importance of the equilibrium position as compared with the ever-shifting transition towards it."

3 Flow blockages of this type were frequently discussed in the writings of Locke and Hume as well as Cantillon, Say and J.S. Mill. Robertson made it operational by formally introducing the lagged adjustment that had always been implicit.

4 A distinction should be made between Hicks' 1933 "Gleichgewicht und Konjunktur" (Hicks, 1980) and Hayek (1933) who placed emphasis on the endogeneity of the quantity of money under fractional-reserve banking and Keynes and Knight who in addition focused on the change in the production structure which required such changed financial conditions: "Producers cannot accurately know the conditions of demand in the present, and still less can they know the demand, of the future time to which their present plan and activities relate. Under modern methods the process of producing goods extends over a *long period of time* . . . one producer does not know what others are planning to do, and they cannot act as a unit." Knight (1933), p. 89. Leon, (1967, pp. 125 ff.) suggests reasons why the "unit" proposition should hold, but also (1981) suggests that not even a firm can be viewed as a unit with coherent goals.

5 "I believe you are wrong in suggesting the common element in the doctrine of Simons and Keynes was the influence of the Great Depression. We all held similar views in the 1920's. They had been more fully elaborated by R.G. Hawtrey who was all the time talking about the 'inherent instability of credit'; but he was by no means the only one . . .". Hayek quoted in Friedman (1969, p. 88n).

6 Sraffa perhaps exaggerates with respect to the English literature, unless he has in mind the opening sentences of Keynes' *Treatise* (he may instead have been referring to the Italian literature where such factors were much better represented). But see H. Withers (1926).

7 Davidson (1972) bases his approach on the forward market analysis of the *Treatise.* Hart (1960, pp. 416–7) stresses that natural values were implicit in the *Treatise* analysis of "normal" and "anticipated normal" prices in spot and forward markets. Tonveronachi (1980) also suggests that the *Treatise* may be interpreted in terms of natural and market prices, thus providing an explanation of the divergence of aggregate spending and the value of output at natural prices sought by Malthus (and Smith?) in his idea of the role of effectual demand.

8 Minsky (1975) has further extended these ideas to accommodate the *debt financing* of positions in durables, i.e. q becomes the income flow of the position and c the financing cost, considerations that Keynes's formal argument assumed away.

9 Townshend (1937) was the first to suggest that Chapter 17 provided the basis for the theory of value in a monetary economy.

10 It should be clear that it is impossible to attribute to Keynes any conception of demand for money based upon the properties of money which are not directly related to the desire for liquidity or the idea of liquidity itself.

11 Lachmann (1956, pp. 74–7) argues that Keynes's result rests on the assumption of rigid prices preventing sufficient adjustment of spot prices. Given, the rate of interest above marginal efficiency of an asset there is some price low enough to generate speculative demand for the commodity sufficient to keep net investment unchanged. This recalls Keynes's *Treatise,* Vol. ii p. 140 argument and requires analysis such as found in Kaldor (1960, pp. 17–58). Since the crucial value is spot relative to future price some implicit assumption must be made as Wicksell did (cf. Kregel 1980b, n. 11) about the rigidity of forward prices.

12 Nell (1978, 1979, 1981); Nina Shapiro (1977) has already pointed out the formal similarity between Kalecki's degree of monopoly and the propensity to consume (p. 544, n. 13).

Asimakopoulos, e.g. (1977) has also investigated the various aspects of Kalecki's approach, usually from a short-period point of view.

13 One method of analysing the process of adjustment is suggested by Lachmann, "The Role of Expectations in Economics as a Social Science", *Economica,* Feb. 1943 (reprinted in Lachmann, 1977, p. 78) in terms of using the elasticity of expectations as a measure of the strength of the gravitational field around a normal position. If long-run forces are strongly believed to determine price then expectations will be highly inelastic, while changes in such forces, indicating an adjustment to a new normal position, will be associated with highly elastic expectations. In such conditions transitory forces may predominate.

14 Although this paper has attempted to suggest that Keynes' approach is in general consistent with such a search it should not be misconstrued as suggesting that Keynes has indeed all but accomplished it. In particular, Keynes's assumption of diminishing returns governing the behaviour of q must be replaced (cf. Hicks, 1936, pp. 231–32 and JMK, xxix, pp. 212–14), as does the analysis of technical change and innovation. Steps along this path have been taken by, for example, Steindl (1952); Lachmann (1977) "A Reconsideration of the Austrian Theory of Industrial Fluctuations", with the introduction of the K and E sectors, and most recently by Pasinetti (1981).-

Chapter 7

EFFECTIVE DEMAND

This is the term used by Keynes in his *General Theory* (1936) to represent the forces determining changes in the scale of output and employment as a whole. Keynes attributed the first discussions of the determinants of the supply and demand for output as a whole to the classical economists, in particular the debate between Ricardo and Malthus concerning the possibility of 'general gluts' of commodities, or what has come to be known as Say's Law of Markets. Indeed, Keynes's theory was intended to replace Say's Law, although the emergence of effective demand from his *Treatise on Money* (1930) critique of the quantity theory of money, and his insistence on its application in what he originally called a 'monetary production economy', suggests that it should also be seen in antithesis to classical monetary theory. For Adam Smith (1776, p. 285), 'A man must be perfectly crazy who . . . does not employ all the stock which he commands, whether it be his own or other peoples' on consumption or investment. As long as there was what Smith called 'tolerable security', economic rationality implied that it was impossible for demand for output as a whole to diverge from aggregate supply. Although Smith (p. 73) did call the demand 'sufficient to effectuate the bringing of the commodity to the market', the 'effectual demand' 'of those who are willing to pay the natural price' of the commodity, the idea referred to divergence of market from natural price of particular commodities and the process of gravitation of prices to their natural values. J.B. Say's discussion of the problem of the 'disposal of commodities' adopted Smith's position. Against those who held that 'products would always be abundant, if there were but a ready demand, or market for them,' Say's 'law of markets' argued 'that it is production which opens a demand for products' (1855, pp. 132–3); if production determined ability to buy, then demand could not be deficient. While excesses in particular markets were admitted, they would always be offset by deficiencies in others. Ricardo used similar arguments against Malthus, who responded by suggesting that:

> from the want of a proper distribution of the actual produce, adequate motives are not furnished to continued production, . . . the grand question is whether it [actual produce] is distributed in such a manner between the different parties concerned as to occasion the most effective demand for future produce . . . (Malthus, 1821)

Malthus argues that the composition of output affects its quantity by producing doubts in the minds of Smith's rational entrepreneurs concerning the 'security' of their future profit.

The final word in the classical debate was J.S. Mill's 'On the Influence of Consumption on Production', which sought exceptions to the proposition that 'All of which is produced is already consumed, either for the purpose of reproduction or enjoyment' so that 'There will never, therefore, be a greater quantity produced, of commodities in general, than there are customers for' (1874, pp. 48–9). Mill accused those who argued that demand limits output of a fallacy of composition, for the individual shopkeeper's failure to sell is due to a disproportion of demand which cancels out for the nation as a whole. Mill also notes that the argument that every purchaser must be a seller presumes barter, for money enables exchange 'to be divided into two separate acts' so one 'need not buy at the same moment when he sells' (p. 70). To avoid this problem 'money must itself be considered as a commodity', for 'there cannot be an excess of all other commodities, and an excess of money at the same time' (p. 71). Mill admits that if money were 'collected in masses', there might be an excess of all commodities, but this would mean only a temporary fall in the value of all commodities relative to money. Similarly to Smith's 'tolerable security', Mill explains an excess of commodities in general by 'a want of commercial confidence', which he denies may be caused by an overproduction of commodities (p. 74).

Mill's defence of Say's Law highlights the importance of the classical quantity theory, which was originally formulated to oppose the undue emphasis given to precious metals as components of national wealth by the mercantilists. Hume noted that labour, not gold, produced the commodities which composed national wealth; that gold was only as good as the labour it commanded to produce output. Thus the classical position that the velocity of circulation of money was independent of its quantity was built on the view that money would only be held to be spent. Money could at best cause temporary general gluts; in the long term, 'rational' men would not choose to hold money rather than spend it.

On the eve of the marginal revolution, classical theory thus admitted the temporary occurrence of general gluts explained by cyclical disproportions in demand for money and commodities due to crises of confidence. It is paradoxical that while the marginal revolution was motivated by the failure of classical theory to give sufficient attention to the role of demand in value theory, it failed to extend its analysis of demand to output as a whole in either the long or the short period. Indeed, the emphasis on individual equilibrium produced by the subjective theory of value which replaced the classical theory, made separate discussion of aggregate supply and demand redundant. Thus Keynes's reference to 'the disappearance of the theory of demand and supply for output as a whole, that is the theory of employment *after* it has been for a quarter of a century the most discussed thing in economics' (Keynes, 1936c).

But it was discussion, not Say's Law, which disappeared from neoclassical economics. Thus Keynes classed economists from Smith and Ricardo to Marshall and Pigou as 'Classical', for despite antagonistic theories of value and distribution, they all held a similar theory of supply and demand for output as a whole.

Keynes suggests that this was due more to the failure of neoclassical economists to heed Mill's warning concerning the extension of the conditions faced by the individual to the economy as a whole, than to positive analysis. If consumers (producers) maximize utility (profit) subject to an income (cost) constraint, reaching the maximum by substituting in consumption (production) goods (inputs) which were cheaper per unit of utility (output), then excess supply of any goods (resource) is due to its price exceeding its marginal utility (productivity). Market competition would lead to relative price adjustments which eliminate excess supply. Since it was impossible for any single good (resource) to be unsold (unemployed), it was natural to extend this analysis to the aggregate level to deny the possibility of general gluts without further analysis.

Any divergence from this position was explained, not by reference to hoarding money due to crises of confidence, but by temporary impediments to the automatic adjustment of relative prices in competitive markets. Thus, despite their new marginal theory of value, Keynes's contemporaries reached a similar result that divergence of employment from its full employment level would be determined by temporary non-persistent causes eliminated in the long run.

From 1921 to 1939 the unemployment rate in the United Kingdom never fell below 10 per cent, peaking in 1932 at 22.5 per cent (over 2.7 million). This exceeded the limits that most economists attributed to short-period frictions. The self-adjusting nature of the neoclassical version of Say's Law that Keynes chose to criticize was thus contradicted by reference to economic events as well as by Keynes's conception of effective demand.

Keynes was not concerned with impediments to the equality of the supply and demand, but with the

> problem of the equilibrium of supply and demand for output as a whole, in short, of effective demand . . . When one is trying to discover the volume of output, and employment, it must be this point of equilibrium for which one is searching.

While the Classics solved the problem by assuming the identity of savings and expenditure on investment goods, neoclassical theory presumed Say's Law 'without giving the matter the slightest discussion' (1936b, p. 215).

Keynes's theory of effective demand thus had to replace Say's Law. To do this Keynes departed from the Classical position on two points. The first was to assume that wages exceed subsistence so that expenditure on consumption goods does not exhaust factor incomes. As expressed in Keynes's psychological law of consumption, this implied that as output increased, the gap between aggregate expenditure and factor costs increased, so that unless investment expenditure expanded to fill the gap, entrepreneurs would experience losses.

The second departure was from the assumption that rationality dictated that entrepreneurs' savings represented productive investment expenditure. If investment could produce losses, or changes in interest rates change capital values, then greater future enjoyment might be assured by not investing; holding money might be 'rational' in such conditions. Further, in a monetary economy, nothing guarantees that maximization of returns in money will maximize either productive capacity or the demand for labour.

In Keynes's theory the propensity to consume and the multiplier produce the proposition that it is the level of output which adjusts saving to investment, rather than the rate of interest, while the explanation of the decisions over the level of investment in a monetary economy requires an explanation of rates of interest in money terms. The two factors are closely related.

In a 1934 letter to Kahn, Keynes gives a 'precise definition of what is meant by effective demand' (1934a, p. 422). If O is the level of output, W the marginal prime cost of production for that output, and P the expected selling price, 'Then OP is effective demand'. The classical theory that 'supply creates its own demand' assumes that OP equals OW, irrespective of the value of O, 'so that effective demand is incapable of setting a limit to employment which consequently depends on the relation between marginal product in wage-goods industries and marginal disutility of employment'. Thus, what Keynes later called (1936a, ch. 2) the two 'classical' postulates limit O at full employment. In contrast,

> On my theory OW ≠ OP for *all* values of O, and entrepreneurs have to choose a value of O for which it is equal – otherwise the equality of price and marginal prime cost is infringed. This is the real starting point of everything.

The key point was thus the impact of different levels of O on the difference between costs and prices, that is on entrepreneurs' profits. Keynes took up this question, in an undated exchange with Sraffa of about the same time (1934b, pp. 157ff). Keynes notes that a non-unitary marginal propensity to consume implies OP ≠ OW for any O, and generates

> the general principle that *any* expansion of output gluts the market unless there is a *pari passu* increase of investment appropriate to the community's marginal propensity to consume; and any contraction leads to windfall profits to producers unless there is an appropriate *pari passu* contraction of investment.

The level of O at which OP = OW will be determined by the level of investment and the propensity to consume. Changes in the rate of investment, based on entrepreneurs' expectations of their future profits, will determine O.

In an early draft of the *General Theory* Keynes put it this way:

> Effective demand is made up of the sum of two factors based respectively on the expectation of what is going to be consumed and on the expectation of what is going to be invested. (1973a, p. 439)

Thus the theory of effective demand required, in addition to explanation of consumption based on the propensity to consume, an explanation of variations in the level of investment. Since neoclassical theory resolved this problem by presuming that investment was brought into balance with full employment saving by means of the rate of interest, Keynes located the 'flaw being largely due to the failure of the Classical doctrine to develop a satisfactory theory of the rate of interest' (1934c, p. 489).

Keynes concentrated his efforts to produce a theory of interest compatible within this theory of effective demand within what he called a monetary production economy. The *Treatise on Money* (1930) had explained changes in prices in terms of households', consumption decisions relative to entrepreneurs' production decisions. If these decisions were incompatible, investment diverged from saving and prices of consumption goods adjusted producing windfall profits or losses. The prices of investment goods were determined separately from this process, by means of the interaction of the bearishness of the public reflecting their decisions to hold bank deposits or securities on the one hand, and the monetary policy of the banking system on the other.

Investment goods are held because their present costs or supply prices are lower than the present value of their anticipated future earnings or demand prices; the larger this difference, the higher the expected rate of return. Since any change in the price of a durable capital asset will influence its rate of return, a theory that explains the price of capital assets also explains rates of return (which Keynes called marginal efficiency). With the demand price of an asset based on the value of expected future earnings discounted by the rate of interest, it is clear why a satisfactory theory of interest is crucial to the explanation of effective demand.

But money was a durable asset like any other, and as such it has a spot or demand price and a supply price or forward price, which determine the money rate of interest. Keynes thus transformed his concept of bearishness into liquidity preference which, together with banking policy, would determine the rate of interest. For Keynes, 'the money rate of interest . . . is nothing more than the percentage excess of a sum of money contracted for forward delivery . . . over what we may call the "spot" or cash price of the sum thus contracted for forward delivery' (1936a, p. 222), it is:

> the premium obtainable on current cash over deferred cash . . . No one would pay this premium unless the possession of cash served some purpose, that is had some efficiency. Thus we may conveniently say that interest on money measures the marginal efficiency of money measured in terms of itself as a unit. (1937a, p. 101)

Since both money and capital assets had marginal efficiencies representing their rates of return, profit-maximizing individuals in a monetary economy would demand money and capital assets in proportions which equated their respective returns. The equilibrium level of output chosen by entrepreneurs would then be represented by equality of the marginal efficiency of capital and the rate of interest (the marginal efficiency of money). The question of the effect of an increase in output on profit raised by a propensity to consume less than unity can now be seen as the effect of an increase in investment on the marginal efficiency of money relative to the marginal efficiencies of capital assets. Since these marginal efficiencies reflect pairs of spot and forward asset prices, the question can also be put as the effect of an increase in investment on relative money prices. Thus Keynes's independent variables, the propensity to consume, the efficiency of capital and liquidity preference, given expectations and monetary policy, interact to determine effective demand.

Since this equilibrium could be described by S = I, or equality between the rate of interest and the marginal efficiency of capital, the level of output which equates aggregate demand and supply also equates marginal efficiency with the rate of interest. To complete his theory of effective demand, Keynes faced the question first raised by Wicksell of the causal relation between the natural and the money rate of interest. Just as Keynes rejected the determination of the level of O at which OP = OW by the equality of the marginal productivity and disutility of labour, he rejected marginal productivity as the determinant of marginal efficiency and the real rate of interest determining the money rate because it was based on 'circular reasoning' (1937b, p. 212).

Keynes argues instead that it is the marginal efficiency of capital assets which adapts to the money rate of interest rather than vice versa. These two points of departure are discussed in chapters 16 and 17 of the *General Theory*, where Keynes points out that the money rate of return to be expected from a capital asset depends on the relation of anticipated money receipts relative to expected money costs, and that there is no reason to believe that these will be related in any predictable way to the asset's physical productivity. Wicksell's natural rate, derived from physical relations of production and exchange, has no application in a monetary economy; Keynes thus substitutes the concept of marginal efficiency.

Keynes also notes that increased investment in particular capital assets increases supply prices and reduces demand prices, causing a decline in marginal efficiencies; an increase in output thus leads to investment in assets with lower rates of return. At some point the marginal efficiency of money will make investment in money as profitable as the purchase of capital assets. At this point the rate of interest equals the marginal efficiency of capital, and any further increase in output would confirm Keynes's 'general principle' that any further expansion in output gluts the market, for increased income is not spent but held in the form of money which becomes a 'generalised sink for purchasing power'.

The question that distinguishes Keynes's theory is thus why money's liquidity premium does not fall as output expands, for this is what prevents investment from rising by just the amount to fill the gap created by the propensity to consume being less than one. To describe these 'essential properties of interest and money', Keynes departs from Mill's position that money is just another commodity. When money is the debt of the banking system its price and quantity behaviour will differ from physical commodities, for it has no real costs of production nor real substitutes. Thus an asset which has a negligible elasticity of production and substitution with respect to a change in effective demand, will have a rate of return which responds less rapidly to an expansion in demand. As long as the rate of interest falls less rapidly than the marginal efficiencies of capital assets, its rate will be the one which sets the point at which further expansion creates losses.

Thus the propensity to consume shows that investment will have to increase by the amount of the gap between incomes and expenditures as incomes rise if entrepreneurs are not to make losses, while the marginal efficiency of capital and liquidity preference in a monetary production economy explain why the behaviour of the rate of interest relative to the marginal efficiency of capital makes it unlikely that the rate of investment should adjust by just that amount. Since entrepreneurs maximize monetary returns, not employment or physical output, there is no reason why their investment decisions should lead to an equilibrium at full employment. Keynes's explanation of the limit to the level of employment permits any level as a stable equilibrium, including full employment; it is thus more general than the classical Say's Law position, in which the only stable equilibrium was the limit set by full employment as given in the labour market.

Bibliography

Keynes, J.M. 1930. *A Treatise on Money*. Reprinted in Keynes (1971).

Keynes, J.M. 1934a. Letter to R.F. Kahn, 13 April. Reprinted in Keynes (1973b).

Keynes, J.M. 1934b. Letter to P. Sraffa, undated. Reprinted in Keynes (1979).

Keynes, J.M. 1934c. Poverty in plenty: Is the economic system self-adjusting? Reprinted in Keynes (1973b).

Keynes, J.M. 1936a. *The General Theory of Employment. Interest and Money*. Reprinted in Keynes (1973a).

Keynes, J.M. 1936b. Letter to A. Lerner, 16 June. Reprinted in Keynes ((1979).

Keynes, J.M. 1936c. Letter to R.F. Harrod, 30 August. Reprinted in Keynes (1973c).

Keynes, J.M. 1937a. The theory of the rate of interest. Reprinted in Keynes (1973c).

Keynes, J.M. 1937b. Alternative theories of the rate of interest. Reprinted in Keynes (1973c).

Keynes, J.M. 1971–83. *The Collected Writings of John Maynard Keynes*. Ed. D. Moggridge. London: Macmillan for the Royal Economic Society: 1971. V and VI. *A Treatise on Money* (1930). 1973a. Vol. VII. *The General Theory of Employment. Interest and Money* (1936). 1973b. Vol. XIII. *The General Theory and After: Part I – Preparation*. 1973c. Vol. XIV. *The General Theory and After: Part II – Defence and Development*. 1979. Vol. XXIX. *The General Theory and After – A Supplement*.

Malthus, T.M. 1821. Letter from Malthus to Ricardo, 7 July, Reprinted in Ricardo (1952) 9–10.

Mill, J.S. 1874. On the influence of consumption on production. In J.S. Mill, *Essays on Some Unsettled Questions of Political Economy*, 2nd edn, reprinted Clifton, NJ: A.M. Kelley, 1974.

Ricardo, D. 1952. *Works and Correspondence of David Ricardo*, Vol. IX. Ed. P. Sraffa with the collaboration of M. Dobb, Cambridge: Cambridge University Press.

Say, J.B. 1855. *A Treatise on Political Economy*. 6th American edn, Philadelphia: J.B. Lippincott.

Smith, A. 1776. *An Inquiry into the Nature and Causes of the Wealth of Nations*. Oxford: Oxford University Press, 1976.

Chapter 8

THE CHANGING PLACE OF MONEY IN KEYNES'S THEORY FROM THE *TREATISE* TO THE *GENERAL THEORY* (*)

In notes prepared for his 1937 lectures Keynes observes that he "reached the conception of effective demand comparatively late on" (1973b, p. 180) and indicates a period after 1932. This would seem to preclude any direct link between Kahn's formulation of the multiplier, worked out in 1930 and published in 1931, and what Keynes called effective demand. Indeed, Keynes distinguished between his "initial novelty" concerning the introduction of the multiplier as the mechanism equilibrating savings and investment which was "independent of my subsequent theory of the rate of interest" and which he formulated "before I had reached the latter theory" of the rate of interest. The analysis of output adjustment to equate savings and investment in terms of the aggregate supply and demand framework left an important monetary variable, the rate of interest, undetermined: "If the rate of interest is not determined by saving and investment in the same way in which price is determined by supply and demand, how is it determined? One naturally began by supposing that the rate of interest must be determined in some sense by productivity — that it was, perhaps, simply the monetary equivalent of the marginal efficiency of capital, the latter being independently fixed by physical and technical considerations in conjunction with the expected demand. It was only when this line of approach led repeatedly to what seemed to be circular reasoning, that I hit on what I now think to be the true explanation" (1973b, p. 212), and Keynes goes on to define the function of the rate of interest as "to modify the money prices of other capital assets in such a way as to equalise the attraction of holding them and of holding cash" (*ibid.*, p. 213). An attentive reader of the *Treatise* would here recognise the determination of investment goods' prices by means of bearishness and the decisions of the banking system to create money transformed into a supply and demand analysis analogous to that for output. The analysis differed, however, in that it now determined the "price" of money, the rate of interest rather than the price of investment goods, and it reversed the *Treatise* order of causation, making the marginal efficiency of capital depend on the money rate of interest, rather than the natural rate being the determinant of investment.

This would suggest that the new, monetary explanation of interest and the theory of effective demand were born simultaneously. Since, in this new theory the rate of interest was expressly a monetary phenomenon, this would suggest that money and effective demand are uniquely correlated in Keynes's theory and quite independent of the conception of the multiplier. This should not be surprising for Keynes was a monetary economist, and he clearly stated that the *General Theory* was exclusively concerned with a monetary economy; indeed the very title of the book may be read as indicating the determinants of the dependent variable, employment. Yet, the role of money and the special features of its rate of interest virtually disappeared in the period after the Keynesian revolution, and played no explicit role in the divulgation and extension of the *General Theory* to the long period by those Cambridge economists and others closest to Keynes during the book's development. This solution to this seeming paradox is to be found in the interconnections between Keynes's revolution in monetary theory and the revolution in value theory which was simultaneously occurring in Cambridge as Keynes worked his way from the *Treatise* to *The General Theory*.

1. Money and the instability of credit.

The *General Theory* is often described as a reaction to the Great Slump, yet Keynes's formative years as an economist covered the 1914 financial crisis, war finance and post-war reconstruction and hyperinflation. While the Slump may have provided the immediate provocation for the book, it may better be seen as the culmination of Keynes's lifelong reflection on the nature of the capitalist system (cf. Vicarelli). Hayek sums up the theoretical environment in which Keynes and his contemporaries started their theoretical investigations of the relations between money and trade cycles: "We all held similar views in the 1920's ... more fully elaborated by R.G. Hawtrey who was all the time talking about the "inherent instability of credit"; but he was by no means the only one" (quoted in Friedman, 1969, p. 88n).

Hawtrey's 1913 *Good and Bad Trade* clearly identified the basic interaction of money and effective demand: "the manufacturer's efforts in producing the goods depends upon their being an effective demand for them. ... It is only because the dealer anticipates ... this effective demand ... that he gives the manufacturer the order ... The manufacturer, in accepting the order, and the banker in discounting the bill, are both endorsing the opinion of the dealer. The whole transaction is based ultimately on an expectation of a future demand, which must be more or less speculative" (p. 78).

Investigations into the interaction of money and the cycle not only inspired the monetary studies of Hayek and Keynes, but also of Robertson, Pigou, Cassel, Schumpeter, Fisher and others. These were the economists to whom Keynes addressed his 1923 *Tract on Monetary Reform* and 1930 *Treatise on Money*. Although subject to criticism, the Quantity theory provided the implicit framework adopted by all these writers; when his *Treatise* openly rejected this common framework, communication with his contemporaries became difficult and Keynes had to look elsewhere for sympathetic criticism.

2. Cambridge value theory in the 1920's: imperfect competition.

In this same period Cambridge economics was undergoing a sharp change as a group of young graduates, Kahn and Joan and Austin Robinson, extended Sraffa's 1926 criticisms of Marshall's theory of value to produce the "Imperfect Competition Revolution". It was to this new generation of Cambridge economists, actively involved in recasting

Marshall's value theory, that Keynes turned for comment and criticism. They differed from his contemporaries in that they had no first hand experience of the earlier "monetary" debates, and they were outrightly sceptical of the Quantity theory (e.g. R.F. Kahn, cf. 1984, p. 52, whose rejection of the dominant Quantity theory led him away from the study of monetary factors which had inspired the earlier generation). These young economists were joined (and on occasion preceded) in elaboration of imperfect competition by others such as Harrod, Kaldor, and Kalecki, all of whom were to make prominent contributions to Keynesian theory. Thus the Cambridge economists who formed the "Circus", and others such as Harrod, who played such an important role in working out the *General Theory*, were all initially involved in the value theory revolution before they were co-opted into Keynes's monetary revolution. It is perhaps not surprising that they should have perceived an inter-relationship, although Keynes's opinion was that these developments in the theory of value had no application to his own efforts. Nonetheless, the new theoretical environment created by Sraffa's arrival in Cambridge in the mid-1920's produced two clear and separate influences on the evolution of Keynes's ideas: R.F. Kahn's analysis of short period supply and Sraffa's conception of commodity rates of interest.

In the *Treatise* Keynes had already disregarded the quantity of money as the determinant of the price level in favour of "real" determinants: efficiency wages and investment, the two terms of the fundamental equations. He had also adapted Hawtrey's position on the importance of the rate of interest, placing emphasis on its indirect influence on the price level via the divergence between saving and investment. Thus, in line with Marshallian theory in which supply prices and demand determined individual prices in the short period, Keynes had reached a position in which costs and expenditures determined the aggregate price level, with only an indirect influence of money on prices via the influence of the long-term rate of interest on saving and investment. Keynes followed Wicksell and called "natural" the rate of interest which equated saving and investment, with a divergent market rate producing windfall profits. But the fundamental equations combined costs and excess demand in a single relation. Kahn's short period analysis was to provide the possibility of completing the analogy with Marshall's theory, separating the two to produce an explanation of output as a whole in terms of separate, but interdependent, aggregate supply and demand functions, while Sraffa was to provide further insight into the role of the rate of interest in producing equilibrium.

3. Imperfect competition and Kahn's short period analysis.

While Joan Robinson's formulation of imperfect competition is better known, Kahn also developed the implication of Sraffa's challenge to Marshall in a way which was closer to Keynes's own interests in his Fellowship Dissertation (1933) which elaborated Marshall's short period in imperfectly competitive conditions. Kahn argued that if firms maintained prices when faced with a fall in demand in an attempt to preserve market share then adjustment would fall on output. This would diminish the virulence of crisis by limiting price competition and bankruptcy, but it would also prolong it. Indeed, Kahn seems to have been the first to suggest Leijonhufvud's "inversion" of the

Marshallian adjustment speeds of prices and quantities as an explanation of persistent under-capacity working. Yet, it was not this early attempt to explain persistent unemployment by price rigidity, nor the reverse L-shaped supply curve which it implied, which influenced Keynes, but rather the idea of a short-period supply curve given productive capacity.

Keynes's fundamental equations had clearly identified expenditure from wages and profits as the source of demand for consumption goods, but there was no ready made conception of the supply of consumption goods to complete the analysis. In his multiplier article Kahn used his earlier study of Marshall's short period to suggest the formulation of a supply curve for consumption goods as a whole: "It was Mr Kahn who first attacked the relation of the general level of prices to wages in the same way as that in which that of particular prices had always been handled, namely as a problem of demand and supply in the short period rather than as a result to be derived from monetary factors" (1939, in 1973b, p. 400, n. 1). Kahn also convinced Keynes that the price of investment goods should be handled in an analogous fashion (cf. the discussion in 1973a, p. 219ff.), thus leading the way to the separation of the demand and supply elements combined in the fundamental equations into an aggregate demand function representing consumption expenditures (all wages are spent on consumption) and investment expenditures and an aggregate supply function to determine the "aggregate" price level. This development was a direct application of the value theory investigations then going on to the problems that Keynes was attempting to resolve in his monetary studies. Kahn had used *Treatise* definitions to formulate the employment multiplier, its elaboration made it clear that definitions, such as "windfall profit", had to be eliminated. Kahn himself (1984, p. 99) considers that his greatest contribution to Keynes's analysis is not the technical multiplier, but rather the demonstration that investment generates the savings it needs to finance it, and thereby convincing Keynes to drop the second term of the fundamental equations in favour of the savings-investment identity, thereby facilitating the application of aggregate supply and demand analysis. Keynes's correspondence also suggests that it was Kahn (e.g. Keynes, 1973a, p. 637) who was instrumental in convincing Keynes to adopt the $S = I$ framework and definitions. Thus despite Keynes's rejection of the formal analysis of imperfect competition, Kahn's elaboration of the Marshallian short period was to provide the implicit framework for the Circus discussions which eventually led to the presentation of the principle of effective demand in terms of aggregate supply and demand prices found in chapter 3 of the book. But, this change had a more important consequence. The *Treatise* attempted to eliminate the direct influence of money on prices by channeling the influence of money through the effect of the rate of interest on saving-investment equilibrium. With the disappearance of the saving-investment term from the fundamental equations money nor the rate of interest had any direct role in the determination of prices. It is for this reason that Keynes suggested that the upshot of the introduction of the multiplier as the equilibrating mechanism for saving and investment "was to leave the rate of interest in the air" (1973b, p. 212). It was Sraffa who would show Keynes how money could be introduced into his emerging theory of effective demand.

4. Sraffa's commodity rates of interest.

Sraffa's influence comes not from the 1926 article, which had stimulated Imperfect Competition, but from his 1932 review of Hayek's *Prices and Production* in which he suggested the concept of commodity rates of interest to criticise Hayek's use of Wicksellian rates of interest which in the *Treatise* assured saving-investment equilibrium. But traditional value theory, and in particular Hayek's monetary theory, implied that in the absence of money the natural rate of interest would always prevail and equate investment to full employment saving. If money could be made "neutral", then Say's Law would necessarily prevail. Keynes thus shifted his attention from direct criticism of the Quantity theory to the implications of the traditional theory of interest for his *Treatise* analysis.

Hayek's definition of "neutrality" required the money rate of interest equal the "equilibrium" (natural) rate so that money savings purchase the same amount of producers' goods as if the supply and demand for capital met in "their natural form".

It is well known that Sraffa had already started work on his *Production of Commodities* in the 1920's, and that his work on Ricardo had already commenced in the 1930's. Thus, it seems likely that Sraffa had a clear idea of the limits to a "natural" rate of profit and of the complications that arose when extended to more than one commodity (although at that time neither the standard commodity nor the corn model interpretation of Ricardo had been worked out, cf. Sraffa, 1960, p. 93 and Roncaglia, 1978).

It must then have been straightforward for Sraffa to point out that "natural" rates may exist for corn or any other commodity implicitly for every commodity, and explicitly whenever there is a forward market. These rates will be uniform in an equilibrium in which "the spot and forward price coincide" for each commodity. But when savings, whether in money or natural form, are positive there may be as many natural rates as there are commodities' "under free competition this divergence of rates is as essential to the effecting of the transition as is the divergence of prices from the costs of production; it is, in fact, another aspect of the same thing" This, Sraffa goes on to note "applies as much to an increase in saving, which Dr. Hayek regards as equivalent to a shift in demand from consumers' to producers' goods, as to changes in the demand for or the supply of any other commodity" (1932, pp. 50–1). It is not the non-neutrality of money, but the competitive process of adjustment in which prices are equated to costs of production which causes the non-uniformity of commodity rates of interest, and of these rates from the money rate: indeed neutrality cannot be defined under the conditions proposed by Hayek.

Sraffa's analysis linking the divergent commodity rates of interest to divergences between costs and prices thus suggested an analogue in terms of divergent interest rates to the profit motive leading to production of goods whose price exceeded costs of production, or projects whose supply price exceeded demand price as represented by discounted future yields or, more generally, in terms of spot prices relative to forward prices. Here was a clear link between the rate of interest and the divergence of expenditures and costs of the fundamental equations. What Sraffa provided was another way of representing the divergence of aggregate supply and demand prices being worked out in Kahn's Marshallian framework, but in terms of the analysis of individual supply and demand (spot and future) prices.

Sraffa's analysis also suggested that even in a non-monetary system the operation of the rate of interest in producing investment equal to full employment savings was less straightforward than the traditional theory had supposed. In a monetary economy, since investors would naturally refer to the relative commodity rates in terms of money, how could the money rate itself bring about the equilibrium position as, for example, Fisher's theory seemed to suggest? The role of money and the money rate of interest in a capitalist economy were clearly crucial to the investment expenditure decisions which would determine its equilibrium position.

5. Interest rate parity and liquidity preference.

If money was to be put on an equal footing with investment in other durable commodities it required a comparable definition of its rate of interest in terms of spot and future prices. Thus Keynes defined the money rate of interest as "nothing more than the percentage excess of a sum of money contracted for forward delivery, e.g. a year hence, over what we may call the "spot" or cash price of the sum thus contracted for forward delivery" (1936, p. 222). The importance of this change was that it allowed Keynes to refer back to his earlier *Tract* analysis of "interest rate parity" (cf. Kregel, 1982, 1984) to argue that the willingness of investors to take positions in any durable good (including money) could be analysed in the same way as decisions to take positions in foreign currencies since every durable will have a spot and forward price in terms of itself as numeraire which determines its "commodity-rate" or "own-rate of own interest": The *General Theory* explicitly makes the analogy that "just as there are differing commodity-rates of interest at any time, so also exchange dealers are familiar with the fact that the rate of interest is not even the same in terms of two different moneys ..." (JMK: VII, p. 224). Just as returns to foreign currency positions had to be evaluated in terms of the home currency, the diverse commodity-rates could only be evaluated in terms of a single commodity defined as "money".

In the foreign exchange currency markets equilibrium was achieved when the forward discount or premium reached equality with the interest rate differential. The forward discount, Keynes, argued, measured the market's "preference" for holding that currency. In the same way the market's "preference" for holding money was also measured by the discount of future over spot money in terms of money: the rate of interest (for example, a position in money is made by selling a 90-day bill for $ 95 spot against $ 100 90 days forward, representing a forward premium (spot discount) for the bill and forward discount (spot premium) for money). Equilibrium can only prevail when the relative advantages of taking positions in different assets are equalised, i.e. when the commodity rates in terms of money were all equal to the rate on money itself, or as stated earlier, "the function of the rate of interest is to modify the money prices of other capital assets in such a way as to equalise the attraction of holding them and holding cash" (*op. cit.*).

It was thus possible for Keynes to give expression to his idea that a monetary economy is characterised by the fact that "changing views about the future are capable of influencing the quantity of employment and not merely its direction" (1936, p. VII), for every decision to invest at prevailing spot prices was crucially dependent on expectations of future conditions as expressed in future prices: the relation of spot to forward prices or supply and demand prices determined the rates of return on investment in durable goods or their marginal efficiency while liquidity preference determined the spot and forward price of money, the rate of interest. Marginal efficiencies and liquidity preference thus reflected this view of the future which was generalised as the state of general expectation. The composition of asset holdings and the overall decisions on expenditure were thus directly influenced by changing views of the future. Since each individual had to reach his own view on the relation between present and future prices to determine the most attractive rate of return in the market, expenditure decisions on investment goods or to hold money would be characterised by diversity of view as to the expected rate. Equilibrium would be established only when the market for any activity was balanced between those whose expectations were more than satisfied and those who were disappointed. In such conditions, as Shackle has stressed, every agent may find his expectations were mistaken and is thus forced to reconsideration of his position, which makes decisions to invest liable to constant fluctuation. It was only possible to produce an equilibrium by presuming a given state of expectations and then working out the static adjustments. In such conditions the effects of increasing investment or of shifts from one activity to another is made in terms of relative rates of return (marginal efficiencies), changes in demand will produce adjustment in spot prices, current production (i.e. net investment) or the degree of liquidity, depending on the type of market and type of activity (cf. Tonveronachi, 1983, pp. 167–8). Changes in expected future conditions would thus lead to divergences in rates of return which would reflect differences between costs of production which would initiate expenditure decisions which would affect both future supply and price. Adjustment would continue until the marginal efficiencies and the rate of interest on money were brought into equilibrium. This position could be represented equally on the aggregate level in terms of effective demand equating aggregate supply and demand prices or in terms of equality of all rates of return produced by the spot and forward prices of all durables.

Keynes still had to show that it was impossible to produce saving-investment equilibrium at full employment by expanding the quantity of money sufficiently to reduce the money rate of interest sufficiently to lead individuals to spend all of their income on current production. Keynes's argument was to suggest that since interest rates represented expectations of future rates such a policy would only succeed if individuals could be convinced that the rate reduction would not be reversed. His simple "square" formula (1936, p. 202) suggested that scepticism (reinforced by the appearance of "semi-inflation" as money wages progressed more rapidly than productivity) would lead rational investors to increased liquidity preference to reduce capital losses, thereby blocking the fall in the rate of interest (and confirming their scepticism) before full employment had been reached.

The orthodox argument was that while increased liquidity preference reduced the demand for goods, if money could be produced by labour then it had no effect on the level of employment. Keynes's "essential properties of money" (cf. Davidson, p. 159, Minsky, p. 77), rather than that of the liquidity trap, or absolute liquidity preference, is meant to deal with this point; it depends on the response of the quantity of money to an increase in the demand for it relative to that for other goods. The elasticities of production and substitution need not be zero only lower than those for any other good.

6. Interest rate parity and aggregate supply and demand.

The development of this line of analysis, opened up by Sraffa's review of Hayek, appears in chapters 16 and 17 of the *General Theory* as Keynes's demonstration (in reply to Hayek) of exactly how a monetary economy in which money is a real factor determining investment decisions by means of the effect of the money rate of interest differs from a neutral or non-monetary economy in which there is no asset which possesses a liquidity premium in excess of its carrying costs. This discussion was initially conceived as describing the indirect influence of money on prices, as suggested in the *Treatise*, for it appears as the second chapter, "The meaning and consequences of "bearishness", of book III "The Determination of Price", in the initial 1932 table of contents and becomes "The factors determining liquidity preference" in the second. In the 1933 Table, however, liquidity preference (the supposed afterthought) is already "determining the rate of interest", while the supply function, the multiplier and real and money wages became chapters 15, 16 and 17 of Book IV, "The Theory of Prices". The discussion of the essential properties of interest and money necessary to give the money rate of interest its predominant role appears as chapters 2 and 3, of Book I, "The Relation of the General Theory of Economics to the Classical Theory". The principle of effective demand first appears in the 1934 Table, with the initial monetary discussion moved to a new Book entitled the "Theory of Investment".

There was thus a steady movement away from early emphasis of money's indirect role in determining prices via the rate of interest to the role of the money rate of interest determining saving-investment equilibrium at less-than-full employment via Sraffa's commodity-rate analysis adapted to a monetary economy. The prominence given to money in the Spiethoff *Festschrift* announcing the "Monetary Theory of Production" (1933) reflecting the 1932 drafting and the titles of Keynes's 1932 and 1933 Lectures is thus replaced at the beginning of the book by the short period framework and the intersection of aggregate supply and demand representing the principle of effective demand, money becoming an integral part of the later discussion of investment. The position and importance of money in the presentation of the theory thus followed Keynes's move towards the identification of investment as the *causa causans* in determining output and employment; while money loses pride of place in the first Book, it gains in importance for it provides the very basis for effective demand and the explanation of the inherent instability on investment in a capitalist economy, as well as its essential properties producing the explanation for persistent unemployment equilibrium. The discussion in terms of Sraffian-inspired own rates thus appears as the summing up of Book IV: "The inducement to invest" (which Kahn, 1984, p. 159 calls "profound"), just before the summary chapter 18 concluding presentation of the basic theory.

Thus, of the two lines of influence on Keynes's presentation of his theory the "Marshallian" formulation of effective demand in terms of aggregate supply and demand prices took on the more visible role as the introductory explanation while the exposition of individual investment decisions determining asset prices reflecting liquidity preference in a monetary economy seemed to take on a secondary position. But, the two approaches have simply exchanged places in the order of presentation, both remained as virtually equivalent explanations of effective demand and unemployment equilibrium.

In the discussion following the publication of the book, it is the aggregate supply and demand aspect which arrested the attention of the profession. The most famous of these reinterpretations, Hicks's *IS-LM,* is simply an alternative to the Marshallian aggregate supply and demand framework, based on aggregation of Walrasian excess demand equations in "bundles" representing "market" equilibria in which equality of the natural and market rate of interest replaces the equality of "aggregate" supply and demand prices of the principle of effective demand. Since the Hicksian approach ignores Keynes's monetary analysis it can produce less-than-full employment equilibrium only by assuming a horizontal range to the *LM* curve. But since the market rate of interest is the only "price" in the model, this is equivalent to assuming fixed prices (and, as is more frequent, wages), both of which Keynes expressly rejected.

In his replies to the reviews of his book (as well as in correspondence with Townshend) Keynes consistently refers to his monetary analysis, which he felt had been overlooked because most commentators had failed to notice its relation to the aggregate supply and demand explanation due to undue emphasis on the difference between expected and actual demand. In his reply to Viner, as well as to those, such as Hicks, who proposed "alternative" monetary theories of interest, and in his 1937 contribution to the Fisher *Festschrift* Keynes reiterates that his readers have not appreciated the importance of his treatment of money and the money rate of interest. Hicks is in particular singled out in this respect (cf. XIV, p. 201 ff.).

For Keynes, in difference from the Quantity theory, money was a real factor which could affect relative prices and outputs in the long period as well as the short, while in difference to the theories of Wicksell and Hayek, the rate of interest was a purely monetary factor completely independent of any connotation of natural productivity: "Put shortly, the orthodox theory maintains that the forces which determine the common value of the marginal efficiency of various assets are independent of money, which has, so to speak, no autonomous influence, and that prices move until the marginal efficiency of money, i.e. the rate of interest, falls into line with the common value of the marginal efficiency of other assets as determined by other forces. My theory, on the other hand maintains that this is a special case and that over a wide range of possible cases almost the opposite is true, namely, that the marginal efficiency of money is determined by forces partly appropriate to itself, and that prices move until the marginal efficiency of other assets fall into line with the rate of interest" (XIV, p. 103). The point is also made in the 1937 reply to Viner: "instead of the marginal efficiency of capital determining the rate of interest, it is truer ... to say that it is the rate of interest which determines the marginal efficiency of capital" (*ibid.*, p. 123). The rate of interest was thus not simple the "monetary equivalent of the marginal efficiency of capital" and Keynes escaped "circular reasoning" by his introduction of money via the own-rate framework. In Hicks's *IS-LM* representation Keynes's adjustment process could only be preserved by assuming that prices and wages were rigid in order to produce the proper horizontal slope to the *LM* curve.

7. Development and extension of the General Theory.

Thus there were two possible lines of development: the extension of the short-period framework to discussion of factors such as capital accumulation, which Marshall had treated under long-period analysis, or extension of the role of money within the context of own rates of own interest. Keynes's younger Cambridge colleagues clearly saw extension of the theory in the former light, while Sraffa abandoned his 1926 reference to imperfect competition and instead produced a theory of prices more in line with his criticism of Hayek than his criticism of Marshall. Sraffa clearly thought there was nothing to be gained in further expansion of Marshall's faulty apparatus, and he was particularly sceptical of the new fangled conceptions required to support the short-period presentation of effective demand via aggregate demand and supply prices.

The work of Kahn, Robinson, Kaldor, Harrod, and Kalecki thus built on the aggregate version of Marshall's short-period apparatus, often building on advances gained in the analysis of imperfect competition, to extend Keynes's theory to the long-period, tackling the problems of capital accumulation and distribution. Thus the Harrod-Domar growth models spawned multiplier-accelerator models, and the analysis of capital accumulation produced the Cambridge theories of aggregate income distribution. It is characteristic of these theories that investment is taken as exogenous, thus eliminating the discussion of effective demand and the monetary elements which Keynes had used in the *General Theory* to explain the level of investment. Thus, while investment and expectations play a crucial role in the post-Keynesian theories of capital, growth and distribution, there is little or no analysis of money, much less liquidity preference or the analysis of chapter 17 which provided the crucial foundations of Keynes's treatment of investment. At the same time the *Treatise* was left to one side and the link between monetary variables and the price of capital assets was therefore eliminated. It is interesting to note that few of these developers of imperfect competition and of a Keynesian long-period theory saw much of value in the *Treatise* analysis. Monetary elements, of little importance in value theory, were also considered of little importance in the extension to Keynes's theories.

By the 1950's there were two Keynesian systems of thought in place: the Walrasian based aggregate supply and demand formulation of the short period via Hicks' *IS-LM* which had supplanted the original Marshallian version, and the extension of this latter formulation to the analysis of long-run capital accumulation. But such long-period analysis could also be produced by reintroducing price flexibility into Hicksian analysis which produced theories which implied the natural establishment of full employment in the long period, thus questioning the generality of Keynes's short-period theory as being limited to cases of wage and price rigidity. Not surprisingly, it was the line of development of Keynes's theory based on the developments of the imperfect competition theorists that was the first to be incorporated into traditional theory, nor is it surprising that the Cambridge criticism of these theories in Marshallian terms had little impact on the profession. In the Cambridge capital theory debates it was eventually necessary to fall back on Sraffa's theory of prices to show that the traditional theory was based on inherent logical contradictions. But this defence still seemed to suggest that Keynes's theory was restricted to conditions of ad hoc rigidity.

Joan Robinson, for example, after spending the best part of a long career pursuing the extension of the Marshallian short-period version of Keynes to the long period finally rejected this approach in favour of the study of "historical" time. Neither does the conception of the long period in terms of natural tendencies or long-period averages appear to permit the introduction of money in any more meaningful way than the neutrality proposed by Hayek. Keynes's extension of Sraffa's commodity-rate analysis to a monetary economy was clearly an attempt to respond to Hayek by showing just exactly how money did affect the economic system. Just as Sraffa went on to develop a similar framework into the specification of the essential logical relations between distributive variables and relative prices, the extension of the interest rate parity theorem can be considered as the identification of the logical relations between the money rate of interest and the level of output and employment in a monetary system. As Roncaglia (1984) has pointed out, Sraffa's relations imply no particular causal relationships, while Keynes's system explicitly proposes money as the causal or "real" variable constraining a capitalist or monetary production system. It is the recognition of this role of money that has been absent from recent attempts to produce long-period theories of effective demand.

A number of economists have recently tried to recover aspects of Keynes monetary analysis. For example, Davidson has built an analysis in terms of spot and future prices which draws as much on the monetary detail of the *Treatise* to support liquidity preference as on the *General Theory*, while Minsky has linked the role of aggregate expenditure to the determination of the price of consumption goods relative to the price of capital assets to reformulate the demand for money and produce a theory of financial instability in the tradition of Keynes's early studies on money and the cycle.

Joan Robinson has recently suggested (1978) that this is insufficient, that such developments should be extended to produce a link between Keynes and Sraffa. This would imply integrating Keynes's essential monetary relationships with Sraffa's. Pasinetti's (1981) discussion of the relation between his natural system and the social structure of monetary relations suggests a possible approach. Attempts to relate the concepts of own-rates in Keynes and Sraffa directly have been studied in Kregel (1982, 1984) and Nell (1983).

It would appear that these are the lines of analysis which should be followed if Keynes's insights are to be preserved, for it is interesting to note that there is only one aspect of Keynes's theory that has not been successfully duplicated in traditional theory: the role of money. Practitioners of the General Equilibrium approach admit that their models cannot provide an explanation of the purely monetary aspects of Keynes's model. In this respect they consider of greatest importance (cf. Hahn, 1977) those monetary aspects discussed in chapters 16 and 17 of the *General Theory* which have been the focus of interest of those economists who have always insisted that Keynes was a monetary economist and that his theory could not be understood independent of its novel contributions to the theory of monetary analysis. From Hicks' reformulation of Keynes's supply and demand analysis in Walrasian terms to Patinkin's recent rediscovery of its original Marshallian foundation, the profession (with the exception of Dillard's exceptional 1954 paper, and more recently the developments in France led by Barrère, 1983, 1984, and the formulation and extension of the theory of the "circuit" by Parquez, e.g. 1982) has considered the principle of effective demand to be a simple expression of the multiplier and somehow independent of Keynes's analysis of the essential properties of interest and money. But Keynes clearly considered them as alternative ways of presenting the same propositions. Recognition of the crucial role of money in Keynes's theory may yet give fulfillment to the revolution in economic theory promised by Keynes's theory of effective demand in a monetary production economy.

Note

* This is the original version of a paper presented to the Annual Meetings of the American Economic Association, Dallas, December, 1984, and at the Convegno Internazionale "Domanda Effettiva, Prezzi e Distribuzione" sponsored by the Gruppo di Ricerca M.P.I. of the Facoltà di Scienze Politiche, Università di Catania, January, 1985. A short summary will appear in the *Papers and Proceedings issue of the American Economic Review*, May, 1985, pp. 133–139.

References.

Barrère A., 1983, 2nd ed., *Diséquilibres et contre-révolution Keynesienne*, Paris, Economica.
—, ed., 1984, *Keynes Aujourd'hui*, Paris, Economica.
Davidson P., 1972, *Money and the Real World*, London, Macmillan.
Dillard D., 1955, "The Theory of a Monetary Economy", in Kurihara, K., ed., *Post-Keynesian Economics*, London, Allen and Unwin, ch. 1.
Friedman M., 1969, *The Quantity Theory of Money*, London, Macmillan.
Hahn F.H., 1977, "Keynesian Economics and General Equilibrium Theory", in Harcourt G.C., ed., *Microfoundations of Macroeconomics*, London, Macmillan.
Hawtrey R.G., 1913, *Good and Bad Trade*, London, Constable.
Kahn R.F., 1931, "The Relation of Home Investment to Unemployment", *Economic Journal*, 41, pp. 173–198.
—, 1983, *L'economia del breve periodo*, Torino, Boringhieri.
—, 1984, *The Making of Keynes' General Theory*, Cambridge, Cambridge University Press.
Keynes J.M., 1973, *The Collected Writings of J.M. Keynes*, Vol. VII, *The General Theory of Employment, Interest and Money*, London, Macmillan.
—, 1973a, Vol. XII, *The General Theory and After, Part I*, London, Macmillan.
—, 1973b, Vol. XIV, *The General Theory and After, Part II*, London, Macmillan.
—, 1979, Vol. XXIX, *Ibid., A Supplement.*, London, Macmillan.
Kregel J.A., 1982, "Money, Expectations and Relative Prices in Keynes' Monetary Equilibrium", *Economic Appliquée*, 35, pp. 449–465.

—, 1983, "Effective Demand: Origins and Development of the Notion", in Kregel J.A., ed., *Distribution, Effective Demand and International Economic Relations*, London, Macmillan.

—, 1984, "Expectations and Rationality within a Capitalist Framework", in Nell E.J., ed., *Free Market Conservatism: A Critique of Theory and Practice*, London, Allen and Unwin, pp. 98–118.

Minsky H.P., 1975, *John Maynard Keynes*, London, Macmillan.

Nell E.J., 1983, "Keynes after Sraffa: The Essential Properties of Keynes's Theory of Interest and Money", in Kregel J.A., *Distribution, Effective Demand and International Economic Relations*, London, Macmillan, ch. 2c.

Parguez A., 1982, "La monnaie dans le circuit ou le voile déchiré", *Economie Appliquée*, 35, n. 3.

Pasinetti L., 1981, *Structural Change and Economic Growth*, Cambridge, Cambridge University Press.

Robinson J., 1980, "Keynes and Ricardo", *Journal of Post Keynesian Economics*, 1, pp. 12–18.

Roncaglia A., 1978, *Sraffa and the Theory of Prices*, Chichester, Wiley.

—, 1984, *Comment on Vianello and Minsky*, Oral Communication to Centro di Studi Economic Avanzati Conference, Trieste.

Sraffa P., 1926, "The Laws of Returns Under Competitive Conditions", *Economic Journal*, 36, pp. 535–550.

—, 1932, "Dr. Hayek on Money and Capital", *Economic Journal*, 42, pp. 42–53.

—, 1960, *Production of Commodities by Means of Commodities*, Cambridge, Cambridge University Press.

Tonveronachi M., 1983, *J.M. Keynes. Dall'instabilità ciclica all'equilibrio di sottoccupazione*, Firenze, La Nuova italia.

Vicarelli F., 1984, *Keynes: The Instability of Capitalism*, London, Macmillan.

Chapter 9

THE MULTIPLIER AND LIQUIDITY PREFERENCE: TWO SIDES OF THE THEORY OF EFFECTIVE DEMAND

I INTRODUCTION

One of the most perplexing facts in interpreting post-war developments of Keynes's theory is his comment on Hicks's now-famous 'Mr Keynes and the Classics'. Although Hicks himself has in recent years become critical of the uses to which his *IS–LM* apparatus has been put, he still stands by it as representing the essence of Keynes's theory and supports his contention by reference to what he interprets as Keynes's tacit agreement with the contents of his 1937 paper: 'Keynes accepted the *IS–LM* diagram as a fair statement of his position' (Hicks, 1977, p. 146).

The present chapter has two goals. The first is to assess Keynes's pointed criticism of the representation of the rate of interest upon which Hicks's 1937 paper was based. The second is to attempt an explanation of *IS–LM* which might be interpreted as a 'fair representation' of Keynes's theory. These two goals permit discussion of what I believe to be the most often overlooked aspect of Keynes's theory, the indissoluble relation between the multiplier and the liquidity preference explanation of money prices.

II KEYNES'S CRITICISM OF 'MR KEYNES AND THE CLASSICS'

The careful reader of Keynes's comments in his exchange of letters with Hicks (*CW*, XIV: pp. 74ff.) will note two points. Hicks centred his comparison of Keynes and the Classics on the effect of an increase in expenditure on the rate of interest. What Hicks calls 'Mr Keynes's special theory', 'yields the startling conclusion that an increase in the inducement to invest, or in the propensity to consume, will not tend to raise the rate of interest, but only to increase employment' (Hicks, 1982, p. 107). Keynes comments on this characterisation of his position:

> From my point of view it is important to insist that my remark is to the effect that an increase in the inducement to invest *need* not raise the rate of interest. I should agree that, unless the monetary policy is appropriate, it is quite likely to. In this respect I consider that the difference between myself and the classicals lies in the fact that they regard the rate of interest as a non-monetary phenomenon, so that an increase in the inducement to invest

> would raise the rate of interest irrespective of monetary policy, – though they might concede that monetary policy was capable of producing a temporary evaporating effect. (*CW*, XIV: p. 80).[1]

Keynes thus rejects the *shape* of the *LM* curve as the focal point of difference between his theory and the classics. Had Hicks accepted this point he should not have insisted 'the most important thing in Mr Keynes's book' is that 'it is also possible to say something about the shape of the [*LM*] curve. It will probably tend to be nearly horizontal on the left, and nearly vertical on the right' (Hicks, 1982, p. 109).[2] Indeed, he could not have found any distinctive feature in Keynes's theory, for without this possibility 'Mr Keynes takes a big step back to Marshallian orthodoxy, and his theory becomes hard to distinguish from the revised and qualified Marshallian theories, which, as we have seen, are not new' (ibid, p. 108).[3]

Keynes concludes his commentary on the 1937 paper by returning to Hicks's interpretation of his theory of the rate of interest:

> I am just about to write a lecture on the question of the relation between my theory of the rate of interest and a theory based, as the Swedish one is, on the demand and supply for loans. In this connection I shall be referring to what you wrote in your review of my book. But you dealt with this very briefly, and I do not really understand what you were driving at. In particular, where you say 'It is a perfectly legitimate method, but it does not prove other methods to be wrong', what exactly are the other methods which you have in mind? (*CW*, XIV: p. 81)

Keynes may have had 'next to nothing to say by way of criticism' of Hicks's 1937 paper, yet he questioned the very point upon which Hicks had centred his comparison of Keynes with the classics and suggested that Hicks had already misunderstood his position on this very point – the theory of the rate of interest – in his earlier review of the *General Theory*. Keynes further promises a formal criticism of the point in what became 'Alternative Theories of the Rate of Interest' (*CW*, XIV: pp. 201 ff.).[4]

In his letter of reply Hicks notes that Townshend (1937) had already pointed out an error in the presentation of Keynes's theory of interest in the review. At the same time as Hicks suggests a correction he attempts to clarify the meaning of his earlier statements on the rate of interest.[5] Hicks concludes, 'Of course what lies behind this rather silly business is a desire to separate the essential content of your theory from its formal arrangement. I am a convinced liquidity preference man, but I do covet some freedom of choice about the way (or ways) the doctrine shall be expressed' (*CW*, XIV: p. 83). Keynes remains unconvinced, and writes in his 1937 *Economic Journal* article of the approach of Ohlin, Robertson and Hicks: 'Some of the writers . . . believe that my theory is on the whole the same as theirs and mainly amounts to expressing it in a somewhat different way. Nevertheless the theories are, I believe, radically opposed to one another' (*CW*, XIV: p. 202). There clearly was no freedom of choice possible in the presentation of Keynes's theory of the rate of interest.

If Keynes had any hesitation concerning Hicks's *IS–LM* representation we must look for it not in the polite comments of Keynes's private correspondence, but in his clearly enunciated public criticism of the point upon which he felt he differed fundamentally from the interpretation given by Hicks in his review of the *General Theory*, and which is the centre about which the comparison of Mr Keynes and the classics is built: the exposition of the rate of interest. Although Keynes's article deals with Hicks as one of a group of proponents of a similar position, Townshend's short note (1937) deals directly with Hicks's exposition of the rate of interest. Keynes's subsequent correspondence with Townshend (*CW*, XXIX: pp. 255ff.) concerning the 'basic postulate' of the Classical theory is also of interest in confirming Keynes's position on the fundamental difference between his theory and the classics as the rate of interest.

What Hicks intended by 'freedom of choice' can be simply summarised (cf. also Kregel, 1982b). If one interprets Keynes's three fundamental psychological variables – the propensity to consume, liquidity preference and the efficiency of capital – as representing 'bundles' or aggregations of individuals' decisions in 'three markets' for goods, money and loans, then there are three equations to 'determine' the prices of goods and the rate of interest in terms of money as the numeraire.

> Thus two of the equations, as you would say, are operative equations, one is a check equation. But it is possible to select any one of the three equations as a check equation, and distribute the operative equations among prices and interest as we choose. Thus there are six possible alternative 'theories'; but if they are correctly stated, they all mean the same thing, and are equally right. (*CW*, XIV: p. 82)

Hicks interpreted the equality of savings and investment (the supply and demand for loans, in Hicks's terminology) as Keynes's choice of the 'check' equation, leaving the supply and demand for goods to determine their prices and the supply and demand for money to determine the rate of interest. But it was also possible to use, for example, the supply and demand for money as the 'check' equation, producing one of the other five 'alternative theories', with the rate of interest determined by the supply and demand for loans (saving and investment) and goods prices determined by the supply and demand for goods.[6] Hicks considered these two formulations identical 'monetary' explanations of the rate of interest and built his comparison of Keynes's theory and the classics via *IS–LM* on the basis of these similar 'alternative' formulations.

Keynes clearly objected to this contention of similarity, for Hicks's alternative theory implied that the rate of interest was determined by savings and investment, and that the 'price' of money was the inverse of goods prices, which appears to be a very precise representation of Say's Law and the Quantity Theory of Money![7] Accepting such an equivalence Hicks could only produce Keynes's result of unemployment equilibrium by means of arbitrarily fixing prices or interest rates. In the *IS–LM* formulation it is the last possibility that is chosen in the horizontal *LM* curve representation of the 'liquidity trap', and which allows Hicks to identify Keynes's 'special theory' as implying that expenditure can change without affecting the rate of interest (indeed, Hicks never provides a citation for this contention). It is, as already noted, precisely this point to which

Keynes objects, and to which he returns in a more detailed fashion in his public criticism of the possibility of 'alternative' monetary theories of the rate of interest, insisting on the distinctive nature of his own 'liquidity preference' approach. Had Keynes not considered this point fundamental to understanding of his theory he certainly would not have taken such pains to correct misunderstanding with those few economists who were most receptive, at least superficially, to his theory through their acceptance of the necessity of a 'monetary' explanation of the rate of interest.

III KEYNES'S CRITICISM OF THE ALTERNATIVE MONETARY THEORIES OF INTEREST

Keynes's 1937 criticism of these 'alternative' monetary theories of the supply and demand for credit or the supply and demand for loans, is that they all reduce supply to 'exactly the same thing as the quantity of saving' and reduce demand to 'exactly the same thing as the quantity of net investment', so that 'we are completely back again at the classical doctrine . . . that the rate of interest is fixed at the level where the supply of credit, in the shape of saving, is equal to the demand for credit, in the shape of investment' (*CW*, XIV: pp. 205–6).

Keynes was right to suspect that Hicks's position fell into this category, for one of Hicks's six alternative combinations of three markets is precisely this case, and it is on the basis of this three-market representation that Hicks represented Keynes's theory in the two market-equilibrium curves, one equation being redundant as the check equation. If Keynes could not accept the horizontal *LM* curve as representative of his 'special theory' then his theory became one of the six variants in Hicks's 'General' theory and was formally equivalent to the traditional approach, as Hicks had already noted.

Accepting Hicks's framework, the argument between Hicks and Keynes then turns on whether one can be 'indifferent' to the choice of which equations determine which variables. Hicks notes that mathematically there can be no difference, while Keynes contends that economically his theory has not been understood. Recall what Hicks calls the 'ordinary method of economic theory'. Here the check equation is the supply and demand for money which determines the price *level*, while the demand and supply for goods determines *relative* prices and savings and investment the interest rate. This implies that changes in the demand for money relative to supply will determine the general price level and be independent of relative prices. Now, Keynes repeatedly insists that his theory differs from the traditional theory in treating money as a 'real' factor (*CW*, XIV: pp. 202–3, note 2), while he considers the rate of interest as a 'monetary' factor (ibid, p. 80), or that money has no 'direct' effect on prices. Rather Keynes insists that it is the rate of interest that determines prices through its effect on the rate of return to assets, i.e. on the relation of their demand prices to their supply prices:

> In so far as [money] has been noticed, the essential nature of the phenomenon has been misdescribed. For what has attracted attention has been the *quantity* of money which has been hoarded; and importance has been attached to this because it has been supposed to have a direct proportionate effect on the price level through affecting the velocity of circulation.

> But the *quantity* of hoards can only be altered either if the total quantity of money is changed or if the quantity of current money income . . . is changed; whereas fluctuations in the degree of confidence are capable of having quite a different effect, namely, in modifying not the amount that is actually hoarded, but the amount of the premium which has to be offered to induce people not to hoard. And changes in the propensity to hoard, or in the state of liquidity preference as I have called it, primarily affect, not prices, but the rate of interest; any effect on prices being produced by repercussion as an ultimate consequence of a change in the rate of interest. (*CW*, XIV: p. 116)[8]

This emphasis on money as a 'real' factor, and the rate of interest as a 'monetary' factor, may cause perplexity to those who believe that Keynes's sole contribution to economic theory was the income multiplier (which he adapted from Richard Kahn's employment multiplier), or have only noticed those passages in Keynes's correspondence – with Harrod, Hawtrey and Robertson – where he states repeatedly: 'The novelty in my treatment of savings and investment consists, not in my maintaining their necessary aggregate equality, but in the proposition that it is, not the rate of interest, but the level of incomes which (in conjunction with certain other factors) ensures this equality' (*CW*, XIV: p. 211), or 'As I have said above, the initial novelty lies in my maintaining that it is not the rate of interest, but the level of incomes which ensures equality between savings and investment' and 'the result . . . was to leave the rate of interest in the air. If the rate of interest is not determined by savings and investment in the same way in which price is determined by supply and demand, how is it determined?' (*CW*, XIV: p. 212).

In Keynes's comments on the possibility of 'alternative' theories, instead of insisting on savings and investment being brought into equality via the multiplier Keynes emphasises his rejection of the view that the 'price' of money is the inverse of the price of goods, denying any direct influence of changes in the demand for money or the velocity of circulation on prices. As Townshend puts it, 'the volume of money is not a directly determining factor . . . of any prices' (1937, p. 158). Instead, Keynes emphasises that it is changes in liquidity preference that will bring changes in the rate of interest; it is the change in the rates of interest which affect the prices of capital assets and their marginal efficiencies, the change in marginal efficiency leading to decisions to increase or decrease holdings of capital goods, i.e. to investment decisions. Changes in investment in their turn affect the rates of return on capital assets as they set in motion the multiplier process which produces the savings required to balance the changes in investment. It is in this sense that money is a 'real' phenomenon: changes in the price of money, the rate of interest, will bring about changes in the rates of return on capital goods and thus cause investment and income to adjust. At the same time, this argument shows clearly that Keynes's theory of interest is simply the other side of the multiplier medal.

Hicks's alternative formulations approach may aid in seeing this interrelation, for if one accepts the 'ordinary method of economic theory' it is formally equivalent to object to the rate of interest being determined by savings and investment and to the supply and demand for money directly setting the level of prices. Rejecting one means rejecting the other. At the same time, insisting that money is a real phenomenon and the rate of interest is a monetary phenomenon means that the money market determines the rate of interest. Savings and investment becomes the check equation, and effective demand determines the *level* of output. The theory of interest and the multiplier thus replace Say's Law and the Quantity Theory of Money. But, in this version it is relative prices which are left hanging in the air. The insistence that money is a real phenomenon that affects prices via the rate of interest means that it is left to liquidity preference to determine *money* prices. The end result may be the same in equilibrium no matter which of Hicks's alternatives is chosen; the process of adjustment to the equilibrium position is not.

Further, Keynes insists that in such a process a change in liquidity preference may affect prices without *any* change in aggregate money holdings. Hicks might better have interpreted Keynes's 'special theory' as proposing that an increase in the inducement to invest may occur without any change in the quantity of money demanded rather than without any change in the rate of interest.[9]

As Keynes reiterates in his contribution to the Irving Fisher *Festschrift* – Keynes credited Fisher with leading him to this position[10] – this is the basic difference from traditional theory:

> Put shortly, the orthodox theory maintains that the forces which determine the common value of the marginal efficiency of various assets are independent of money, which has, so to speak, no autonomous influence, and that prices move until the marginal anciency of money, i.e. the rate of interest, falls into line with the common value of the marginal efficiency of other assets as determined by other forces. My theory, on the other hand, maintains that this is a special case and that over a wide range of possible cases almost the opposite is true, namely, that the marginal efficiency of money is determined by forces partly appropriate to itself, and that prices move until the marginal efficiency of other assets fall into line with the rate of interest. (*CW*, XIV: p. 101)

Thus Keynes's insistence, in his discussions with Hicks, that the distinctive feature of his theory compared with the classics was to be found in treating money as a 'real' factor (*CW*, XIV: p. 203), and that the rate of interest is not determined by 'real' factors such as the productivity of real capital, but is a monetary phenomenon (*CW*, XIV: p. 80, 206; *CW*, VII: pp. 214–15), leading to his position that the money rate of interest as determined by liquidity preference sets the rate of return on real assets, which is just the opposite of Wicksell's theory, for example. This, of course, is the basis of Keynes's theory that the money rate of interest rules the roost, spelled out in chapters 16 and 17 of the *General Theory*.

It is important to note that Keynes's insistence on the importance of the rate of interest comes from his repeated denial that money enters the determination of prices and demand for goods via changes in the demand for money (or changes in hoarding, or changes in the velocity of circulation) affecting the effective quantity of money. This further testifies that Keynes did not consider his theory of liquidity preference as an improved specification of the demand-for-money function. Yet it is precisely this point that Hicks emphasises in his 1937 characterisation (although not in 1936) and which is now commonly accepted by both neoclassical and post-Keynesian writers. At best, Keynes's position might be described as a theory of shifts in the demand for money. What Hicks and others have interpreted as an improvement in the specification of the demand for money Keynes considered to be a revolutionary approach to the determination of money prices via the influence of money on the rate of interest.

IV THE MULTIPLIER, LIQUIDITY PREFERENCE AND MONEY PRICES

There can then be no difference between Keynes's insistence that it is the level of income via the multiplier that equates savings and investment and his insistence that it is the degree of liquidity preference which determines the rate of interest. Placing emphasis on the latter 'equation' leads more clearly to what Keynes called the main point of difference with the classical theory: that money is a *real* phenomenon, for if the rate of interest is a monetary phenomenon then money enters the determination of prices via the rate of interest. As Fisher had emphasised, every rate of interest can be conceived of as two prices, present and future. Thus, Keynes's theory implied not a 'time preference' explanation of prices, but a 'liquidity preference' theory of *money* prices, or as Townshend (1937, p. 160) suggested in his note, a correction of the marginal theory of value.

It is now easy to see that if the multiplier and liquidity preference are two sides of the same coin, then the liquidity preference theory of money prices must be an integral part of the explanation of the changes in the demand for investment goods which is necessary to bring about the adjusting action of income on saving via the multiplier. To split the multiplier from liquidity preference is to deprive the income adjustment mechanism of its motor force – profit opportunities caused by movements in relative money prices.

The impossibility of separating liquidity preference from the multiplier was already suggested in a note in Hicks's 1937 article (1982, p. 107, note 4). Hicks rewrites his representation of Keynes's theory, retaining the Quantity Theory demand for money equation. The famous three equations thus become: $M = kY$; $I = f(i)$; $I = S(Y)$. Hicks notes that now the 'multiplier is shorn of its wings. For since Y still depends only on M, I now depends only on M, and it is impossible to increase investment without increasing the willingness to save or the quantity of money. The system thus generated is therefore identical with that which, a few years ago, used to be called the "Treasury View". But Liquidity Preference transports us from the "Treasury View" to the "General Theory of Employment".'

Keynes's theory replaced not just Say's Law, but Say's Law *and* the Quantity Theory which formed a unified whole (cf. Kregel, 1983, pp. 52 ff.). It thus had to replace *both* if it were to be creditable. And just as Say's Law and the Quantity Theory formed a unified system, the theory of income adjustment and liquidity preference formed a unified whole.

Keynes was further concerned (especially in his post-1936 writings) to point out not only the equivalence of income equating saving and investment and his monetary theory of the rate of interest producing real effects; he also stressed that this latter was not simply an alternative explanation of changes in the level of hoarding (or the velocity of circulation, or the quantity of money demanded). This was because traditional theory had argued that an increase in the demand for money would reduce the velocity of circulation, the reduced effective money supply leading to lower prices, leaving saving, investment and the rate of interest unchanged.

Thus Keynes argued the extreme case that a change in liquidity preference could cause a change in prices and output without any change in the quantity of money. As Townshend puts it:

> Any quantity of money, however small, will in theory support any price, however high, provided it circulates fast enough. And any quantity of money, however large, is consistent with zero prices, provided it does not circulate at all, or with indefinitely low prices if it circulates slowly enough. Thus the limitations, whatever they may be, of the stock of money cannot suffice to prevent expectations from raising (or lowering) the money-prices of all durable goods and assets (not, of course, equally) without limit of speed – that is to say, to an arbitrary extent even in the shortest period. (Townshend, 1937, p. 161)

The change in prices in Keynes's approach comes instead from the effect of a change in liquidity preference on the rate of interest relative to the rates of return on other durable assets. Following Fisher, Keynes defines the rate of interest in terms of two prices, for present and future delivery. It is to emphasise this point that Keynes starts his criticism of the alternative monetary theories of interest by stating 'The liquidity preference theory of the rate of interest which I have set forth . . . makes the rate of interest to depend on the present supply of *money* and the demand schedule for a present claim on money *in terms of a deferred claim on money*' (*CW*, XIV: p. 202, italics added), or 'Interest on money *means* precisely what the books on arithmetic say that it means; that is to say, it is simply the premium obtainable on current cash over deferred cash, so that it measures the marginal preference (for the community as a whole) for holding cash in hand over cash for deferred delivery' (*CW*, XIV. p. 101).

In chapter 17 of the *General Theory*, Keynes had put it: 'The money rate of interest – we may remind the reader – is nothing more than the percentage excess of a sum of money contracted for forward delivery, e.g. a year hence, over what we may call the "spot" or cash price of the sum thus contracted for forward delivery' (*CW*, VII: p. 222). The rate of interest is thus the difference between two prices, the spot price and the price for forward delivery per cent. Keynes goes on to note, 'It would seem, therefore, that for every kind of capital-asset there must be an analogue of the rate of interest on money' (ibid) each involving the spot and forward price of the asset or good in question. On the basis of Sraffa's (1932) suggestions, Keynes works out the analysis of this point in terms of what he called the 'own rates of own interest' (or the marginal efficiency in terms of the asset) which are defined in terms of spot and forward (or demand and supply) prices.

Changes in liquidity preference will thus change the relation between spot and forward prices of all assets: 'it would seem that it is essential to take liquidity into account in order to discuss *any money* prices. For even if certain assets have so little liquidity-premium that changes in it do not affect their money-prices, variations in the (large) liquidity-premium of money will do so – operating of course on the conditions of new production of the assets' (Townshend, 1937, p. 161). The relation of the spot to forward price of all durable goods are thus seen to be determined by the rate of interest: 'The function of the rate of interest is to modify the money prices of other capital assets in such a way as to equalise the attraction of holding them and holding cash' (*CW*, XIV: p. 213). Keynes's 'novelty' could thus be expressed as a theory of money relative prices determined by the rate of interest. Townshend correctly concludes, 'Now, if Mr. Keynes' views . . . be accepted, it would seem that the considerations governing the prices of monetary assets must also, pro tanto, apply to determine the prices of other durable assets. For the latter have, as Mr. Keynes puts it, "monetary attributes in a varying degree". A kind of liquidity-premium attaches to them also' (Townshend, 1937, p. 159).

Thus relative money price changes lead to profitable investment opportunities and to new investment decisions which produce income adjustment via the multiplier. At the same time as the multiplier adjusts income to equate savings and investment, it adjusts the relation of present to future prices so as to produce 'net balance in the minds of wealth-owners between the conflicting desires to retain *purchasing power* (in any form) and to exercise it' (ibid), or to equate the marginal efficiency of all durable stores of value with the marginal efficiency of money: the rate of interest (Keynes development of this theory is more fully spelled out in Kregel, 1982a).

In chapter 14 of the *General Theory*, Keynes criticises those theories 'which attempt to make the rate of interest depend on the "marginal efficiency of capital"' (*CW*, VII: p. 184), noting that although they'll be equal in equilibrium, the correct calculation of the latter depends on the former. The factor which determines their equality is the level of income, and it is thus the same adjustment process that equates savings and investment which operates to adjust relative prices and thus brings the rate of return of capital investments (the marginal efficiency of capital) and the rate of interest into equality. A change in liquidity preference is thus capable of changing prices and output independently of any change in the quantity of money held by the public, as the multiplier process equates saving and investment at the same time as it adjusts present to future prices so as to equate the marginal efficiency of capital to the new rate of interest resulting from the initial change in liquidity preference.

Keynes's theory thus substitutes both Say's Law and the Quantity Theory with his Liquidity-Preference–income-multiplier theory. Much of the post-war literature has emphasised *only* the income-expenditure adjustment process, substituting a traditional demand for money formulation for the theory of liquidity preference. Ironically, although this is how Hicks represented liquidity preference, he was also the first to recognise that it was inappropriate to split that theory from the multiplier.[11] The theory of liquidity-preference-determined money prices cannot be separated from the 'novelty' of income adjusting saving to investment, because they are part of one and the same process.[12]

I have elsewhere (Kregel, 1983) argued that the money prices so determined will, in stationary equilibrium, be compatible with what have come to be called 'Sraffa prices'. Whether or not this view is accepted, we must conclude that the novelty of the multiplier cannot be separated from the theory of liquidity preference without losing what Keynes considered to be his main difference from the traditional theory – the determination of the rate of interest by monetary factors representing the direct influence of money on real factors, rather than vice versa. As Hicks saw, divorcing liquidity preference from the multiplier and adding a simple demand for money function leads back to the Treasury View (or forward to modern monetarism).

The recognition that liquidity preference and the multiplier are but different sides of the same coin also provides an explanation for those who have been bothered by the aggregate representation of demand, enquiring how individual entrepreneurs can be expected to formulate (or why they should be expected to formulate) a schedule of aggregate demand for output as a whole. What the individual entrepreneur faces is a series of supply prices for different levels of activity, and what he formulates is a series of anticipated prices or marginal efficiencies, and he acts in order to bring them into equality. Keynes's effective demand is an attempt to give an economy-wide representation of this fact. For a discussion of the idea that prices lie behind the idea of aggregate demand, cf. Parrinello (1980).

V REINTERPRETING *IS–LM*

It is the relation between money, the money rate of interest and money prices which will distinguish Keynes's theory from Hicks's representation of it. It is thus interesting to go back to Hicks's initial 'three market' model to see how his 1937 rendering of Keynes was developed. His 1935 attempt to dynamise his *Theory of Wages* (1932) dealt with the markets for labour, loans, and goods (bread). If bread is taken as the standard, there are three market equilibrium relations to determine the wage rate and the rate of interest. 'Of these three equations (as in the system of Walras) one follows from the other two. But it is completely indifferent which of the three equations we strike out in this way; convenience seems to dictate that we should strike out the equation relating to loans' (1982, p. 77). Within this framework Hicks presumes that 'bread' wages increase. The result is that 'the total demand for bread will rise, and the rate of interest will rise' (ibid, p. 78). This causes a reduction in the demand for labour, the expected response to an increase in the 'price' of labour.

Hicks notes the fact that the rate of interest and the wage rate moving in the same direction is unusual. This occurs because the bread rate of interest is determined by the equations for the supply and demand for bread. There is no independent 'price' of bread in the model; since bread is the numeraire,

> the world that we have been analysing is a world in which wages are paid in bread, and the rate of interest is a 'bread' rate of interest; in the real world wages are paid in money, and the rate of interest is a money rate. This affects our analysis in two ways. On the one hand, since the enterprise does its calculations in money . . . we have to take into account . . . the current price of the product, and the expected movement of that price. . . . On the other hand, since money is now taken as the standard of value, it is the equation of demand and supply for money which is available to determine the rate of interest. The 'consumption-good' equation which we used before is now no longer available, for it is fully occupied in determining the prices of consumption goods. This means that the reactions through

> interest are monetary reactions, and will depend in practice on the monetary system. (ibid, pp. 78–9)

This seems very like Keynes's theory.

As Hicks points out, at this stage he had not yet seen the *General Theory*, but 'I must certainly have heard that Keynes was determining the rate of interest by the supply of money. I was curious to test out this doctrine on the model with which I was working' (1982, p. 10). Let us follow the adjustments suggested by Hicks. To account for 'money' there will now be four 'markets' – loans, bread, labour and money – to determine interest rates, prices and wages, money now serving as numeraire. As in the original analysis the equation for loans is dropped, leaving the supply and demand for bread to determine the price of bread, the demand and supply of labour to determine the wage rate, and the demand and supply of money to determine the interest rate. In this framework a change in wages affects the demand for bread *and* the costs of producing bread; the rate of interest rises as the nominal value of bread increases if this raises the demand for (transactions balances) money given the supply. The effect on employment depends on the effect of the change in wages relative to prices on bread output, and the effect of the rate of interest on future bread production plans; or on the positive effect of higher wages on consumption relative to the negative effect of the higher interest rate on investment on the demand side, and the negative effect of the change in relative prices on current production and expected profits.

Hicks later explained that such a mechanism might be called 'orthodox Keynesian':

> If there is not enough money to support full employment at the enhanced level of money wages, the rate of interest will rise, employment will *therefore* fall, and (probably) real wages will rise, since a smaller volume of labour is being applied to an unchanged capital stock. This is not so very far away from the classical analysis of the same problem; after all, it is a rather 'classical' problem, with which classical theory ought to be better able to cope. Both are agreed that the rise in money wages will now lead to a rise in real wages and a fall in employment. (Hicks, 1965, pp. 360–1)

On the other hand, if Hicks's 'monetised' 1935 bread model takes wage units as the numeraire and drops the labour market equation, this leaves three equations to determine the prices of goods, the rate of interest and the price of money. Since the latter is the 'purchasing power of money' or the inverse of the price of goods, there are just two unknowns to be determined by three equations. This seems to be the formulation that Hicks had in mind when he wrote the review (Hicks, 1936) of Keynes's book, rather than the suggested 1935 adjustments. The difference is the introduction of the wage-unit as numeraire, something which Hicks could not have foreseen in 1935.

Problems arise, however, in equating Keynes's scheme with this one, for as Hicks notes, Keynes's two 'prices' were rather different: 'Keynes also appeared to have two parameters – his Y (income in terms of wage units) and r, the rate of interest' (1982, pp. 320–1). As noted, reference to wage-units as numeraire allowed the elimination of the labour market. The rate of interest posed no problem as it appeared in Hicks's earlier version of the model determined by the money market. But income did not fit in, for in Hicks's bread model the output of bread was assumed to be given within the 'period'. Thus, in order to adapt his scheme, Hicks was forced to substitute income for goods prices. This, in fact, involved taking physical output as given; money income was thus determined by the supply and demand for goods determining prices. The equilibrium relations in the money, loans, and goods markets were thus available to determine the interest rate and the 'price' of a physically given aggregate output (Hicks might have referred to Keynes's aggregate demand price, but did not). Given Keynes's assumption that savings equal investment, the loans market became the check equation, leaving supply and demand for money to determine the rate of interest and the supply and demand for output to determine the level of income: *LM* and *IS*.

It is in elaborating this latter relation that Hicks, as he now recognises (Hicks, 1980–1), ran into trouble. Instead of adopting Keynes aggregate supply and demand structure of effective demand, this market becomes completely demand-determined, physical supply being given within the period. Since demand was composed of consumption and investment, and saving is the inverse of consumption, the equality of savings and investment for any level of income would also determine aggregate demand for that level of income. Thus the multiplier relation could be represented by means of two equations, one linking investment to the marginal efficiency of capital and the other linking saving to the level of income. Since in equilibrium the marginal efficiency of capital equals the rate of interest, different values of the rate of interest (equal to the marginal efficiency of capital) will then produce different levels of consumption and investment and different equilibrium levels of income. It would be possible to derive from this equilibrium a relation between the rate of interest rate (marginal efficiency of capital) and the level of income.[13] The *LM* curve would then show the relation between income and the money rate of interest. The *IS–LM* diagram will then have the money-rate of interest (always equal to the marginal efficiency of capital) on the vertical axis and the level of income on the horizontal axis. Equilibrium is described by the level of income at which the rate of interest which produces equilibrium in the money market is equal to the marginal efficiency of capital. To the left of the intersection of the *IS* and *LM* curves the rate of interest is below the marginal efficiency, profitable opportunities for investment lead entrepreneurs to increase their demand for investment goods, and the multiplier adjusts income to the level at which savings equals investment and prices have adjusted so as to eliminate further profit opportunities to entrepreneurs.

A change in liquidity preference, given the supply of money, will shift the *LM* curve. Since the *IS* curve is drawn up on the assumption that interest equals the marginal efficiency and saving responds to the rate of interest as well as the level of income, the *IS* curve will also shift. A reduction in liquidity preference shifts the *LM* curve to the right. Since the effects of lower interest rates will also affect the investment for any level of income, the *IS* curve will also shift to the right. Thus income will expand until the marginal efficiency read off the *IS* curve equals the rate of interest determined in the money market. If the shifts are equiproportional we have precisely the case that Hicks described as Keynes's 'special theory': Income expands at an unchanged rate of interest. At the same time, Keynes's requirement that income and prices are affected without a change in money holdings initiating the change, is also satisfied. Keynes could hardly have objected to *IS–LM* had he interpreted it in this way.

But this is not what Hicks presented in his 1937 paper. In his 1936 review he had already warned: 'This monetary character of interest is, of course, no novelty; it has been generally recognised at least since the time of Wicksell. But the way of expressing it used by Wicksell and his followers has, of course, to be abandoned by Mr Keynes –since a "natural rate" of interest would be a concept foreign to the whole present trend of his ideas' (1982, p. 92). Yet, in his 1937 presentation, Hicks makes no distinction between the rate of interest which equates saving and investment – the "investment rate of interest" – and the rate of interest determined in the money market, until his concluding summary where he notes: 'when characterised in this way, Mr Keynes's theory begins to look very like Wicksell's . . . if *IS* is horizontal, we do have a perfectly Wicksellian construction; the investment rate becomes Wicksell's *natural* rate, for in this case it may be thought of as determined by real causes' (1982, p 114).

In this explanation, income adjusts neither saving and investment nor the rate of interest and the marginal efficiency of capital so as to adjust money prices. The rate of interest is a strictly monetary phenomenon, but it has no real effects – these are determined solely by the natural rate of interest. Hicks provides no explanation of the link between the 'real' and the money rate of interest other than a reference to Wicksel's cumulative inflationary process. Indeed, what Hicks has implicitly done in giving this Wicksellian interpretation is to shift his underlying 'three market' model. Now savings and investment determine the 'real' or 'natural' rate of interest, while the supply and demand for money determines the money rate of interest; effective demand has become the check equation determining the level of income. There is only one level of effective demand compatible with stable prices, but clearly this is not what Keynes was attempting to demonstrate.

One can certainly understand that Keynes was unclear about which 'alternative' theory of interest Hicks was assuming, even though Hicks demonstrated the indifference as to which equation serves as the check equation for the equilibrium result. Keynes was thus concerned to insist that the description of the process of adjustment of the system was of fundamental importance, especially with respect to policy formation.

Economists have spent the last forty years investigating, criticising, and expounding the multiplier adjustment process in Hick's *IS–LM* framework. This has masked the other side of the adjustment process – the role of the rate of interest in determining prices and the role of income in adjusting relative prices. One of the most important tasks of Keynesian monetary theorists must be the pursuit of Keyne's theory of the determination of money prices within the theory of liquidity preference, and his theory of price adjustment within the theory of the income adjustment process of the multiplier; both sides of the income adjustment coin should carry equal importance.

Notes

1 Keynes here refers to those who determine the rate of interest by means of physical productivity of capital, the roundaboutness of production or natural factors: e.g., Böhm Bawerk and Wicksell, cf. *CW*, vII: pp. 213ff.

2 Compare this with Tobin's (1972, p. 853) comments on Friedman: "In terms of the Hicksian language of Friedman's two articles I thought (and I still think) . . . the main issue. . . was the shape of the *LM* locus" Friedman (1972, p. 913) insists that both he and Tobin accept a positive slope, rejecting a vertical or horizontal *LM* curve.

3 Which offers a clear explanation of why post-Keynesian monetary theorists consider Tobin and Friedman's work to be similar and only tenuously linked to Keyne's theory.

4 Since there is no explicit discussion of this point in the 1937 paper it would have been impossible to criticise it directly. Yet Keynes clearly took this to be the most important point at issue, challenging Hicks to clarify and differentiate his position from that of Ohlin and Robertson, which Hicks did not feel to be necessary.

5 (*CW*, XIV: pp. 82–3) This represents an expansion of Hick's comments in the 1936 review: cf. Hicks (1982, pp. 92–4).

6 Hicks calls this 'alternative' the "ordinary method of economic theory" in his 1936 review (1982, p. 92). In his full explanation given in his letter to Keynes (*CW*, XIV: p. 82), Hick's second alternative has goods prices determined by the supply and demand for money, with effective demand the check equation. Below we suggest that this was the model which finally came to charcterise *IS–LM*. Hick's first alternative was his characterization of Keyne's approach.

7 If the supply and demand for money is the check equation, then the demand for money relative to supply determines the price level, while the supply and demand for goods determines relative prices.

8 This passage clearly indicates that Keynes did not consider liquidity preference as a new, improved explanation of the demand for money. Keynes wanted to distance his position from those who explained cyclical changes in prices by means of changes in hoarding or the velocity of circulation affecting the effective quantity of money, because such an explanation based on changes in the quantity of money demanded preserved the direct link between the quantity of money and the price level of the Quantity Theory. This intention can also be seen in the following passage from R. B. Bryce's "Introduction to a Monetary Theory of Employment" (*CW*, XXIX: p. 142): "It is through its effect on the rate of interest that the quantity of money actually affects investment, incomes, employment and prices. The relationship of the quantity of money to any of these latter elements is rather complex so that it is no wonder that simple directness of the quantity theory of money could shed so little light on what actually happens."

9 As Hicks notes (*CW*, XIV: p. 82), "Mr. Townshend seems to object against the loans theory that it leaves out the possibility of a general rise in the price of securities without any borrowing or lending." Cf. Townshend (1937, p. 158).

10 'I find, looking back, that it was Professor Irving Fisher who was the great-grandparent who first influenced me strongly towards regarding money as a "real" factor' (*CW*, XIV: p. 203).

11 Hicks assesses Keynes's difference from the classics as follows: 'Mr Keynes' three equations . . . differ from the classical equations in two ways. On the one hand, the demand for money is conceived as depending upon the rate of interest (Liquidity Preference). On the other hand, any possible influence of the rate of interest on the amount saved out of a given income is neglected. Although it means that the third equation becomes the multiplier equation this second amendment is a mere simplification and ultimately insignificant. It is the liquidity preference doctrine which is vital' (Hicks, 1982, p. 107).

12 Townshend (1937, p. 164) notes, however, that before the adjustment process comes to an end, 'in general further (similar or opposite) spontaneous changes in the liquidity premiums . . . will have taken place; obviously the physical production . . . can never take place fast enough for its effects on prices to catch up with people's purely *mental* revaluations of existing ones. Of course, in practice, the *possibility or prospect* of new production bringing down again the *money*-price . . . is present in people's minds, and operates to diminish optimism or to cause a wave of optimism to be followed by a wave of pessimism.' Thus the theory of 'shifting equilibrium' (cf. Kregel, 1976) which is constrained by short-period production factors (cf. Kregel, 1978).

13 Hicks puts it this way: 'For it is now the rate of interest, not income, which is determined by the quantity of money. The rate of interest set against the schedule of the marginal efficiency of capital determines the value of investment; that determines income by the multiplier. Then the volume of employment (at given wage-rates) is determined by the value of investment and of income which is not saved but spent upon consumption goods' (Hicks, 1982, p. 107). Thus

$I = f$(MEC) and $S = f(Y)$. Taking into account the possible influence of interest on saving, and the fact that when $I = S$, i = MEC the equilibrium becomes $I = S(Y, i)$ and the marginal efficiency drops out of the story, as does the adjustment of prices as Y changes in adjusting MEC to i. Support for this interpretation is also found in Hicks's later reflections. Cf. Hicks (1977, p. 66).

It is interesting to compare this summary quotation from Hicks with the very similar one produced by Harrod (*CW*, XIII: p. 553) to convince Keynes of his full understanding of the theory. This did not prevent Harrod from producing (Harrod, 1937) a summary of the *General Theory* based on three 'market equations' which fails to consider what Keynes called the essential point of difference from the classicals and which completely ignored effective demand!

References

Friedman, M. (1972) 'Comments on the Critics', *Journal of Political Economy*, vol. 80 (Sept/Oct).
Harrod, R. F. (1937) 'Keynes and Traditional Theory', *Econometrica*, vol. 5 (Jan).
Hicks, J. R. (1932) *Theory of Wages*, 2nd edn. 1965 (London: Macmillan).
—(1936) 'Review of the General Theory', in Hicks (1982) pp. 83–99.
—(1937) 'Mr Keynes and the Classics', in Hicks (1982) pp. 100–15.
—(1977) Economic Perspectives (Oxford: Clarendon Press).
—(1980–1) 'IS-LM -An Explanation', in Hicks (1982) pp. 318–31.
—(1935) 'Wages and Interest: The Dynamic Problem', in Hicks (1982) pp. 64–79.
—(1982) *Collected Essays*, volume Il (Oxford: Blackwell).
Keynes, J. M. (VIl) *The General Theory of Employment, Interest and Money*, 1971.
(XIII) *The General Theory and After*: Part I, 1973.
(XIV) *The General Theory and After: Part Il*, 1973.
—(XXIX) *The General Theory and After: A Supplement*, 1979. All volumes from *Collected Writings of John Maynard Keynes* (London: Macmillan).
Kregel, J. A. (1976) 'Economic Methodology in the Face of Uncertainty', *Economic Journal*, vol. 36 (June).
—(1978) 'La teoria keynesiana della domanda effettiva e la teoria classica', *Economia Internazionale*, vol. XXXI (Feb–May).
—(1982a) 'Money, Expectations and Relative Prices in Keynes' Monetary Equilibrium', *Economie Appliquée*, vol. XXXV, no. 3.
—(1982b) 'Microfoundations and Hicksian Monetary Theory', *de Economist*, vol. 130, no. 4.
—(1983) 'Effective Demand: Origins and Development of the Notion', in *Distribution, Effective Demand and International Economic Relations* (London: Macmillan).
Parrinello, S. (1980) 'The Price Level in Keynes' Effective Demand', *Journal of Post Keynesian Economics*, vol. Ill (Fall).
Sraffa, P. (1932) 'Dr Hayek on Money and Capital', *Economic Journal*, vol. XLII (March).
Tobin, J. (1972) 'Friedman's Theoretical Framework', *Journal of Political Economy*, vol. 80 (Sept./Oct).
Townshend, H. (1937) 'Liquidity-premium and the Theory of Value', *Economic Journal*, vol. XLVII (March).

Chapter 10

MONEY, EXPECTATIONS AND RELATIVE PRICES IN KEYNES' MONETARY EQUILIBRIUM(*)

I. BACKGROUND: KEYNES AND THE 1914 CRISIS

According to Hicks (1977, p. 45) monetary economics differs from other branches of economics because "a large part of the best work on Money is topical ... prompted by particular episodes, by particular experiences of the writer's own time". This reflects his earlier (1967, p. 156) opinion that "monetary theories arise out of monetary disturbances. This is obviously true of the *General Theory,* which is the book of the Great Depression - the World Depression - of the nineteen-thirties".

Yet the great slump could have had only a relatively small impact on Keynes' work in monetary economics which had started well before the generalised conditions of either British or World depression. A relatively more important influence must have been the "monetary disturbance" of 1914.

Indeed, Keynes at the early age of thirty-one was piloted from Cambridge to London in the side-car of his brother-in-law's motor cycle in order to advise the government on the incipient bank crisis at the outbreak of the First War. It was as a result of this activity that he literally became the international financial system during the war period: "I was in the Treasury throughout the war and all the money we either lent or borrowed passed through my hands" (JMK, XVI, p. 3, the editor of the volume comments "He hardly exaggerated, as he was directly concerned with the strategy of financing Britain's war expenditure and that of her allies, and finally took charge of a division of his own responsible for all of Britain's inter-allied financial arrangements").

This early experience of the 1914 financial crisis introduced Keynes to certain features of the monetary system which were to remain a permanent part of his theoretical approach to economic analysis. One characteristic feature of this system was that "the bill upon London was an international currency which could be negotiated anywhere ... A mountain of credit of unprecedented size was reared up internally upon the reserve of the Bank of England, and that reserve was amazingly small" (Feaveryear, 1931, p. 299.) In general terms the City operated just as an international bank relending to the Empire the proceeds of their export surpluses on England which were held on deposit in sterling (an excellent analysis of the operation of the system is given in de Cecco,

---

* This paper summarises part of a seminar given in the University of Ottawa and I am grateful for comments received there. It draws on two previous pieces (Kregel, 1976 a, and 1980).

1974). Trade bills or acceptances played a pivotal role as did the institutions that dealt in them: "the bill of exchange is not only a beautifully simple and efficacious device for financing commerce, but it is also an ideal form of investment for bankers and others who are obliged by the nature of their business to keep their reserves ... readily convertible into cash" because they can be readily discounted (Withers, 1926, p. 46). Bills represent *par excellence* that aspect of the money market as "the place in which money down is exchanged for the promise of money some day" (*ibid.*, p. 4) and the extent to which sterling debt had replaced gold and foreign legal tender as international stores of value and media of exchange. They also reflect the importance of confidence in the issuer and guarantor of the debt and anticipations of financial condition at maturity, or more simply of money as a two-way debt-credit relation.

The creation of money in such a world system was primarily determined by foreign decisions to hold sterling deposits rather than gold allowing bills on London to adapt to the needs of trade. Confidence in London was crucial to the international financial mechanism in general and to the acceptance market in particular. It was this confidence that Keynes held primary in his analysis of the effects of a suspension of gold payments during the crisis.

When political actions in August 1914 created panic in European financial centres and suspension of trading it became difficult, if not impossible, for foreigners to settle bills due in London. This in turn put pressure on the acceptance houses and discount houses who were liable for settlement. At the same time stockbrokers dealing on account for foreigners became technically insolvent because these customers could not settle (cf. de Cecco, 1974, pp. 130-31). As Morgan (1952, p. 3) points out, foreigners could acquire sterling credits by selling goods, supplying gold, selling securities or refinancing debt in London. The fear of hostilities eliminated the first two possibilities, the closing of the Stock exchange the third. Since the finance houses were unable to meet their commitments to the commercial banks the response of the latter was to attempt to strengthen their position by calling loans rather than increasing them and increasing their gold reserves to meet the expected increase in demand for legal tender by a public made nervous by their losses. Thus, the failure of overseas settlement due to the war produced a severe shortage of sterling credits and a sharp increase in the demand for gold by the banks which decreased the ability of the Bank to meet demand with sterling credits.

In the event the expected demand for gold by the public did not materialise and Keynes commented that the "system was endangered, not by the public running on the Banks, but by the banks running on the Bank of England" (quoted in Morgan, 1952, p. 30). His concern, expressed some months earlier, in an analysis of the adequacy of the Bank's gold reserve, was not over the "improbable" event "that the big banks will come to grief", but rather that "the main loss which the community suffers is due to forced realisations on the Stock Exchange of international securities" (1971, p. 4) and thus on international finance and activity (cf. his comments on the effects of the crisis in France, *ibid.*, p. 45). Keynes was thus led to defend maintenance of gold payments by the Bank, recommending sufficient credit in sterling be made available to satisfy both the sudden rise in international demand caused by the blockage of settlements and demand for gold by the commercial banks.

The potential paradox of Keynes' involvement in, and concern for, international financial affairs and his ultimate use of a closed system in the *General Theory* has also been explained by Hicks who notes that Ricardo, Keynes and Wicksell must be distinguished from "the general run of monetary writers because 'each of them'" ... "was content to work with a model that was *closed*. The model was closed, because the world is closed" (1977, p. 47). Hicks might have said that in Keynes' time the British Empire could be treated as a closed, world system!

It would thus seem reasonable to recognise "topical" aspects such as the 1914 Crisis and Keynes participation in war-time finance and commodity markets on behalf the British Treasury as relevant to his subsequent monetary analysis.

In particular such experience might have indicated the importance of debt as means of payment and store of value and thus the importance of the general state of confidence as well as anticipations of future market conditions as reflected in the present and future prices of debt. Finally, the crisis indicated very clearly the consequences of sudden shifts in confidence and anticipations on asset holding decisions. Indeed, Keynes turns to a theoretical analysis of holdings of foreign currencies in his first post-war writings (1922, subsequently collected in a book, *A Tract on Monetary Reform* (1923)).

II. ANALYSIS OF DEBT HOLDING: INTEREST RATE PARITY IN FINANCIAL MARKETS

"If dollars one month forward are quoted cheaper than spot dollars to a London buyer in terms of sterling, this indicates a *preference* by the market, on balance, in favour of holding funds in New York during the month in question rather than in London, - a *preference* the degree of which is measured by the discount on forward dollars" (Keynes, 1922, p. 12, reprinted in *Tract*, p. 123, italics added).

Keynes goes on to show how dollar holders can earn a return equal to $(p_f - p_s)/p_s$ by selling dollars spot for sterling at $\$p_s/£$ and selling forward the sterling thus acquired at $\$p_f/£$ – a sterling premium ($p_f > p_s$), this difference per cent per annum representing the return to taking a position in sterling, or the measure of what the market is willing to forego for its *preference* for holding dollars in New York.

Differentials in interest rates on positions in different currencies were, in Keynes' view, the determinants of this preference: "the most fundamental cause is to be found in the interest rates obtainable on 'short' money. … If by lending dollars in New York for one month the lender could earn interest at the rate of 5½ per cent per annum whereas by lending sterling in London for one month he could earn at the rate of 4 per cent, then the preference for holding funds in New York rather than London is wholly explained. That is to say, forward quotations for the purchase of the currency of the dearer money market tend to be cheaper than spot quotations by a percentage per month equal to the excess of the interest which can be earned in a month in the dearer market over what can be earned in the cheaper." *(Ibid.*, p. 12, *Tract*, p. 124.)

This relation can be recognised as the now well-known "interest rate parity theorem" (cf. McKinnon, 1979, pp. 102-3) in which interest rate differentials are equated by the premium or discount of the future relative to the spot price. For purposes of this discussion this relation may be written as $i_\$ \ (- f_\$) = i_£ + f_£$ where f is the forward discount or premium (and $f_\$ = 0$ when quotations are taken in dollars) and $f_£ = ({}^\$p_f/£ - {}^\$p_s/£)/(\$p_s/£)$ (Keynes example is obviously taken from the point of view of a holder of dollars in London where foreign quotations are given in dollars per pound sterling rather than in terms of the domestic currency per unit of the foreign currency as is more common in other financial centres. In this latter case the dollar discount would be given as ${}^£p_s/\$ > {}^£p_f/\$$ and $f_\$ = ({}^£p_f/\$ - {}^£p_s/\$)/({}^£p_s/\$)$; $i_\$ - f_\$ = i_£ + f_£$ (with $f_£ = 0$)).

This framework identified the factors determining the movements of funds in and out of London as relative money interest rates and the future conditions in money markets as reflected by the relation of spot to future prices. It is quite obvious that sterling was the centre of this system, international liquidity being determined by the rate of interest on sterling (Bank rate) and the forward estimates of these rate differentials as reflected by the forward premium or discount. It also reflects the primary role of the debt relations: money today for money tomorrow and thus the importance of future conditions on current decisions to hold money and issue contracts for the future delivery of money.

Following the idea that the *General Theory* can be viewed as a "closed" system in Hicks' sense or of the British Empire as a closed world system, it is clear that the above international analysis could be adapted for a closed system by making e.g. sterling deposits *the* "money" of the system with durable assets comprised of foreign currencies. The interest rate parity theorem then provides an explanation of the "preference" for "liquidity" (sterling) influencing decisions to take positions in other (foreign currencies) assets in terms of their spot and forward prices relative to sterling.

Indeed, this is precisely the way Keynes defines the rate of interest on money, the most liquid of all durables: "Interest on money *means* precisely what the books on arithmetic say that it means ... the premium obtainable on current cash over deferred cash, so that it measures the marginal preference (for the community as a whole) for holding cash in hand over cash for deferred delivery. No one would pay this premium unless the possession of cash served some purpose, i.e. had some efficiency. Thus we can conveniently say that interest on money measures the marginal efficiency of money measured in terms of itself as a unit" (1937, p. 101) or "the money-rate of interest - one may remind the reader - is nothing more than the percentage excess of a sum of money contracted for forward delivery, e.g. a year hence, over what we may call the 'spot' or cash price of the sum thus contracted for forward delivery" (1936, p. 222).

Just as the "preference" for a position in a foreign or national currency is determined by the relation of the spot to the future price the "preference" for a position in money (or a preference for liquidity or, as it became, "liquidity preference") could be measured by the rate of interest, or the "premium" the market is willing to pay for its preference for liquidity.

Keynes also extends his earlier analysis to other durables: "it would seem, therefore, that for every kind of capital-asset there must be an analogue of the rate of interest on money" (ibid.). Since "there is no reason why the(se) rates of interest should be the same" (ibid., p. 223) the parity analysis can be applied to produce a configuration of demands for the various durable assets which equates their rates of interest or their "marginal efficiencies" with that on money as determined by the market's preference for liquidity.

The failure to recognise liquidity preference as a general theory of asset choice has led some economists (e.g. Tobin, 1971, pp. 229 and 242) to interpret Keynes' theory as dealing with only the choice of money versus bonds, leaving open the explanation of what is now called the portfolio balance of money and a range of financial assets. On the other hand it has led some economists to claim that there is no theoretical explanation of the rate of interest which "is determined by nothing else but uncertainty of future interest rates" and "seems to leave interest hanging by its own bootstraps" (Hicks, 1939, p. 164).

But, such criticism has never been made of the interest-rate parity theorem, and in just the same way as Keynes tried to isolate the fundamental factors determining the foreign exchange market's preference for holding debts denominated in a particular currency he also provided an explanation of the factors which determined the preference for money over other assets capable of preserving command over future consumption as well as the size of that preference. For this Keynes required the equivalent for durable goods of international interest rate differentials. This was provided in his theory of the "marginal efficiency" of durable assets, based on Sraffa's (1932) conception of "commodity rates of interest".

III. ANALYSIS OF ASSET HOLDING: INTEREST RATE PARITY IN DURABLE GOODS MARKETS

Sraffa had elaborated this idea in criticism of Hayek's (1931) use of the concept of monetary neutrality and natural interest rates. Keynes adopted the idea, calling it the "own rate of own interest". Just as money rates of interest on national currencies vary across countries, so would the own rates of own interest for different durables. Just as international interest-rate differentials were brought into equality by forward discounts and premiums, taken in terms of a common currency unit, the various different own rates of own interest should also be equalised in equilibrium when they are calculated in a common unit of value. It was thus necessary to convert all "own rates" to a single (money) standard.

In the *General Theory* Keynes gives as an example the case of wheat. If the money rate of interest is 5 per cent (£ 105/£ 100), the forward price of wheat is £ 107/100 bushels and the spot price is £ 100, the own rate of interest (or the own rate of interest of wheat in terms of wheat) can be calculated by noting that the future provision of 100 bushels worth £ 100 spot can be purchased for £ 107, while the future provision of the £ 100 to pay for them costs £ 105. Thus, the 100 bushels can be sold spot for £ 100 which can be sold forward for the delivery of £ 105, which will become available for the purchase of wheat for forward delivery at a price of £ 107/100 bushels. Thus 105/107 x 100 = 98 bushels can be purchased forward for 100 bushels spot representing a –2 per cent preference of the market for being in wheat. Thus, 'the difference between the "future" and "spot" contracts of a commodity, such as wheat, [...] bears a definite relation to the wheat rate of interest, but, since the forward contract is quoted in terms of money for forward delivery and not in terms of wheat for spot delivery, it also brings in the money rate of interest' (1936, 233). That the relation is exactly similar can be seen from the definition of the 'forward contract' for money in terms of the sum contracted for forward delivery relative to the spot price of that sum. The formal equivalent for wheat would be in terms of bushels contracted forward relative to bushels to be given spot, that is, $\frac{98-100}{100}$ and not $\frac{107-100}{100}$.

Thus Keynes defined the rate of interest on money as the difference between the spot price of a contract for the future delivery of a sum of money (or liquidity) and the sum itself. It was thus the *expected* conditions at this future date which would determine the size of the offer to repay money in excess of the sum borrowed in the same way as the expected future conditions in commodity or foreign exchange markets determined their forward prices. If the money rate of interest was held up by its own bootstraps then so was the price of any other durable commodity traded in competitive conditions on organized markets! As Sraffa pointed out, 'It will be noticed that under free competition, this divergence of rates is as essential to the effecting of the transition as is the divergence of prices from the costs of production; it is, in fact, another aspect of the same thing.' It is only 'in equilibrium' that 'the spot and forward price coincide' and the analysis can proceed without express reference to future conditions (Sraffa 1932, 50) (or if the future is known).

Neither did this imply that *either* money *or* bonds would be held by investors. Instead, given the differences in own-rates (account taken for the fact that their observed future prices are for the delivery of money rather than the commodity at the future date) holdings of durables will be determined by the movement in their relative prices (premiums or discounts) making each equally attractive in terms of rate of return calculated in a common standard. Any position characterised by the holding of "only" money or bonds (or any other single durable) should lead to an adjustment in its own rate of return via adjustment in either its spot or future price. Thus, as long as both had a positive rate of interest (as long as the markets' preference for liquidity kept pf $\geq$ ps) money would be held along with *all* other durables, not only bonds!

Up to this point, which durable is chosen as money has no particular importance. It need not serve as the common unit used to evaluate the various rates of return. Yet, just as sterling has a very special position in the financial system of the pre-1914 Empire, money held a special role because, as Sraffa put it, of "Those characteristics which are set forth at the beginning of every text-book on money. That is to say, that money is not only the medium of exchange, but also a store of value, and the standard in terms of which debts, and other legal obligations, habits, opinions, conventions, in short all kinds of relations between men are more of less rigidly fixed" (Sraffa, 1932, p, 43).

Thus, there will be a crucial role played by "a general fall, or rise, of prices" (ibid., p. 44) in terms of money. As is now well known due to the work of Davidson (e.g., 1972, and 1980) and Minsky (e.g., 1975) Keynes differentiates the factors determining an asset's marginal efficiency in terms of q, its net yield, c, the carrying cost (including user cost) and l, the liquidity premium. Capital goods are predominantly q-influenced, while financial assets are primarily l-influenced.

Any durable, however, may increase or decrease in price relative to the standard. Thus the ranking of own rates of return for all assets must include a factor ± a measuring "the expected percentage appreciation (or depreciation)".

Every durable will have a measure of its own rate of return in terms of money (its marginal efficiency) given by $\pm$ a + $(q - c) + l$ (with a = 0 in the case of money). In equilibrium, the extension of the interest-rate parity theorem suggests that they should be equal across all commodities and equal to the rate of interest on money. If they were not arbitraging could take place and profit could be made.

This framework could be used to show the effect of a "shift in liquidity preference" similar to the shift e.g. that occurred in the Clearing Banks' preferences during the 1914 Crisis. Such a shift would have two effects, one on the issue department of the Bank of England, the second on the discount market and thus on the stock market. Both would have the effect of pushing up interest rates by reducing the spot prices of existing assets relative to forward prices. In Keynes' 1914 analysis this led to forced liquidation and insolvency of some parts of the financial and business community due to the effect of the fall in spot prices on capital values. The immediate impact on trade and employment was obvious, but not considered irreparable or permanent (cf. Lachmann, 1956, pp. 74-5). Of greater importance was the weakening of London's control of international finance that would be caused by the loss of confidence due to suspension of gold payments.

In the *General Theory* however, Keynes had extended his use of the spot-forward price equilibrium scheme to the analysis if investment in newly produced assets: "those assets of which the normal supply-price is less than the demand price will be newly produced; and these will be those assets of which the marginal efficiency would be greater (on the basis of their normal supply price) than the rate of interest (both being measured in the same standard of value whatever it is). As the stock of the assets, which begin by having a marginal efficiency at least equal to the rate of interest, is increased, their marginal efficiency ... tends to fall. Thus a point will come at which it no longer pays to produce them *unless the rate of interest falls* pari passu. When there is *no* asset of which the marginal efficiency reaches the rate of interest, the future production of capital assets will come to a standstill" (1936, p. 228, cf. the discussions in Davidson, 1972, pp. 69 ff., and Minsky, 1975, pp. 93 ff.).

Liquidity preference must adjust in a particular way if output and employment are to expand to the limits of capacity. Not only will sudden shifts in liquidity preference disturb equilibrium, but its failure to adjust so as to cause the rate of interest to fall at least as fast as the marginal efficiency of other assets given the state of expectation may produce equality of rates of return with excess labour and or capacity.

The contribution of Keynes' monetary production analysis was to argue that there was no reason for liquidity preference to adjust in this way. The reason can be better understood by first recalling that the marginal efficiencies of capital assets are determined primarily by q, which is subject to diminishing returns as given by technical factors, while that of money is given by, l, its liquidity premium which is determined primarily by the money market conditions expected to prevail at futures dates. This type of expectation is due, primarily to price speculation - will asset prices rise or fall?

The supply of contracts for future delivery thus depends on the fact of the future (capital) value of money being more easily predictable than other financial assets.

Real assets, with minimal liquidity are dominated by q, which is determined, via the present value formula, by technical conditions of production and expected future prices of the output produced. The uncertainty over the future price of these assets is due, not to expectations over their prices at future dates, but over the price and quantity sold of their output. Such uncertainty generates a demand for contracts for the future supply of money as a precaution against the possibility that in some future period expected yields may not be realised. Here money serves not as protection against changes in the prices of the assets, but as a precaution against the possibility that in some period gross receipts will fail to cover running costs (cf. Minsky, 1975, chapter 4). Liquidity preference, l, is thus linked via the "speculative" and "precautionary" motives to uncertainty over future capital values in financial markets and the uncertainty over future net yields in commodity markets respectively.

Money can only provide this function if its value is more stable (i.e., it marginal efficiency is less variable, or falls more slowly) than other assets and the net sales value of future output.

It is here that the means of payment function of money joins that of store of value for as a generalised means of payment holding money becomes equivalent to holding a porrtfolio of all other assets, and diminishes the effect of an unexpected change in the relative price of any one or group of them. The demand for this service thus depends on the uncertainty concerning the prices of all durable goods and their yields.

V. MONEY, DEBT AND PRODUCTION EQUILIBRIUM

It was this definition of the essential properties of money (cf. the work of Davidson, 1972 and Minsky, 1975) which Keynes used to justify the movements of the rates of interest of money being "reluctant to decline as output increases" 1936 (p. 229), i.e. the negligible elasticities of production and substitution.

In equilibrium the money rate of interest $\mathrm{i} = \pm \mathrm{a} + (q - c) + l$ for every other durable. If i declines less rapidly than $(q - c) + l$ for other durables as their output expands then a must be rising, i.e. the spot prices of these durables are falling relative to their future prices in terms of money or the exchange value of money rises relative to the wage unit.

The cost of using money for exchange thus rises and some other durable might be substituted which has lower costs. In this way a durable with a lower or faster falling $(q - c) + l$ might be substituted, thus allowing expansion to continue. But, Keynes notes "the peculiarity of money that its utility is solely derived from its exchange-value" implies that "as the exchange value of money rises" so does its utility (1936, p. 231). At the same time "low (or negligible) carrying costs of money play an essential part" in giving stability "to the prospective value of money at future dates" (p. 233) thus allowing it to satisfy the speculative and precautionary motives. Thus, expectations of money's future value presume the expectation that substitutes will not replace it as medium of exchange, an eventuality which would imply high carrying costs exceeding the liquidity premium, i.e. Keynes' definition of a 'non-monetary' economy (p. 239).

The elasticity of production condition relates to the fact that for normal durables a rise in demand and price relative to cost implies the potential for profitable expansion of output (and thus employment) leading to a fall in its own rate. This is possible for commodity monies but not for bank debt which has virtually no cost of production and requires no labour in production. But, in this latter case even if money expands in step with demand there is no reason for the rate of interest to fall nor affect employment. Since the price of liquidity is simply the price of a contract to supply money at some future date an attempt to reduce prices by an increase in supply whether inside or outside the banking system, need have no effect on employment or on the price of future contracts for the ability of the system to absorb them has no objective constraint if the public considers them as costless at the prevailing price (e.g. short sales).

> "In other words, beyond a certain point money's yield from liquidity does not fall in response to an increase in its quantity to anything approaching the extent to which the yield from other types of assets falls when their quantity is comparable increased" (1936, p. 233).

Thus, "Suppose there is a change in the distribution of demand between various (durables) ... some will rise in price, and others will fall ... after a certain time, the supply of the former will increase, and the supply of the latter will fall, and accordingly the forward price, for the date on which equilibrium is expected to be restored, will be below the spot price in the case of the former and above it in the case of the latter, in other words, the rate of interest on the former will be higher than on the latter" (Sraffa, 1932, p. 50). Once the adjustment is completed the rates will come back to equality: except when the durable in question is money whose rate of interest will not be influenced by the change in quantity demanded because its output is in dependent of demand for labour.

> "Now, in the case of assets having an elasticity of production the reason why we assumed their own-rate of interest to decline was because we assumed the stock of them to increase as the result of a higher rate of output ... that money cannot be readily produced by labour gives at once some prima facie presumption for the view that its own-rate of interest will be relatively reluctant to fall" (1936, p. 231).

The money rate of interest thus takes on a special significance in determining the equilibrium rates of return on all other durables and thus on investment, output and employment in Keynes' theory of monetary production. By viewing Keynes' system as being applicable to (and inspired by) conditions other than those of depression and a closed economy it becomes clear that it is crucially linked to the operation of a debt economy where every durable has a present and a future price, and both relative prices and the general level of prices play a crucial role. It was for these reasons that Keynes could argue that his own approach gave the crucial role to money and expectations: "Put shortly, the orthodox theory maintains that the forces which determine the common value of the marginal efficiency of various assets are independent of money, which has, so to speak, no autonomous influence and that prices move until the marginal efficiency of money, i.e. the rate of interest, falls into line with the common value of the marginal efficiency of other assets as determined by other forces. My theory, on the other hand maintains that this a special case and that over a wide range of possible cases almost the opposite is true, namely, that the marginal efficiency of money is determined by forces partly appropriate to itself, and that prices move until the marginal efficiency of other assets falls into line with the rate of interest" (JMK, XIV, 1937, p. 103). Or that in a monetary production economy the rate of interest, determined by liquidity preference, will set the limit to the rate of profit as determined by the marginal efficiencies of the various durable assets which will be uniform in equilibrium![1].

Note

1 This analysis is consistent, as I have previously argued (1967 a, 1980) with Sraffa's statement (1960, p. 33) concerning the relation between the money rates of interest and the rate of profits. It implies that Sraffa's (1960) analysis can be used to complete the theory of relative prices which already exists in Keynes' (1936) amplification of Sraffa's (1932) analysis. Rymes (1980) takes a similar position. That Keynes' analysis in chapter 17 provides the basis for a theory of value as well as output is not new. See Townshend's (1937) "Liquidity-premium and the theory of value": "The theory of value in a capitalist economy is the theory of money-prices" (p 167) "Prices - even relative prices - are therefore not to be regarded as wholly determined by supply and demand at the margin of production" since "new production never catches up with the continuous spontaneous variation in the liquidity premiums attaching to the existing stocks" (p. 168). Finally, Latouche (1970) previously used Sraffa's analysis to clarify Wicksell's interest theory.

REFERENCES

P. Davidson (1972), *Money and the Real World*, London, Macmillan, 2nd ed., 1978.

———. (1980), "The Dual-Faceted Nature of the Keynesian Revolution: Money and Money Wages in Unemployment, and Production Flow Prices", *Journal of Post Keynesian Economics*, 2, Spring.

M. de Cecco (1974), *Money and Empire*, Oxford, Blackwell.

A.E. Feaveryear (1931), *The Pound Sterling*, Oxford, Clarendon Press.

F.A. Hayek (1931), *Prices and Production*, London, Routledge.

J.R. Hicks (1939), *Value and Capital*, Oxford, Clarendon Press.

———. (1967), *Critical Essays in Monetary Theory*, Oxford, Clarendon Press.

———. (1977), *Economics Perspectives*, Oxford, Clarendon Press.

J.R. Hicks (1980), "Equilibrium and the Trade Cycle" translation of "Gleichgewicht und Kunjunktur", 1933, *Economic Inquiry*, 18, Oct.

J.M. Keynes (1922), "The forward Market and Foreign Exchanges", *Manchester Guardian Commercial supplement*, "Reconstruction in Europe", April 20, pp. 11–15, incorporated in Keynes (1923).

———. (1923), *A Tract on Monetary Reform*, Vol. IV of *Collected Writings*, London, Macmillan, 1971.

———. (1930), *A Treatise on Money*, V and VI of *Collected Writings*, London, Macmillan, 1971.

———. (1936), *The General Theory of Employment, Interest and Money*, Vol. VII of *Collected Writings*, London, Macmillan, 1973.

———. (1937), "The Theory of the Rate of Interest", reprinted in Vol. XIV of *Collected Writings*, London, Macmillan, 1973.

———. (1971), Vol. XVI of *Collected Writings: Activities 1914–19: The Treasury and Versailles*, London, Macmillan.

———. (1979), Vol. XXIX of *Collected Writings: The General Theory and after: supplement*, London, MacMillan.

J.A. Kregel (1976 a), "Sraffa et Keynes: Le Taux d'interet et le Taux de Profit", Actes du Collogue Sraffa, *Cahiers d'Economie Politique*, n° 3.

———. (1976 b), "Economic Methodology in the Face of Uncertainty", *Economic Journal*86, June.

———. (1980), "Expectations and Rationality within a Capitalist Frame-23. work", paper presented to the Annual Meetings of the American Economic Association, Denver, Colo, Sept.

L.M. Lachmann (1956): *Capital and its Structure*, London, Bell.

S. Latouche (1970), "Taux Reel et Taux Monetaire", *Revue d'Rconomie Politique.*

R.I. McKinnon (1979), *Money in International Exchange*, New York, Oxford University Press.

H.P. Minsky (1975), *John Maynard Keynes*, New York, Columbia University Press.

E.V. Morgan (1952), *British Financial Policy 1914–1925*, London, Macmillan.

T.K. Rymes (1980), "Sraffa and Keynes on Interest Rates", *Carleton Economics Papers* 80–09, Ottawa.

G.L.S. Shackle (1975), "Keynes and Today's Establishment in Economic Theory: A View", *Journal of Economic Literature*, 11, June.

P. Sraffa (1932), "Dr Hayek on Money and Capital", *Economic Journal*, 42, March.

———. (1960), *Production of Commodities by Means of Commodities*, Cambridge University Press, Cambridge.

J. Tobin (1971), *Essays in Economics*, Vol. I: Macroeconomics, Amsterdam, North Holland.

H. Townshend (1937), "Liquidity-Premium and the Theory of Value", *Economic Journal*, 47, March.

H. Withers (1926), *The Meaning of Money*, (1st edition 1909), London, John Murray.

Part Three

PRICE THEORY, THEORY OF INTEREST AND FINANCIAL MARKETS

Chapter 11

IRVING FISHER, GREAT-GRANDPARENT OF THE *GENERAL THEORY*: MONEY, RATE OF RETURN OVER COST AND EFFICIENCY OF CAPITAL

Irving Fisher is frequently credited, in the *General Theory*, in articles written immediately after its publication, and in private correspondence, by Keynes as having been an important influence on his work. These influences refer to two points: Keynes' treatment of money as a real factor in the determination of economic equilibrium and Keynes' concept of the marginal efficiency of capital.

For example in "Alternative theories of the rate of interest", one of a number of articles published in 1937 to distinguish his position, Keynes indicates the authors who most influenced his work: "I regard Mr Hawtrey as my grandparent and Mr Robertson as my parent [...] I might also adopt [...] Wicksell as my great-grandparent, [...] I find, looking back, that it was Professor Fisher who was the great-grandparent who first influenced me strongly towards regarding money as a "real" factor" (JMK: XIV, pp. 202–3, n. 2). In "The Theory of the Rate of Interest", published in a Festschrift for Fisher, Keynes writes: "I have thought it suitable to offer a short note on this subject in honour of Irving Fisher, since his earliest and latest contributions have been concerned with it, and since during the whole thirty years that I have been studying economics he has been the outstanding authority on this problem" (JMK: XIV, p. 101, n. 1). Indeed, it is in this same article that Keynes set out the difference between his own approach and that of traditional theory in terms of money being a "real" variable in his own theory: "Put shortly, the orthodox theory maintains that the forces which determine the common value of the marginal efficiency of various assets are independent of money [...] My theory, on the other hand, maintains that this is a special case and that [...] almost the opposite is true ..." (*Ibid.*, p. 103).

The second area of Fisher's influence appears in the following footnote in the same article; Keynes reconfirms an affirmation originally made in the *General Theory*, crediting Fisher with "The [...] "marginal efficiency of capital" [...] first introduced by Irving Fisher in his *Theory of Interest* (1930), under the designation "the rate of return over cost". This conception of his is, I think, the most important and fruitful of his recent suggestions" (*Ibid.*).

Considering Keynes' early representation of the consumption decision as depending on "time preference", it is possible to consider Fisher as important an influence on the *General Theory* as Marshall, for he may be linked to all three of Keynes' innovations:

liquidity preference, the efficiency of capital and the propensity to consume. The present paper initiates an assessment of this possibility. The evidence presented supports Keynes' expression of indebtedness to Fisher for his recognition of money as a real factor, while the development of the three independent variables, in particular the marginal efficiency of capital, probably owes more to Hayek's criticism of the treatment of capital theory in the *Treatise* and Sraffa's refutation of Hayek's alternative approach.

MONEY, VALUE AND BUSINESS CYCLE

It is now widely recognised that R.G. Hawtrey was the instigator of the interest of almost all major economists in the integration of the theories of value and money as represented by the theory of business cycles. Indeed, his 1913 book, *Good and Bad Trade* represented the revival of interest in the concept of effective demand that Keynes was later to lament. In a 1961 Preface to the Kelley reprint of this book Hawtrey explains his early interests as follows: "I began writing this book in March 1909, when the depression which followed the American crisis of 1907 was still unrelieved [...] It struck me that the extinction of profit could be explained if the price level fell in the interval between the incurring of costs and the sale of product. And if traders borrowed at interest to finance profit-making business, they could pay a higher rate of interest when prices were rising and a lower rate when prices were falling. A falling price level makes a given market rate of interest more onerous, and a rising price level less so. Here, I thought, was a discovery, but I was disillusioned when I learnt from an economist friend that the principle was one already recognised, and had been expounded in Irving Fisher's work, *The Rate of Interest*" (Hawtrey, 1913, p. VII). On the basis of Harrod's biography Sue Howson confirms that "The "economist friend" was probably Keynes of whom Hawtrey saw much at that time" (Howson, in Harcourt, 1985, p. 145).

Keynes' debts to Robertson date from shortly afterward. After reading Robertson's Fellowship Dissertation (which became *A Study of Industrial Fluctuation*) Keynes wrote to Robertson: "your work has suggested to me what appears at first sight a superb theory about fluctuations" (letter of 20 September 1913, JMK: XIII, p. 1). Keynes eventually developed this "superb theory" in *How far are bankers responsible for the alternations of crisis and depression?* which directly criticises the "'ordinary theory' [...] chiefly associated perhaps with the name of Professor Irving Fisher" (JMK: XI, p. 2). Keynes' explanation of Fisher's position repeats that which he had presented in his 1911 *Economic Journal* review of Fisher's *Purchasing Power of Money* (JMK: XI, pp. 375–81). Reference to Keynes' reading lists and the notes for his early lectures on the theory of money (given from 1909–1913) indicate that he was familiar with Fisher's published work. It is thus clear that Fisher's analysis of how a change in monetary factors influenced the rate of interest and how the rate of interest influenced the movement in the level of activity served as a background to Keynes' discussions with Hawtrey and Robertson as they sought an explanation of cycles within the doctrines of traditional value theory.

Fisher's theory depended on the reactions of businessmen and bankers to a rise in prices exceeding temporarily the rise in the rate of interest; in his review Keynes criticised Fisher for never explaining clearly "*how* new gold raises prices *in the first instance*, and is content with showing by the quantity theory that new gold *must* raise them somehow" (*Ibid.*, p. 377). This is a concern which finally motivated his outright rejection of the quantity theory approach in the *Treatise:* "The fundamental problem of monetary theory is not merely to establish identities or statical equations relating (e.g.) the turnover of monetary instruments to the turnover of things traded for money. The real task of such a theory is to treat the problem dynamically, analysing the different elements involved, in such a manner as to exhibit the causal process by which the price level is determined, and the method of transition from one position of equilibrium to another" (JMK: V, p. 120).

THE REAL INFLUENCE OF MONEY ON PRICES AND INVESTMENT

The dynamic determination of prices thus became the subject of Keynes' *Treatise.* In substitution for the quantity theory's equation of exchange, Keynes proposed a Fundamental Equation in terms of wage costs and demand to determine the price of consumption goods which could be elaborated through the introduction of the exogenously determined price of capital assets to explain the price of output as a whole. The prices of capital assets, which were explained independently of the fundamental equations, resulted from the combination of what Keynes called the bearishness of the public (the demand for savings deposits) and the behaviour of the banking system in creating these deposit liabilities. This explanation of the determination of asset prices which seemed to group together the prices of physical capital goods (which might have been more appropriately explained by an equation similar to that for consumption goods, *i.e.*, by costs and demand) and financial assets generated perplexity in quarters as diverse as the "Cambridge Circus" and Hayek's LSE. Yet, Keynes seemed convinced of the correctness of his overall approach, and yielded very little to his critics.

Perhaps the strength of Keynes' views on the importance of monetary factors in the determination of asset prices can be explained by the fact that they had their roots in his first experience of financial crisis on the eve of the '14-'18 war: "Although it is our current income and not our capital that is threatened, there is a false and misleading appearance, through the destruction of paper values, of an enormous and widespread loss of the latter. This is due to a violent change of equilibrium in the immediate exchange values of the three categories — capital goods, money and consumable goods. This change is due to two more or less distinct influences, the one arising out of the state of finance, the other out of the state of consumption. It is the business of financiers to hold their assets, through the medium of title deeds, bonds and securities, in the form of goods, partly consumable but mainly fixed; while their liabilities, on the other hand, are in the form of promises to pay sums of money. If the financiers are called on to fulfill their liabilities at a time when for reasons of prudence or panic people generally do not choose to have more of their resources than they need in the form of fixed capital goods, they are forced at any cost to themselves to turn their assets into money, even though they know well enough that the future money value of their assets is certain to be far higher than the present money value [...] With a fall of £ 188,000,000 between July 20th and

July 30th in the money value of securities, we learn not, as with the destruction of Liège or Louvain, of a loss in the world's real wealth, but only of the financial world's extreme urgency for money. [...] We experience, therefore, a sudden and violent change in our relative valuation of present and future income. Where formerly we equated against 100 units of present goods 117 units of goods due three years hence we now prefer 100 of present goods to 124. [...] This shows itself in the rate of interest and in the number of years' purchase of each future year's income from the capital goods which the present exchange value of these capital goods represents. But the actual future income from the capital goods may remain exactly what it was" (JMK: XI, p. 268–271).

Here Keynes clearly accepts that the current prices of capital assets may in certain circumstances be determined, not by their ability to produce future outputs, or as one might today want to put it, by their physical productivity, but rather by the unwillingness of people to run the capital risk associated with holding them, an unwillingness which will depend on their needs for other assets capable of discharging debt, *i.e.* by their need to be liquid. This is, of course, the clear forerunner of the "bearishness" theory of the financial circulation worked out more fully in the *Treatise*. It should also be clear the extent to which this theory is an attempt to complete the attempt to link money, the rate of interest and the level of real activity, for here changes in the industrial and financial circulations affect not only the price level, but the decisions to produce investment and capital goods. As Keynes eventually admitted to Hawtrey, this led him to the verge of a full-fledged theory of output: "The question *how much* reduction in output is caused [...] is important, but not strictly a monetary problem. I am primarily concerned with what governs *prices* [...] I repeat that I am not dealing with the complete set of causes which determine the volume of output. For this would have led me an endlessly long journey into the theory of short-period supply and a long way from monetary theory; — though I agree that it will probably be difficult in the future to prevent monetary theory and the theory of short-period supply from running together" (JMK: XIII, pp. 145–6).

It is not surprising then that when his analysis of the determinants of the level of output led him to the realisation that saving and investment would be equal at all levels of income so that they could not determine the rate of interest, Keynes had a ready explanation of the determinants of the rate of interest. "If the rate of interest is not determined by saving and investment in the same way in which price is determined by supply and demand, how is it determined? One naturally began by supposing that the rate of interest must be [...] in some sense [...] independently fixed by physical and technical considerations [...] It was only when this line of approach led repeatedly to what seemed like circular reasoning, that I hit on what I now think to be the true explanation [...] that the rate of interest serves to equate the demand and supply of hoards — *i.e.* it must be sufficiently high to offset an increased propensity to hoard relatively to the supply of idle balances available" (JMK: XIV, p. 212–3). That is, the bearishness of the public relative to the policy of the banks, is replaced by liquidity preference and the money supply, only now it is the rate of interest (spot and future asset prices) on money which is being determined, rather than asset prices directly.

MONEY'S "REAL" INFLUENCE ON ASSET AND DEBT PRICES

Thus, although monetary factors represented by the need for liquidity will have an influence on asset prices which will lead rational individuals to refrain from investing all their savings, the correspondence with the bearishness theory is not exact. Keynes explains the difference as follows: "Whilst liquidity-preference due to the speculative-motive corresponds to what in my *Treatise on Money* I called "the state of bearishness", it is by no means the same thing. For "bearishness" is there defined as the functional relationship, not between the rate of interest (or price of debts) and the quantity of money, but between the price of assets and debts, taken together, and the quantity of money. This treatment, however, involved a confusion between results due to a change in the rate of interest and those due to a change in the schedule of the marginal efficiency of capital [...]" (JMK: VII, pp. 173–4).

Thus Keynes limits the effects of the need for liquidity to the price of debts, *i.e.* interest rates charged for the creation of balance sheet liabilities; but this left the price of assets (capital goods) undetermined. The shift from the *Treatise* theory of bearishness to the liquidity preference theory of the *General Theory* was accomplished by separating the determination of capital goods prices from the rate of interest. Keynes' solution was to identify the marginal efficiency of capital, which was to be considered independent of the rate of interest, as the determinant of capital goods demand prices.[1]

Let us consider the importance of this distinction between asset prices and liability prices by reference to the most important type of bank liability: a demand deposit. We are not used to thinking of having to pay a price, an interest rate, to obtain a demand deposit, but this is indeed how the greatest proportion of the money supply is created. As Withers (*The Meaning of Money*, 1926) puts it: Loans make deposits. Thus the creation of money arises from the creation of book credits by banks which produce deposit liabilities and their price, the rate of interest, says Keynes, must be such that it "equalises the advantages of holding cash and a deferred claim on cash" (JMK: XIV, p. 206) which is precisely the role of the loan rate charged by banks who accept a deferred claim on cash for a current account deposit. Of course nothing limits this process to banks, for private individuals can also exchange present for future claims on money.

Now what about assets? Assets are the existing physical assets or the prospective income earning assets which lead to the creation of the liabilities, things like land, houses, paintings, existing capital equipment and investment projects. We would want to include here common stocks for although they are found on the liability side of the balance sheet they are considered as part of equity, not debt. Now, if we think back to Keynes' reference to the difference between a change in the value of stocks and the destruction of cities by war, in the *General Theory* he no longer accepts that the price of assets should be linked to their potential to perform real services, but rather their expected ability to generate future income will determine their values, irrespective of real capabilities; a change in prices may then be produced by a change in prospects, which may be independent of either their real productivity or of the rate of interest. At the same time, given prospects, their prices will be affected, as in the *Treatise*, by a change in the need for liquidity and thus in the rate of interest used to capitalise the expected income.

Liabilities, on the other hand, have streams of interest payments, not receipts, attached to them, streams which are usually perfectly certain in amount and established at the time of contract. There is thus a distinction to be drawn between the determination of asset values (prices) and interest rates attached to liabilities. It is only with respect to debt that liquidity preference is a direct determinant, while it is indirect via the interest rate on assets and may be offset by shifts in the state of expectation. Thus, in place of the bearishness of the public and the policy of the banks of the *Treatise*, *The General Theory* has two "psychological variables", the efficiency of capital and liquidity preference, which combine with the policy of the banks and the state of expectation to determine asset prices and liability prices (in the form of rates of interest).

In difference from the *Treatise*, where it was the financial circulation which determined asset *and* liability prices and where a change in the quantity of money, or of its distribution between the industrial and financial circulations, would lead to changes in asset prices, in the *General Theory* it is "fluctuations in the degree of confidence" which modify, "not the amount that is actually hoarded, but the amount of the premium which has to be offered to induce people not to hoard. And changes in the propensity to hoard, or in the state of liquidity preference as I have called it, primarily affect, not prices, but the rate of interest; any effect on prices being produced by repercussion as an ultimate consequence of a change in the rate of interest" (JMK: XIV, p. 116).

The novelty of this explanation with respect to the *Treatise* is not so much the liquidity preference theory of the rate of interest, but the new theory of capital goods prices based on marginal efficiency. As Keynes remarked to Harrod, "the discovery of the definition of the marginal efficiency of capital looks very slight and scarcely more than formal, yet in my own progress of thought it was absolutely vital" (JMK: XIII, p. 549). Its introduction was made necessary by the recognition that traditional theory usually confounded the rate of interest and the rate of return on capital. If the rate of interest no longer equated savings and investment, then it no longer represented the return to capital in equilibrium; if the rate of interest was determined by liquidity preference and the policy of the banks, then it was the rate of return on capital assets that was left hanging in the air. It was the role of the efficiency of capital to cut the link, not only to Wicksell's "natural" rate, but also to the marginal productivity of capital.

FISHER AND MARGINAL EFFICIENCY

The argument up to this point suggests that it was the recognition of money as a real factor which eventually led Keynes to recognise the need to reconsider the determination of capital asset prices (but not the essence of the determination of debt prices) that he had presented in the *Treatise*. It is this reconsideration which produced the marginal efficiency of capital. Yet Keynes seems to give Fisher direct credit for suggesting this concept. "Although he does not call it the "marginal efficiency of capital", Professor Irving Fisher has given in his *Theory of Interest* (1930) a definition of what he calls "the rate of return over cost" which is identical with my definition. "The rate of return over cost", he writes, is that rate which, employed in computing the present worth of all the costs and the present worth of all the returns, will make these two equal. Professor Fisher explains that the extent of investment in any direction will depend on the comparison between the rate of return over cost and the rate of interest. [...] Thus Professor Fisher uses his "rate of return over cost" in the same sense and for precisely the same purpose as I employ the "marginal efficiency of capital"" (JMK: VII, pp. 140–1).

It is the last sentence that raises doubts concerning any direct contribution of Fisher's work in Keynes' development of the *General Theory* for, as argued above, Keynes requires the marginal efficiency explanation of capital goods prices for precisely the same reason he employs the liquidity preference theory of interest rates, to break the equality between the "real" return (or marginal productivity) of capital and the rate of interest, which provides the possibility for money to play an independent role as a "real" factor affecting the level of investment through its impact on the rate of interest. To preserve this role for money also required the separation of the "prices" of assets and the prices of liabilities, for one could not dominate the other, could not "rule the roost", if they were determined by the same factors. Indeed, Keynes had already criticised Fisher's "appreciation and interest" theory of the real rate of interest in a 1933 draft chapter (JMK: XXIX, pp. 83 ff.), as well as its implications for the investment behaviour of entrepreneurs. This criticism, in slightly reduced form, was preserved in the final version of the book in the section immediately after the one crediting Fisher for his rate of return over cost explanation!

Irrespective of whether or not Keynes' marginal efficiency concept and Fisher's rate of return over cost concept are formally similar (see the discussion between Alchain (1955) and Romney Robinson (1956), it is clear, as Richard Kahn has noted (1984, pp. 146–7), that Fisher's analysis presumed the absence of uncertainty.[2] Further, it has recently come to light that Keynes appears to have inserted this reference to Fisher's rate of return over cost after being alerted to the similarity to the marginal efficiency by Redvers Opie via Guillebaud and Kahn (cf. the note appended to the "Discussion" of Moggridge's paper in Patinkin and Leith, p. 89, n. 6). There is thus no available evidence to indicate that Keynes had read the 1930 book by Fisher or that his development of marginal efficiency was influenced by it.

One is thus led to conclude that Keynes' claim of Fisher as great-grandparent is not misplaced, for as we have seen in Keynes' 1911 reviews, it was Fisher's theory of the role of the rate of interest on prices in producing cyclical fluctuations which appears to have been the source of his own interest in the problem and which motivated his assessment of both Hawtrey's and Robertson's efforts. If Keynes judged their work against the background of Fisher's theory, and considered their work as precursor of his own, then one can credit the validity of his classifying Fisher as antecedent to Hawtrey and Robertson who were antecedent to Keynes' own work. It is as a result of the consideration of money as a real factor that Keynes' own approach eventually felt the need to develop distinct theories of asset and liability prices. The creation of the marginal efficiency of capital to resolve the determination of capital goods prices appears to have been independent of any direct contribution of Fisher's ideas. There is no analytical or archival support for the claim that Fisher had preceded Keynes in discovering the independence of the rate of interest from the prices of capital goods which made necessary the separation of the determination of asset and debt prices and thus the creation of the marginal efficiency to accompany liquidity preference. Indeed, Keynes' criticism of Fisher's real rate of interest theory shows that Fisher had not intended his rate of return over cost to be used for the same purpose.

THE GENEALOGY OF THE MARGINAL EFFICIENCY OF CAPITAL

If Fisher cannot be credited with precedence in this matter, it does raise the question of where the concept of the marginal efficiency of capital came from. Here, as I have previously suggested (Kregel, 1985), one has to look to the discussions on capital theory that Hayek initiated upon reading the *Treatise* and which led to Sraffa's 1932 critique of Hayek's own attempt to explain the relationship between money, interest rates and prices, by means of the concept of commodity rates of interest.

In the *Treatise* Keynes had been primarily interested in prices of consumption goods and capital assets, with the latter, including both capital goods and financial assets including bank deposits, determined independently of the fundamental equations by the "bearishness" of the public and the supply of deposits created by the banking system. But, as Keynes pointed out in his 1932 lectures, "banking and money markets are dealers in debts and not in capital goods proper e.g. materials". In "pure theory" Keynes then assumed that the best the banks could do would be to determine the price of debts, *i.e.* the rate of interest at which "the amount of debts is equal to the quantity of money where the preference of individuals for money rather than debt is fulfilled. [...] Price of capital assets comes in only indirectly. They are dealt in between the public. They come in only by altering preference of public for money now rather than hence, *i.e.* only indirectly" (Bryce: 31/10/32).

The decision to purchase a capital good thus comes by "comparing their prospective yield with that of a debt. [...] Hence to get value of asset we need both quasi rent and also rate of interest. [...] Hence we can capitalise the estimated value of the asset. If this is greater than the cost of production we will get investment" (Bryce: 7/11/32). Thus in place of a theory of asset prices in the *Treatise* there is a theory of debt prices and capital goods prices. But these two prices have different dimensions, one is a rate of interest, the other is a demand price. The direct comparison could be facilitated if both could be reduced to either a price or a rate of interest. If the first route were to be followed they would have to be spot prices, for demand prices of investment goods had to be compared to present supply prices, but the spot price of money was identically equal to unity. Direct comparison could only be made by reducing capital goods prices to a rate of return, which is precisely what the marginal efficiency of capital is, the rate of discount which equates the expected future proceeds to the present costs.

Keynes thus substitutes rates of return for prices in the *General Theory*, emphasising the nature of the money rate of interest as a relation between spot and future prices being equivalent to the relation between the spot and future prices of newly produced capital goods. Already in the last 1933 draft Keynes stated that "the entrepreneur is guided, not by the amount of product he will gain, but by the alternative opportunities for using money having regard to the spot and forward price structure taken as a whole" (JMK: XXIX, p. 83). Now, this is precisely the way Sraffa worked out his critique of Hayek in terms of commodity rates of interest which Keynes employs, referring the reader to Sraffa and his own prior work on spot and future prices with respect to foreign exchange markets, in his Chapter 16 and 17 explanation of the real influence that money may have via the rate of interest on the level of investment. Thus although naming the concept marginal efficiency had to wait until 1934, the essence was already present in the adaptation of spot and forward prices to produce rates of return which could be compared and which demonstrated that if the rate on debt were more sticky than that on assets the production of assets might not achieve the full employment level.

Thus we may conclude that Fisher remains a distant ancestor of the Keynes of the *General Theory* only to the extent that his work provoked Keynes into developing a theory in which money was a real factor in that the money rate of interest determined the rate of return on capital investment; it was this theory that required the development of the marginal efficiency which was more likely developed on the basis of Schumpeter's work[3] and the discussions which were initiated by Hayek's criticism of the absence of capital theory in Keynes' *Treatise*.[4]

Notes

1 It is interesting to note the chronology here: liquidity preference appeared in Keynes' 1932 lectures, its limitation to debt prices produced a simultaneous discussion of a determinant for capital assets prices (first quasi-rents) which only received the name efficiency of capital in late 1933 along with the propensity to consume, which is called the propensity to spend. Their combination to produce effective demand only follows in 1934 (although the term is used earlier to express the ratio of disbursement to income). This is consistent with Keynes belief that the weak point in the traditional theory was the rate of interest and the criticism be received over his treatment of capital goods prices in the *Treatise* (cf. JMK: XIII, pp. 201 ff.). It does not support those who consider the multiplier to be the starting point which left the rate of interest hanging, implying that liquidity preference was an afterthought.

2 As I have stressed in a number of places (Kregel, 1976 b, 1977) Fisher did not ignore the importance of uncertainty, but when he faced the analysis of uncertainty, like so many other economists, he resolved the problem not as Keynes did by assuming a given state of expectations of an uncertain future (cf. Kregel, 1976 a), but that "expected income is foreknown with certainly and the rate of interest is foreknown" (Fisher, 1906, p. 202).

3 "In the case of fixed capital it is easy to understand why fluctuations should occur in the rate of investment. Entrepreneurs are induced to embark on the production of fixed capital or deferred from doing so by their expectations of the profit to be made. Apart from the many minor reasons why these should fluctuate in a changing world, Professor Schumpeter's explanation of the major movements may be unreservedly accepted" (JMK: VI, p. 87), there follows a summary of Schumpeter's *Business Cycles* which Keynes borrows from Wesley Mitchell!

4 In revising this paper I recalled a point originally raised in Kregel, 1976 b, p. 43–4, which notes that an analysis very similar to commodity rates of interest is also present in Fisher (1930, e.g. p. 42). It appears that neither Opie, Guillebaud, Hayek, Sraffa nor Keynes credited Fisher with paternity for this particular concept.

REFERENCES

Alchian, A. (1955), "The Rate of Interest, Fisher's Rate of Return over Costs and Keynes' Internal Rate of Return", *American Economic Review*, Dec.

Bryce, R.B. (1932, 1933), "Notes of Keynes Lectures", mimeo, Cambridge.

Fisher, I. (1906), *The Nature of Capital and Income*, New York, Macmillan.

Fisher, L (1930), *The Theory of Interest*, Philadelphia: Porcupine Press Reprint, 1977.

Harcourt, G.C. (ed.) (1985), *Keynes and His Contemporaries*, London, Macmillan.

Harrod, R.F. (1951), *The Life of J.M. Keynes*, London, Macmillan.

Hawtrey, R.G. (1913), *Good and Bad Trade*, New York, Kelley Reprint, 1962.

Howson, S. (1985), "Hawtrey and the Real World", in HARCOURT.

Kahn, R.F. (1984), *The Making of Keynes' General Theory*, Cambridge University Press.

Keynes, J.M. (JMK), *The Collected Writing of J.M. Keynes*, London, Macmillan for the Royal Economic Society: V, VI: A Treatise on Money, 1971.

VII: *The General Theory of Employment, Interest and Money*, 1973.

XI: *Economic Articles and Correspondence: Academic*, 1983.

XIII: *The General Theory and After: Part I. Preparation*, 1973.

XIV: Part II. *Defense and Development*, 1973.

XXIX: *A Supplement*, 1979.

Kregel, J.A. (1976 a), "Economic Methodology in the Face of Uncertainly", *Economic Journal*, June.

Kregel, J.A. (1976 b), *Theory of Capital*, London, Macmillan.

Kregel, J.A. (1977), "On the existence of expectations in English Neoclassical Economics", *Journal of Economic Literature*, June.

Kregel, J.A. (1985), "Hamlet without the Prince", *American Economic Review*, Papers and Proceedings, May.

Patinkin, D. and J.C. Leith, *Keynes, Cambridge and the General Theory*, London, Macmillan, 1977.

Robinson, R. (1956), "The Rate of Interest, Fisher's Rate of Return over Costs and Keynes' Internal Rate of Return: Comment", *American Economic Review*.

Withers, H. (1926), *The Meaning of Money*, London, John Murray.

Chapter 12

CAPITAL AND INCOME IN THE THEORY OF INVESTMENT AND OUTPUT: IRVING FISHER AND JOHN MAYNARD KEYNES

The second war produced a watershed in twentieth-century economics. Together with the dominance of the profession by purely academic economists came the disappearance of what might be called financial macroeconomists whose principal concern was the explanation of the interaction of finance and investment in the context of economic fluctuations. Although there has been a renewed interest in business cycles, it has concentrated on 'real' factors, while 'finance' has become a separate discipline concentrating on the microeconomics of efficient markets and some aspects of rational expectations.

One of the founders of the financial macroeconomics approach was Irving Fisher. He was part of a group of economists which included Hayek, Böhm-Bawerk, Schumpeter, Wicksell, Hawtrey, Robertson and Keynes to name a few. Although these economists came from diverse theoretical backgrounds, a common denominator was active participation in financial markets, either through private or public sector experience. This background of institutional knowledge provided support for their distinctive theoretical approach, which recognized that monetary and financial factors are important determinants of the behavior of the economy. This common background may also be noted from the fact that despite theoretical difference, Keynes was outspoken in acknowledgment that 'it was Irving Fisher who ... first influenced me strongly towards regarding money as a "real" factor' (1973, pp. 202–203, n.2). In particular, Keynes suggested that his theory of investment, based on the marginal efficiency of capital, 'was first introduced by Irving Fisher in his *Theory of Interest* (1930) under the designation "the rate of return over cost". This conception of his is, I think, the most important and fruitful of his recent conceptions' (Fisher, 1930, p. 103). Indeed, the modern financial analyst would be surprised to discover in *The Nature of Capital and Income* (1906) and *The Theory of Interest,* most of the basic tools of time value analysis of investment including spot and forward yield curves.

It is unfortunate that much of this part of Fisher's work has fallen from the standard economics curriculum. In the post-war view of economics, Fisher is generally characterized as a forerunner of modern monetarism in which money has no permanent influence, and as the proponent of the rule that nominal interest rates reflect the adjustment of underlying, stable real rates of interest to rationally anticipated inflation. These suggest the rather extreme position that the rate of interest is determined by productivity and that monetary factors have no permanent impact.

But, anyone who has studied Fisher's work will recall the importance of his definition of income for his entire work, as well as the scientific caution in which Fisher always couched his positions. In particular his concern to combat the extreme positions of the 'psychology school' or the 'productivity school' (1930, p. 312), by joining time preference and investment opportunity as dual determinants of the rate of interest. They will also recall his admonition that his theory was only representative of 'rational tendencies', that are based on 'rational and empirical laws ... analogous to rational and empirical laws of physics and astronomy' (p. 321).

Outside these conditions, where actuarial risk is replaced by uncertainty and in which the value of money is unstable Fisher recommended that 'We must ... give up as a bad job any attempt to formulate completely the influences which really determine the rate of interest' (p. 321). Although he did consider it possible to take steps to reduce the problems caused by unstable money, and made numerous proposals to that effect.

Before someone questions my representation of Fisher as an expert in the operation of financial markets by reference to his role as the public antidote to Roger Babson's continued predictions of an impending stock market crash in early September 1929 and his subsequent declarations that stock prices remained undervalued, I will also draw attention to the fact that Fisher quickly learned from the experience and by 1931 has worked out his theory of debt deflation. Indeed, it is interesting to note the absence of a conference session devoted to this topic. This approach lives on in the work of a small group of Wall Street analysts who rediscovered it through Hyman Minsky's financial instability hypothesis. Although Minsky's theory is often presented as Keynesian, his use of Keynes and Kalecki is primarily the aggregate profits equation, and serves more to explain why 1929 has not recurred, than why it is still a clear and present danger. The endogenous generation of depression from excessive lending and the process by which reducing indebtedness increases indebtedness are both clearly derived from Fisher. And like Keynes, Minsky has clearly acknowledged this debt to Fisher.

However the particular Fisherian themes that I would like to emphasize will perhaps surprise you. It is "time". Indeed, time is a factor unites the group of prewar financial macroeconomists. These economists took the impact of time seriously. To draw on an aphorism of Dennis Robertson, the short-run is not the same length in both directions, forward and back. By which I assume he meant that what is unclear in anticipation, appears obvious and self evident in retrospect. What has been done in anticipation can never be recovered. Fisher's theory of capital is based on the distinction between the theory of what occurs during the passage of time, and what occurs at a point in time. Thus the distinction between capital as a stock, income as a flow, and the value of capital as the value at a point in time of the income flow expected from it. Indeed, at one point Fisher suggests that the theory of capital might better be described as a theory of income. It is a flow theory, a theory that occurs over the passage of time. And the rate of interest is of crucial importance to theory because it is the linkage between two points in time, it brings the future to the present point in time that allows the calculation of capital values. Since the rate of interest relates to flows over time, its specification requires at least two points in time.

The rate of interest on a loan is thus the price of a spot-forward swap of money, or what we today would call a repo contract. Interest can be represented by swap points over spot, as in a foreign currency swap, or repo agreement. Or Fisher would say, by the excess over par. Alternatively, it may be represented by the discount from the maturity or face value, as in a foreign exchange bill or a Treasury bill. Both come to the same thing. It is instructive to note that Keynes also defined the rate of interest as 'nothing more than the percentage excess of a sum of money contracted for forward delivery – over what we may call the "spot" or cash price of the sum thus contracted for forward delivery' (Keynes, 1936, p. 222).

Since there are spot-forward swaps of different maturity, there will be interest rates referring to different periods, extending not only from today to different future dates, but from future dates to farther future dates. It was following this line of reasoning that led Fisher to the concepts of zero-coupon rates as well as forward rates which have come to play such an important role in modern financial analysis. But, more importantly, Fisher also notes that there is no reason why 'interest rates' cannot also be applied to individual commodities, so that a spot-forward swap of say gold or wheat would also produce a rate of interest, only it would be measured in terms of the commodity itself. Fisher thus notes that

> We thus need to distinguish between interest expressed in terms of money and interest expressed in terms of other goods. But no two forms of goods can be expected to maintain an absolutely constant price ratio towards each other. *There are, therefore, theoretically just as many rates of interest expressed in terms of goods as there are kinds of goods diverging from one another in value* (emphasis in original, 1930, p. 42).

To keep the comparison with Keynes, the sentence that follows the one quoted above reads: 'It would seem, therefore, that for every kind of capital asset there must be an analogue of the rate of interest on money' and he goes on to specify a wheat-rate of interest and a steel-plant rate of interest, finally referring the reader in a note to Sraffa's use of the concept in his debate with Hayek.

Starting from this specification of the rate of interest it is easy to see how Fisher extended it to his opportunity theory of investment and the concept of rate of return over cost. It is important to remember that the discussion is in terms of project selection. The rate of return over cost is that rate which equalizes the net present value of the stream of cash flows from two alternative opportunities of investment. The decision to use the option of an alternative opportunity will then be determined by comparing it to the market rate of interest. The concept is also used to determine incremental investments in a single line, similar to the decision over capital intensity of a project. It also generates what we would now call 'switching' rates of return, that is, changes in market rates of interest which cause one project to be preferred to another. There are also indications that Fisher entertained the possibility of reswitching, caused by multiple solutions and increasing returns, but discarded them as unlikely curiosa.

When Keynes deals with the concept, it has been reduced to the option of shifting from a fixed interest security to an additional unit of a capital investment project and the marginal rate of return over cost becomes the marginal efficiency of capital. But, the important point for both of them is the independent determination of the rate of interest (leaving aside any differences between the psychological determinants of time preference and liquidity preference) and the rate of return over costs (or the efficiency of capital) which allows the determination of equilibrium in terms of the equality between the two. It also leads, for both, to the importance of distinguishing between short and long rates of interest. Fisher cites as a corollary of his theory 'the necessity of positing a theoretically separate rate of interest for each separate period of time ... the divergence between the rate for short terms and for long terms' (1930, p. 313) and Keynes' belief in the difference between short and long-period expectations, citing 'The mistake of regarding the marginal efficiency of capital primarily in terms of the *current* yield of capital equipment, which would be correct only in the static state where there is no changing future to influence the present ...' pointing out in a footnote that 'the relation between rates of interest for different periods depends on expectations' (1936, p. 145).

Up to this point, both Keynes and Fisher propose an equilibrium determined by the equality of the appropriate rate of interest with the return on investment, and propose a similar procedure to decide on the investment project which will be implemented. The specification of this equilibrium raises another important point – given the possibility noted by both of specifying rates of interest in terms of individual commodities there is the question of whether arbitrage across different rates will produce the same results when specified in different standards. Fisher notes that the arbitrage process cannot determine the rate of interest, but it only 'enables us ... to calculate the rates in other standards' on the assumption 'that the rate of *some one* standard is already known' (1930, p. 45). Keynes also notes 'that even when calculating own rates, since they are quoted in money terms, "it also brings in the money-rate of interest"'. Thus, some rate has to be known from outside the system, and that rate for both is the money rate of interest.

First, let us consider the arbitrage process. Fisher argues that the market arbitrage should act to eliminate any changes in the relative values of the standards used to express the multiple possible rates of interest. Thus if there are two commodities, say gold and wheat, each showing the same ratio between spot and forward prices, but one of them, say wheat, is appreciating in terms of gold, then there should be a market preference to hold wheat, irrespective of the preferences for the two goods. The increased demand for wheat would then drive up its spot price relative to its forward price, reducing its premium over par and causing a reduction in its interest rate. (Keynes would have identified this as backwardation). The rate of interest on wheat thus adjusts until it is brought into equality with the rate on gold.

Now, one of the implications of considering the interest rate as a spot-forward swap is that it creates a known future value. It fixes a future action and thus makes the future less difficult to predict. But, even if every economic action takes the form of a spot and a predetermined forward transaction, this does not mean that the future is perfectly known or that it will represent a position of equilibrium. Fisher always starts out his theory by assuming perfect foresight, and then explains why this is impossible, even in the presence of forward contracting.

Thus Fisher's description of the arbitrage process between gold and wheat argues that if the forward price of wheat were perfectly known to be at a 10% premium, while the forward price of money were known to be at a 4% premium (the spot and forward price of wheat in money is 1:1, then the arbitraged forward price of wheat in money is 1.10/1.04), it would pay to borrow money at 4%, buy a bushel of wheat at the current spot price which can be lent today against 1.10 bushels forward. The wheat can then be sold for 1.10 to repay the money loan with interest of 1.04, giving a positive carry of 6%. If the forward price ratio between gold and wheat is fixed at unity, this would drive up the current price of wheat until it stood at 1.10 / 1.04 = 1.057 premium over money. 1.057 in money invested at 4% just yields 1.10.

Now, this is the relation that Keynes worked out in the *Manchester Guardian* and republished in the *Tract on Monetary Reform*, known today as the interest rate parity theorem. I have suggested (Kregel, 1997) that it forms the core of Keynes' analysis of income determination. If we substitute dollars for gold and marks for wheat, with the dollar interest rate 4% relative to the mark interest rate of 10% it says that the proportional difference between the spot and forward prices of the two currencies should be the spot rate times 1 plus the dollar interest rate divided by 1 plus the mark interest rate or 1 times (1.04/1.10). In Fisher's example the forward dollar mark rate is fixed at 1:1, so we have to rearrange the formula to find the spot rate as the forward rate times 1 plus the mark interest rate divided by 1 plus the dollar rate or 1 times (1.10/1.04). Thus, wheat sells at a spot premium or a forward discount. This means that wheat bought at 1.057 can only be sold at 1 at the end of the contract. It is clear that the arbitrage may occur via adjustment of either the spot or forward prices, i.e. the rate of appreciation or depreciation of one standard in terms of the other, or in terms of the rates of interest in each standard, or in all three.

Of course, the determination of the rate of interest in Fisher's approach to the theory of income is the rate which brought about equality of present and future incomes. It is the extension to real income of the arbitrage process described above that leads directly to the relation between money and real rates of interest. As noted, there are three factors at work, the appreciation or depreciation of one standard in terms of the other, which we can clearly recognize as the rate of inflation, when measured in terms of the money standard, the rate of interest in terms of money and the rate of interest in terms of time preference for present over future income.

Now, if we substitute income for 'wheat' and money for 'gold', then Fisher's arbitrage argument says that it is only possible that the money rate of interest should be 4% when the (real) income rate of interest is 10% if money is expected to exchange for 5.8% more income in the future than in the present so that 1.0578·1.04 = 1.10. Thus, if there is a forward discount on income (the inverse of the forward premium of 1: 1.057 on money), the rate of return on income (10%) must be higher than that on money (4%), but if income is at a forward premium, then the rate of return on money must be higher than the return on income. This, of course, is just reversing the process noted above, by substituting money and income, for gold and wheat, or for dollars and marks. The relation between the real and the money interest rates given by the rate of appreciation of the standard thus descends directly for the arbitrage relation that insures that the rate of interest is equal to the rate of return over costs or from the interest rate parity theorem.

Now, this precise formal equivalence between Fisher's and Keynes's analysis of the equality between rates of interest and rates of return is really not such a great discovery. Everyone who has taught a course in international finance draws a four-comer diagram in which the two corners of one side (usually the top) represent Keynes's (covered) interest rate parity theorem and Fisher's real-nominal interest rate relation. And that is what we have just done here.

This is the standard proposition from interest rate parity.

Of course, the actual process of adjustment can come in any of the variables. For example, if the interest rate on income and the discount or premia are fixed, then all of the adjustment must come in the money rate of interest. On the other hand, if only the return on income is fixed, say by time preferences, then the money rate will have to adjust to any changes in the forward discount or premium on money. The proposition that $(1 + p)(1 + r) = (1 + i)$, where p is the rate of inflation, r the rate of increase in real income, and i the rate of interest on money, is just a different way of expressing the interest rate parity theorem for a closed economy, or that there is full arbitrage. Rewriting the relation as $(1 + p) = (1 + i)/(1 + r)$, and writing S as the spot rate of exchange of money for wheat and F the forward rate of exchange of money for wheat, then $F/S = 1 + p$ and we have $F = S\,[(1 + i)/(1 + r)] = 0.945\,S$ or given $F = 1$, $S = 1/0.945 = 1.057$, which is the price of wheat in money terms that eliminates arbitrage profit.

But not only is there a formal similarity, Keynes also accepted the general validity of the empirical data in support of Fisher's proposition in the form of what has come to be known as the Gibson Paradox – higher rates of inflation tend to produce higher rates of interest. However, despite this similarity in approach, and agreement on the empirical basis, Keynes takes issue with Fisher on the relation between the rate of interest and the rate of inflation. Thus, there is more than a Gibson Paradox, there is the paradox of how two economists who adopted virtually similar basic analytical systems could reach radically opposed solutions.

Part of the solution to the paradox is to be found in Fisher's discussion of the relation between the rates of interest measured in terms of the various possible commodity standards. He notes the difficulty in transferring the idea of a rate of interest on an individual commodity to income as a whole. In principle 'a rate of interest in terms of fundamental income itself would seem to come as near as we can practically come to any basic standard in which to express a real rate of interest' (1930, pp. 42–3), however, in the absence of such a measure, the practice is to fall back on the use of 'a practical objective standard' represented by 'a cost of living index' which Fisher spent most of his career trying to perfect.

> By means of such an index number we may translate the nominal, or money rate of interest, into a goods rate or real rate of interest, just as we translate money wages into real wages. The cost of living plays the same role in both cases although the process of translating is somewhat different and more complicated in the case of interest from what it is in the case of wages, for the reason that interest involves two points of time, instead of only one; so that

> we must translate from money into goods not only in the present, when the money is borrowed, but also in the future, when it is repaid (1930, p. 42).

Fisher was concerned by this point because in his theory the rate of interest to which rate of return over cost should be equated was determined by present relative to future income-time preference. Keynes did not have this problem because liquidity preference referred to present relative to future delivery of money.

This difference is important because the definition of a rate of return in terms of 'fundamental income' (or of an amount of nominal income which can be deflated by a price index) eliminates any possibility of a market-based process of arbitrage which ensures the equilibrium relation. Since there are no markets for 'fundamental income', it is impossible to argue that individuals will buy and sell fundamental income spot against forward or to arbitrage it against a money relative given by a price index. A theory which is based on a real financial market process of arbitrage when applied to individual commodities, has no direct counterpart when looked upon in the aggregate. But, it is precisely such an arbitrage process that Fisher invokes to establish the inflation adjustment of nominal interest rates.

Fisher's solution of 'fundamental income' and aggregate price indices is subject to the criticism of von Mises and Hayek concerning the inadequacies of index numbers, as well as Sraffa's criticism of Hayek's use of a 'neutral' rate of interest. Attempts to deal with these difficulties have moved economists in two directions. Both seem to converge on the same point.

The first is to find a suitable measure of 'fundamental income'. The concept of fundamental income is related to Ricardo's invariable standard of value, and links up with Sraffa's standard commodity and Hicks's definition of income and its 'average period' in his *Value and Capital* (Chapter XIV and note). At this point, we may note that it is a bit more complicated than finding the appropriate price index by which to deflate nominal income.

The second is to analyze the importance of the assumption of perfect foresight for the arbitrage process which establishes the equality of real and nominal rates. This is where Keynes had difficulties with Fisher's version of interest parity (cf. *Treatise on Money,* Volume II, pp. 202–203 and *General Theory,* pp. 142–143). Keynes argues that Fisher's argument that the money rate of interest should automatically reflect a perfectly foreseen rise in the rate of inflation overlooked the impact on long-term bond prices of a rise in interest rates. While it would be true that a perfectly foreseen rise in inflation for the coming year of 2% producing a 2% rise in interest rates on one-year Treasury bills would keep real returns constant, the same would not be true of a holder of a longer-term instrument if it were sold after one year (or even if it were held to maturity). But, it should be true that the one-year return should be the same for any instrument held for one year.

Keynes uses the example of a £100 par value British consol paying £10 per annum to yield 10% which falls to £81.96 (a decline of 1.8% and a capital loss of over £18) when interest rates rise to 12.2%. While the 'variations in the rate of interest earned during the year in question are too small to make much difference' (e.g. the extra 2.2%

on the £10 coupon), the holder of fixed interest assets will have a substantial capital loss. The investor will have the benefit of being able to invest the future £10 interest coupon payments at the higher rate of 12.2%, but over a single year this will not be sufficient to cover the £18 decline in the capital value of the bond, and thus by definition could not compensate for any rise in the inflation rate equal to the increased rate of interest. Thus, Keynes suggests that Fisher's relation goes in the wrong direction to the extent that a higher inflation rate increases bond yields and causes absolute losses in capital values which more than offset the rise in the rate of interest which is supposed to compensate for the fall in the value of money. Full inflation coverage should provide for an adjustment in capital value as well as in the income from the bond. But, here we are led back to the concept of income. Keynes is arguing that since the principal value of the bond is impaired even when interest rates adjust to inflation, an individual will have a lower total real income from the original investment. This is particularly easy to see in the case of the consol, for its price is permanently reduced.

The point seems obvious, given Fisher's concern to derive capital values from income flows. Yet, it is the theory of income that prevents Fisher from taking it into account. This is because, if capital is just discounted future income, then an appreciation or depreciation of capital value, i.e. a capital gain or loss, must represent an increase or decrease in expected future income. But, this has no impact on present income. Fisher notes that

> Consols and rentes fluctuate in value every day with every change in the money market. Yet the income they actually yield flows on at the same rate. ... A rise in the market is a capital gain, but it is not income (1930, p. 27).

Fisher had already discussed the point in *The Nature of Capital and Income*:

> Expressed in a single sentence, the general principle connecting realized and earned income is that they differ by the appreciation or depreciation of capital. It is thus possible to describe earned income as realized income less depreciation of capital, or else as realized income plus appreciation of capital. We may therefore state anew the fallacy of confusing realized income with earned income: the fallacy consists in reckoning depreciation of capital as a part of outgo, or appreciation of capital as a part of income. (1906, p. 238).

Thus, the case of a capital loss caused by an increase in the rate of interest is equivalent to the case of realized income exceeding earned income, or the depreciation of capital, due to the rise in the rate of interest. In order to keep capital constant, a deduction will have to be made to income received in future periods. This is the reduction to future income which is represented by the capital loss. A higher rate of inflation, which reduces real future income will also require an increase in future income to offset it.

An alternative way of looking at the problem would be to note that insofar as capital gains and losses for the economy as a whole net to zero, there should be no impact on either present or future income streams due to the change in nominal interest rates. Thus, there need not be any impact on the overall rate of time preference linking present and future incomes. This seems to be what Hayek had in mind with his conception of neutral money, for the money rate of interest would then be managed so as to leave the real rate unchanged. This suggests the second difference, and that is that Fisher implicitly assumes that real incomes are unchanged, while Keynes is looking at a theory to explain the movement in incomes.

> Indeed Professor Fisher's theory could be best rewritten in terms of a 'real rate of interest' defined as being the rate of interest which would have to rule, consequently on a change in the state of expectation of the future value of money, in order that this change should have no effect on current output (1936, p. 143).

Keynes then goes on to make his basic criticism of Fisher's relation, that the most important impact of inflation will be not in the interest rate, but on the incentive to invest – the marginal efficiency of capital. Fisher's account of the impact of a rise in the rate of inflation makes no mention of the impact on either long-term bond values or on the rate of return over costs.

This brings us back to the question of the definition of fundamental income, or just exactly what it means to have income constant when changes in interest rates have an influence on capital values. This is the question that Hicks sought to answer in his 'average period' of income and is now better known as 'Macauley duration', which was worked out in an attempt to assess the Fisher relation with respect to the Gibson Paradox.

Against this background it is interesting to assess Fisher's theory of debt deflation, for here it seems quite clear that he accepted that income would not be constant. Fisher had already noted that his theory required that 'the performance of contracts corresponds to promises and expectations' and that 'because of defaults, the equations fail of being precisely true' (1930, p. 320), and this is precisely the case of debt deflation. This process is propagated by a failure of interest rates to fall in order to keep real rates constant, and thus produces an increase in real indebtedness. This requires the process of forced liquidation which drives prices down. '... the liquidation of debts cannot keep up with the fall of prices which it causes. In that case, the liquidation defeats itself. While it diminishes the number of dollars owed, it may not do so as fast as it increases the value of each dollar owed.' ... *'The more debtors pay, the more they owe'* (1933, p. 344, emphasis in original). Which is simply another way of saying that nominal interest rates have not fallen sufficiently rapidly and have not become sufficiently negative. The failure of lenders to make direct payments to borrowers means that they experience the reduction in terms of default and total loss of principal. The result is that income does not remain constant. The general implication is that when interest rates fail to keep up with inflation there is a boom and when they fail to keep down with deflation there is a debt deflation. Which looks very much like Wicksell. When the interest-inflation rule is met, then income is stable, which looks very much like Hayek. And despite the formal similarities between this rule and the interest rate parity theorem and their investment theories, it does not look at all like Keynes.

REFERENCES

Fisher, I. (1906), *The Nature of Capital and Income*, New York, Macmillan.

Fisher, I. (1930), *The Theory of Interest*, New York, Macmillan.

Fisher, I. (1933), 'The debt-deflation theory of great depressions,' *Econometrica*, 1, 337–357.

Keynes, J.M. (1930), *Treatise on Money*, 2 volumes, London, Macmillan.

Keynes, J.M. (1936), *The General Theory of Employment, Interest and Money*. London, Macmillan.

Keynes, J.M. (1973), *The General Theory and After: Part II: Defense and Development*, edited by D. Moggridge, Volume XIV of Keynes' Collected Writings, London, Macmillan.

Kregel, J.A. (1988), 'Irving Fisher, great-grandparent of the *General Theory*: Money, rate of return over cost and efficiency of capital,' *Cahiers d'Économie Politique*, 14–15, 59–68.

Kregel, J.A. (1997), 'The theory of value, expectations and chapter 17 of the *General Theory*' in G.C. Harcourt and P. Riach (eds), *A Second Edition of the General Theory*, London, Routledge, 261–282.

Chapter 13

QUERIES ABOUT COINCIDENCES AND CORRELATIONS BETWEEN FISHER AND KEYNES, THE GIBSON PARADOX AND THE IDEA OF *DURATION*

Interrogation #1.

Q. What is the difference between the Keynesian demand for money and the Classical?
A. The speculative demand for money.
Q. What is the speculative demand for money?
A. The impact of changes in the rate of interest on the capital value of long-term bonds held in investment portfolios. It is a question of interest and capital.
Q. Who was the world's best known expert on the relation between capital and interest in the first half of the 20th century?
A. Irving Fisher.
Q. So, Fisher must have adopted a Keynesian theory of the demand for money?
A. No, he was a pure classical quantity theorist.

Interrogation #2.

Q. Was Keynes a good empirical economist?
A. No, every empirical regularity he identified turned out to be a special case.
Q. Such as?
A. The best known is the relation between prices and output, or the impact of diminishing returns leading to an inverse relation between changes in the level of employment and output on one hand and the level of real wages on the other. Dunlop, Tarshis and Kalecki all provided statistical evidence to the contrary. Fortunately, this had no major consequences for his theory.
Q. Is that all?
A. Well, he got the same thing wrong in a number of different ways. He also considered the positive relation between wholesale commodity prices and yields of British consols one of the most completely established facts in all of empirical economics.
Q. And it is not?
A. Not only does it appear to have no foundation, but Keynes fudged the figures in a way that would have made Milton Friedman proud.

Interrogation #3.

Q. If Keynes and Fisher disagreed about monetary theory they must have disagreed about most things in economics?

A. No, they agreed about the "Gibson Paradox", that there was an unequivocal relation between prices and interest rates.

Q. Then they were both wrong?

A. No.

Q. No?

A. They had different explanations to explain the relationship that didn't exist. Fisher's was wrong. Keynes just had the right explanation for the wrong problem. He needed to find the right problem to explain.

Q. And that was?

A. The decision to hold money or hold bonds.

Q. And what was the difference?

A. You should have guessed by now. The impact of interest rates on capital values.

Interrogation #4.

Q. Where did Fisher go wrong in his explanation?

A. As you can read in any economics or finance textbook, Fisher argued that when there was an increase in the inflation rate, lenders would require an increase in return. If the rate of interest was r, they expected 1+r at the end of the investment period. If, during the period prices had risen by p, then they would require that their funds be indexed and the return would have to be (1+r)(1+p).

Q. But, what determined the r that they got before calculating the depreciation of money due to inflation?

A. Ah, there's the rub. r was the "real rate" of interest. If lenders always got the inflation adjustment, then the real rate remained constant.

Q. What has all this got to do with the demand for money?

A. Good question. Remember that the speculative motive is based on changes in capital values caused by changes in interest rates. If all interest rate changes due to changes in inflation are offset by nominal rate adjustment such as to leave the "real value" of capital unchanged, then there are no "real" capital value adjustments because "real" interest rates are unchanged. Or at least this seems a plausible explanation of why the world's expert on interest and capital could overlook the impact.. in real terms there was none.

Q. You mean that if nominal interest rates always adjust so as to offset changes in inflation then the real value of capital assets are constant and have no impact on the demand for money?

A. Now you're catching on. Yes, this seems to have been Fisher's explanation. But, remember, there is no theoretical or empirical foundation for this proposition. It all seems to have been based on the statistical anomaly created by Gibson.

Interrogation #5.

Q. But, how can you be so sure that Gibson was wrong?

A. An exhaustive study of the course of interest rates and bonds yields in the United States since 1856 and of the statistical relations of those rates and yields to one another, to stock and commodity prices, to the physical and monetary volume of trade, and to credit and banking conditions published in a 1938 National Bureau of Economic Research Study by Frederick R. Macauley.

Q. And what did Macauley show?

A. First, that the data do not support Gibson -- there is no reason to accept the proposition that there is an empirical relation. Second, that there are severe logical inconsistencies with the explanations for its existence.

Q. But then both Keynes and Fisher were wrong?

A. Yes, Macauley is merciless in showing how both of them continually fudged their positions. He even quotes Keynes' *Treatise on Probability* to show that Keynes once knew better.

Q. What else did Macauley do?

A. Since Keynes and Fisher used slightly different versions of the Gibson idea, Keynes dealing with yields on consols, Fisher with short-term rates, Macauley raised the question of just exactly what was meant by yield on long and short term instruments.

Q. And what did he discover?

A. First, that the concept of yield to maturity commonly used to classify interest returns is virtually meaningless. Since it is based on discounted value it presumes what now would be called a flat yield curve, that all interest payments can be reinvested at the common yield to maturity, no matter how far in the future they may lie. Yield to maturity thus more resembles a "promised" rate of return than a "secure" or certain return.

Q. You mean that when I buy a bond with a 10% yield to maturity I'm not certain of the 10% return?

A. Not at all. You get 10% only if you manage to reinvest all the coupons from now to maturity at 10%.

Q. With Alan Greenspan at the helm that seems hardly likely.

A. You said it.

Q. But, aside from the implications for my retirement, why is this important?

A. Remember that Gibson's relation linked the yield on consols and wholesale prices. What Macaulay pointed out was that these were simply an average of a whole range of interest rates, what the Austrians would have called an "aggregate" rate with no direct market referent. Thus to argue that the market responded to inflation by adjusting yield was like saying that the economy adjusted to inflation by changing its marginal propensity to consume. It might be true in the aggregate, but there is no individual decision rule that makes it so.

Q. But what interest rates should be used?

A. Here Fisher was probably closer to the mark. Short rates are probably the best response to changes in expected prices. What Macauley then tried was to work out what would happen if individuals perfectly forecast short-term changes in commodity prices and adjusted their short-term borrowing and lending behaviour accordingly. He argued that this should then have an impact on long term rates since investors always had the choice between operating short term or buying long term and selling before maturity (Note how changes in capital values come back in here). What he discovered was that long term rates did not come anywhere near what would be required on the assumption that inflation could be foreseen and that investors would be indifferent between say a six-month Treasury and buying a twenty-year Treasury bond and selling it after six months.

Q. So that got rid of Fisher's explanation. What about Keynes?

A. Well, one of the things Macaulay tried to do was to provide a measure of what was a long and what a short maturity. His idea was that the difference in investor behaviour between short- and long-term bonds was precisely in the fact that changes in capital values did not adjust so as to make the six-month bill equal to the holding period return on the twenty-year bond over six months. He argued that some bonds of similar maturity may be longer term than others, precisely because of the defect noted above in the use of yield to maturity as a measure of return. Bonds with different coupons or different premia and discount will react differently to changes in the rate at which their interest payments can be reinvested. To take an extreme, what is now called a zero coupon bond pays no coupon and thus has no uncertainty over the rate at which they will be invested. At the other, a bond with a very high coupon gets reinvested more quickly and thus has rates that are closer to the hypothesised yield to maturity. On the other hand, low coupon bonds or deep discount bonds are more like zeros in that their payoff comes at the end of their life. Macauley tried to take these things into account. He developed a concept called "duration" to measure the effective maturity of a bond with respect to the risk of a change in reinvestment rates.

Q. That must have been a very important concept?

A. Yes, but it was almost totally ignored. Hicks, working from the hints in Keynes, developed his own version in Part II of *Value and Capital*, (1939) but then no one ever reads anything but Part I, dealing with Statics. It was more or less rediscovered by Paul Samuelson in a 1945 article dealing with the impact of higher interest rates on the stability of the banking system, and implicitly formed the basis for the analysis in Homer and Leibowitz, *Inside the Yield Book*, the Salomon Brothers bond traders' bible which launched modern bond trading management in the 1970s and is the basis for modern financial innovations in risk management. In particular, stripping Treasury bonds into their individual components.

Interrogation #6

Q. OK, I don't want to appear ignorant, especially where Salomon Brothers is involved. But, what is the big deal with the duration idea and the Gibson paradox?

A. Remember that Gibson had used the yield on British consols to compare with the wholesale price index. Macauley reconstructed the series (this was in the days when the NBER did serious work on cycles). What he discovered was that for the years 1901 to 1903 the prices used were for a new stock issue, announced in 1888, to replace the existing 3% consols. This new stock was to pay 3% until April 5, 1889, 2.75% until April 5, 1903, and 2.5% until 1923. After that date it could be called at par. Yet, Gibson assumed that this stock would continue to pay over its entire life the interest rate payable at any particular date, without taking into account the changes in the rate which would occur over the life of the bond. Thus, the rate he calculated for 1901 was based on 2.75%, and ignored the fact that lower rates would be paid after April 5, 1903.

Q. You mean he treated the rate then current as if it were the yield to maturity?

A. Now you're catching on real fast. That is precisely it. Indeed, one could go so far as to imagine that Macauley discovered the idea of duration by looking at how Gibson had treated a bond in which the reinvestment rate was set out in advance at a rate which was different from the stated yield to maturity. It was clear that a bond that had a rate schedule attached could not have a yield to maturity equal to any of the preannounced coupon rates, and thus it could not have reinvested its coupons at a fixed rate. Indeed, this was the case with any bond, yet this is what yield to maturity refused to contemplate.

Once he had recognised this, it seemed obvious that there could not be much relevance in a relation between rates of commodity price increase and yields to maturity on consols. At the very least, one would have had to have looked at consols with the same duration. Or simply restricted the analysis to short rates.

Interrogation #7

Q. But didn't Keynes and Fisher use different rates? Keynes consol yields and Fisher short rates? What about the relation between short and long-term rates? Isn't there an explanation of long rates which says that they are determined by expected short rates?

A. Good point. This is the part of Hicks' analysis which has in fact survived in the form of what has come to be called the "expectations" explanation of the slope of the yield curve relating the yield to maturity and the time to maturity of a bond.

Hicks points out that a long-term loan can be viewed as a "spot" loan for one week (you remember that Hicks always uses a "week" as the standard period), and a series of forward one-week loan transactions, each involving relending the principal and interest for a further week. A two-week loan will then be compounded out of the spot rate and the rate expected to prevail one-week forward. The long-term rate of interest can thus always be unbundled into the shortest-term spot rate and a series of expected forward rates for the same term.

From this basis, if short rates expected to rule in future weeks are higher than the rate for the current week, then long-term rates will be higher than the current short rate since an investor can always invest for a single week, and then reinvest the proceeds next week at the expected higher rate, giving a compound weekly return which is higher than this week's short rate. Since long rates have to compete with this rate, they will rise until the return from investing long is equivalent to the compound rate achieved by investing week by week for a similar term. Thus, the "yield curve" slopes upward. If rates for future weeks are expected to be lower, then the curve slopes downward. This is what is meant by the idea that long rates are "explained" by anticipated movements in short rates. But, Hicks also points out that short rates can be explained by expected long rates which refer to a finite holding period. The holding period return for a perpetuity (that is, a consol with no redemption date) will be determined by the interest coupons, adjusted for the rise or fall in the market price of the bond. Thus, the rate of interest for a week is determined by the fixed coupon adjusted for anticipated changes in the future prices of the long bond. With a rise in long rates, holding period returns for short periods may fall to zero, and can easily become negative, i.e. the loss in capital value exceeds the interest coupon. Hicks argues that this will lead lenders to use shorter maturity lending whenever possible, and that they would be willing to pay something for eliminating the potential of a reduced or negative return in the form of lower rates of return. So we are back to the relation between capital and interest, or better, how the change in interest affects capital value relative to yield.

The important point, however, is not so much that expected short rates determine long rates, or vice versa, but the process which determines the formation of the expectations of the rates which will prevail in future. Hicks deals with this in terms of the "elasticity of expectations".

Macauley takes a more direct approach. He notes that the explanation of the Gibson paradox in which short rates rise with inflation because lenders require a higher future income to offset their loss in purchasing power implies that investors are able to form perfect forecasts of inflation over the short-term future. That is, it is the expectation of future prices which determines the expectation of future interest rates.

Q. Does that make a difference?

A. Not much. Macauley adopts the strong assumption that expectations are correct. Today we would say that expectations are "rational". He then argues that this assumption implies that short-term interest rates will be a function of the *rate of change* of prices, rather than the *level* of prices.

Q. Why is that?

A. Say the interest rate is 4% and prices are stable, so the real and the money rate of interest are both 4%. Now, assume that prices start to rise by one percentage point per annum, perfectly foreseen. In the first year the rate of interest will rise to (1.04*1.01 -1 =) 5.04%. The nominal rate will rise by 1.04 percentage points each year. 6.08% for the second year when inflation is 2%, 7.12% when it is 3% and so forth. Now, assume that inflation peaks in the 6th year at 6%, with an interest rate of 10.24%. The inflation rate starts to fall back by 1 point per year, as does the interest rate. However, the price level, which had risen by nearly 23% over the first six years, will continue to increase. After 12 years prices will be 42%

higher, but interest rates will be back at 4%. Interest rates will have peaked half way through the inflationary cycle, when the rate of increase of prices, not the price level, reached its maximum value.

Q. OK, but didn't Fisher eventually adopt the link between interest rates and rates of change of prices in his explanation of the paradox?

A. True, but it doesn't help. Macaulay generalises the argument, assuming the inflation rate takes on a periodic motion in the form of a sine curve on a log scale, such that 12 years of rising prices is followed by 12 years of deflation. He first points out that when deflation hits 6%, interest rates should be about -2.24%, although no supporter of the theory had ever suggested that symmetry should prevail and borrowers would force lenders to pay them negative rates to reimburse them for the increase in the real value of their debt! More seriously, he notes that the peak of interest rates occurs after the first quarter (after 6 years) of the full motion when the slope of the price curve is at a maximum, while the price peak occurs after the first half (12 years), so that under these assumptions interest rates would lead prices by a quarter of the cycle period.

Q. And the link between short and long rates?

A. That's easy. Macauley compares them when inflation is stable, i.e. at the inflection points of the periodic motion. A stable six percent inflation rate corresponds to a stable 10.24% short-term interest rate. But, the same inflation coverage could be obtained by an alternative route of buying a long-term bond and selling it at the end of the year. Remember Hicks' representation of the relation between short and long-term yields. In the absence of price changes, the return on bonds over the year would be given by the coupon yield or the current yield. If the current yield on bonds were less than 10.24% then bond prices would be rising throughout the year (causing the current yield to fall) so that the holding period return for the year would be just 10.24%.

On the other hand, if the bond's yield to maturity were less than then short-term rate, the yield to maturity would also have to decline, but its price need not rise, and indeed might fall.

Since short-term rates are likely to be higher than current bond yields when prices have been rising, current yields will be falling and bond prices rising after short-term rates have peaked, but commodity prices are still rising. The same will be true of yield to maturity on bonds (but not necessarily of prices) which will continue to fall as long as short-term yields are higher. Bond yields will only stop falling when prices have reached the top of the sine curve.

Thus, in conditions in which price changes are perfectly foreseen, short rates should lead prices by a quarter of a cycle and the cyclical movement of long rates should show a perfect negative correlation with the price cycle (and thus lag the peaks of price rates of change by a quarter cycle). Thus even if Fisher's hypothesis concerning the real rate of interest is fulfilled, it does not provide an explanation of positive correlation with either short or long rates.

Q. I noticed something interesting here. When short rates are rising to offset inflation, long yields may have to be falling (bond prices are rising) to keep long bonds competitive, so the difference between the two rates or the spread should be falling or negative. Isn't that an inversion of the slope of the yield curve? Or a negative slope? But doesn't Hicks argue that this is based on expectations of falling forward short rates? Isn't that contradictory? And isn't change in the slope supposed to mean something about the future of prices?

A. Good. Lots of questions. A change in the spread is certainly supposed to mean something about the future. But, we are not sure of what or why. Now that Mishkin has become head of the New York Fed research function, everyone is aware that the yield spread between short and long rates is a good predictor of turning points in economic activity. Harvey is also a backer of this hypothesis. It is based on a different version of a stable real rate of return. Rather, it assumes that agents maximise intertemporal utility when incomes are stable over time. They thus engage in investment activities which produce income smoothing. If I expect my income to fall because of an anticipated fall in future economic activity I will seek investments which produce income to fill the expected future shortfall in income. (Note that the same argument can be made for business firms, who will reduce their longer-term investments, and thus longer-term borrowing to finance them, if they expect future conditions to be depressed. The supply of longer-term securities will then fall as demand rises.) Thus, the demand for financial instruments that cover the period of expected decline in activity will rise, increasing their prices and reducing their yields; if these increased longer holdings are financed by the sale of shorter maturity instruments, short rates will rise. Thus, longer rates fall relative to current yields, causing a decline in the spread; if this continues the yield curve eventually inverts on the expectation of a downturn in activity. Note that we could substitute an anticipated fall in real income caused by expected inflation for a decline in income due to an anticipated fall in the level of activity, and find that expectations of rising prices produce inverted yield curves, and vice versa. And that this would produce expectations of lower future short rates relative to current short rates, so Hicks' conjecture is also preserved. In fact, this is just what Macauley deduced.

However, we have to be careful here to distinguish between a change in the slope and a change in the level of rates. The slope of the yield curve may change while both short and long rates are rising, or vice versa or when they are moving in opposite directions. This should also make it clear that the result we get depends on the hypothesis we make about expectations. Hicks was very clear on this point. The inversion of the yield curve in the face of currently rising prices is the result of the assumption that future inflation (or economic conditions) can be perfectly predicted. (Or in the case of the change in the spread on the idea that the anticipations of private agents are more quickly expressed in interest rates than in any other economic variables) Macauley went on to test that too, and discovered that it perfectly cannot be predicted! Thus, there may not be any stable relation between short and long rates.

Interrogation #8.

Q. OK, I see how Fisher came to grief if there is no relation between short and long rates, and long rates calculated by means of yield to maturity are not the relevant expression of the interest rate. But, what about Keynes. Isn't he just as badly off as a result of Macauley's duration?

A. Let's look at Keynes's criticism of Fisher's explanation (*Treatise on Money*, II, pp. 202-3). Fisher argues that a rise in the rate of inflation by 2% will cause bond yields to rise by approximately 2%. (If inflation is initially zero and bonds pay 10% the bond holder now needs (1.10)*(1.02)= 1.122 or a rate of 12.2% to retain his 10% yield in real terms) But Keynes argued that Fisher overlooked the negative impact on existing holders of rising interest rates on bond prices (a consol with a £100 par pays £10 per annum to yield 10%, at a 12.2% rate of interest its market value falls to £81.96 or a decline of 1.8% and a capital loss of over £18) so that an investor will be worse off "whilst the variations in the rate of interest earned during the year in question are too small to make much difference". We can presume that the last phrase refers to the higher interest rates that can now be earned on reinvesting the coupon interest on the bonds. Instead of reinvesting each £10 interest payment received is now invested at 12.2%, rather than 10%; this covers the decline in the value of money, but not the change in the capital value of the bond. So it makes no difference at all.

His argument is that Fisher's relation goes in the wrong direction. To the extent that a rising inflation rate increases bond yield it causes absolute losses in capital values which more than offset the rise in the rate of interest which is to compensate for the fall in the value of money. Full inflation coverage should provide for an adjustment in the capital value as well as in the income from the bond.

Q. I know inflation is a bad thing, but what does all this have to do with duration?

A. An alternative method of understanding duration is the time that it takes for the increased interest earned on the reinvestment of interest due to a rise in the rate of interest to offset the fall in capital value. What Keynes is arguing here is that in the short term (where Fisher set his argument) this cannot in general take place.

Q. So Keynes got it right?

A. Not quite, and not yet. What he forgot to figure in was the coupon itself. At the end of the period the investor has not only his capital position, he also has the year's interest payments to offset against the rise in the price level. The calculation still holds, but it is not quite as extreme as it looks at first sight.

Interrogation #9

Q. And why was Keynes so interested in all of this?

A. Remember that all of this discussion of the Gibson paradox appears in the *Treatise on Money*. Keynes provides an explanation by means of his "fundamental equations". Also recall that he is trying to explain a slump, and the behaviour of falling prices an interest rates, not on inflation. He is also trying to justify an expansionary monetary policy, even though it seems not to be working. He thus argues that if the money rate of interest is too high, and the monetary authority is too slow in adjusting to the lowered level of the natural rate, then saving will be continually running ahead of investment and there will be what he called a "profit deflation", which eventually leads into an "income deflation". This implies that falling interest rates will accompany a falling price level.

Q. But how does that support the role of expansionary monetary policy?

A. It allows him to argue that the low interest rate policy has not gone far enough, that a policy "à outrance" would be necessary to get the money rate down to the natural rate and bring about a return to stability.

Q. And where does the business of capital values of bonds come into all this?

A: "It happens that on this occasion when, if I am right, one of the conditions limiting the open-market operations *à outrance* does not exist; for it is not an occasion -- at least not yet-- when bonds are standing at a price above reasonable expectations as to their long-term normal, so that they can still be purchased without the prospect of a loss. Not until deliberate and vigorous action has been taken along such lines as these and has failed, need we, in the light of the argument of this Treatise, admit that the Banking System can *not*, on this occasion, control the rate of investment and, therefore, the level of prices" (*Treatise on Money*, Vol. II, p. 387). To get prices to stabilise and then rise, interest rates have to go down. But, Gibson says it can't be done. Keynes thus has to show why Fisher's explanation of inflation adjusted rates will not be valid. This he does by pointing to the beneficial effect of falling interest rates on capital values.

But this creates an unexpected counterargument to his own theory. What happens if bond yields cannot be further reduced, such that bond values cannot be further increased? The passage just quoted is from the conclusion to the *Treatise*, and it looks very much like saying, given the level of bond prices relative to what they are expected to be in normal conditions this is not likely to occur, or that 'there is currently no liquidity trap'.

Interrogation #10

Q. So, that's the end of the story?

A. Not quite. You will have recognised that the Gibson paradox has a life of its own and in some form or other is still alive and well in most of the world's central banks and in most bond houses. They all believe that higher inflation produces higher long-term interest rates -- this is what motivates the so-called "bond market vigilantes" who push up long-term bond interest rates whenever they think inflation is about to rise, and the Fed, which puts up short rates whenever it thinks that inflationary pressure is about to appear, in the hopes of forestalling the rise in long rates, or even causing them to come down.

Q. That's not what I meant. What about the Keynes and Fisher story?

A. Well, in the *General Theory* Keynes makes the same criticism of Fisher. But, there is also a strange passage in which he actually makes the calculation of the break-even point between the impact of higher interest rates on the capital value of a bond and the increase in interest earned on the reinvested coupon payments. This is the "square rule" which says that if the rate of interest is expected to rise by the square of itself, then the loss in capital value on a bond will just offset the coupon interest received from owning the bond, leaving the investor with a zero annual yield. Clearly, if the rise in the rate of interest is imposed in order to compensate for an equal rise in the inflation rate, then the investor clearly is not being very efficient in protecting against the loss in real purchasing power due to the higher rate of inflation.

Q. You mean that the interest rate would have to rise by more than the inflation rate?

A. Yes, but every increase in the interest rate produces an increasing fall in capital value, and since the coupon rate is fixed, you can never get there from here -- it can't work. Thus, in such conditions you cannot insure an investor that his real return will be protected -- Fisher offered a contract which could not be honoured. This is the chain of ideas which eventually produced the liquidity trap, and the motivation for the speculative demand for money.

Q. And duration?

A. Keynes never mentions it. And Macauley never mentions the *General Theory*. Hicks does mention Keynes, but he never mentions duration, or Macauley.

Interrogation #11

Q. But, Hicks published his book after Macauley. How did Hicks get into all this?

A. Remember that Hicks' contribution appears in his presentation of "dynamic" theory, or better his prelude to dynamic theory in the form of temporary equilibrium in which there are transactions which occur across "weeks". He had already been working on this theory when Keynes's book came out, and he tells us that he quit when he read Keynes, as it had all been done. Well, he eventually changed his mind.

One of the points he makes is that income is not an appropriate concept for dynamic theory. This is because it is extremely difficult to give a precise definition of income when some of income is composed of fixed income securities resulting from long-term borrowing and lending. If income is defined as what an individual can consume without impoverishing himself, there are a number of ways this idea can be expressed. It could be the expenditure that leaves the present value of his future net receipts constant, or it could be the amount that can be spent in perpetuity (recall the assumption of constant income through time in the spread theory), this either in nominal or real terms. Now, what happens to income when there is a change in the rate of interest? Or the rate of inflation? Take the former. A rise in the rate of interest increases the income from investment, so that expenditure may rise if capital is being reinvested each week. But, if it is invested for a number of weeks, then possible expenditure can rise by less. Thus two individuals with the same earned income and capital position will be affected differently by a change in the rate of interest depending on whether they have invested long or short-term.

Q. How will they be affected?

A. This is the point, and it will depend on the impact of higher interest rates on capital values relative to the higher incomes from reinvesting at a higher interest rate. To solve this problem, amongst others, Hicks defines what he calls the "average period" to measure a standard stream of income. He takes the actual expected income stream, and calculates the net present value of that stream at the current rate of interest (on the standard assumption that the yield curve is flat). He then asks what constant income stream would produce the same present value, given the same current rate of interest. This is the "standard stream". Changes in the rate of interest will change the present value of both the actual and the standard stream. Income will increase if the change in the rate of interest changes the present value of the actual stream by more for an increase, or less for a decrease, than it changes the standard stream.

Q. And how can you decide this?

A. Hicks's entire theory is built on substitution and complementarity. He thus looks at the interest elasticity of the two definitions of income. The answer thus depends on the relative elasticities. If the actual income has an interest elasticity which is greater, then a fall in the rate of interest (Hicks in fact works with the discount factor, one over one plus the rate of interest) will increase actual income more than standard income and the individual will be better off as a result of the change in the interest rate. This elasticity is defined as the "average period" of the income stream and represents "the average length of time for which the various payments are deferred from the present, when the times of deferment are weighted by the discounted values of the payments" (p. 186). A comparison of the average periods of the standard and actual income will determine the impact of changes in the rate of interest on income. If the average period of actual income is greater, then a fall in interest will increase income, and a rise decrease it.

Q. That's very interesting -- but very complicated, and seems to have nothing to do with investment or the demand for money.

A. What Hicks does is to use the concept of average period to analyse flows of net income from production plans and investment projects. He notes that the Austrian theory is based on a theory of the average period of these income flows which is unweighted. His average period is weighted by its "distance" in time. He thus proceeds to measure the "capital intensity" of production plans in terms of their "average periods" as follows. Calculate the average period of the flows of periodic net surplus at the ruling rate of interest. Allow the rate of interest to change, and allow entrepreneurs to rearrange the production plan. Recalculate the average period of these flows using the old rate of interest. If the average period is longer, then a lower rate of interest leads to a longer "average period" of production. The Austrian theory turns out to be right.

Q. Wait a minute. Aren't we going way off track here? This is Sraffa and Cambridge capital theory controversies stuff.

A. Exactly. Isn't it interesting how one thing leads to another? Hicks sets up his analysis precisely in order to show that a rise in the rate of interest brings about a decrease in the average period (e.g. all periodic surpluses are positive). But, he also notes that there may be exceptions to this result. If surpluses are concentrated at the beginning and the end of the production plan, or are complementary, or if there is a large risk factor attached to the far-dated surpluses such that increasing risk overwhelms the influence of interest rates then the average period may not increase. He considered these as improbable in practice. On analogy with the analysis of the period of individual income, one would have thought that movement in one way was as likely as the other. But, Hicks is so intent on validating the Austrian theory that he discards them. What is even more interesting is that there is no theory that says that duration will rise when interest rates rise. Indeed, if Hicks had put the question that way, we probably all would have been saved the capital theory controversy!

Interrogation #12

Q. But, wasn't Samuelson in on this capital theory controversy? And on the same side as Hicks? Didn't you say he also discovered duration? And he also got the capital theory part wrong?

A. Samuelson looking at the difference between anticipated and unanticipated changes in interest rates. He made the very simple point that the negative impact of rises in rates can be avoided if they are indeed foreseen, but if they are not they can but increase your lifetime wealth. Higher rates must thus be a good thing, even when the future is not foreseen. Of course, Samuelson was arguing in the absence of perpetuities, so that all long-term bonds would eventually pay off at par, and any interest receipts would now be invested at a higher rate, so that lifetime accumulation would be higher.

Q. So where did duration come in?

A. When applied to a financial institution the problem is one of the impact of interest on its receipts and payments. He thus generalised the proposition by defining the average time period of the sum of the discounted receipts and payments weighted by the time period in which they take place. He could then argue that a rise in the rate of interest would benefit any institution which had a weighted average of disbursements greater than its receipts.

Q. And the capital theory debate?

A. Well, if disbursements are given a minus sign and receipts a plus sign, the lower the net value of the average time period, the greater the benefit of a higher rate of interest. This gives an inverse relation between time period and impact of raising the rate of interest, which is similar to Hicks.

Q. Yes, Hicks. What does Samuelson say about his use of duration?

A. Nothing. Despite using the exact same average period terminology. Nor does he say anything about Keynes. Or Macauley, or anyone else! Honour among thieves.

Interrogation #13

Q. And bond traders still believe in the Gibson thing AND use duration? And economists use duration AND still believe that capital intensity is inversely related to the rate of interest?

A. Of course. Don't you know the aphorism about consistency and small minds? Besides, they have encouragement. For example, Shiller and Siegel have confirmed that the Gibson relation does hold using spectral analysis, but they do not mention any of the problems raised by Macauley concerning the relation between bond maturity and duration and the relevance of the long rates used to test the relation.

Q. But, what is the point of all this correlation and coincidence?

A. You should be able to guess by now. First, Keynes appears to be the first to discover duration, and it plays an important role in his theory and his investment activity. Second, that it is much more important than most economists and financial analysts have suspected. And third, that we might have avoided a great deal of debate and misunderstanding if this had been recognised earlier.

Appendix: Duration and the Square Rule

Keynes argues that an investor will choose to hold money rather than assets when the potential for capital loss per annum on assets exceeds their expected coupon yield per annum. The condition is thus dP-C=0, where dP is the annual cumulative change in price of a perpetual bond, and C its coupon. The price of a perpetual bond is given by its present value, or C/r, where r is the current yield to maturity. The change in price may then be given by the result of multiplying price times the change in the rate of interest, dr, times the modified duration of the bond. For a perpetual bond duration is given by D = (1+r)/r and modified duration by D/(1+r) which reduces to 1/r. Thus dP=P*dr*MD, which can be rewritten as dP= (C/r)*dr*(1/r) = dr * (C/r^2). dP-C=0 thus can be expressed as dr * (C/r^2) - C = 0 which resolves to dr = r-squared as the condition under which dP=C and is simply Keynes' square rule.

The duration of a perpetual bond paying an annual coupon is given by the formula (1+r)/r so that a 4% consol selling at par of 100 and paying a £4 coupon has a duration of 26 years. The modified duration, defined as D/(1+r), which measures the volatility of bond prices, is then 25 years. The change in the price of the 4% par consol is calculated by multiplying modified duration by the current bond price and the result by the change in the bond's yield to maturity. In the case of a 16 basis point rise in the yield from .04 to .0416, the value of the bond will fall by 25*100*.0016 = £4, which is precisely the value of the bond coupon. For any higher increase in interest rates, the fall in the bond's value will exceed the current coupon yield of the bond, producing net losses for the holder. It is this case that Keynes defines as the liquidity trap, for the investor should prefer to hold cash rather than bonds if his expectation is for a rise in interest rates by more than the square of the rate.

This point can also be described in terms of the break even point on the bond. Any change in yield on a bond affects both capital value, and reinvestment income, but in opposite directions. Duration gives the point at which the fall in value is just offset by the increased reinvestment income of the bond's coupons. Thus, the lower the rate of interest, the higher the value of the bond's duration and the longer it takes to recover the fall in capital values with increased reinvestment earnings. At 3% the duration rises to 34.33 years and at 2% to 51 years. At 1% it is 101 years. Thus Keynes' dictum that the lower the rate of interest, the more likely the liquidity trap. However, it should be clear that this does not rule out the existence of a liquidity trap at higher rates. At 8% duration is 13.5 years and modified duration, 12.5 years. A rise in the rate of interest to .0864 would produce a fall in the price of a par 8% consol of 100*12.4*.0064 = £8 which is exactly the coupon value. An expectation of a rise in interest rates of more than 8% then leads to the decision to remain liquid. The expected percent rise in interest (or equivalently, the expected percentage fall in the price of the bond) is however, twice as high as in the case of 4% rates. However, these should be judged relative to recent changes in bond prices. If 8% lies outside of the range given by two standard deviations from the mean of rate changes over the recent past, then it would be just as rational to remain liquid at 8% as it was at 4% in similar conditions of volatility.

However, as rates rise, duration measures become increasingly lower. At a 20% yield to maturity duration falls to six years and modified duration to five years. At 60%, similar to rates paid in Mexico in crisis periods, duration is 2.67 years, so an investor can recover his lost capital value from the reinvested earning on higher interest rates in less than three years. If there is any basis for the interest elasticity of the demand for money, this is it. However, it also suggests that the elasticity will be based on expectations, and that expectations will be based on recent volatility of rates. In a volatile rate environment, it will become more difficult to use changes in interest rates to influence the demand for money.

As rates rise, the square rule produces larger and larger absolute changes in the interest rate, and the use of modified duration to calculate the change in price becomes less and less accurate. The full calculation of the change in the bond price will require the calculation of convexity. It is interesting to note that Hicks, 1939, p. 261, note 2, reproduces the square rule, and notes that it is very likely that returns will be negative, since the fall in capital values will be even greater if changes in risk are taken into account.

References:

Fisher, Irving *The Rate of Interest*, New York: Macmillan, 1907.

———— *The Theory of Interest*, New York: Macmillan, 1930.

Harvey, Campbell, "Forecasting Economic Growth with the Bond and Stock Markets," *Financial Analysts Journal*, Sept/Oct. 1989.

Hicks, J.R. *Value and Capital*, Oxford, 1939.

Homer, Sidney and Martin L. Leibowitz *Inside the Yield Book: New Tools for Bond Market Strategy*, New York: Prentice-Hall, 1972.

Keynes, J.M. *A Treatise on Money*, London: Macmillan, 1930.

———— *A General Theory of Employment, Interest and Money*, London: Macmillan, 1936.

Macauley, Federick R. *The Movements of Interest Rates, Bond Yields and Stock Prices in the United States Since 1856*, New York, National Bureau of Economic Research, 1938.

Estrello, Arturo and Federic S. Mishkin "The Yield Curve as a Predictor of U.S. Recessions, *Current Issues in Economics and Finance*, Federal Reserve Bank of New York, June, 1996.

Samuelson, P. "The Effect of Interest Rate Increases on the Banking System", *American Economic Review*, March, 1945.

Shiller, Robert. J. and J. J. Siegel, "The Gibson Paradox and Historical Movements in Real Interest Rates", *Journal of Political Economy*, Vol. 85, 1977.

Chapter 14

FISHER'S RELATION, PURCHASING POWER PARITY AND THE INTEREST RATE PARITY THEOREM (INCLUDING COVERED AND UNCOVERED INTEREST ARBITRAGE)

Fisher's question: If the price of wheat in terms of gold rises at a rate d per period, and the rate of interest on gold is i = 10% per period and the rate of growth of wheat is j = 4% per period, what is the relation between i and j that must be paid to lenders to make them indifferent between denominating the loan contract in gold or wheat.

	today = t_0	tomorrow = t_1
Gold	1D	D(1 + i)
Wheat	1B	B(1 + j)
Price	1B = 1D	1B = D(1 + d) or B(1 − d) = 1D

Being indifferent means lending either 1D or 1B today and receiving either D(1 + i) or B(1 + j) at the end of the period, or D(1 + i) = B(1 + j). Since B = D(1 + d) this can be rewritten as D(1 + i) = D(1 + d)(1 + j) substituting for B. Simplifying yields the Fisher relation for the rate of inflation of the price of wheat in terms of gold that would leave lenders indifferent between lending in gold or wheat:

$$i = (1 + d)(1 + j) = j + d + dj \text{ which simplifies to } i = j + d \text{ since dj will be small.}$$

If we use the rates assumed above, then 0.10 = 0.04 + d + 0.04 d or
0.10 − 0.04 = 1.04 d
0.06 = 1.04 d
d = 0.577 or money must depreciate in terms of purchasing power by 5.77% relative to wheat.

The same result can be reached on the basis of a market arbitrage:
Borrow 1B of wheat today and sell it for 1D of gold.
Lend the gold to receive 1.10D gold at the end of the period.
Buy 1.04 B of wheat for 1.04D
Repay wheat loan and interest of B(1.04)
Keep the difference in Profit of 1.10D − 1.04D = 0.06D

	today = t_0	tomorrow = t_1
Borrow B	+1B	−B(1 + j)
Sell B	1D = −1B	
Lend D	−1D	+ D(1 + i)
Buy (1 + j) B		−D(1+j)= +B(1+j)
IF		iB = 1D
NET O		D(1+i)-D(i+j) = ij = 0.10 − 0.04 = 0.06D

To eliminate this arbitrage profit, either the cost of wheat in terms of money today will have to fall or will have to rise tomorrow to eliminate the 6% arbitrage profit. If the rate of inflation is 5.77% as given above, then

	today = t_0	tomorrow = t_1
Borrow B	+1B	−B(1 + j)
Sell B	1D = −1B	
Lend D	−1D	+ D(1 + i)
NOW	1B = (1 +d)D	
Buy (1 +j)B		−D(1+j)(1+d) = +B(1+j)
NET 0		D(1+i)−D(i+j)(1+d) = i−(j+d+jd)
		0.10−(0.04 + 0.577 + 0.231) = 0.0D

Alternatively, if the spot (t_0) price of wheat in terms of gold had adjusted we would have:

	today = t_0	tomorrow = t_1
NOW	1B = [1/(1 + d)]D	1B = 1D

note: the current price of wheat in money rises by (1+d) to reach 1 and [1/(l+d)]* (1+d) = 1

Borrow 1B	+1B	−B(1 +j)
Sell 1B	[1/(1−d)]D= −1B	
Lend D	−[l/(l−d)]D	+ D[l/(1−d)](1+i)
Buy (1 +j)B		−D(1+j) = +B(1+j)
NET	0	D[1/(l+d)](1+i) − D(1 + j) = (1+i)/(1+d) − 1+j
		1.10/1.577 − 1.04 = 1.04 − 1.04 = 0.0D

Note the original question that is being asked: "what is the relation between i, j and d that would leave you indifferent between lending in gold and wheat" with the second question, which is: "what is the rate of inflation that would eliminate free market arbitrage if i and j were given".

Finally, note that there is another question that can be asked, and that is: "if d and j are given, what is the interest rate on gold that would be produced". This is the natural question to ask if you believe that the rate of inflation is given by the formula MV = PT, as Fisher clearly did. In that case, the Fisher relation gives the money or nominal rate of interest as $i = j + d + jd$. Since j is considered to be a "real" rate (the rate of growth of wheat say) then the nominal rate of interest is determined by the rate of inflation and Fisher can argue that the rate of interest is not reduced when the quantity of money is increased, as in a simply supply and demand analysis, but that interest rates are HIGH when money is in excess supply and thus have to be explained by his own theory of Impatience and Investment Opportunity.

Another Question

Once we start asking these type questions there are a number of additional possibilities. What if we are concerned not about loan contracts denominated in two different standards, but about the real value of contracts denominated in two different currencies. If we assume that we want to be able to buy one bushel of wheat at the end of the period and that $i = 4\%$, $j = 10\%$ at home and the rate of inflation of foreign money with respect to wheat is zero because in the foreign country $i^* = j^* = 4\%$ then

	today = t_0	tomorrow = t_1
Dollars	1D	D(1 + d)
DM	1DM	DM(1+d*) (d* = 0)
Price	1D=1DM	1DM = D(1 + k)
Exchange rate	D/DM = 1	D(1+k)/DM

Then we will be indifferent between being paid in either currency when D(1 + d)=DM(1+d*); substituting this becomes D(1+d) = D(1+k)(1+d*). When $d^* = 0$ the rate of inflation of the DM (decline in purchasing power of the Dollar) must be equal to the rate of inflation (decline of domestic purchasing power) or $d = k$. When $d > d^* > 0$ then $d = d^* + k + d^*k$ or the rate of appreciation of the DM (depreciation of the dollar) is $k = d - d\$ - d^*k$, or the change in the exchange rate is determined by the relative rates of inflation in the two countries. This is what is better known as **Purchasing Power Parity** (PPP).

There is also an arbitrage argument that supports this proposition.

today = spot = t_0	tomorrow = forward = t_1
Buy German B for forward delivery	−1DM
Import German B	1B
Sell German B in US	+ D(1 + d)
Buy 1 DM to pay for B	−1D=1DM
IF	1D = 1DM
NET 0	D(1 + d)−D = dD = 0.577D

Of course, neglecting transport and other carry costs. To eliminate the arbitrage the price of DM has to change to D(1+k)

today = spot = t_0	tomorrow = forward = t_1
Buy German B for forward delivery	−1DM
Import German B	1B
Sell German B in US	+ D(1 + d)
Buy 1 DM to pay for B	−(1+k)D=1DM
NOW	(1+k)D = 1DM
NET 0	D(1+d)−D(1+k) = (d−k)D = 0

So, under purchasing power parity, exchange rates are such that you would be indifferent to receive payment in either currency and there is no incentive to import or export similar goods, i.e. there should be no intra industry trade, unless exchange rates depart from PPP.

Again, note that if d is determined by rates of monetary growth, k is also determined by money growth. This is the source of the monetary approach to the balance of payments. If money growth drives up domestic prices, then foreign goods become relatively cheap and a negative foreign balance builds up, putting downward pressure on the currency. The exchange rate and the balance of payments will only be in equilibrium when the rates of money growth in the two countries are similar. It is also the source of the idea that domestic prices and the exchange rate will be stable in a floating exchange rate regime if the domestic money supply grows at a constant rate equal to that of the country's trading partners.

Another Question

We really fudged part of the problem in working out the PPP when we set the foreign interest rates to equality with domestic rates. What happens when they are not the same? Then we have the same question that we started out with above, except now instead of gold and wheat we will have dollars, D, and Deutsche Marks, DM, and instead of gold and wheat interest rates we will have US, i, and German, i*, interest rates, and instead of the price of wheat in terms of gold, we will have the price of a DM in terms of dollars. The question then becomes, what is the appreciation (deflation) or depreciation (inflation) of the dollar that will make lenders indifferent between denominating loan contracts in dollars or DM.

	spot = t_0	forward = t_1
Dollar	1D	D(1 +i)
DM	1DM	B(1 +i*)
Exchange Rate	1D=1DM	D(1 + d) = 1 DM

Being indifferent means lending either 1D or 1DM today and receiving either D(1 + i) or DM(1 +i*) at the end of the period, or D(1 + i) = DM(1 + i*). Since DM = D(1 + d) this can be rewritten as D(1 + i) = D(1 + d)(1 + i*) substituting for DM. Simplifying yields the Fisher relation for the rate of inflation of the DM in terms of the Dollar (depreciation of the Dollar) that would leave lenders indifferent between loan contracts in DM or Dollars:

$i = (1 + d)(1 + i^*) = i^* + d + di^*$ which simplifies to $i = i^* + d$ since di^* will be small.
If we use the rates assumed above, then if $i = 0.10$ and $i^* = 0.047$
$0.10 = 0.04 + d + 0.04d$ or
$0.10 - 0.04 = 1.04\,d$
$0.06 = 1.04\,d$
$d = 0.577$ or the dollar must depreciate in terms of purchasing power over the DM by 5.77%.

The same result can be reached on the basis of a market arbitrage:
Borrow 1DM today and buy 1D.
Lend the 1D and receive 1.10D at the end of the period.
Buy 1.04 DM for 1.04D
Repay the DM loan and interest of DM(1.04)

Keep the difference in Profit of 1.10D−1.04D = 0.06D

	spot = t_0	forward = t_1
BorrowDM	+1DM	−DM(1 +i*)
Sell B	1D = −1DM	
Lend D −1D	+D(1 + i)	
Buy (1+i*) DM		−D(1+i*)= +DM(1+i*)
IF	1D= 1DM	
NET	0	D(1+i)−D(i+i*) = i−i* = 0.10−0.04 = 0.06D

To eliminate this arbitrage profit, either the cost of DM in terms of spot dollars today will have to fall or will have to rise in terms of forward dollars to eliminate the 6% arbitrage profit. If the rate of depreciation is 5.77% as given above' then

today = t_0	tomorrow = t_1
Borrow DM +1DM	−DM(1 + i*)
Sell B 1D = −1DM	
Lend D −1D	+ D(1 + i)
NOW 1DM = (1 +d)D	
Buy (1 +i*)DM	−D(1+i*)(1+d) = +DM(1+i*)
NET 0	D(1+i)-D(i+i*)(1+d) = i−(i*+d+i$d)
	0.10−(0.04+0.577+0.231)=00D

Now, the value of d that we have derived is the inflation in the cost of DM that is required to offset its lower rate of return, but in the foreign exchange market it is called the premium of the D M forward over spot.

Recall that the rate of interest was defined as the premium of a forward dollar over a spot dollar 1D is spot, D(1+i) is the forward price, and the rate of interest is the difference between Forward and Spot per cent or $F_{(t,T)} - S_{(t)} / S_{(t)} = D(1+i) - D/D = i$. What we are looking for is the equivalent relation for the foreign exchange market, the premium or discount of DM for forward delivery over spot DM as $F_{(t,T)} - S_{(t)} / S_{(t)} = [D(1+d) - D]/D$ so $F_{(t,T)} = S_{(t)}(1+d)$

If we take $D(1 + i) = D(1 + d)(1 + i^*)$ and solve for d we get
$D(1+d) = D(1+i)/(1+i^*)$

or $d = (1+i)/(1+i^*) - 1 = 5.77\%$ so a DM for forward delivery sells as a premium of 5.775 over its spot price of \$1 and the forward price is \$1.577: $S_{(t)} * (1.577) = F_{(t,T)} = 1.577$.

We can ask another question about the forward rate. What would you charge a client who asked you to make available 1 DM at the end on the period? If you are a US bank and don't have DM you would Borrow 1D

Buy 1DM at the spot rate of D/DM = 1
Lend DM forward in return for DM (1+i*)
Receive DM (1+i*) which you would have available for your client.
This is in fact more DM than is required so you could
Borrow only 1D/(1+i*) dollars
Buy 1DM/(1+i*)
Lend 1DM/(1+i*) forward for a return of [DM/(1+i*)]* (1+i*) = 1 DM which is what you require.

Your cost in addition to the Spot rate of D/DM = 1 are the cost of the borrowed dollars or $F_{(t,T)} = S_{(t)} [(1+i)/(1+i^*)]$

Now, when would your client be indifferent between buying forward DM in the forward market and producing forward DM by borrowing dollars and lending DM?

If $F_{(t,T)} = S_{(t)}(1+d) = S_{(t)} [(1+i)/(1+i^*)]$,
or $S_{(t)}(1+d) = S_{(t)}[(1+i)/(1+i^*)]$,
(which is equivalent to $D(1+d) = D(1+i)/(1+i^*)$ derived above, substituting $S_{(t)}$ for D the dollar price of a DM or the spot exchange rate)
or $(1+d)(1+i^*) = (1+i)$,
or $(1+d+i^*+i^*d) = (1+i)$,
or $1 + d(1+i^*) + i^* = 1+i$
or $d(1+i^*) + i^* = i$
or $d(1+i^*) = i - i^*$

or $d = (i - i^*)/(1+i^*)$ which is the normal version of the **Interest Rate Parity Theorem.** It says that the difference between spot and forward delivery as a rate will be determined by the interest rate differentials between the two currencies. appreciation or depreciation of the currency will be determined by the interest rate differential between the two currencies. When forward rates are used to cover an interest rate arbitrage position it is called CIA: Covered Interest Rate Arbitrage. When there is no forward cover used it is Uncovered interest rate arbitrage, and the presumption is that expectations are that the exchange rate will not appreciate by more than the interest rate differential.

Thus we have three relations that come from the original question:

Fisher Relation determined by interest rate differentials in different standards: i = p + j+ pj p = i j − pj
(and for a foreign country p* = i*j*−p*j*)
Purchasing Power Parity determined by inflation rate differentials p = $S_{(t)}$ p* or $S_{(t)}$ = p/p* or
$S_{(t)}$ = (i− j − pj)/ (i*j*−p*j*)
Interest Rate Parity determined by international interest rate differentials in different currencies:
d = (i−i*)/(1+i*) or substituting
$F_{(t,T)}$ = $S_{(t)}$ [(1+i)/(1+i*)] = [(i j − pj)/ (i*j*−p*j*)] * [1+(1+p)(1 + j)]/[1+(1+p*)(1+j*)].

The j's are exogenous, the p's are given by money supply growth and the i's are given by money supply through inflation rates. Thus, Fisher provides a complete theory of prices, interest rates and foreign exchange rates on the basis of the quantity theory of money, the theory of impatience and investment opportunity!

Chapter 15

ASPECTS OF A POST KEYNESIAN THEORY OF FINANCE

Unlike other postwar interpretations, the Post Keynesian approach starts with a "monetary" theory of production. Keynes introduced this terminology to emphasize the fact that money was not a "veil," but a "real" factor determining production decisions in a modern economy. Not only was this approach innovative in its treatment of money, it built on Keynes' original formulations of a number of basic propositions in the theory of finance. In addition to the well-known "finance motive," Keynes employed his original theory of interest rate parity and carried out his analysis in terms of forward, futures, and options contracts. Economists working in the Keynesian tradition have usually chosen to ignore these aspects of Keynes' work, while finance theorists have incorporated them into their basic theory and instead concentrate on Keynes' approach to probability, dismissing it as based on a "subjective" approach.[1]

This essay calls attention to Keynes' contributions to the modern theory of finance that might serve in the development of a Post Keynesian approach to finance. Three areas are highlighted. The first is the treatment of expectations, and inevitably, the relationship between risk and uncertainty. The second is the importance of this diverse approach to expectations for the determination of prices, in particular of financial assets. The third is the reciprocal of the theory of asset price formation as found in the theory of interest, and in particular the explanation of the yield curve.

The theory of monetary production: the influence of changing views about the future

> A monetary economy . . . is essentially one in which *changing views about the future* are capable of influencing the quantity of employment and not merely its direction. But our method of *analysing the economic behaviour of the present under the influence of changing ideas about the future* is one which depends on the interaction of supply and demand, and is in this way linked up with our fundamental theory of value. [Keynes, 1936, p. vii, emphasis added]

The characteristic feature is that "changing ideas about the future" have a determinant influence on present decisions. The first requirement for a theory of monetary production is thus specification of the way the "changing ideas about the future" are formulated.

Expectations, risk, and uncertainty

The modern approach to the formulation of expectations under uncertainty considers the problem as similar to gambling (see Bernstein, 1996). In this approach, expectations emerge from the theory of statistical inference. It tells us how to evaluate the expectation that a sample statistic represents a population parameter in terms of a probability. But the expectations that are formed are not of future conditions, but of how well a sample statistic predicts an unchanging population parameter on the basis of limited current information. The theory is based on repeated random sampling with replacement of a known and defined population of potential events. In simple terms, what is sought is a "reliable" estimate of the frequency distribution of the population. This provides a view about the future only because the population is unchanging through time, so that predicting the current value is also predicting the value at any past or future date.

To deal with temporal sampling from the population, it is assumed that a stationary stochastic process produces realizations that are equivalent to random sampling with replacement. The same statistical procedures can then be used to estimate the frequency distribution and form expectations of the likelihood of particular realizations of the process, just as we do with an urn of colored balls or the results of the spin of the roulette wheel. But, Keynes warns us, "When the capital development of a country becomes a by-product of the activities of a casino, the job is likely to be ill-done" (1936, p. 159). We might paraphrase this to say that, when the formation of expectations in economics becomes the byproduct of the statistical analysis of gambling, it is likely to be ill done. Keynes clearly had something else in mind. He proposed a different "method of analysing" behavior based on the idea of "rational belief." Since "beliefs" are considered by definition to be "subjective," the juxtaposition with rational was meant to highlight the difference in the method of analysis in the same way that money was proposed as a "real" factor of analysis.

It is in the nature of statistical populations to be comprised of objects or events, and it is the nature of objects or events to be "objective." An object is or it is not, an event occurs or it does not, no belief or subjective interpretation is required, just application of a definition of an event and a set of rules called "scientific" observation. A coin is a head or a tail, prices go up, or down, or stay constant. Given the "objective" definition of an occurrence, we arrive quickly at an expectation based on the probability that the sample statistic represents a population parameter. If that event is associated with a payoff to which we can attach a measure such as utility, we have its "expected value," which serves as a basis for rational investment decisions to maximize net wealth.

An obvious criticism is that the uncertainty faced in "real" life[2] is unlike the uncertainty over the outcomes of games of chance, because there is no possibility of random sampling with replacement. What G.L.S. Shackle (1955) called a "crucial experiment" can never be repeated to a sufficient number of realizations to insure statistical significance since its realization changes the underlying structure of the system. A corollary is that individuals taking decisions in the "real" world, unlike gamblers in Monte Carlo, will not be able to specify fully the relevant population of possible outcomes. Shackle thus emphasizes the role of "imagination," or Austrian "purposive action," in taking decisions on less than complete information that change the population from which observations are drawn, and thus the potential outcomes in ways that are inherently unpredictable.[3] Clearly, if the underlying population is not constant, there is no possibility of forming a sample statistic based on expectation of the frequency distribution, irrespective of whether there is sampling with replacement at a given point in time, and no expectation of the likely occurrence of specific realizations can be formed on the basis of standard statistical methods.[4]

Paul Davidson has extended this line of criticism by emphasizing the difference between the processes that generate the realizations that satisfy the requirements of statistical theory,[5] and those processes that produce events that Shackle classified as "unique" or "crucial," about which statistical theory can say nothing. This shifts the criticism from the events themselves to the processes or relationships that produce them. Davidson argues that, since most events of interest to economists are produced by nonstationary, nonergodic processes, the standard theory of statistics cannot be applied.

These criticisms leave the possibility that the standard theory may be applied to any series of realizations that does exhibit (or can be massaged to exhibit via differencing or some other procedure) the necessary stochastic properties. Thus, while most economists accept these criticisms, they nonetheless argue that they do not apply to the vast majority of economic events, such as the behavior of asset prices, because long time series representing repeated realizations do exist and it is possible for these series to be tested to determine whether they come from a stationary stochastic process. A well-known process is a white noise series called a random walk. If asset prices exhibit this property, then standard statistical methods could be justified to provide estimates of means and variances, and expectations of occurrences can be made. In this way the realizations are themselves used to decide whether the characteristics of the underlying population are constant through time, even if its individual components are constantly being renewed.

But it would be totally inappropriate to conclude that since some series of events may be shown to have been produced by an ergodic process that the traditional approach to expectations formation can be retained for these processes. Keynes' idea was that the theory of expectations formation does not relate primarily to "objects" or events or realizations, but instead to the complex of factors that produce the events and realizations. Even if an ergodic process produces a stationary series of realizations, we may nonetheless be uncertain about the specification of that particular process relative to alternative specifications. In Keynes' alternative method of analysis of probability, it is not the estimation of the frequency distribution of events or the occurrence of objects that is at issue, but rather the estimation of the probability that a particular specification of the process has actually produced the events that are observed. Expectation formation does not concern the realization of a particular event from a set of possible events (e.g., whether the coin will come up heads or tails or the die will produce snake eyes), but of the theory explaining the occurrence of the event (e.g., how a particular combination of muscle movements and bend of the elbow will produce a head or a tail).[6]

The means by which these expectations are formed is not random, nor is it subjective. "A proposition," Keynes argued, "is not probable because we think it so. When once the facts are given which determine our knowledge, what is probable or improbable in these circumstances has been fixed objectively, and is independent of our opinion. The theory of probability is logical, therefore, because it is concerned with the degree of belief which is rational to entertain in given conditions, and not merely with the actual beliefs of particular individuals, which may or may not be rational" (Keynes, 1973, VIII, p. 4). This "logical probability" or degree of "rational belief" is defined as follows: "Let our premises consist of any set of propositions *h*, and our conclusion consist of any set of propositions *a*, then, if a knowledge of *h* justifies a rational belief in *a* of degree α, we say that there is a probability-relation of degree α between *a* and *h*" (Keynes, 1973, VIII, p. 4).[7] Expectations are formed as "rational beliefs" concerning a proposition when knowledge of it is not certain.

Keynes considers two ways in which rational belief about a proposition may be reached when perfect knowledge is not available. The first is based on the formulation of a probability reached on the basis of uncertain information, or of "doubtful arguments" (Keynes, 1973, VIII, p. 3). In the second, it is impossible to determine a rational belief. In this case, it is "rational" to allow "animal spirits" to determine actions. It is precisely these two types of uncertainty that traditional theory excludes by assuming that individuals have full or certain knowledge of what Keynes calls the "primary proposition" that one seeks to validate.

The evaluation of the evidence relative to a proposition is thus extremely important in expectations formation. "As the relevant evidence at our disposal increases, the magnitude of the probability of the argument may either decrease or increase, according as the new knowledge strengthens the unfavourable or the unfavourable evidence; but something seems to have increased in either case—we have a more substantial base upon which to rest our conclusion. I express this by saying that an accession of new evidence increases the weight of the argument" (Keynes, 1973, VIII, p. 77). When Keynes evokes the role of confidence in the discussion of how "changing ideas of the future" influence the present decision to undertake an investment in chapter 12 of the *General Theory,* it is the "weight of the argument" that he has in mind (Keynes, 1973, VII, pp. 148–149). This weight is the determining factor in deciding whether to act on the basis of the probability of a proposition. Animal spirits will determine the moment at which the weight of the argument attached to a proposition is sufficient to make it dominant over all other possible propositions and make it the object of the "spontaneous urge to action rather than inaction."[8] It is important to note that Keynes insists that this does not mean that decisions depend on "waves of irrational psychology" (Keynes, 1973, VII, p. 162), but, rather, that this type of decision is securely founded in "rational spirits" (see Kregel, 1987, p. 526), by "our *rational* selves choosing between the alternative as best we are able, calculating where we can, but often falling back for our motive on whim or sentiment or chance" (Keynes, 1973, VII,p. 163, emphasis added).

It is difficult to endogenize this process of expectations formation, and as Keynes notes, "the state of long term expectation . . . cannot be inferred from the given factors" (Keynes, 1973, XIII, p. 480) so that these decisions must be considered as being taken outside the "realm of the formally exact"(Keynes, 1973, XIV, p. 2). In such conditions, Keynes suggests that decision makers fall back on their common sense as reflected in "the actual observation of markets and business psychology" (Keynes, 1973, VII, p. 149), rather than on the calculus of statistical probability. Thus, entrepreneurs will first consider their past experience and may presume that "the existing state of affairs will continue indefinitely, except in so far as we have specific reasons to expect a change" (p. 52). Conscious of the lack of information and of the reliability of their individual judgments, entrepreneurs will "fall back on the judgement of the rest of the world which is perhaps better informed" in such a way that behavior permanently conforms to that of the majority or the average, and "the psychology of a society of individuals each of whom is endeavoring to copy the others leads to what we may strictly term a conventional judgement" (Keynes, 1973, XIV, p. 114). It is against this background that Keynes' remark that, "in practice we have tacitly agreed, as a rule, to fall back on what is, in truth, a convention" (Keynes, 1973, VII, p. 152) should be interpreted. Finally, entrepreneurs may admit that the "existing state of opinion" as expressed by the evaluation of the market is the only one that should be considered the "correct summing up of future prospects" (Keynes, 1973, XIV, p. 114). But included in this market evaluation will be "all sorts of considerations ... which are in no way relevant to the prospective yield" (Keynes, 1973, VII, p. 152). In fact, in these conditions, the calculations of agents count for less than their "nerves and hysteria, and even digestions and reactions to the weather" (p. 162).

It thus becomes easier to understand why "ideas about the future" may be "changing" in ways that are impossible for the throw of dice, and are subject to sudden, sometimes violent, changes, marked by waves of optimism and pessimism. From this perspective, the conventional methods of calculation are "compatible with a considerable measure of continuity and stability in our affairs, so long as we can rely on the maintenance of the convention" (Keynes, 1973, VII, p. 152). Expectations may thus be extremely volatile but need not be violently unstable. However, the appearance of new fears and new hopes "will, without warning, take charge of human conduct. The forces of disillusion may suddenly impose a new conventional basis of evaluation" (Keynes, 1973, XIV, p. 115). Thus, even in the most extreme conditions of uncertainty, Keynes rejects purely subjective or random decision making. That his approach to decision making has been termed "irrational" is due to the failure to recognize that the traditional definition of "rationality" does not apply in such conditions.[9]

In place of the "statistics" that provide the expectations of the parameters of the distribution of the population of events, Keynes instead introduces convention, self-reference, reflexivity, and self-reinforcing processes, which may quickly jump from one conventional view to the other (in modern terminology, they may bifurcate). The processes that form the expectations need not be uncertain, they may be perfectly known and discoverable—indeed, that is what his theory of probability was meant to do. Yet, they do not produce predictable behavior or stationary stochastic series. Now, this is precisely the type of behavior that one might expect of a chaotic system. The generating function may be perfectly known, yet its realizations may not be statistically predictable.

How changing ideas about the future influence prices

The theory of expectations formation was required to explain how ideas about future conditions influence present decisions and lead to changes in the level of activity. Keynes thought that his earlier *Treatise on Money* had failed to take this factor into account and, as a result, "failed to deal thoroughly with the effects of *changes* in the level of output. My so-called 'fundamental equations' were an instantaneous picture, taken on the assumption of a given output. They attempted to show how, assuming given output, forces could develop which involved a profit-disequilibrium, and thus required a change in the level of output. But the dynamic development . . . was left incomplete and extremely confused." Since profit-disequilibrium represented a divergence of prices from their "normal" values as given by the "fundamental equations," the most important "dynamic development" left unanswered was whether the price adjustments set in motion by the profit-disequilibrium would automatically eliminate the imbalance or whether it would lead to changes in the level of output and employment.

Keynes' discussion of this process is in a short section on the "short-period theory of prices" in volume II of the *Treatise*. Keynes argued that, if a fall in prices below their "normal" levels, due to an excess of stocks, generated expectations of further declines, then factors determining the normal prices of the fundamental equations (i.e., current costs of production and supply and demand conditions) would become irrelevant because market supplies were dominated by decisions to sell from existing stocks, rather than by production decisions. Ideas about future conditions would then overwhelm current information, and current prices would continue to fall as long as producers believed they could minimize losses by selling today at a price below normal, but higher than the price at which their expectations suggest they will be able to sell tomorrow. Prices would continue to fall until they reached the level at which entrepreneurs could expect to make a competitive return by waiting to sell at a better price at a future date. In such conditions the movement of current short-period prices is completely determined by the "ideas of the future" prices.

The fall in prices would only come to a halt when it was sufficient to produce the expectation that a competitive return could be earned by buying (or holding) existing stocks at the reduced current, or spot, price, and holding them for sale at the normal future or forward price.[10]

Keynes' idea can be seen more clearly by considering a commodity such as wheat. Today, at time t, its current market (spot) price is S_t. The decision to sell today or hold for sale at some future date will be determined by the expectations formed about the future spot price, S^*, expected to prevail at some future date, $t+T$, T days distant. If there is a market where the commodity may be sold for delivery T days forward, the forward price, $F_{t,T}$, quoted today at time t, for delivery at $t+T$ must be sufficiently above S_t in order to cover the cost of holding the commodity for T days. This cost of "carry" may be defined as cS_t. If $F_{t,T}-S_t$ were more than this, a profit could be made by buying the commodity today at the current spot price and simultaneously selling it for forward delivery at price $F_{t,T}$, holding it for T days, and making delivery at $t+T$. The carry cost will include the costs of financing, maintenance, storage, insurance, etc. In a balanced market, $F_{t,T} - (1+c)S_t = 0$ and the present value of the commodity will then be given by $(F_{t,T})/(1+c) = S_t$. The expected spot price should also equal the forward price, so $S^*_{t,T} = F_{t,T}$. If the changing ideas about the future suggest a lower expected spot price, a decision not to sell today incurs not only the cost of carry but also a loss due to sale at the lower expected price. Loss minimization would thus lead to the spot sale of all existing stocks. Even agents who foresee a future need for wheat will minimize their costs by selling today and buying wheat for forward delivery since this is cheaper than holding wheat.

In the *General Theory,* Keynes coined the term "user costs" to make the importance of the expectation of future conditions on present prices more explicit. Since stocks are being held because they are expected to yield a return equal to the difference between their current or "spot" price and the expected normal, or "forward," price, a decision to "use" them (i.e., either as an input in production or by selling them at the current spot price) will eliminate the possibility of realizing this expected future gain. The implicit cost associated with using stocks today rather than holding them is thus the present value of the expected net future return that could be realized by waiting to sell at the expected normal price.[11]

Since the decision not to "use" a commodity is equivalent to retaining the privilege of doing so in future, the decision to hold includes the equivalent of the value of a call option which provides the owner with the right, but not the obligation, to purchase the commodity at a future date or dates at a "strike" price equal to the spot price prevailing when the decision to hold is taken. The evaluation of current costs should thus take into account the "user" costs as reflected in the value of the option. To see this more clearly, consider the owner of wheat who wants to sell (use) today without losing the possibility of a future profit that would result should there be a rise in price. He or she could do so by purchasing a call option with a strike equal to the current spot price. If the price rises, the loss due to the precipitous decision to sell can be reversed by exercising the option, which will have a payoff equal to the difference between the sale price and the now higher price. Thus, the calculation of the "supply price" of the commodity should add the option price, representing user cost, to the sale price.[12] Keynes considered that his major theoretical innovation in the *General Theory* was "the introduction of the concepts of user costs and the marginal efficiency of capital" (1936, p. 146), although he admitted that the latter was not really his own invention.

User costs are often presented as an elaborate calculation of depreciation, or as the difference between the current costs involved in the operation or use of assets relative to the maintenance costs of keeping them idle.[13] But such an interpretation makes no recognition of the role of user costs in expressing the impact of the future on present returns through the appropriate adjustment to supply prices.[14] Given the impact of the future on the present, current costs of production will no longer be relevant to the supply price of existing capital goods, since the costs incurred in the use of existing capital goods cannot be ignored. User costs provide the solution to this problem by defining the cost of using existing capital goods as the difference between the cost of holding them idle (i.e., the cost of keeping them in good productive condition plus interest charges) and the expected net return from using them to produce output in the future. The rate of discount that equates the expected stream of future returns to the cost of producing new capital goods, thus, has to compete with the rate of discount that equates the expected stream of future returns to the supply prices of existing capital goods as determined by user costs. Just as in the short-period theory of the *Treatise,* if the prime cost of using existing capital is below the flow supply price for newly produced capital goods, because their prices are expected to continue to fall, no one will demand new investment goods and investment expenditures will fall.[15]

Thus, Keynes could declare that "[t]he marginal efficiency of capital is of fundamental importance because it is mainly through this factor (much more than through the rate of interest) that the expectation of the future influences the present" (1936, p. 145). And this is because that impact is reflected in the supply prices of capital goods through the specification of the net present value of an investment. Recognizing the possibility of evaluating user costs through option prices provides a response to those who argue that the appropriate futures markets required for Keynes' theory (for example, for second-hand capital goods) will not exist, or that the specification of the expectations that determine forward prices is purely subjective and thus irrational. Thus, instead of saying that supply prices have to be adjusted for user costs, we could say that supply prices that are corrected for the impact of the future on the present should include the appropriately calculated values of the imbedded options.

Note that, while "ideas of the future" enter both the demand and supply sides, the rate of interest also enters into the calculation of demand prices through the specification of the appropriate rate of discount, and it enters supply prices through the impact of the interest cost of carry on user costs. Hence, Keynes' admonition that it is necessary to give "full weight to the importance of the influence of short-period changes in the state of long-term expectations as distinct from changes in the rate of interest" by separating them. It was for this reason that Keynes considered a major difference between the *General Theory* and the *Treatise on Money* the introduction of a distinction between the determinants of the marginal efficiency of capital and the rate of interest (see Keynes, 1936, p. 173). With the newly defined "marginal efficiency" to determine the rate of return on capital goods, liquidity preference, built on the concept of "bearishness" from the *Treatise,* was to determine the rate of interest.

Liquidity preference and the concept of the "liquidity premium" have both caused difficulty in interpretation of Keynes' theory. However, once the concept of user costs is understood as representing the influence of the future in determining the relative costs of holding or using a commodity in production or sale, it seems straightforward to apply it to the decision to hold or use money. Buying investment goods, or consumption goods, or buying financial assets (which includes bank lending to either households or entrepreneurs), or repaying debt means that money will no longer be available to be "used" at a future date when the prices of the assets or goods will be different. The "user cost" of expending money today can then be defined as the present value of the potential future gain or loss that has been foregone or avoided by parting with money today. This future gain or loss will depend on the expected prices of investment goods, consumption goods, and financial assets at future dates. The user cost of money could thus be defined as the equivalent of a call option on a deposit at the current interest rate. Alternatively, holding money uninvested in a portfolio allows you to avoid the sale of an investment asset to meet an unanticipated need for liquid funds. This is equivalent to the value of a put on the investment position written at the expected future appreciation (or depreciation) of the asset. With respect to other financial assets, the user cost of money is the foregone gain (or loss) that could have been earned (or avoided) by waiting to purchase financial assets at lower (higher) prices and higher (lower) yields.

If the "use" of money is defined as becoming "illiquid," then the premium that is required to convince individuals to become illiquid and to part with money is the equivalent of the "user cost" of money. Liquidity preference determines this liquidity "premium" and is thus also a clear expression of the impact of the expectation of the future movement of asset prices on present prices. The rate of interest can then also be represented by the relation between the spot price and the expected future prices of money. Although few textbooks put it this way, no one should be surprised, for Keynes insisted that his definition of the rate of interest, unlike the "real" rate determined by the forces of productivity and thrift in traditional theory, was "nothing more than the percentage excess of a sum of money contracted for forward delivery, e.g., a year hence, over what we may call the 'spot' or cash price of the sum thus contracted for forward delivery" (Keynes, 1936, p. 222).

The complete specification of the monetary production economy in which the changing ideas about the future have an influence on the present thus requires the application of user costs to money as well as commodities and produced current and capital goods. In this context, the question of the determinants of the level of employment would be posed in terms of the returns from the decision to employ labor and produce output relative to the returns from the alternatives, which would include holding money as given by the user cost of money, of holding capital goods (or any other durable) idle in terms of the return as given by user costs, and the return from using the capital goods with labor to produce consumption or investment goods as given by the marginal efficiency of capital. Only if the return on the employment of labor and capital to produce output could be held above all other types of "investment" would capital accumulation take place and employment be provided. Expanding employment would require the appropriate manipulation of user costs, that is, expected future prices, and interest rates (which were also determined by expected future price movements). Thus, the "state of expectations" was not a subjective or irrational assessment of what might occur, but the expression of the anticipated costs of alternative courses of action as expressed in their influence on current market prices. The explanation that Keynes offered of underemployment equilibrium thus turns on the different behavior of supply and demand prices as supplies change, relative to the way financial asset prices respond.[16]

The rate of interest and the yield curve

The implications of Keynes' diverse approach to expectation and price formation can be seen directly with respect to the determination of interest rates. The currently accepted explanation of interest rates is based on expectations of future goods prices relative to present goods prices as expressed in the expected rate of inflation or deflation of goods prices. It is the expected future evolution of inflation that then determines the yield curve. This theory is based on a proposition presented in Irving Fisher's *The Theory of Interest* (1930), that was strictly limited to conditions in which "rational tendencies" were based on "rational and empirical laws . . . analogous to rational and empirical laws of physics and astronomy" (Fisher, 1930, p. 321), that is, on conditions in which statistical procedures could be applied. Outside these limited conditions, where actuarial risk is replaced by what Fisher considered "uncertain" conditions and the value of money is unstable, "We must . . . give up as a bad job any attempt to formulate completely the influences which really determine the rate of interest" (p. 321). These are precisely the conditions that Keynes' approach to uncertainty was designed to analyze.

Aside from these differences, Fisher's approach is very similar to that of Keynes. Both specify the rate of interest on a loan as the price of a spot-forward swap of money, or by the excess of the forward price over the par or spot price. Fisher also recognized that, since there will be spot-forward swaps for different maturities, there will be interest rates referring to different periods extending not only from today to different future dates, but from various future dates to further future dates.[17] More importantly, Fisher, like Keynes (and Sraffa), notes that it is possible to use a spot-forward swap of gold or wheat to produce a rate of interest that could be measured in terms of the commodity itself, and that this makes it necessary "to distinguish between interest expressed in terms of money and interest expressed in terms of other goods. But no two forms of goods can be expected to maintain an absolutely constant price ratio towards each other. *There are, therefore, theoretically just as many rates of interest expressed in terms of goods as there are kinds of goods diverging from one another in value*" (1930, p. 42, emphasis in original).[18]

What is the relation between these different (in chapter 17 of the *General Theory*, Keynes called them "own-rates of own interest") interest rates? Fisher argues that market arbitrage should act to eliminate any changes in the relative values of the standards used to express the multiple possible rates of interest. For example, *if the forward price of wheat were perfectly known* to be at a 10 percent premium to spot, while the forward price of gold were known to be at a 4 percent premium, there would be a preference for wheat that would be expressed by using present stocks of gold (or borrowing gold at 4 percent) to buy wheat at the current spot price, lending the wheat against 1.10 bushels forward. The forward wheat received is then exchanged for 1.10 units of gold to replenish own stocks (or repay the gold loan) with an excess 0.04 units representing a positive carry of 6 percent. If the forward price ratio between gold and wheat is fixed at unity, this would drive up the current price of wheat until it stood at 1.1/1.04 = 1.057 percent premium over gold (if the spot and forward price of wheat in terms of gold is 1:1, then the arbitraged forward price of wheat in money is 1.10/1.04). 1.057 of gold invested at 4 percent just yields 1.10.[19]

In Fisher's approach to the theory of income, the rate of interest represents time preference, not liquidity preference, and its variation brings about the equality of present and future incomes, not of liquidity and illiquidity. Fisher extends the arbitrage process described above to "real income." This leads directly to the "Fisher relation" between monetary and real rates of interest that now underlies monetary policy and dominates the theoretical explanation of the shape of the yield curve.

As noted, there are three factors at work in the process, the appreciation or depreciation of one commodity standard in terms of the other, which we can clearly recognize as the rate of inflation, the rate of interest in terms of the money standard, and the rate of interest in terms of the commodity (now the "real income") standard, representing individuals' time preference for present over future income. If we substitute "real income" for "wheat" and "money" for "gold" in the above example, then the arbitrage of competitive markets implies that it is only possible that the money rate of interest should be 4 percent when the (real) income rate of interest is 10 percent, if money is expected to exchange for 5.8 percent more income (i.e., purchasing power of money increases through a deflation) in the future than in the present so that 1.0578*1.04 = 1.10. The relation between the real and the money interest rates given by the rate of appreciation of the standard thus descends directly from the arbitrage relation that insures that the rate of interest is equal to the rate of return over costs (or from Keynes' interest rate parity theorem).[20] The Fisher relation in which the monetary rate of interest is the real rate corrected for the rate of inflation, that is,

$$(1 + p)(1 + r) = (1 + i),$$

where p is the rate of inflation, r the rate of increase in real income, and i the rate of interest on money, is just a different way of expressing the operation of this arbitrage relation.[21] Fisher notes that the arbitrage process by itself cannot determine the rate of interest, but simply "enables us . . . to calculate the rates in other standards" on the assumption "that the rate in *some one* standard is already known." (Fisher, 1930, p. 45). Thus, one rate has to be given outside the system; for Fisher it is the real rate and for Keynes it is the money rate of interest. Given the money short rate, as set by the central bank or by the user cost of money, it is then possible to derive rates of interest, not only in terms of all commodities, but also for all future periods, which allows the specification of the full yield curve.

Given these remarkable similarities in approach, why did Keynes object to Fisher's relation between the rate of interest and the rate of inflation? First, because it relied on the assumption of perfect foresight for the arbitrage process which establishes the equality of real and nominal rates (see *Treatise on Money*, vol. II, pp. 202–203, and *General Theory*, 1936, pp. 142–143). Second, because Fisher's argument that the money rate of interest should automatically reflect a perfectly foreseen rise in the rate of inflation overlooks the negative impact of a rise in interest rates on the prices of financial assets. While it is true that a perfectly foreseen rise in inflation for the coming year of 2 percent, producing a 2 percent rise in interest rates on one-year Treasury bills, would keep real returns constant, the same would not be true of a holder of a longer-term instrument if it were sold after one year (or even if it were held to maturity). Yet, market arbitrage should ensure that the return should be the same for any instrument (even thirty-year bonds sold one year after purchase) held for one year.

Keynes uses the example of a £100 par value British consol paying a £10 coupon that falls to £81.96 (a decline of 1.8 percent and a capital loss of over £18) when interest rates rise to 12.2 percent. While the "variations in the rate of interest earned during the year in question are too small to make much difference" (e.g., the extra 2.2 percent on the £10 coupon), the holder of fixed interest assets will have a substantial capital loss. The investor will have the benefit of being able to invest the future £10 interest coupon payments at the higher rate of 12.2 percent, but over the year this will not be sufficient to cover the £18 decline in the capital value of the bond, and thus by definition could not compensate for any loss in purchasing power resulting from a rise in the inflation rate equal to the increased rate of interest. Thus, Keynes argues that, for existing bond holders, Fisher's relation goes in the wrong direction since the higher yields required to preserve real yields causes capital losses that more than offset the increased interest earnings. Full inflation coverage would have to provide for an adjustment in capital value as well as to the income from the bond.

Thus, the discussion is led back to the concept of income. Keynes argues that, since the principal value of an existing bond is impaired when interest rates adjust to reflect anticipated inflation, an individual bond holder will have a lower total real income from the original investment. This is particularly easy to see in the case of the consol, for its price is permanently reduced. This provides the basis for Keynes' basic criticism of Fisher's relation, that the most important impact of inflation will be not on the interest rate, but on the prospective earnings from employing capital goods, the incentive to invest—the marginal efficiency of capital. Fisher's account of the impact of a rise in the rate of inflation makes no mention of the impact either on long-term bond values or on the rate of return over costs, that is, on real returns, which Fisher thought remained unaffected. Keynes suggests that there is no reason for this to be the case if money is the "real" factor and real returns adjust to reflect changes in expectations of future conditions.

Keynes builds on this criticism of Fisher when he specifies the determinants of the speculative demand for money in the *General Theory* (Keynes, 1936, p. 202) in terms of the so-called "square rule." Keynes argues that a "rational" investor deciding whether to hold money or a financial asset will always balance the increase in interest earned against the change in capital value when there is a change in the rate of interest. A rational investor chooses to hold money rather than assets when the potential for capital loss per annum on his or her assets exceeds the expected coupon or dividend yield per annum. The breakeven condition for a perpetual bond is thus $\Delta P – C = 0$, where ΔP is the annual cumulative change in price, and C is its annual coupon interest. The price, or present value, of a perpetual bond is C/r, where r is the current yield to maturity and C the coupon. The change in price may then be represented as the result of multiplying price times the change in the rate of interest, Δr, times the modified duration of the bond. For a perpetual bond duration is given by $D = (1 + r)/r$ and modified duration by $D/(1 + r)$ which simplifies to $1/r$. Thus, $\Delta P = P^*\Delta r^*MD$, which can be rewritten as $\Delta P = (C/r)^*\Delta r^*(1/r) = \Delta r * (C/r^2)$. $\Delta P – C = 0$ can thus be expressed as $\Delta r * (C/r^2) – C = 0$ which simplifies to $\Delta r = r^2$ as the condition under which $\Delta P = C$. This is simply Keynes' square rule.[22]

This point can also be described in terms of the breakeven point on the bond. Any change in a bond's yield affects both its capital value and the income from reinvestment of the coupons, but in opposite directions. Duration gives the point at which the change in capital value is just offset by the opposite change in interest income from reinvesting coupon interest at the higher or lower interest rate over the remaining time to maturity of the bond. Thus, the lower the rate of interest, the higher the bond's duration and the longer it takes to recover the fall in capital values from the increased reinvestment earnings. At 3 percent, the duration rises to 34.33 years and at 2 percent to 51 years. At 1 percent it is 101 years. Hence Keynes' dictum that the lower the rate of interest, the more likely the liquidity trap. However, it should be clear that this does not rule out the existence of a liquidity trap at higher rates. At 8 percent, duration is 13.5 years and modified duration, 12.5 years. A rise in the rate of interest to 0.0864 would produce a fall in the price of a par 8 percent consol of 100*12.4*0.0064 = £8, which is exactly the coupon value. An expectation of a rise in interest rates of 8 percent then leads to the decision to remain liquid. The expected percentage rise in interest (or, equivalently, the expected percentage fall in the price of the bond) is, however, twice as high as in the case of 4 percent rates. However, these should be judged relative to recent changes in bond prices. If 8 percent lies within two standard deviations from the mean change in rates over the recent past, then it would be just as rational to remain liquid at 8 percent as it was at 4 percent in similar conditions of volatility.

However, as interest rates rise, *ceteris paribus,* duration falls. At a 20 percent yield to maturity, duration falls to six years and modified duration to five years. At 60 percent, as with interest rates paid in Mexico in the Tequila crisis period, duration is 2.67 years, so an investor can recover his or her lost capital value from the reinvested earnings on higher interest rates in a little over two and a half years. If there is any basis for the interest elasticity of the demand for money, this would appear to be it. However, it also suggests that the elasticity will be based on expectations of future bond prices, and that expectations will be based on recent volatility of rates. In a volatile rate environment, it will become more difficult to use changes in interest rates to influence the demand for money, since they will have to be larger in order to produce an impact.[23]

Here, all Keynes is doing is formalizing the relation between the user cost of money and the rate of interest. Holding money gives a zero interest return, but holding a consol for one year when the rise in the interest rate is expected to exceed the square of itself will mean a return that is negative since the capital loss more than offsets the interest received, the user cost of money is negative, and money will dominate consols in portfolios. It is now possible to extend the reasoning to various holding periods (or to abandon the hypothesis of consols and allow bonds of different maturity) that will be associated with different values of duration. Bonds of longer duration will have a longer time to the breakeven point at which the increased reinvestment yield offsets the capital loss. This explains a positively sloped yield curve, since the risk of capital loss relative to coupon interest is higher, the higher the duration on a bond. Note that the shape of the yield curve then depends on the expectation of changes in prices of longer-term bonds, not the simple extrapolation of expected short yields, as in the traditional Hicksian expectations hypothesis. This does not mean that short rates will not have an impact on the yield curve, only that the traditional Hicksian explanation of the yield curve based on expected future short rates determined by expected future inflation rates leaves out a very important aspect of the expectations that are relevant to bondholders (and bond traders).

The shape and reaction of the yield curve will then be affected by the type of expectations (is the change in rates once over, or expected to continue?) and the holding period of the investor (an investor who holds until maturity will be unaffected by changes in capital value, while a short-term trader will be predominantly interested in capital values). Richard Kahn (1954) draws attention to this latter aspect by noting the importance of the difference between investors' sensitivity to income and capital risk. If all bond investors are widows and orphans who hold to maturity for income (as in Victorian novels), then short-term changes in capital value are unimportant. On the other hand, if markets are dominated by investment banks with leveraged bond portfolios managed to generate short-term proprietary trading gains, changes in capital values will be crucial. The Fisher relation is based on the dominance of widows and orphans, investing on the basis of confidently expected constant real returns on assets they expect to buy and hold. The Keynes-Kahn approach, on the other hand, emphasizes the impact of interest rates on asset prices and of interest rates on the cost of carry of bond portfolios, and thus seems more appropriate to modern capital market conditions. Here, it is the expected future long rate that influences the demand for short-term funds, because the expected capital gains determine the size of the portfolio to be financed by borrowing short-term funds through repos of the bonds. The level of short rates, thus, influences the costs of accessing these capital gains through the costs of carry. The shape of the yield curve is determined by expectation of changes in long rates relative to the short borrowing rate. Monetary policy, which can only influence short rates, can influence the shape of the yield curve, and thus long rates, to the extent that it is capable of influencing expectations of changes in long rates. That is, by influencing the estimates of the future that determine present prices. This need have nothing to do with expectations of future inflation rates, unless the central bank reaction function suggests that changes in short rates are an indicator of future changes in inflation. Nor need it have anything to do with a constant, exogenously determined, expected real return. However, because changes in interest rates change the carry on levered bond positions, and thus the profitable arbitrage possibilities for market makers and speculators, they will also have an influence on long rates. Not through inflation premia, or short-term expectations, but by changing the cost of financing a levered portfolio. By reducing the spread between short and long rates, it reduces the running yield in the form of the positive carry, relative to the expected change in capital values. Which is simply an application of the two component elements of the square rule.

Conclusion

The combination of Keynes' new method of analyzing expectations and the proper calculation of prices through the inclusion of user costs provides the basis for a monetary theory of production in which changing ideas about the future influence present production decisions. It also provides a theory of asset prices that is "linked up with our fundamental theory of value" and provides the basis for a Post Keynesian theory of finance.

Notes

1 This line starts with Hicks's early work on risk, which took definitive form in his *Value and Capital* (1939), and is further developed by Tobin in "Liquidity Preference as Behavior

towards Risk" (1958), which played a seminal part in the development of the modern theory of finance (see Bernstein, 1996, pp. 69–70). Bernstein considers Keynes as highlighting the subjective evaluation of outcomes, and thus with the expected utility tradition. A linkage between money and finance based on Tobin's work was attempted by Moore's *Money in a Theory of Finance* (1968).

2 Keynes drew a distinction between analysis of an economy "subject to change, but where all things are foreseen from the beginning" and "the problems of the *real world* in which our previous expectations are liable to disappointment and expectations concerning the future affect what we do to-day" (Keynes, 1936, pp. 293–294, emphasis added).

3 Another way of looking at this point is that the population being sampled is time-dependent. This is the basis of the idea behind the Post Keynesian insistence that time is important, and irreversible.

4 In Bernstein's (1996) version of these events, even if there is mean reversion, it is impossible to know the mean value at any point in time since it is continuously changing.

5 And to which economic analysis should be restricted according to the approach of rational expectations.

6 This is what a stock analyst does when he or she justifies his expectations of a stock's future price. He has a theory about what determines the price, and expectations are formed about that "theory" relative to the alternative explanations of other analysts, not about the probability that the actual stock price will be 100 or 50 based on past behavior of the price. This is even true of "technical analysis" based on hypotheses about the underlying behavior that is expressed the objective form of charts of price movements.

7 Keynes writes the probability relation thus defined as $a \backslash h = \alpha$.

8 Keynes (1936), p. 173. It is at this point in the decision-making process that the subjectivity that resides in the evaluation of different individuals may become dominant, since it is individual experience that will determine the weight assigned to new information. It is necessary to point out that the notion of "weight" poses the problem of the determination of the point in time at which a decision will be made. Keynes excludes the idea of a maximum weight corresponding to the existing set of available information, arguing that it is not possible to equate the cost of additional information with an increase in weight in such a way that traditional theory relates an increase in information with an increase in certainty: "There clearly comes a point when it is no longer worthwhile to spend trouble, before acting, in the acquisition of further information, and there is no evident principle by which to determine how far we ought to carry our maxim of strengthening the weight of our argument" (Keynes, 1973, VIII, p. 83.)

9 It would certainly not be correct to interpret the idea that asset prices are determined by convention as indicating that expectations are slow to change, and that as a result there will be stability of interest rates through time (see Bernstein, 1992, p. 69), even though Keynes clearly did believe that high interest rates could represent a dissipative structure a la Prigogine.

10 To explain this, Keynes produced a reduced form relation, $pq = xy$, (where q is the proportionate reduction in normal output due to the fall in price, x is the cost of carry as a proportion of the expected normal price, y is the time period until the return to normal conditions, and p is the proportionate fall in the spot price relative to the expected future price) which summarized the factors that determine the depth and the length of the cyclical downturn, as well as the evolution of prices.

Of course, the cyclical evolution of prices may itself bring about changes in the factors that determine "normal" prices and quantities, which is the dynamic aspect that Keynes recognized subsequently as missing from his analysis in the *Treatise*.

11 A decision to "use" the commodity today, either by selling it or as an input in production means foregoing the gain in value that will occur between t and $t+T$, which is given by the present value of $F_{t,T} - S^*_t$, or uS_t. This is the "user cost" associated with the commodity.

12 On the other hand, if price is expected to fall, a covered call option could be written at the current spot price. If the price falls, the premium is retained. If the options were traded in the market, the price of the option would be set by the balance of those who expect prices to rise and those who expect prices to fall, just as user costs are determined by the expectation of price rises and price falls. For the covered call, writers will be supplying the options for the buyers at a premium that is fixed by the balance between them.

13 Davidson (1987) is the major exception, but he notes that the concept has been primarily employed in the analysis of depletable natural resources.

14 Here it is important to note that, while Keynes' theory was grounded in effective demand, he himself identifies his major departures from traditional theory in the analysis of supply. Recall the argument that labor had no way of choosing its desired position on the labor offer curve. User costs made a similar point concerning the supply curve of output. This point is important, not only because one of the supposed failings of Keynes' theory that led to the crisis in Keynesian economics of the 1970s was the absence of the analysis of supply factors. Thus, the specification of the theory of effective demand also implies a basic difference in the specification of the supply side.

15 This is the condition described as "backwardation" in the *Treatise on Money* (and which has gained a place in the finance literature on futures prices). In normal conditions of balanced supply and demand, this will occur when prices for future delivery are driven below current spot prices because long hedgers seeking cover dominate short hedgers and speculators. In conditions of a slump, this requires that the prime costs (user costs of operating) of existing equipment be greater than the prime cost of producing new capital goods so that, given the expectations of the recovery of prices, it is cheaper to order new capacity for future delivery than to buy existing capital goods to hold until future recovery. In the language of the futures market, flow supply prices are below futures prices, which are below spot prices, so the most profitable action is to sell capital goods futures, hedging by producing them for sale at maturity, rather than buying them spot.

16 Looked at from this perspective, the key to recovery is to produce conditions in which current spot prices stand in relation to future prices such that it again becomes more profitable to purchase newly produced goods rather than existing goods (i.e., "backwardation" exists in the market). The short-period price analysis suggests that the easiest way to do this would be to reduce the rate of interest (to reduce the carrying costs) and to increase demand for existing stocks, by monetary expansion or by government expenditures.

17 It was by following this line of reasoning that Fisher developed the concepts of zero-coupon rates as well as forward rates that have come to play such an important role in modern financial analysis.

18 Note the similarity with Keynes, who follows the definition of the rate of interest given above by noting, "It would seem, therefore, that for every kind of capital asset there must be an analogue of the rate of interest on money." He goes on to specify a wheat-rate of interest and a steel-plant rate of interest, finally referring the reader in a note to Sraffa's use of the concept in his debate with Hayek.

19 It is easy to see that this is just Keynes' interest rate parity theorem which forms (see Kregel, 1996) the core of Keynes' analysis of interest rates and income determination. If we substitute dollars for gold and Deutsche marks for wheat, with the dollar interest rate 4 percent relative to the mark interest rate of 10 percent, the proportional difference between the spot and forward prices of the two currencies should be the spot rate times 1 + the dollar interest rate divided by 1 + the DM interest rate or 1 * (1.04/1.10). In Fisher's example, the forward dollar mark rate is fixed at 1:1, so we have to rearrange the formula to find the spot rate as the forward rate times 1 plus the mark interest rate divided by 1 plus the dollar rate or 1 * (1.10/1.04). Thus, wheat sells at a spot premium or a forward discount. This means that wheat bought at 1.057 can only be sold at 1 at the end of the contract. It is clear that the arbitrage may occur via adjustment of either the spot or forward prices, that is, the rate of appreciation or depreciation of one standard in terms of the other, or in terms of the rates of interest in each standard, or in all three.

20 Note the precise formal equivalence between Fisher and Keynes' analysis of the equality between rates of interest and rates of return. This is really not such a great discovery; anyone who has taught a course in international finance has drawn the four-corner equivalence diagram in which the two corners of one side (usually the top) represent Keynes' (covered) interest rate parity theorem and Fisher's real-nominal interest rate relation.

21 That this is formally equivalent to the interest rate parity theorem can be seen by rewriting the relation as $(1 + p) = (1 + i)/(1 + r)$, writing S as the spot rate of exchange of gold for wheat and F the forward rate of exchange of gold for wheat, then $F/S = 1 + p$ and we have $F = S[(1 + i)/(1 + r)] = 0.945S$, or given $F = 1$, $S = 1/0.945 = 1.057$, which is the price of wheat in terms

of gold that eliminates arbitrage profit and 1.057 — 1 = 0.057 is the rate of price deflation of wheat in money that brings the own rates of gold and wheat into equality.

22 The duration of a par perpetual bond with a £4 coupon is 26 years. Modified duration, defined as $D/(1 + r)$, which measures the volatility of bond prices, is 25 years. The change in the price of the 4 percent par consol is thus calculated by multiplying modified duration by the current price and the change in the bond's yield to maturity. In the case of a 16 basis point (4 basis points squared) rise in the yield from 0.04 to 0.0416, the value of the bond will fall over the year by 25*100*0.0016 = £4, which is precisely the bond coupon. For any greater increase in interest rates, the fall in the bond's value will exceed the current coupon of the bond, producing net losses for the holder. If an investor expects interest rates to rise by more than the square of the current rate, Keynes says the investor should prefer to hold cash rather than bonds. In such conditions, attempts to lower the rate of interest by increasing the purchase of bonds will find ready buyers at the prevailing interest rate, and the attempts of the monetary authority to lower rates will be prevented by a "liquidity trap."

23 As rates rise, the square rule produces larger and larger absolute changes in the interest rate, and the use of modified duration to calculate the change in price becomes less and less accurate. The full calculation of the change in the bond price will require the calculation of convexity. It is interesting that Hicks (1939, p. 261, n. 2) reproduces the square rule and notes that it is very likely that returns will be negative, since the fall in capital values will be even greater if changes in risk are taken into account.

References

Bernstein, P. *Capital Ideas.* New York: Free Press, 1992.

———. *Against the Gods.* New York: Wiley, 1996.

Davidson, P. "Rational Expectations: A Fallacious Foundation for Studying Crucial Decision-Making Processes." *Journal of Post Keynesian Economics*, Winter 1982–83, *5* (2), 182–198.

———. "User Cost." *The New Palgrave Dictionary of Economics*, vol. 4. London: Macmillan, 1987, p. 766.

———. "Is Probability Theory Relevant for Uncertainty? A Post Keynesian Perspective." *Journal of Economic Perspectives*, Winter 1991, *5* (1), 29–43.

Fisher, I. *The Theory of Interest.* New York: Macmillan, 1930.

Hicks, J.R. *Value and Capital.* Oxford: Clarendon Press, 1939.

Kahn, R.F. "Some Notes on Liquidity Preference." In *Essays on Employment and Growth.* Cambridge: Cambridge University Press, 1972.

Keynes, J.M. *The General Theory of Employment, Interest and Money.* In *The Collected Writings of John Maynard Keynes*, vol. VII. London: Macmillan, 1973 (originally published 1936).

———. "The General Theory of Employment." *Quarterly Journal of Economics.* In *The General Theory and After, Part 2: Defence and Development, The Collected Writings of John Maynard Keynes*, vol. XIV. London: Macmillan, 1973 (originally published 1937).

———. *Treatise on Probability.* In *The Collected Writings of John Maynard Keynes*, vol. VIII. London: Macmillan, 1973.

———. *Essays in Biography.* In *The Collected Writings of John Maynard Keynes*, vol. X. London: Macmillan, 1972.

———. *The General Theory and After, Part I: Preparation.* In *The Collected Writings of John Maynard Keynes*, vol. XIII. London: Macmillan, 1973.

Kregel, J.A. "Money, Expectations and Relative Prices in Keynes' Monetary Equilibrium." *Economie Appliquée*, 1982, *36* (3), 449–465.

———. "Rational Spirits and the Post Keynesian Macrotheory of Microeconomics." *de Economist*, 1987, *4*, 519–531.

———. "Keynesian Stabilisation Policy and Post-War Economic Performance." In E. Szirmai, B. van Ark, and D. Pilat (eds.), *Explaining Economic Growth.* Amsterdam: Elsevier, 1993.

———. "The Theory of Value, Expectations and Chapter 17 of the *General Theory*." In G. C. Harcourt and P. Riach (eds.), *A Second Edition of the General Theory*. London: Routledge, 1996.

———. "Instability, Volatility and the Process of Capital Accumulation." *Proceedings of International Conference in Memory of Fausto Vicarelli*, G. Gandolfo and F. Marzano, eds. London: Macmillan, 1998.

Moore, B. *An Introduction to the Theory of Finance*. New York: Free Press, 1968.

Shackle, G.L.S. *Uncertainty in Economics*. Cambridge: Cambridge University Press, 1955.

Tobin, James, "Liquidity Preference as Behaviour Towards Risk." *Review of Economic Studies*, February 1958, *67*, 65–86.

Chapter 16

KEYNES'S INFLUENCE ON MODERN ECONOMICS: SOME OVERLOOKED CONTRIBUTIONS OF KEYNES'S THEORY OF FINANCE AND ECONOMIC POLICY

Introduction

It is often argued that Keynes's *General Theory* dealt with macroeconomic aggregates of the real economy in conditions of depression. As a result, many argued that the theory was not general and required the addition of discussions of the economy in "normal conditions" as well as a discussion of the determinants of the nominal price level. In the postwar period, this was achieved through the discussion of the individual or "microeconomic" decisions that produced the economic aggregates in terms of the addition of classical individual optimization theory, what came to be called the "micro" foundations of macroeconomics. The problem of nominal prices was addressed through the addition of the short-run Phillips curve. The result was what came to be called the "Neoclassical Synthesis" and the "monetarist counterrevolution," which paved the way for the rational expectations revolution and the revival of pre-Keynesian classical economics.

Keynes's policy proposals were eviscerated in a similar way, in what has come to be known as "hydraulic" Keynesianism, the use of government tax and expenditure policies to ensure that the level of aggregate expenditure is sufficient to produce full employment. In the 1950s, the emergence of stagflation, the simultaneous occurrence of rising unemployment and rising prices, and high levels of inflation in the 1970s, created a policy paradox in which fiscal policy could not be simultaneously expansive to support full employment levels of demand and restrictive to reduce excess demand and fight inflation. This brought a return to monetary policy as the instrument seen as most appropriate to fight inflation and produce price stability, supported by supply-side tax incentives as the instrument most appropriate to sustain employment and economic growth. Keynes's approach to monetary policy by influencing expectations of long-term interest rates was replaced by control of the growth of monetary aggregates. Keynesian fiscal policy ceased to have a macroeconomic objective and was instead directed toward increasing private incentives through the reduction of the role of government in the economy and the reduction of marginal tax rates to increase investment incentives. Thus, the overall level of fiscal stimulus and interest rates became residual, completely reversing Keynes's approach.

The failure of monetarist money growth targeting eventually forced recognition of the endogeneity of money and a return to policy focus on interest rates and expectations. However, this focus was not on expectations of long-term rates but rather on expectations of future inflation rates in the form of "inflation targeting." The failure of supply-side tax reductions, and reductions in government activities to provide fiscal balance, led to ad hoc budgetary rules to ensure that any new fiscal expenditures were matched with new funding measures.

However, the sharp declines in activity and asset prices during the collapse of the dot-com bubble, the post–September 11 downturn, and the current subprime crisis have created frequent breaches of these principles in favor of a naive type of pre-Keynesian policy in which direct income transfers to support private expenditure and direct liquidity injections to support financial institutions, have become the rule rather than the exception. Policymakers appear to have returned to the hydraulic form of Keynesian policy, but have lost the theoretical basis that supports it. The reason stems from the initial belief mentioned above, that Keynes's theory was based on the ability to forecast the reaction of economic aggregates expressed in real terms to expenditure policy measures. However, a review of the body of Keynes's work shows that this emphasis on the behavior of real economic aggregates does not represent his contribution to economic theory or policy. This chapter will review the innovative contribution of Keynes's major works and show how they were unified in his *General Theory* (CWK 7) in a policy that is radically different from that normally presented, criticized, and currently employed as Keynesian theory.[1]

The financial building blocks of the *General Theory*

The Tract *and interest rate parity*

The theory that emerges in the *General Theory* contains essential elements of Keynes's contribution to finance theory that were developed in his earlier work, starting with the *Tract on Monetary Reform* (CWK 4). In this book, Keynes addresses the practical problem of what shape monetary policy should take in a world that has abandoned the gold standard. He follows Cassel's proposal that stabilization of the international purchasing power parity of the national monetary unit should replace stabilization of the purchasing power of gold as the principal aim of monetary policy. This was a straightforward attempt to replicate the essential features of the gold standard. Under the gold standard, the free movement of gold would lead profit-maximizing agents to exchange gold for the goods of countries where gold was overvalued due to low domestic prices. This would bring an increase in imports of gold to exchange for commodities in countries where prices were lower than average (and an increase in the export of their products) and a decrease in prices (and an increase in imports) in countries where they were above average. Equilibrium would be achieved when gold and goods stopped moving because the purchasing power of gold was the same in all countries; changes in domestic gold supplies brought gold prices of internationally traded goods into equality, adjusting for transactions costs.

The idea was to design a monetary policy for the domestic currency that would produce the same results. This could be done by linking the domestic creation of money to the relative international purchasing power of money. The link to the quantity of money is obvious, simply representing a shift from controlling the money supply to produce domestic price stability to producing stability in the international purchasing power of money—purchasing power parity. Indeed, Keynes, following Marshall, endorses the general validity of the quantity theory. However, he notes that the expositors of the quantity theory usually have failed to present it in the appropriate form, and he provides a version that moves well beyond the traditional representation. He also provides what are now the traditional provisos concerning the general applicability of purchasing power parity.

More important, he notes a major difference between the new approach and that operating under the gold standard. Under the gold standard, despite large seasonal variations, "The daily balance was adjusted by the movement of bankers' funds. . . . But now it is no longer a purely bankers' business, suitably and sufficiently rewarded by arbitrage profit. If the banker moves credits temporarily from one country to another, he cannot be certain at what rate of exchange he will be able to bring them back again later on. . . . [H]e has learned from experience that unforeseen movements of the exchange may involve him in heavy loss. . . . In fact, the seasonal adjustment of credit requirements has ceased to be arbitrage banking business, and demands the service of speculative finance. Under present conditions, therefore, a large fluctuation of the exchange may be necessary before the daily account can be balanced, even though the annual account is level" (CWK 4, pp. 109–110).

This is because there was implicit protection against exchange rate risk given by the automatic arbitrage within the gold points, and private short-term arbitrage flows had generally ensured that the movement of exchange rates would be well within the gold points precisely because of the limit on fluctuations given by the possibility of physical movements of gold. This assurance would not be present under a managed currency standard, since there would be no limit to fluctuations in the event a central bank was not able to operate according to the new operating standard of stabilizing purchasing power parity.

To remedy this deficiency, Keynes recommended the use of forward foreign exchange markets to provide exporters with a means of hedging the increased risk of fluctuating exchange rates on trade flows. In explaining how the operation of the forward market would provide cover against exchange rate risk, Keynes develops the interest rate parity theorem, according to which the forward discount or premium to the spot exchange rate will be determined by the interest rate differential between the currencies.[2]

The method that Keynes uses is similar to the concept of portfolio replication that has been the basis of the advances in financial engineering since the introduction of floating exchange rates in the 1970s. Keynes notes that a commitment to provide foreign currency against domestic currency at a future date at a rate to be determined today can be made with certainty only by borrowing the domestic currency today, converting it into foreign currency at the current spot rate, and investing it at the foreign interest rate until the future date at which it has to be delivered in order to meet the obligation. The cost is thus, the spot cost of buying the currency, plus the difference between the interest earned on the deposit of the foreign currency and the interest paid to borrow the domestic currency. Keynes notes that the forward premium derived in this way "indicates a *preference* by the market, on balance, in favour of holding funds" in one market rather than another (CWK 4, p. 123), and that "The difference between the spot and forward rates is, therefore, precisely and exactly the measure of the *preference* of the money and exchange market for holding funds in one international centre rather than another" (ibid., p. 124; emphasis added).

The important point to note here is the formulation of the problem in terms of spot versus forward prices representing the preference for holding one asset rather than another, and the idea that a change in interest rates will create an incentive to take action that brings the relation back into equality. Thus, if a change in the domestic interest rates causes the interest rate differentials to change, it will be profitable to act in the forward market to arbitrage the discrepancy between the forward market and the loan markets in the two countries. If there is a decline in domestic interest rates, the cost of providing forward cover falls, so the existing quote for the forward rate is overvalued, and profit can be made by selling foreign currency in the forward market, and by borrowing domestic currency, and selling it at the spot rate for foreign currency, investing it at the foreign interest rate, and delivering it forward. Doing so will increase the supply of forward foreign exchange, driving down the forward rate, and increase the demand for spot foreign exchange, pushing up the spot rate. At the same time, it increases the demand for domestic borrowing and the supply of foreign loans, increasing the interest rate on the former and decreasing it on the latter. This combination of actions corrects the mispricing of forward foreign currency. If the domestic borrowing rate is fixed, then it is the foreign rate and the spot and forward prices that adjust. In the period in which Keynes was writing, sterling was the global currency, so it could be assumed that the sterling bank rate was fixed by the Bank of England, and the rates of interest on other currencies and their spot rates would be the factors of adjustment.

The **Treatise** *and the theory of futures prices: normal backwardation*

In the *Treatise on Money,* Keynes (1930) continues his investigation of the relation between spot and forward prices (as well as his concern for the reform of the international financial system). However, he rejects the quantity theory as the basis for the impact of money on prices, instead formulating fundamental price equations for available and unavailable outputs, and makes a strong recommendation against returning to the gold standard. In particular, he shifts the focal point of his analysis from the impact of the demand for money on prices to the effective economic decisions in the economy, and in particular on the "effort of producers and the expenditure of consumers" (CWK 5, p. 120).

However, of major interest is Keynes's emphasis on the relation between money and prices. While the fundamental equation for available outputs looks very much like a cost plus (windfall) profits (normal profits were included in costs) pricing model, with prices given by efficiency wages and the divergence between investment and saving determining windfall profits, of greater interest is the neglected theory of short-period prices outlined in the discussion (in CWK 6, pp. 140ff.) of the behavior of prices in commodity markets.

Keynes notes the important influence of how the market eliminates excess stocks on the behavior of prices and on decisions to engage in new production. Again, working from the point of view of today's spot price and a future price, he notes that markets for excess stocks of commodities do not operate in the same way as markets for flow supplies. Instead of falling prices reducing production and increasing demand to restore equilibrium, just the opposite may occur. If the price in the future is expected to be lower than the current spot price, then it will be profitable to sell stocks today to avoid further loss; even if they are needed for production, it would be profitable to sell since it is expected that they can be repurchased at a lower price in the future. This will create additional downward pressure on current market prices, further depressing expected future prices and increasing the incentive to sell existing stocks. Thus, the question is how the market reverses this declining spiral of prices in order to allow prices to return to normal and provide incentives for new production.

As a solution to this problem, Keynes proposed what he called "neglected" theory of short period prices expressed in the reduced form equation $pq = xy$.[3] The implication of the equation is as follows: the higher is x, the carrying costs as a share of the normal price, and the higher is y, the time to recovery, the larger the required fall in price to bring the decline in prices to a halt. The implication is that if you want a more rapid return to normal, you reduce carrying costs as much as possible, i.e., you reduce interest rates. The higher is the fall in production or rise in consumption produced by a fall in price, both expressed in q, the lower the required fall in price before recovery. The implication is to take measures to reduce the excess stocks as rapidly as possible, by the creation of buffer stock schemes, measures to reduce the increase in production, or other types of government expenditures to decrease the time to recovery and increase the responsiveness of consumption to a fall in price.

Keynes then goes on to "restate the argument in terms of the 'forward market'" (1930, vol. 2, p. 142). He notes that in organized commodity markets there are always two prices, one for current delivery and another for delivery at some future date, and that it is the latter that is of importance to the producer. If the producer can earn his normal profit on his costs of production at this price, "then he can go full steam ahead, selling his product forward and running no risk." However, this relation may be disturbed by the impact of existing stocks on prices for current delivery. If there are no redundant stocks, then "the spot price may exceed the forward price (i.e. in the language of the market there is a 'backwardation')." This means that there is excess demand for current output that can only be met by increasing output. The spot price will then rise until it becomes advantageous to buy for future delivery rather than trying to access the increasingly deficient current supply. This drives up demand for future output, at the same time as it creates an incentive for producers to go full steam ahead and produce output for future sale.

However, Keynes points out that it is not necessary to have abnormal shortages of current stocks for backwardation to exist. He notes that in conditions of balanced supply and demand, there should be no difference between spot and future prices; however, normally there will be an imbalance between producers seeking to sell forward relative to those seeking to hedge against price increases. This will create an excess supply of contracts to deliver the commodity in the future, driving the future price below the spot and creating what has come to be called "normal" backwardation. As long as the price for future delivery remains above existing supply prices, production will continue to take place.

In this context, the existence of surplus stocks impedes current production, for it makes backwardation impossible; if backwardation existed along with excess stocks, it would always be profitable to sell today for future delivery, rather than hold the stocks and incur the costs of warehousing, insurance, and so forth. Indeed, Keynes argues, the existence of surplus stocks must cause the forward price to rise above the spot price, i.e., to establish, "in the language of the market, a 'contango'; and this contango must be equal to the cost of the warehouse, depreciation and interest charges of carrying the stocks." That is, the cost of selling spot and buying back for future delivery must be equal to the costs borne by the speculator who buys the stocks and holds them until the future delivery date. As a corollary, the textbook explanation of futures prices emerges as the spot price plus carrying costs for the term of the contract.

However, the important point is the negative impact of redundant stocks on new production and Keynes's observation that "efforts to get rid of surplus stocks aggravate the slump, and the success of those efforts retards the recovery" (CWK 6, p. 145) because of "the additional element of uncertainty introduced by the existence of stocks and the additional supply of risk bearing which they require. . . . In other words, the quoted forward price, though above the present spot price, must fall below the anticipated future spot price by at least the amount of normal backwardation; and the present spot price, since it is lower than the quoted forward price, must be much lower than the anticipated future spot price" (p. 144). Thus, there is no incentive to engage in current production for future sale, and the short-period price analysis gives the conditions required to return to normal production and normal price as given by the fundamental price equation for available goods.[4]

The monetary theory of production

In the interval between the *Treatise* and the *General Theory* (CWK 7), Keynes took a major step toward using these financial concepts to represent the way investment decisions determine the behavior of the economy. Keynes defines the "efforts of producers" as the decision "whether it is expected to pay a firm in possession of capital equipment to spend money on incurring variable costs, i.e. whether the result of spending money on employment and of selling the output is expected to result in a larger net sum of money by the end of the accounting period than if the money have been retained" (CWK 29, p. 66). He also notes with approval Marx's assertion that decisions in a capitalist economy are determined by the relation M-C-M′, that is, by spending money today to produce commodities to sell for a larger net sum of money in the future, irrespective of the impact on C, which might be higher or lower. This emphasis on present expenditure compared with future receipts fits quite naturally with the prior analysis of the relation between spot and future prices necessary to ensure profitable production.

Keynes points out to his readers that one of the major changes between the *Treatise* and the *General Theory* is the shift from a theory of a given level of output with well-anchored expectations of normal prices given by the fundamental equations, to a theory of changes in the level of output with uncertainty over the level of future prices. Thus, in the *Treatise,* departures from normal positions are represented by unforeseen windfall profits or losses that produce a departure of current prices from the fundamental price equation for available goods. However, windfall profits or losses should bring about changes in normal values, just as the *q* and *c* factors in the short-period theory of prices bring about temporary changes in output and consumption. In the *General Theory,* Keynes thus, gives up the theory of normal prices with well-anchored expectations of normal values and natural interest rates and investigates how divergence from equilibrium determines adjustment and uncertainty in the system.

He also tells us that splitting up the determination of the rate of interest and the return on investment is an important step in his thinking. However, the form of both these concepts conforms to his prior analysis of relations between spot and forward rates. The differentiation is in terms of the explanation given for liquidity preference and the marginal efficiency of capital. For the former, there is no analysis of the supply-side; for the latter, Keynes introduces the idea of user costs.

References in the *General Theory* to prior financial building blocks

In the *General Theory,* Keynes makes direct and indirect reference to his prior work on financial analysis. This is particularly evident in chapters 16 and 17, where Keynes undertakes his analysis in terms of spot and forward markets. For example, the definition on the first page of chapter 17 of the "[t]he money-rate of interest, we may remind the reader, is nothing more than the percentage excess of a sum of money contracted for forward delivery, e.g. a year hence, over what we may call the 'spot' or cash price of the sum thus contracted for forward delivery" (CWK 7, p. 222). Keynes also notes that every commodity can be expressed in this fashion and that "for every kind of capital-asset there must be an analogue of the rate of interest on money" (ibid., pp. 222–223).

Keynes then uses his analysis of different currencies in the *Treatise?* as a template for the analysis of the different own rates on the individual efforts of investors. Indeed, he alerts the reader that he is doing this by pointing out that "It may be added that, just as there are differing commodity-rates of interest at any time, so also exchange dealers are familiar with the fact that the rate of interest is not even the same in terms of two different moneys, e.g. sterling and dollars. For here also the difference between the 'spot' and 'future' contracts for a foreign money in terms of sterling are not, as a rule, the same for different foreign moneys" (ibid., p. 224).

In precisely the same way as he had analyzed interest parity, Keynes notes that just as the forward discount or premium on sterling brings the return on investment in currencies with different national rates of interest into equality, there will be an expected appreciation or depreciation in terms of the standard of account that brings the individual own rates of return into equality when evaluated in terms of the standard. This is the *a* factor that Keynes introduces in chapter 17. In difference from the foreign currency markets, where the only factor is interest differentials, in the analysis of the whole economy, investors will have a range of investment choices that provide different returns that will be characterized by other factors.

For example, Keynes's analysis of future prices made very clear the important role of carrying costs in determining the relation between spot and forward prices for stocks of commodities. Keynes thus, introduces this factor as *c* in determining the returns of such commodities. Keynes also notes that the investment efforts of entrepreneurs can be represented as the difference between the money spent on producing output, and employment and the money return, identified as *q*, the net return. However, this net return differs from the returns considered in comparing currencies in that there is no single forward or future price but rather, a series of future returns. This means that the future stream of returns has to be reduced to a single "price" to preserve the formal relation with interest parity. Keynes does this by proposing to use the net present value of stream of yields, with the expectation of the future yields in each future period representing the impact of the future on the present.

However, he notes that the spot price of an investment must also be corrected for the impact of the future on the present. Keynes defines this as "user cost." Understanding user costs has been difficult for most interpreters of Keynes, and the concept has all but disappeared from macroeconomics. However, it can be quite easily understood with reference to Keynes's work on future prices, described above. Indeed, Keynes again directs his readers to this effect: "The calculation [of user costs] is exhibited in its simplest and most intelligible form . . . in the case of a redundant stock of a raw material such as copper, on the lines which I have worked out in my *Treatise on Money*, vol. II. chap. 29" (1936a, p. 70). However, there is a difference, and Keynes notes that

> "In the case of raw materials the necessity of allowing for user cost is obvious; if a ton of copper is used up to-day it cannot be used to-morrow, and the value which the copper would have for the purposes of to-morrow must clearly be reckoned as a part of the marginal cost. But the fact has been overlooked that copper is only an extreme case of what occurs whenever capital equipment is used to produce. . . . It is an advantage of the concepts of user cost and supplementary cost that they are as applicable to working and liquid capital as to fixed capital. The essential difference between raw materials and fixed capital lies . . . in the fact that the return to liquid capital consists of a single term; whereas in the case of fixed capital, which is durable and used up gradually, the return consists of a series of user costs and profits earned in successive periods" (ibid., p. 73).

Thus, "User cost constitutes one of the links between the present and the future. For in deciding his scale of production an entrepreneur has to exercise a choice between using up his equipment now and preserving it to be used later on. It is the expected sacrifice of future benefit involved in present use which determines the amount of the user cost, and it is the marginal amount of this sacrifice which, together with the marginal factor cost and the expectation of the marginal proceeds, determines his scale of production" (ibid., pp. 68–70).

User cost can be "arrived at . . . by calculating the discounted value of the additional prospective yield which would be obtained at some later date if it were not used now" (ibid., pp. 69–70). With user cost built on the analysis of futures prices, the calculation of the net return *q*, or the marginal efficiency of an investment decision, will require an adjustment to costs that incorporates expectations of the future just as the calculation of the sales proceeds will require expectations of future market conditions. Indeed, Keynes considered the addition of user costs as his only original contribution to the theory of investment. And it comes in the definition of the supply price of capital, rather than the demand price.

Finally, Keynes introduces liquidity preference in the form of a "premium" that attaches to assets as determined by a preference to hold them rather than other similar assets. As noted above, the interest rate that measures the premium for possessing money is already specified in terms of spot and forward prices. Note that Keynes frequently refers to the liquidity premium as the marginal efficiency of money. This is because the analysis of chapter 17 deals with the decisions that bring the own returns of all assets into equality; and because the return on money can also be analyzed in terms of user costs. Here the difference from the analysis of futures prices is not that money has a multiperiod return but rather that it has no carrying costs. However, if money is to be lent, the future price will be above the spot price – i.e., since this contango cannot be explained by the traditional carrying costs of the theory of future prices, which Keynes assumes to be zero on money, it must be determined by some other factor that Keynes defines as its liquidity. Just as Keynes noted that normal backwardation did not require a shortage of stocks, contango in the market need not be caused by an excess supply of money, but it could be caused instead by an imbalance between those seeking to become liquid (to borrow i.e., to supply forward money) relative to those willing to become illiquid (to lend, i.e., to demand forward money). The difference between selling money today against future receipt of money produced both a price risk, given by the possible change in the capital value of the security received, and the risk of being unable to meet contractual commitments. Alternatively, user cost can be measured as the forgone income that is the result of lending today rather than waiting to lend at high future interest rates.[5]

Thus, Keynes provides a full specification of the returns that will attach in some degree to all investments, as given by the difference between spot and forward prices in terms of the three attributes, *q*, *c*, and *l*, all of which are themselves expressions of the impact of the future on the present. The adjustment to equilibrium comes via an analysis of the movement of the *a* factor. This provides a system in which the own rate of own return for every investment possibility, *r*, is adjusted by *a*, the discount or premium, and will be determined by the relative importance of *q*, *c*, and *l*. Keynes describes this process as follows:

To determine the relationships between the expected returns on different types of assets which are consistent with equilibrium, we must also know what the changes in relative values during the year are expected to be. Taking money (which needs only to be a money account for this purpose, and we could equally well take wheat) as our standard of measurement, let the expected percentage appreciation (or depreciation) of houses be a_1 and of wheat a_2. . . . [I]n equilibrium the demand-prices of houses and wheat in terms of money will be such that there is nothing to choose in the way of advantage between the alternatives;—i.e. $a_1 + q_1$, $a_2 - c_2$ and l_3 will be equal. The choice of the standard of value will make no difference to this result because a shift from one standard to another will change all the terms equally, i.e. by an amount equal to the expected rate of appreciation (or depreciation) of the new standard in terms of the old. . . .

. . . Now those assets of which the normal supply-price [read "production" price] is less than the demand-price [read "forward" price] will be newly produced; and these will be those assets of which the marginal efficiency would be greater (on the basis of their normal supply-price) than the rate of interest (both being measured in the same standard of value whatever it is). As the stock of the assets, which begin by having a marginal efficiency at least equal to the rate of interest, is increased, their marginal efficiency . . . tends to fall. Thus, a point will come at which it no longer pays to produce them, unless the rate of interest falls *pari passu*. When there is no asset of which the marginal efficiency reaches the rate of interest, the further production of capital-assets will come to a standstill.

Let us suppose (as a mere hypothesis at this stage of the argument) that there is some asset (e.g. money) of which the rate of interest is fixed (or declines more slowly as output increases than does any other commodity's rate of interest); how is the position adjusted? Since $a_1 + q_1$, $a_2 - c_2$ and l_3 are necessarily equal, and since l_3 by hypothesis is either fixed or falling more slowly than q_1 or $-c_2$, it follows that a_1 and a_2 must be rising. In other words, the present money-price of every commodity other than money tends to fall relatively to its expected future price. Hence, if q_1 and $-c_2$ continue to fall, a point comes at which it is not profitable to produce any of the commodities, unless the cost of production at some future date is expected to rise above the present cost by an amount which will cover the cost of carrying a stock produced now to the date of the prospective higher price (1936a, pp. 227–228).

Note here that Keynes is just describing the conditions in which producers can go "full speed ahead" because the spot prices of production are below forward prices, and if producers do so, they will create changes in their forward prices that reduce the gap between production prices and future prices, and their returns, shifting production and investment to sectors where money returns are higher.

Keynes notes that rather than the money rate of interest setting "a limit to the rate of output, . . . it is that asset's rate of interest which declines most slowly as the stock of assets in general increases . . .]. As output increases, own-rates of interest decline to levels at which one asset after another falls below the standard of profitable production;—until, finally, one or more own-rates of interest remain at a level which is above that of the marginal efficiency of any asset whatever" (ibid., p. 229).

This gives Keynes his formal definition of a monetary economy, i.e., one in which expectations of the future determine present decisions, as one in which there is an asset whose rate of return declines more slowly than all others in the presence of an increase in demand (or, alternatively, the definition of a nonmonetary economy as one in which there is no asset whose liquidity premium is greater than its carrying costs). In such an economy, there is no guarantee that all rates of return will come into equality at a level of investment that produces full employment. Conversely, where this conditions is not met, investment will continue until all resources have been employed—which might require an increase in the employment of labor to produce money. Indeed, Hayek (1943) had argued that this might be the case, and the various composite commodity currency proposals were designed in order to ensure that a demand for money produced an increase in income and employment.

What is money in the monetary production economy?

As Keynes notes, the definition of a monetary economy leaves open the definition of what serves as money, it could be any non-reproducible durable good, but he notes that in modern economies it comes closest to what he defined as "representative" money in the *Treatise* (1930, vol. 1, pp. 9–11). Representative money will have some particular characteristics that cause its return to fall less rapidly or not at all when there is an increase in demand for it. He defines these characteristics in terms of the low or negligible elasticity of production and substitution. Note that this should not be interpreted as an acceptance that money is exogenous. Keynes clearly believed that money was a debt-credit relation and was endogenously determined. What was important was that an increase in the demand for money, even if this caused an increase in its supply, would not bring about a decline in its liquidity return, or provide a demand for more employment to produce it.

This is a radical departure from the traditional analysis of the value of money that relies on the intrinsic value of the money commodity or the backing that is provided for fiduciary money. It is interesting that the year in which Keynes announced his "Monetary Theory of Production" (Keynes 1933) was also the year that gold ceased to play the role of money and thus no longer performed the role of the real backing for fiduciary money. If money is considered as a debt-credit relation, this raises the question of how debts are going to be settled if there is no ultimate real external asset – or Hy Minsky's question of why he could not get anyone to accept his personal IOUs in the settlement of his debts. The answer to this question is found in recognizing that it is necessary not for there to be an ultimate real asset that will settle all debt relations, but rather for there to be some entity that can issue a liability that can be used in settlement of its own debts.

Keynes dealt with the question in his early work on money, and the answer is to be found more explicitly in what is better known as the "state" or "chartalist" theory of money associated with the names of Friedrich Knapp (1924) and Mitchell Innes (1913, 1914). In this approach, money is not a real asset but results from the ability of the state to unilaterally impose a liability on it citizens in the form of a tax that can be liquidated only with the promises to pay that are issued by the state. This meets the contention noted by Innes, that the very nature of credit throughout the world lies in the right of the creditor to hand back to the debtor the latter's acknowledgment or obligation.

It thus follows that the creation and destruction of money depends on the goods and services that the state seeks to buy from its citizens, relative to the tax liabilities imposed by the state on them. If the state runs a balanced budget, citizens as a whole can just meet their tax liabilities (although some individuals may not be able to do so). Conversely, if the state spends less than it taxes in an attempt to run a surplus, citizens as a whole will not be able to meet their tax liabilities (although some individuals may be able to do so) unless there are accumulated money balances held over from prior periods in which the state ran a deficit. Here the circuit analysis is important for determining the viability of the system; by tracing the process by which the state employs the national bank or national treasury to create the money that it uses to acquire goods and services from its citizens and, likewise, the way that its citizens employ the money they receive in these transactions to meet their tax obligations. This analysis makes the important point that if the economy is to grow, the state must be running a budget deficit. However, it cannot determine the amount of money that will be held in individuals' money reserve balances. There are a number of reasons why individuals may choose to hold money balances. The example of a government surplus is one of them, for reserve balances allow the system to meet its tax liabilities. But what is clear is that an increase in the demand for money cannot bring about an increase in its supply, unless it brings about an increase in the government budget deficit. This approach thus, joins monetary policy and fiscal policy as part of the same policy decision.

It also allows an understanding both of why monetary production economies have unemployment and of the role of liquidity preference and fiscal policy. If the public wants hold of more money than the state is willing to create through its budget deficits, individuals will cut expenditures and lower effective demand, causing a reduction in private sector activity and creating unemployment. There is a contango on money, and an increase in the demand for money does not bring about an increase in its supply nor does it increase employment. A monetary economy is thus defined as one in which unemployment may be an equilibrium position. Conversely, it also shows that in the absence of money, or if there is only asset money on the wing that is never held, money can never be in contango, and the economy will automatically produce the level of effective demand compatible with full utilization of resources.

Notes

1 To add a personal note similar to that provided by Marcello de Cecco: in January 1966, I had not yet read the *General Theory*, but upon starting graduate school at Rutgers rather than Chicago, Paul Davidson quickly introduced me to the *Treatise* and the *General Theory*. My interest in Keynes's financial contributions started when Davidson challenged his students to explain the four types of speculative markets in chapter 15 of the *Treatise* (1930, vol. 1, pp. 252–253). This led me to the pricing equation in vol. 2 and then to the own-rates discussion in the *General Theory*. I arrived in Cambridge in 1968, eager to employ these tools, only to find that the discussion had moved on to long-period growth and distribution theory. My first attempt to use the tools of chapter 17 was in an endeavor to link Keynes and Sraffa (Kregel 1976), a suggestion that I continued to pursue for some time (e.g., Kregel 1983) without much success. The discussion herein is a summary of a number of papers (e.g., Kregel 1988b, 1993, 1998a, and 1998b) that have tried to show the cohesiveness of Keynes's work through

his contributions to financial analysis. I have also tried to show the similarity of the work of Keynes and Fisher (with diametrically opposed results) in this regard (Kregel 1988a, 1999a).

2 The interest rate parity theorem was originally proposed in a 1922 supplement on *European Reconstruction* to the *Manchester Guardian* that Keynes was editing (Keynes 1922a, 1922b).

3 The full derivation is given in Kregel 1993.

4 Indeed, the point Keynes is analyzing is whether an excess of saving over investment could be offset by the decline in the prices of available goods causing an increase in demand to hold them as liquid capital investments.

5 Note that the "carry cost" on money can most easily be thought of as the user cost of money and can be measured by an option premium—e.g., if money is "used" by selling (lending) it today for future delivery, a put option is bought at today's strike price; then if future prices rise, the option can be exercised at the higher price even though a sale has been made for future delivery at a lower price. The option premium would then measure the user cost of money, the cost of being illiquid.

References

Keynes, J. M. 1919. *The Economic Consequences of the Peace.* London: Macmillan; CWK 2.

———. 1921. *A Treatise on Probability.* London: Macmillan; CWK 8.

———. 1922a. "The Forward Market in Foreign Exchanges." *Manchester Guardian Commercial,* Series of Supplements: *Reconstruction in Europe* 1 (April 20): 11-18; repr. with modifications in CWK 4, 94–115.

———. 19226. "The Theory of the Exchanges and 'Purchasing Power Parity'." *Manchester Guardian Commercial,* Series of Supplements: *Reconstruction in Europe* 1 (April 20): 6-8; repr. with modifications in CWK 4, 70–80 and 164-169.

———. 1923. *A Tract on Monetary Reform.* London: Macmillan; CWK 4.

———. 19256. Notes on fundamental terminology, for a lecture given on April 25; CWK 29, 35–39.

———. 1930. *A Treatise on Money.* Vol. 1: *The Pure Theory of Money;* Vol. 2:
The Applied Theory of Money. London: Macmillan; CWK 5 and CWK 6.

———. 1931. *Essays in Persuasion.* London: Macmillan; CWK 9.

———. 1933. "A Monetary Theory of Production." In G. Clausing, ed., *Fest- schrift fur Arthur Spiethoff,* 123–125. Munich: Duncker & Humblot.

———. 1936a. *The General Theory of Employment, Interest and Money.* London: Macmillan; CWK 7.

———. 1937. "The General Theory of Employment." *Quarterly Journal of Economics* 51(2): 209–223; CWK 14, 109-123.

———. 1971–1989. *The Collected Writings of John Maynard Keynes* (CWK), ed.
D. E. Moggridge. 30 vols. London: Macmillan. CWK CWK 5. *A Treatise on Money.* Vol. 1: *The Pure Theory of Money.*

CWK 6. *A Treatise on Money.* Vol. 2: *The Applied Theory of Money.* CWK 7. *The General Theory of Employment, Interest and Money,* 1936. CWK 8. *Treatise on Probability.*

CWK 9. *Essays in Persuasion.*

CWK 10. *Essays in Biography.*

CWK 12. *Economic Articles and Correspondence. Investment and Editorial.*

CWK 13. *The General Theory and After.* Vol. 1: *Preparation.*

CWK 14. *The General Theory and After.* Vol. 2: *Defence and Development.*

CWK 20. *Activities 1929–1931. Rethinking Employment and Unemployment Policies.*

CWK 22. *Activities 1939–1945: Internal War Finance.*

CWK 24. *Activities 1944–1946: The Transition to Peace.*

CWK 25. *Activities 1940–1944. Shaping the Post-War World. The Clearing Union.*

CWK 26. *Activities 1941–1946. Shaping the Post-War World. Bretton Woods and Reparations.*

CWK 28. *Social, Political and Literary Writings.*

CWK 29. *The General Theory and After.* A Supplement.

Kregel, J. A. 1976. "Sraffa et Keynes: le taux d'interet et le taux de profit." *Cahiers d'Economie Politique* 3: 135–163.

———. 1983. "Effective Demand: Origins and Development of the Notion." In *Distribution, Effective Demand, and International Economic Relations*, 50–68. London: Macmillan.

———. 1988a. "Irving Fisher, Great-Grandparent of the General Theory." *Cahiers d'Economie Politique* 14–15: 59–68.

———. 19886. "The Multiplier and Liquidity Preference: Two Sides of the Theory of Effective Demand." In A. Barrère, ed., *The Foundations of Keynesian Analysis*, 231–250. London: Macmillan.

———. 1993. "Keynesian Stabilisation Policy and Post-War Economic Performance." In E. Szirmai, B. van Ark, and D. Pilat, eds., *Explaining Economic Growth*, 429–445. Amsterdam: Elsevier.

———. 1998a. "Aspects of a Post Keynesian Theory of Finance." *Journal of Post Keynesian Economics* 21(1): 113–137.

———. 1986. "Instability, Volatility and the Process of Capital Accumulation." In G. Gandolfo and F. Marzano, eds., *Economic Theory and Social Justice*, 149–167. London: Macmillan.

———. 1999a. "Capital and Income in the Theory of Investment and Output: Irving Fisher and John Maynard Keynes." In H.-E. Loef and H. G. Monissen, eds., *The Economics of Irving Fisher: Reviewing the Scientific Work of a Great Economist*, 271–283. Cheltenham, UK: Edward Elgar.

———. 19996. "A New Triffin Paradox for the Global Economy." In *Production, Distribution and Trade Alternative Perspectives* Edited By Adriano Birolo, Duncan Foley, Heinz D. Kurz, Bertram Schefold, Ian Steedman 2010 London Routledge

———. 2006. "Understanding Imbalances in a Globalised International Economic System." In J. J. Teunissen and A. Akkerman, eds., *Global Imbalances and the US Debt Problem. Should Developing Countries Support the US Dollar?*, 149–173. The Hague: Fondad.

———. 2009. "Some Simple Observations on the Reform of the International Monetary System." The Levy Economics Institute of Bard College Policy Note 2009/8. Available at: www.levy.org/pubs/pn_09_08.pdf.

Chapter 17

INSTABILITY, VOLATILITY AND THE PROCESS OF CAPITAL ACCUMULATION

INTRODUCTION

It is ironic that the breakdown of the golden age of post-war capital accumulation in the 1970s should have signalled the crisis of Keynesian economics. Ironic, for as Fausto Vicarelli pointed out, Keynes's entire theoretical edifice was constructed in order to interpret the instability of capitalism, indeed 'the stimulus to his analysis was always some moment of capitalist crisis'. In contrast to those announcing the 'crisis of Keynesian economics' in the face of the increasing instability of the 1970s, Vicarelli argued forcefully 'that Keynes's thought has direct relevance to the present moment of capitalist crisis' (Vicarelli, 1984, p. 184). Yet, as a result of the crisis, the majority of economists have abandoned Keynes's theory in favour of what has come to be called the 'New Classical' economics, which seems to exclude instability by definition, or the inappropriately named 'New Keynesian' economics, which seems to rely on the failure of the perfectly competitive market to allocate information efficiently.

Vicarelli's carefully argued case that Keynes's economics was even more appropriate to periods of crises than to the Golden Age of post-war stability has been completely ignored by most professional economists. The present paper will try to recall and reinforce some of Vicarelli's arguments, drawing on his interpretation of Keynes to integrate it with some more modern theory.

THE EXPLANATION OF ECONOMIC INSTABILITY

Even before Keynes wrote there was broad agreement that economic instability was caused by 'imperfections' which were represented by mistaken forecasts of the future and associated disappointment in expectations (cf. Kregel, 1977), or from mistaken government policies (extending to the very existence of government) producing inappropriate expectations (which is what the Treasury View seems to have been), or most simply the absence of competitive conditions. By and large they tended to be maintained after Keynes and were still prevalent at the time of the 'crisis in Keynesian economics'. All of these explanations implicitly accepted the self-adjusting operation of the market mechanism. This explains why the rational expectations hypothesis had such a powerful and immediate impact, for it simply brought expectations formation within the already accepted self-adjusting mechanism. If information was also a commodity (Stigler), then a perfectly competitive market should eliminate any information failures such as erroneous expectations, whether from the private sector or by government intervention. If the automatic equilibration of supply and demand by prices in competitive markets is accepted, and economic agents are assumed to have the cognitive ability of the average first-year economics student with a middling competent instructor, then sooner or later, but nonetheless eventually, there should no longer be mistaken forecasts of the influence of economic events on prices. And the impact of government policy decisions should also be anticipated. Thus, at a stroke, the existing explanation of instability was eliminated. Exogenous supply side Shocks become the only possible explanation. It is not surprising that the New Keynesians counter-attacked in the area of the economics of information and that their response was in terms of an 'impossibility theorem' concerning the existence of perfect competitive markets for economic information.

Yet, Vicarelli did not base his explanation of Keynes's instability on the failure of the operation of the market for information. Indeed, when Keynes realized that his *General Theory* was being interpreted in terms of the differences between effective demand and income'[1] he declared that the theory of 'effective demand is substantially the same if we assume that short-period expectations are always fulfilled' (XIV, p. 181).[2] Indeed, in the *General Theory* Keynes had already suggested that 'the existing market valuation, however arrived at, is uniquely *correct* in relation to our existing knowledge of the facts . . .' (1936, p. 152; see also, XIV, p. 114). And this is not an isolated passage. Throughout his writings Keynes appears to accept even the strong form of the informational efficiency of markets.

In Keynes's view, the source of instability was not to be found in informational market failure, any more than it was to be found in the existence of uncompetitive product markets or labour markets. Instead, Keynes's analysis of instability was based on his belief that there was a basic difference in the way the price mechanism operated with respect to consumption goods and to capital, or investment goods. This is evident from the fact that, in contrast to acceptance of the assumption that short-term expectations were always realized, he considered that it would be inappropriate to assume that long-term expectations, which determine 'what the entrepreneur can hope to earn in the shape of future returns if he purchases (or, perhaps, manufactures) "finished" output as an addition to his capital equipment' (p. 47), could be assumed to be realized. The reason for this difference is that 'it is the nature of long-term expectations that they cannot be checked at short intervals in the light of realized results' (p. 51).

Since the stability of the price mechanism is based on an error correction mechanism which causes mistaken expectations to be eliminated, if it is impossible to determine whether or not long-term expectations are correct, then it is also impossible for the error correction mechanism to automatically produce adjustments converging towards a uniquely correct valuation on the basis of existing information. In the long run, not only are we all dead, but no purposive action or reaction based on realization or disappointment of expectations can take place.[3] Thus, the 'nature' of the operation of the price mechanism as it applies to investment decisions must be different.

Keynes notes that the problem could be avoided by assuming 'a world in which economic goods were necessarily consumed within a short interval of their being produced' (XIV, p. 113). But this would imply a world without growth and capital accumulation.

Another alternative would be to reduce long-term expectations and the corresponding results of the decisions based on them to a time dimension similar to that applied to short-term expectations, such as are implicit in the Swedish *ex-ante* and *ex-post* approach. But, Keynes also rejects this approach as impracticable. In any case, Keynes notes that the comparison of expectations with realizations is only of importance if this causes expectations to be changed. However, 'the original expectations . . . which led the firm to acquire the capital equipment' will no longer be relevant if conditions have changed after the investment decision has taken place, since 'current decisions will most appropriately be based on current expectations'. Thus, only if conditions are unchanged through time will comparison of expectations with realizations be relevant, but this would require that expectations are always fulfilled or that decisions based on erroneous expectations have no impact on current conditions. This solution, Keynes argued, was the equivalent of considering only the 'current yield of capital equipment, which would be correct only in the static state where there is no changing future to influence the present' and 'has the result of breaking the theoretical link between today and tomorrow' (p. 145). All this was caused by the diverse nature of the accumulation because 'It is by reason of the existence of durable equipment that the economic future is linked to the present' (p. 146).

If it was impossible to determine whether the expectations concerning an investment were satisfied, then the self-adjusting competitive market mechanism could not be applied to the investment decision. Indeed, he argued that in the application of the competitive mechanism to investments 'facts and expectations were assumed to be given in a definite and calculable form. . . . The calculus of probability . . . was supposed to be capable of reducing uncertainty to the same calculable status as that of certainty itself' (XIV, pp. 112–13).

While the appropriate treatment of the impact of the future on current economic decisions was the subject of much debate at the time of the publication of the *General Theory*, by the end of the war economists' concerns had been diverted to the empirical estimation of Keynesian consumption functions, investment functions, income multipliers and the like. Again, ironically, these exercises employed econometric theory which was based on the same 'calculus of probability' that Keynes had rejected as the basis for decision-making (cf. Hamouda and Rowley, 1996).

KEYNES AND INSTABILITY

Keynes believed that the problems caused by the decision to invest could only be recognized in what he called a 'monetary production economy' and defined as an economy 'in which changing views about the future are capable of influencing the quantity of employment and not merely its direction'. (1936, p. vii). It is only by recognizing the importance of changing views on the operation of the price mechanism that the instability of the capitalist system could be explained.

Although the theory of effective demand in a monetary production economy had all but disappeared in the post-war golden age of Keynesian economics, Fausto Vicarelli was among the small group of economists who continued to recognize their importance.

Even before the advent of the rational expectations hypothesis, he had recognized that the instability that Keynes was discussing could not be explained by errors in expectation or imperfection in information. This is evident not only in his book but also in his assessment of the contributions of the New Classical Economics which had been erected on the basis of rational expectations. In one of his last published articles (1985–86) Vicarelli does not direct his criticism of the approach to the assumptions made about expectations, instead he draws attention to the restoration of the idea that capitalist accumulation is based on 'natural laws', which would naturally establish the expansion of investment which would produce full employment. Once this automatic mechanism is accepted, Vicarelli argues, it really makes no difference how expectations are introduced for, following Hicks, the problem simply becomes specification of the means by which agent expectations come to reflect the objective facts of the economy. As Keynes had argued, it is as if the process of adjusting expectations to their correct values had no impact on the current conditions in the economy. If there are 'natural' or 'objective' laws producing current economic conditions, independently of agents' expectations, then there will be objective probability distributions which can be estimated with increasing certainty by standard statistical procedures. But the real point of difficulty concerned the existence of the natural law, the specification of the objective process generating the results which expectations would reflect, not with the process of predicting them.

In his book Vicarelli notes the importance for Keynes's ideas on instability of the debate between Hayek and Keynes over the existence of a neutral monetary policy. It is important because it is based on a similar point. The existence of a 'neutral' monetary policy requires the existence of an objective, or 'real', system based on an automatic adjustment mechanism which exhibited endogenous stability, and which could be disturbed by 'monetary' factors. By demonstrating that there was no reason for an economy absent money to be stable, Sraffa showed a neutral monetary policy to be, not impossible, but irrelevant to the goal of economic stability.

Even if expectations are perfect, if there are no natural forces at work to produce equilibrium in the system, instability will exist; errors and imperfections and incomplete knowledge cannot then be the cause of instability. This is the monetary production economy in which monetary and real factors cannot be distinguished. Following Keynes's idea that a new kind of price mechanism dealing with investment goods is needed, Vicarelli suggests that the appropriate response to the New Classical economics based on the rational expectations hypothesis is 'A Keynesian microeconomic theory, based on the particular features of a monetary economy' (p. 312).

THE BEGINNINGS OF THE NEW MICROTHEORY

The beginning of Keynes's concern with the difference between the determination of the prices of current output and investment goods, and thus with how future conditions impinge on current supply and demand, is in the criticism he received from his younger colleagues for the inconsistency in the explanation of the determination of the prices of consumption goods and capital goods in the *Treatise on Money*. 'Richard Kahn, a pupil of Keynes's . . . noted an unjustified asymmetry between the price level theory for consumption goods . . . and that for capital goods . . . the price level for consumer goods was said to be determined by demand and supply, while the price level for investment goods was attributed to "external" causes . . .' (Vicarelli, 1984, p. 101). Despite the encouragement of the younger economists, schooled in Marshall's price theory, to make the price of investment and consumption goods symmetric, Keynes resisted. The basic reason, Vicarelli notes, was that 'Keynes had, however, long ceased to consider savings as automatic demand for investment. It was futile, therefore, to expect him to ferret out a symmetry between reciprocal excesses of demand and supply in the two sectors' (*ibid.*, p. 102). That is, the demand for investment goods could not be discovered in looking at what was left from income after the demand for consumption goods had been satisfied (the definition of saving), without particular assumptions about the characteristics of the supply curve of investment goods. Vicarelli points out that Keynes chose to make neither adjustment.

Keynes instead sought to incorporate the importance of the future on the present, the diverse determination of the prices of investment goods, the impossibility of comparing expectations with realizations, by 'the introduction of the concepts of user costs and the marginal efficiency of capital' (*ibid.*, p, 14(6) into the Marshallian theory of supply and demand. This reworking of supply and demand is Keynes's new 'microtheory' for a monetary production economy.

MARGINAL EFFICIENCY AND USER COSTS

The marginal efficiency of capital, as Keynes was quick to admit, was not a real innovation, for this approach is already to be found in the work of Veblen, Marshall, Myrdal, Schumpeter and many others. Leaving aside specifics, marginal efficiency is based on the idea that the calculation of the return on an investment project can be handled in the same way as the yield to maturity is calculated on a fixed coupon bond, or, as Keynes suggests, as the value of a finite series of periodic annuity payments. Just as the yield to maturity calculates an average rate of discount that equates the purchase price of a bond to the present value of its periodic coupons, the efficiency of capital calculates the average rate of discount that equates the purchase price of the investment to the present value of its expected future net receipts. Formally, this is correct, but as a measure to represent the impact of a series of future events on the present, it has substantial drawbacks.

This is because the calculation of the internal rate of return of any stream of net periodic payments relies on the assumption that the reinvestment rate of interest is known and constant, implying a flat yield curve or that the risk of the investment is constant over its life. It also fails to deal with the fact that bonds and investment projects differ in the certainty over the size of the future net receipts and the possibilities of changing the shape of the flows of these receipts through shut down or delay of the project. Finally, when there is variation in the size of the expected future receipts, or fluctuations in interest rates or slope in the yield curve, are allowed, there may be multiple internal rates of return, precluding any precise definition of the yields which must be compared across different investments.

The reswitching debate should have taught economists what finance theorists have always known when they discuss the drawbacks of the internal rate of return as a reliable tool in capital budgeting. Keynes must have been aware of these problems for he quickly shifts his discussion from the internal rate of return definition of marginal efficiency to comparison of the demand and supply prices of capital goods, better known today as 'net present value' analysis. This eliminates the ambiguities caused by multiple internal rates of return, but the other difficulties surrounding the calculation of the present value of the future costs and receipts from a project remain. For example, the difference caused by the fact that bond coupons are perfectly known and the periodic net proceeds of an investment still remain, as do the difficulties concerning the appropriate discount rate. Formulating the appropriate course of future interest rates in the form of changes in the shape of the yield curve will be no easier than the estimates of the expected periodic net yields. Keynes recognizes this problem when he speaks of the 'complex of interest rates for various terms which will rule in the future' being reflected in the 'complex of rates which will rule today' (p. 143). Today we would simply talk of the spot yield curve. In addition, there is the question of the appropriate discount rate to be used.[4] Despite all these complications, of which Keynes seems to have been aware, his basic point is simply to emphasize 'The marginal efficiency of capital is of fundamental importance because it is mainly through this factor (much more than through the rate of interest) that the expectation of the future influences the present' (p. 145). Keynes also warns that it is only 'after giving full weight to the importance of the influence of short-period changes in the state of long-term expectation as distinct from changes in the rate of interest, [that] we are entitled to return to the latter as exercising, at any rate, in normal circumstances, a great, *though not a decisive,* influence on the rate of investment' (p. 164, italics added). It is perhaps unnecessary to highlight the difference between this position and the determination of investment in the standard Keynesian model by means of changes in the rate of interest relative to a fixed state of expectations.

The second aspect does, however, present a real innovation: the introduction of user costs into the calculation of supply prices. User costs are often presented as an elaborate calculation of depreciation, or as the difference between the current costs involved in the operation or use of assets relative to the maintenance costs of keeping them idle.[5] But, such an interpretation makes no recognition of the role of user costs in expressing the impact of the future on present returns through the appropriate adjustment to supply prices.[6]

The necessity of specifying the role of user costs in entrepreneurial decision making is expressed in this passage from an early draft of the *General Theory*:

> The employment of the factors of production to increase output involves the entrepreneur in the disbursement, not of product, but of money. The choice before him in deciding whether or not to offer employment is a choice between using money in this way or in some other way or not using it at all . . . The only question . . . is to choose . . . that way which will yield the largest profit in terms of money. It must be remembered that future prices, in so far as they are anticipated, are already reflected in current prices, after allowing for the various considerations of carrying costs and of opportunities of production in the

> meantime which relate the spot and forward prices of a given commodity. Thus we must suppose that the spot and forward price structure has already brought into equilibrium the relative advantages, as estimated by the holder, of holding money and other existing forms of wealth. Thus if the advantage in terms of money of using money to start up a productive process increases, this will stimulate entrepreneurs to offer more employment . . . For the entrepreneur is guided, not by the amount of product he will gain, but by the alternative opportunities for using money having regard to the spot and forward price structure taken as a whole.
>
> *(Keynes, 1936, XIII, pp. 82–3)*

It is necessary to calculate the appropriate supply price incurred in production of output and the present value of the net sum received per unit of output (the demand price or forward price), in order to identify the 'actual nature of the business decision' as the comparison of the spot prices, current supply prices and forward prices. If the return available from engaging in current production to be sold at the expected future price is greater than the return available from buying existing output at the prevailing spot price and holding it for sale at the expected future price (or simply selling for future delivery at the forward price) then employing labour will provide a return greater than any 'alternative opportunities for using money' (or the costs of borrowing the money expended) and decisions will be taken to create output and provide employment. This comparison of the alternative rates of return provided by holding capital idle, using existing capital equipment to produce output, or ordering new capital equipment, was thus the key to determining the offers of employment.

The calculation of 'whether it is expected to pay a firm in possession of capital equipment to spend money on incurring variable costs' to produce either consumption or investment goods will then require a precise calculation of the amount of money spent on 'the employment of a given volume of labour by an entrepreneur'. This will be given by 'the amounts which he pays out to the factors of production for their current services' and 'the amounts he pays out to other entrepreneurs for what he has to purchase from them' plus 'the *sacrifice* which he incurs by employing the equipment instead of leaving it idle, which we shall call the user cost of the employment in question' (1936, p. 23, italics supplied). User cost plays a central role in determining supply price, but not so much in terms of maintenance costs, as the 'sacrifice' related to the decision to produce or not produce.

The calculation of the future return expected (whether it is expected to 'pay') by a firm from operating its existing equipment to produce output by employing labour will be based on the difference between the expected sales value of the output and the sum of costs paid to factors, including the user costs of non-labour inputs: 'in a given situation of technique, resources and factor cost per unit of employment, the amount of employment, both in each individual firm and industry and in the aggregate, depends on the amount of proceeds which the entrepreneurs expect to receive from the corresponding output'.

The origin of the concept of user cost is the analysis of short-period price adjustment in volume two of the *Treatise on Money*.[7] The problem that Keynes was trying to resolve was how the price adjustment mechanism would operate to restore equilibrium in conditions of excess supply. If future prices were expected to fall, then it would be rational to sell excess stocks as soon as possible, aggravating conditions of excess supply. The only way to stop a fall in price would be for prices to have declined to a point at which expectations were reversed. If prices were expected to rise, then it became rational to hold supplies off the market in the hope of selling them at higher prices in the future. However, holding supplies for future sale involved costs, of financing, storage, insurance, and so on. The expected rise in price would have to be sufficient to cover these costs before it would become rational to hold back supplies. This would cause supply to contract and start the process of price recovery. If the expected price rise more than covered the costs of storage, then a decision to sell at the current price would mean the 'sacrifice' of the higher net profit from holding to sell at the higher expected future price. This sacrifice of potential gain, Keynes argued, should be included among the prime costs of supplying commodities today. In this way, expectations of future conditions had a direct impact on current supply prices and decisions to sell or hold a commodity should be made by comparing current selling prices with costs including the prospective future gain.[8] Thus the prime costs of using the commodity today would be the sum of the factor cost, which in this case is its current market value, plus the benefit which will be sacrificed by its current use, or its user cost. In this case prime costs are greater than the current market value, so it is more profitable to hold the commodity for future sale or use in production. User cost is then the present value of the increased return that could have been earned if the use of the commodity had been postponed to a future date. In this way the future exerts an influence on the present supply via the inclusion of user cost. Alternatively, if spot prices are expected to be lower in future, user costs would be negative and would act to reduce supply prices relative to current spot prices. It is thus profitable to 'use' current stocks by selling at current prices, leading to conditions of excess supply and downward pressure on prices. Thus, the response to the question that Keynes had posed in the *Treatise*, whether there was any automatic tendency for prices to move so as to restore equilibrium prices, was that it would depend on expectations of future prices and the costs of carry, primarily, the rate of interest. There was an appropriate combination of expectations and interest rates which would produce adjustment, but there were more combinations which would produce market breakdown and collapse.

Thus, the present value of expected future returns produced the influence of the future on the present demand prices of capital goods, while user costs produced the influence of the future on present supply, prices.[9] This is the new microtheory of supply and demand that Keynes proposed as a substitute for the traditional theory which was only concerned with current conditions and the calculation of current yields.

However, one additional step was required, before the choice facing the entrepreneur in using his wealth could be fully specified. The rate of interest enters into the calculation of demand prices through the specification of the rate of discount and it enters supply prices through the impact of the cost of carry on user costs. Recall Keynes admonition to give 'full weight to the importance of the influence of short-period changes in the state of long-term expectations as distinct from changes in the rate of interest.'

It was for this reason that the *General Theory* differed from the *Treatise on Money* by the introduction of a distinction between the determinants of the marginal efficiency of capital and the rate of interest (compare 1936, p. 173). With the newly defined marginal efficiency to determine, the rate of return on capital goods, liquidity preference, built on the concept of 'bearishness' from the *Treatise,* was to determine the rate of interest. Liquidity preference and the concept of the 'liquidity premium' have also caused difficulty in interpretation, but it seems clear that they are a straightforward extension of the idea of user costs to determine whether it is profitable to hold money for future use, rather than using it today to purchase investment or consumption goods. If money is 'used' today to buy investment goods, or consumption goods, or to buy financial assets (which includes bank lending to either households or entrepreneurs) to gain a return this means that the money will no longer be available to be 'used' at a future date when the prices of the assets or goods will be different. The 'user cost' of spending money today to acquire an asset or good will then be the present value of the potential future gain or loss that has been foregone or avoided by parting with money today. This future gain or loss will depend on the expected forward prices of investment goods, consumption goods and financial assets.

With respect to other financial assets, the user cost of money is the foregone gain (or loss) that could have been earned (or avoided) by waiting to purchase financial assets at lower (higher) prices and higher (lower) yields. The use of money is defined as becoming 'illiquid'. The premium which is required to convince holders of money to become illiquid is thus the equivalent of the 'user cost' of money. Liquidity preference will determine this liquidity premium and is thus linked directly to the expectation of the future movement of prices. The rate of interest can then also be represented as the relation between the spot price and the expected future prices of money. But, no one should be surprised by this, for Keynes insisted that his definition of the rate of interest, in difference from the 'real' rate determined by the forces of productivity and thrift in traditional theory, was 'nothing more than the percentage excess of a sum of money contracted for forward delivery, *e.g.* a year hence, over what we may call the "spot" or cash price of the sum thus contracted for forward delivery' (1936, p. 222). The complete specification of the new microtheory for the monetary production economy in which the future has an influence on. the present thus requires the application of user costs to money as well as capital goods. It was thus possible to answer the question of whether it would. 'pay' to employ labour and produce output by comparing the returns from holding money as given by the user cost of money, of holding capital goods (or any other durable) idle in terms of the return as given by user costs, and the return from using the capital goods with labour to produce consumption or investment goods as given by the marginal efficiency of capital. Only if the return on the latter could be held above the two former types of investment, would capital accumulation take place and employment be provided. This would require the appropriate manipulation of user costs, that is, expected future prices, and interest rates (which were also determined by expected future price movements). The explanation that Keynes offered of underemployment equilibrium turns on the different behaviour of supply and demand prices as supplies change, financial assets prices behaving in a different way than the prices of produced goods.

FROM INSTABILITY TO VOLATILITY AND BACK

The instability of the system then was the result of the fact that it was impossible to compare expectations with results, that there was no 'objective' referent upon which expectations might be based. The representation by means of user costs of this position provides us with an alternative way of seeing this point. Recall that one of the criticisms of the net present value calculation taken over from bond valuation was that it did not take into account the possibility of a variable holding period, for example, a decision to postpone an investment, or shut down a plant during its expected operating period. It thus ignores the value of 'imbedded' options in investment projects.[10]

Note that the decision not to 'use' a commodity or capital equipment in production is the equivalent retaining the privilege of doing so in future. Thus, the value of the decision to hold includes the equivalent of the value of a call option written at a strike price equal to the current spot price. The value of the position is thus its current spot market value plus the value of the option. This is precisely equivalent to the argument that prime costs should include user costs. At the same time, the user cost of money is equivalent to a call option on a deposit at the current interest rate. Alternatively, holding money uninvested in a portfolio allows you to forgo the sale of an investment asset to realize an unanticipated need for liquid funds. This is equivalent to the value of a put on the investment position written at the expected future appreciation of the asset.

Alternatively, anyone wanting to sell without losing the possibility of future profit could do so by purchasing a call option with a strike equal to the current spot price. Thus, if the price rises he can always reverse his prior sale at no net gain or loss by exercising the option and then sell at the now higher market price. On the other hand, if price is expected to fall, a covered call option could be written at the current spot price. If the price falls the premium is retained. If the options were traded in the market, the price of the option will be set by the balance of those who expect prices to rise and those who expect prices to fall, just as user costs are determined by the expectation of price rises and price falls. For the covered call, writers will be supplying the options for the buyers at a premium which is fixed by the balance between them. However, option pricing theory allows the value of options to be fixed without the existence of actual markets to set prices with reference to market conditions. This provides a response to the criticism of those who argue that the appropriate futures markets will not exist, or that the specification of expectations is purely subjective and thus irrational. Thus, instead of saying that supply prices have to be adjusted for user costs, we could say that supply prices which are corrected for the impact of the future on the present include the appropriately calculated values of the imbedded options.

This provides us with an understanding of why Keynes might have considered expectations relatively unimportant with respect to the short-period decision to produce. Consider the relation between spot and forward prices. If a commodity is purchased today to be held for sale in the future, interest costs will be incurred to finance the spot purchase. If expected future prices exceed current spot prices by more than this amount there is a profit to be made by buying spot and holding for forward, sale. This would represent the user cost of the position.[11] If contracts can be drawn for forward delivery, then there is a profitable arbitrage trade of buying spot and selling forward if forward prices exceed spot prices by more than the interest costs less the convenience yield. This will eventually bring the spot and forward prices into a relationship in which the market expectation of the forward price is given by the current spot price and the carry costs given by the rate of interest and convenience yield.

The calculation of present values requires the specification of future prices, discounted at the rate of interest. If future prices are given by spot prices plus the inclusive carry costs, then dividing them by the rate of interest will give spot prices. There is no need to formulate expectations about future prices – knowledge of current interest rates and current spot prices is sufficient to place a value on the commodity in any future period.[12] The present value of the expected future returns can be determined directly from spot prices without reference to expectations of future conditions, and from the appropriate interest rates. All reference to the relationship between expectations and realizations can then be eliminated.

In fact, once the idea of user costs as an option is recognized it is possible to go one step further and calculate the value of the ownership of productive capacity as equivalent to owning the plant and equipment, valued at the existing spot or scrap price, plus an option on the returns that could be generated from hiring labour to produce and sell the output from operating the plant. The exercise price of this option would be the payment of the prime costs of production, primarily wages and inputs.[13] Thus, the value of capital equipment could be determined directly from current spot prices and the value of the option to use the plant to produce future incomes.

Again, the absence of markets is no particular problem, as the formula for option values only requires information on the maintenance costs of the plant, its current operating costs, current output prices and any costs related to starting if the plant is not currently operating. All of this is currently available information and in no way requires specification of expectations or relies on comparing expectations with realized results.

But, there is one crucial additional piece of information which is required in order to calculate the option values. This is the volatility of output prices. The standard deviation of product prices is the only value which is not expressed in current market prices. It is the only 'unknown' which we still have to solve. But, this is precisely what is not, and cannot, be known, This is Keynes's point with reference to traditional theory. Only if the future replicates the past, only if we can use the calculus of probability and assume that realizations come from a stochastic process with zero mean and normally distributed errors, can we assume that past volatility is a good guide to future volatility. This, indeed, is the world of rational expectations. If we are not, and the future has an impact on the present, then Keynes's theory is fundamentally different from the traditional theory. If, as Davidson (1982–83) has argued, the world is not ergodic, or as Minsky has argued, if conditions of stability lead to endogenous changes in risk assessments, then volatility cannot be predicted from the past and there is no basis upon which we may produce an estimate of what it will be in the future. But, if volatility cannot be predicted correctly, then options prices cannot be calculated correctly. We are thrown back to the problem of how changes in the state of expectations are produced. It is the determination of price volatility which determines whether or not the economy is stable or unstable. Volatility will then determine stability and with it the process of capital accumulation. This is just another way of putting Keynes's basic point, that it is not realization of expectations, but whether or not their formation has an impact on the evolution of economic affairs, which is of importance.

This is the explanation which Fausto Vicarelli gave. It was based on the impact on expenditures which results from the failure of households to calculate correctly the user cost of money generating an income multiplier process which changes conditions and thus causes a shift in expectations. Or by a failure on the part of bankers to calculate the user cost of money correctly yielding an expansion of loans and the money supply producing an auto-regressive impact on those decisions.

Obviously, Keynes's own explanation of expectations formation is based on his *Treatise on Probability*. It is important to note that Keynes distinguishes between the probability of the occurrences of possible states of the world and the probability of propositions concerning explanations of those states. The former relates to the objective occurrences of a natural process, while the latter relates to hypotheses upon which to base action. The former will produce stability, the latter instability because the former allows the prediction of future volatility from past volatility, the latter does not.

Notes

1 'Income, i.e. realized results as distinct from effective demand' (XIV, p. 180).
2 Keynes notes that 'a producer estimates what he will get for a product when it is finished when he decides to begin producing it to-day with the existing plant' on the basis of his short-term expectations' (1936, p. 148; see also pp. 46–7).
3 As a rough analogy, it is impossible to determine if a long-distance train will arrive on time by comparing its average speed at any point during the journey with that required by the timetable, for it is always possible for it to make up or lose time until the scheduled arrival time is past. Indeed, it may require variable speeds in order to obtain open track.
4 Where Keynes also notes that this risk adjustment will tend to be variable, falling as the economy expands and thus reinforcing a boom and rising in a decline, reinforcing the duration of a slump.
5 Davidson (1987) is the major exception, but he notes that the concept has been primarily employed in the analysis of depletable natural resources.
6 Here, it is important to note that while Keynes's theory was grounded in effective demand, he himself identifies his major departures from traditional theory in the analysis of supply. Recall the argument that labour had no way of choosing its desired position on the labour offer curve. User costs made a similar point concerning the supply curve of output. This point is important, not only because one of the supposed failings of Keynes's theory which led to the crisis in Keynesian economics of the 1970s was the absence of the analyses of supply factors, but also, as Vicarelli points out, because the basic point of disagreement with the new Classical economics based on the rational expectations hypothesis concerns the specification of the supply curve (Vicarelli, 1985, p. 305) and the natural rate of interest. Thus, the specification of the theory of effective demand also implies a basic difference in the specification of the supply side.
7 This analysis is converted into spot-future price form in Kregel (1993).
8 To those unaccustomed to thinking in terms of spot and forward prices the idea may be seen by considering a commodity such as wheat. Today, at time t, the value of the commodity is given by its current market (spot) price S_t. To determine whether the commodity should be sold or held for future sale will be determined by the spot price, S*, expected to prevail at some future date, t + T, T days distant. Alternatively, if there is a market where the commodity may be contracted for future delivery, the forward price quoted today at time t, for

delivery in T days, will be $F_{t,T}$. In general the difference $F_{t,T} - S_r$ must be sufficient to cover the cost of holding the commodity for T days. This 'carry' cost may be defined as cS_t. If the difference $F_{t,T} - S_t$ were more than this a profit could be made by simultaneously buying the commodity spot and selling it forward, holding it for the T days to be delivered at $t + T$. The carry cost will include the costs of financing, maintenance, storage, insurance, etc. In a balanced market, $F_{t,T} - (1 + c)S_t = 0$ and the present value of the commodity will then be given by $(F_{t,T})/(1 + c) = S_t$. The expected spot price should also equal the forward price, so $S^*_{t,T} = F_{t,T}$. However, if there is imbalance in the market and there are expectations of say a rise in price which is greater than c per period, then $S^*_{t,T} > F_{t,T}$ and the difference represents the profit sacrificed by current use, u. Then c must be adjusted for u to yield $(c - u)$ as the carry cost for holding. This is also often called the 'convenience yield' of a stock of a commodity.
A decision to 'use' the commodity today, either by selling it or as an input in production means foregoing the gain in value which will occur between t and $t + T$, which is given by the present value of $F_{t,T}$-S^*_t, or uS_t. This is the 'user cost' associated with the commodity.

9 Note that user costs enter the calculation of both investment and consumer goods supply prices for the decision facing the producer of investment goods is the same as that facing the producer of consumption goods, to evaluate appropriate the prime costs of production including those from using non-labour inputs and capital equipment to produce today rather than in the future,

10 This analysis builds on an interpretation of Chapter 17 that I shared with Fausto Vicarelli. Its most recent version is Kregel (1996).

11 Recall that this cost is the equivalent, with opposite sign, of what is called the 'convenience yield' of holding stocks of a commodity. When we are dealing with capital equipment, excess capacity may indeed have a 'convenience yield' similar to stocks of primary inputs which should also be included in the 'user costs' of using current equipment at 'full capacity'.

12 If there is a convenience yield, then the appropriate discount rate would be the marginal user cost.

13 Cf. the analysis suggested in Brennan and Schwartz (1985).

REFERENCES

Brennan, M. and Schwartz, E. (1985) A New Approach to Evaluating Natural Resource Investments, *Midland Corporate Finance Journal* **3**, 37–47.

Davidson, P., 1982–83, Rational Expectations: A Fallacious Foundation for Studying Crucial Decision-Making Processes, *Journal of Post Keynesian Economics* **5**, 182–98.

Davidson, P. (1987) User Cost, in *The Palgrave-Dictionary of Economics*, London, Macmillan.

Hamouda, O. and Rowley, R. (1996) Ignorance and the Absence of Probabilities, in C. Schmidt (ed.), *Uncertainty in Economic Thought*, Cheltenham, E. Elgar.

Keynes, J.M. (1930) *A Treatise on Money*, London, Macmillan.

Keynes, J.M. (1936) *The General Theory of Employment, Interest and Money*, London, Macmillan.

Keynes, J.M. (1973a) *The Collected Writings of John Maynard Keynes, Vol. XIII, The General Theory and After, Part I, Preparation*, London, Macmillan.

Keynes, J.M. (1973b) *The Collected Writings of John Maynard Keynes, Vol. XIV, The General Theory and After, Part II, Defence and Development*, London, Macmillan.

Kregel, J.A. (1977) On the Existence of Expectation in English Neoclassical Economics, *Journal of Economic Literature* **15**, 495–500.

Kregel, J.A. (1993) Keynesian Stabilisation Policy and Post-War Economic Performance, in E.Szirmai, B. van Ark and D. Pilat (eds), *Explaining Economic Growth*, Amsterdam, Elsevier, 429–45.

Kregel, J.A. (1996) The Theory of Value, Expectations and Chapter 17 of *The General Theory*, in G. Harcourt and P. Riach (eds), *The Second Edition of Keynes' General Theory*, London: Routledge, 251–72.

Minsky, H.P. (1986) *Stabilizing an Unstable Economy*, New Haven, Yale University Press.

Vicarelli, R (1984) *Keynes: The Instability of Capitalism*, Philadelphia, University of Pennsylvania Press.

Vicarelli, F. (1985) From Equilibrium to Probability: A Reinterpretation of the Method of the *General Theory*, in F. Vicarelli (ed.), *Keynes's Relevance Today*, London, Macmillan.

Vicarelli, F. (1985–86) Natural Laws and Economic Policy: Some Considerations on the Theoretical Foundations of the New Classical Macroeconomics, *Journal of Post Keynesian Economics* VIII, 298–314.

Chapter 18

RATIONAL SPIRITS AND THE POST KEYNESIAN MACROTHEORY OF MICROECONOMICS(*)

1 RATIONAL AND NON-RATIONAL THEORIES OF ECONOMIC BEHAVIOUR

According to Dornbusch and Fisher (and the editors who requested a survey of 'non-rational (*sic*) theories of the formation of expectations related to the microfoundations of macroeconomics') the post Keynesian 'rejection of individual rationality and maximization as a basis of behaviour by firms and households has kept the approach at odds with the mainstream of the profession that has been attempting to bring macroeconomics into closer touch with microeconomics' (1984, p. 571). This interpretation of post Keynesian theory as rejecting the assumption of rational agents, the *homo economicus* of Classical theory, appears to be based on two factors. First, and probably the most pervasive, is the pre-eminent role given to 'animal spirits' in the determination of the level of investment. The second is the rejection of any possibility of bringing Keynes' theory into 'closer touch' with traditional microeconomics, reflecting Hicks' view that the investigations of the microfoundations of macroeconomics have demonstrated that it is the former which is the branch of theory most in need of foundations. Post Keynesian theory thus proposes the macrofoundations of microeconomics, and the development of a theory of the behaviour of money prices based on liquidity preference. The two points are related by the fact that Keynes' explanation of the 'rational' response to uncertainty is the use of money as a store of value, the price of money being determined by the effect of uncertainty on liquidity preference and the decisions to hold positions in all other goods then determining their prices so as to bring their rates of return into equality with the money rate of interest.

The idea of a macrofoundation for microeconomics within post Keynesian theory in fact predates the modern microfoundations discussion and can be found in the work of Kalecki on the degree of monopoly, Andrews on full-cost pricing, Weintraub on the stability of the mark-up and, more in general, the use of these approaches to provide a microfoundation for the macroeconomic models of economic growth linked to the names of Robinson, Kaldor and Pasinetti. As this brief essay cannot cover the entire range of work in this area we simply note the representative work of Marris, Eichner, Wood, and Earl and concentrate on a simplified presentation of the relation between uncertainty, money and Keynes' theory of value.

2 KEYNES AND 'RATIONAL SPIRITS'

For most interpreters Keynes' concept of 'animal spirits' is purely subjective, without any basis in the objective occurrence of events. It is thus incapable of theoretical generalisation and, as emphasised by Shackle in particular, incapable of being described in terms of the theory of mathematical probability based on a frequency distribution of randomly occurring perfectly known events. It is thus said to be incapable of 'rational' representation.

Few proponents of this view (but see Dow and Dow for an important exception) seem to have taken the trouble to follow Keynes' explicit references linking the concept to his earlier work on the subject in his *Treatise on Probability*. There he clearly states that decisions will be based on the probability of a proposition determined by means of a process which 'is not ... subject to human caprice. A proposition is not probable because we think it so. When once the facts are given which determine our knowledge, what is probable or improbable in these circumstances has been fixed objectively, and is independent of our opinion. The theory of probability is logical, therefore, because it is concerned with the degree of belief which it is *rational* to entertain in given conditions, and not merely with the actual beliefs of particular individuals which may or may not be rational' (1921, p. 4, emphasis in the original). It is important to note that Keynes is not here arguing that every individual will attach the same probability to a proposition, for different individuals will have different facts at their disposal and will have different past experiences (he even suggests that 'the constitution of the human mind may vary in some degree from man to man,' *ibid.* p. 18). Thus 'What we know and what probability we can attribute to our rational beliefs is, therefore, subjective in the sense of being relative to the individual, but given the body of premises which our subjective powers and circumstances supply to us, and given the kinds of logical relations, upon which arguments can be based and which we have the capacity to perceive, *the conclusions which it is rational for us to draw, stand to these premises in an objective and wholly logical relation'* (*ibid.* p. 19, emphasis added). Keynes thus considers his theory to be both objective and rational in the sense that any two individuals, faced with the same evidence and with the same experience, would place the same degree of rational belief in a proposition as expressed in an identical probability.

The problem that concerns Keynes is how individuals reach rational beliefs when their knowledge of propositions is not certain. Keynes considers two cases of determination of rational belief when knowledge is 'uncertain.' The first relates to the formulation of a probability which is based either on uncertain information or 'doubtful arguments' (*ibid.*, p. 3), while the second concerns the case in which it is impossible even to formulate a rational belief, in which case it is rational to allow 'animal spirits' to prevail. In his *General Theory* Keynes argued that traditional theory excludes both types of uncertainty, that it analyses typical human decision-making as if all individuals had certain knowledge of what he calls primary propositions. In Keynes' terms this might be expressed as follows.

Let h be the evidence obtained from direct experience about a primary proposition p, such that a secondary proposition p/h expresses the highest degree of rational belief, *a, i.e.* that associated with certainty: 'The peculiarity of certainty is that knowledge of a secondary proposition involving certainty, together with knowledge of what stands in this secondary proposition in the position of evidence, leads to *knowledge of,* and not merely *about,* the corresponding primary proposition' (*ibid.,* p. 15). Since this knowledge is also presumed in statistical probability theory Keynes criticised it as an adequate method to describe 'uncertain' events.

Keynes' analysis of the probability of an event, heads, of a fair coin, would include in *h* the facts that the coin is fair and has one head and one tail, as *p* the proposition that heads will appear in 50% of an infinite number of events, in order to determine the degree of rational belief or the probability, *a,* expressed in a secondary proposition $p/h = a$. Here we note that Keynes is not concerned with the probability of the occurrence of a perfectly described set of possible events, but with the probability of the proposition *p* which asserts a probability for the event, *i.e.* whether, and in what degree, it is rational to believe *p.* The uncertainty reflects the inconclusive basis of our knowledge explaining the occurrence, not of the existence of the occurrence.

The probability expressed by this secondary proposition, as any other statement of probability, Keynes argues, is relative to *h,* the favourable and contrary evidence; the probability will measure the balance of, and thus be relative to, this evidence. When *h* contains an infinite number of repetitions there is no evidence unfavourable to the proposition and the probability asserted by the secondary proposition is unity. In Keynes' sense the certainty expressed by the secondary proposition implies knowledge of the primary proposition. The experience (the infinite number of events) that is included in *h,* which Keynes calls direct, is not obtained by argument. But once it has been used to obtain a probability it can be dispensed with, *e.g.* once we have made the experiment of tossing the coin and the secondary proposition asserts a probability of certainty we have direct knowledge of the primary proposition which is considered as true in the same way as if we had direct knowledge of it.

There is, however, a second type of uncertainty. Keynes argues that in certain circumstances it may be impossible to assert a probability, to formulate the degree of rational belief in a proposition: 'Is our expectation of rain, when we start out for a walk, always *more* likely than not, or *as* likely as not? I am prepared to argue that on some occasions that *none* of these alternatives hold, and that it will be an arbitrary matter to decide for or against the umbrella. If the barometer is high, but the clouds are black, it is not always rational that one should prevail over the other in our minds, or even that we should balance them, – though it will be rational to allow caprice to determine us and to waste no time on the debate.' ... 'It is not the case here that the method of calculation, prescribed by theory, is beyond our powers or too laborious for actual application. *No* method of calculation, however impracticable, has been suggested' (*ibid.,* p. 32). If no probability can be expressed in a secondary proposition, or where it is possible to attach a probability but it cannot be expressed in such a way which allows comparison with the probability attached to another proposition, the rational decision-maker will have to follow his animal spirits. Although Lawson (1985) limits the definition of uncertainty to only those cases where no probability can be attached, Keynes appears to consider incalculability and incomparability as equivalent as expressions of uncertainty.

Post Keynesian criticisms of the use of the frequency theory of probability to describe uncertainty have tended to combine, and sometimes confuse, these two arguments. For example, Shackle has argued that the investment decision is a 'crucial' decision which does not bear repetition: *h* cannot include repeated 'trials.' Further, it may be impossible for the entrepreneur to identify all the possible sides of the coin as part of the direct experience included in *h*. The sum of the probabilities of all propositions, *p*, envisaged thus cannot be constrained to unity.

It is in this respect that Shackle's objection to the use of statistical probability based on a frequency distribution to represent the uncertainty associated with an investment decision can be recognised. Investment decisions will in general relate to conditions in which secondary propositions express uncertainty. But, if it is possible to calculate a probability through the formulation of a secondary proposition concerning the primary proposition *p* that an investment will yield a certain rate of return for a given *h*, Keynes' approach suggests that every entrepreneur faced with this same situation (and with the same mental capacity) will attach the same degree of rational belief to the proposition and act on it in precisely the same way. If they do not, it must be because of the subjective differences which attach to different individuals including differences in their evaluation of the content of *h*. While Shackle defines such decisions as 'irrational,' they are only irrational within the statistical theory of probability; within Keynes' terminology such conditions simply represent a case of less than certain rational belief. It does not imply the necessity of caprice or irrationality within Keynes' theory. It is thus important not to confuse the inability to calculate a *statistical* probability based on a frequency distribution, which simply leads in Keynes' theory to a degree of rational belief which is less than certain, with the more extreme proposition that it is impossible to form a degree of rational belief, because there is no relevant experience available so that it is impossible to assign a probability, or that it is impossible to compare degrees of rational belief in a way which allows the formulation of a decision without reference to the rationality of animal spirits or what one might call 'rational spirits.'

In this respect we may note that the emphasis that the theory of rational expectations places on the basis for forming expectations does appear to meet Keynes' insistence that the theory of probability should refer not to the occurrence of events, but to our assertions about the occurrence of those events, to the formation of expectations. Rational expectations might thus be described as a theory concerning the formulation of secondary propositions containing primary propositions that are statistical probabilities of events generated on the basis of an economic model and which have probability approaching certainty as the observations of the events occurring over time included in *h* become large. Here the certainty of rational belief derives from the presumption that the subjective probability distribution of the value of the predicted variable contained in the experience related to the secondary proposition $p|h = a$ conforms to the objective distribution which generates the actual values of the variable. But, as Davidson (1982–83) has pointed out, this will only be the case generally if the process generating the events about which individuals have to form expectations are ergodic.[1] In Shackle's view this is equivalent to assuming there are no 'crucial experiments.' Or, in Keynes' terms, in a stochastic system which is ergodic every secondary proposition would have to express a certain rational belief, which also produces knowledge of the primary proposition, given that *h* includes all available information. Individuals would thus also have direct knowledge of the objective process. It is then not necessary to assume that the economic model which furnishes the primary propositions is coincident with the real world, for it may be a transform, or a reduced form, which is only remembered after the structural equations have been forgotten. Thus, although rational expectations do address the problem of the formation of expectations in terms of the probability of rational belief expressed by secondary propositions, they are limited to ergodic processes.

It would thus appear that the term 'rational,' as used by traditional theory, can only refer to the limited conditions of certainty of rational belief in a world governed by ergodic stochastic processes; the possibility of decision or choice in uncertain conditions is thus excluded, or classified as 'non-rational.'[2] But, as seen above, Keynes attempted the formulation of a theory of expectations formation in conditions in which the degree of rational belief in propositions is less than certain. It is clear from Chapter 12 of the *General Theory* that the investment decision is the most important application of such a theory. It is indeed unfortunate that commentators who have not bothered to follow Keynes' explicit references to his work on probability consider this chapter as exhibiting the heights of his journalistic style and being devoid of theoretical content rather than representing an attempt to simplify a complex argument concerning the basis of human knowledge!

In this economic application of his theory Keynes appears to adopt the view that while it is in most cases possible, indeed necessary, to express the probabilities asserted by secondary propositions concerning any investment decision, these probabilities will not in general be comparable because the facts of experience which enter *h* for the various primary propositions differ or may not exist: 'Our knowledge of the factors which will govern the yield of an investment some years hence is usually very slight and often negligible. If we speak frankly, we have to admit that our basis of knowledge for estimating the yield ten years hence of an investment] amounts to little and sometimes to nothing' (1936, pp. 149–150).

Where there is no direct knowledge, *h* is empty, and Keynes suggests that rational behaviour will in fact be based on conventional behaviour – by reference to average opinion. For the more general, but formally identical case, where *h* is not empty, but the resulting probabilities of competing secondary propositions cannot be compared, Keynes suggests that a second aspect of probability, the 'weight of the argument,' will become dominant. (*Cf.* Hoogduin, 1987, p. 57, ff., who puts this view in contrast to Lawson.) As Keynes put it, 'It seems that there may be another respect in which some kind of quantitative comparison between arguments is possible. This comparison turns upon a balance, not between the favourable and the unfavourable evidence, but between the *absolute* amounts of relevant knowledge and of relevant ignorance respectively. ... As the relevant evidence at our disposal increases, the magnitude of the probability of the argument may either decrease or increase, according as the new knowledge strengthens the unfavourable or the favourable evidence; but *something* seems to have increased in either case, – we have a more substantial base upon which to rest our conclusion. I express this by saying that an accession of new evidence increases the *weight* of the argument' (1921, p. 77). It is precisely to the weight of the argument that Keynes refers when he discusses the role of confidence in the investment decision: 'The state of long term expectation, upon which our decisions are based, does not solely depend, therefore, on the most probable forecast we can make. It also depends on the *confidence* with which we make this forecast ... The *state of confidence* ... is a matter to which practical men always pay the closest and most anxious attention. But economists have not analysed it carefully ... The state of confidence is relevant because it is one of the major factors determining [the schedule of the marginal efficiency of capital], which is the same thing as the investment demand schedule' (1936, pp. 148–149). Thus when it is impossible to give expression to rational belief, it is the weight of the argument which becomes the dominant factor which allows alternative investment decisions to be assessed and decisions taken. Here the subjectivity of individual differences may become dominant, for an individual's experience will determine the weight to be attached to new evidence.

It seems that this is the point at which animal spirits come into play in the *General Theory*, in deciding when the weight of the argument of a proposition is sufficient to make it prevail over all other propositions, by the 'spontaneous urge to action rather than inaction' which makes it seem irrelevant to gather additional information to increase the weight of the argument and thus the state of confidence.

After outlining both the role of convention and spontaneous urge in the investment decision, Keynes goes on to assure the reader he 'should not conclude from this that everything depends on waves of irrational psychology' for, as argued above, these decisions are decidedly based on "rational spirits": 'our rational selves choosing between the alternative as best we are able, calculating where we can, but often falling back for our motive or whim or sentiment or chance' (1936, pp. 162–163).

Given the importance of the 'state of expectation' in determining the level of investment it should be stressed that in contrast to traditional probability theory, additional evidence will produce a new secondary proposition (because it changes *h)* which may assert either a higher or lower probability, and which may or may not be comparable with the probability of the initial proposition, but which will have a greater weight and thus provide a better means of decision. Postponing a decision in order to acquire more information thus need not increase the probability, but it will increase the confidence in the probability asserted by a proposition and thus increase the basis for making a decision. In the case of statistical probability there is always a sufficient amount of information available to produce a certain basis for decision-making, one has simply to wait for the passage of time to produce more observations or be willing to pay the cost of gathering the additional information. On Keynes' view, however, even if the information exists it may not enable the individual to take a decision because he cannot evaluate it or has no basis for comparing it. The only course which is then open is to increase the weight of the argument. But unlike the logical probability, the weight of the argument has no limits such as certainty or impossibility. When is the weight of the argument sufficient to lead to a decision to act on its basis? To this question Keynes provides no answer, and suggests that there is none for it is not possible to balance the cost of additional information against increased weight as it is possible to balance the cost of additional information against increased certainty in the traditional approach.

Whether the post Keynesian theories are 'rational' or 'irrational' depends then not so much on the definition of the term 'rational' as on the definition of the process which governs the events about which we must form expectations. If it is an ergodic stochastic process then animal spirits are not only not rational, they are unnecessary; if it is non-ergodic then the failure to use 'rational spirits' is not only irrational, but the use of statistical probability would in most cases produce consistently erroneous predictions. Or, in Shackle's view: 'If choice is originative, it can give a thrust to the course of things intended to secure its ends. In order to secure its ends, choice must apply a knowledge of what will be the consequence of what. But the sequel of an action chosen by one man will be shaped by circumstances, and its circumstances will include the actions chosen now and actions to be chosen in time to come by other men. If, therefore, choice is effective, it is unpredictable and thus defeats, in some degree, the power of choice itself to secure exact ends' (1974, p. 1). Thus, if each individual's decisions can change the course of events and they cannot be predicted, the information required in h will not exist when it is required to make a probability calculation. Yet, this does not mean that probabilities will not be calculated or that there is no basis for rational belief capable of leading to decision and choice.

This view of uncertainty and 'rational spirits' provides an explanation of why Keynes chose to present his theory, not by starting with a theory of perfect certainty, and then attempting to introduce aspects of uncertainty, but rather by accepting the ubiquitous nature of uncertainty, formulating this theory in terms of a constant state of long term expectations and then introducing shifting expectations (*cf.* Kregel, 1976). At any point of time entrepreneurs will have attached probabilities to a series of investment propositions and each will also have a weight of the argument expressed as the state of confidence. A different state of confidence, implying a different state of long term expectation will thus give a different combination of investment decisions and a different position to the marginal efficiency of capital curve. In order to trace out the implications of a given level of investment, it was thus necessary to assume a given state of confidence in order to keep the weight of the argument from changing and producing a varying set of investment decisions. This given state of expectations may be expressed as the assumption that for every investment decision taking place, the weight of the argument is just sufficient to produce a decision to undertake the investment under consideration at a point in time.

But how does all this fit in with microfoundations? The answer is to be found in why the information required for certain propositions is not available, in why the system is non-ergodic. The simplest answer, as suggested in the quotation from Shackle given above, is because the events that have to be predicted in economic analysis are not parts of the objective physical universe, but are the results of decisions of other individuals which are currently being taken and which will be taken in future. Now, if we could assume that all individuals were identical both in respect to their physical make-up and their experience we could expect that in similar circumstances they would formulate similar propositions, *i.e.* we could predict $p|h$, and on the basis of Keynes' theory of probability predict the probability that would be assigned and the associated weight of the argument, thereby predicting their 'rational' decision. But, as Shackle has taken great pains to point out in criticism of Keynes' theory, this objectivity is illusory because individuals are not the same. Each will have a different background and experience, will produce different propositions and have different evaluations of evidence. As Adam Smith long ago pointed out in his *Theory of Moral Sentiments,* this is private information which cannot be transmitted and therefore cannot be known. At best it can be imagined. The information which determines the outcome of economic propositions, as Shackle would say, is invented in the very process of making a decision. It is for this reason that waiting for additional information does not increase the degree of rational belief since it provides a new set of decisions and new propositions. As Keynes himself put the point: 'The pseudo-analogy with the physical sciences leads directly counter to the habit of mind which is most important for an economist proper to acquire. I also want to emphasize strongly the point about economics as a moral science. ... it deals with introspection and with values. I might have added that it deals with motives, expectations, psychological uncertainties. ... It is as though the fall of the apple to the ground depended on the apple's motives, on whether it is worth while falling to the ground, and whether the ground wanted the apple to fall, and on mistaken calculations on the part of the apple as to how far it was from the centre of the earth' (1973, p. 300).

The 'non-ergodicity' of the system then ultimately results from the fact that individual actions are constrained by the actions of other individuals which cannot be predicted with certainty and thus when taken together form an aggregate or global or macroeconomic constraint which is not the simple, linear, and therefore predictable summation of individual behaviour. Thus it is not macroeconomics that has to be brought into closer touch with microeconomics, but rather one must try to formulate a macrofoundation for uncertain individual decisions.

3 RATIONAL SPIRITS, MONEY AND THE THEORY OF VALUE[3]

This macrofoundation can only be found in the role of money in the economic system. In his much read, but little understood 1937 *Quarterly Journal of Economics* article, Keynes repeats his 'philosophical disquisition on the behaviour of mankind,' and concludes that the first implication to be drawn is the 'treatment of money and interest' (Keynes, 1937, in 1973 p. 115). After noting that in conditions of certainty there is no possible explanation, for 'anyone outside a lunatic asylum,' to hold money as a store of value, Keynes goes on to note that in reality, 'our desire to hold money as a store of wealth is a barometer of the degree of our distrust of our own calculations and conventions concerning the future. ... The possession of actual money lulls our disquietude; and the premium which we require to make us part with money is the measure of the degree of our disquietude' (*ibid.*, p. 116). This premium, the liquidity premium, is the rate of interest, determined by what Keynes dubs liquidity preference. Here one might be tempted to instantly draw an inverse relation between the state of confidence and the degree of liquidity preference, thereby linking the decision to hold money directly to the analysis of decision-making given above.

Keynes goes on to emphasise that it is not the quantity of money which will influence prices, but rather 'fluctuations in the degree of confidence,' which 'are capable of having quite a different effect, namely, in modifying not the amount that is actually hoarded, but the amount of the premium which has to be offered to induce people not to hoard. ... changes in the propensity to hoard, or in the state of liquidity preference as I have called it, primarily affect, not prices, but the rate of interest.' It is the role of the rate of interest to determine 'the price of capital assets,' for the owner of wealth has two alternatives, he may invest or remain liquid. In equilibrium these alternatives must offer equal advantage which 'is brought about by shifts in the money prices of capital assets relative to the prices of money loans. The prices of capital assets move until, having regard to their prospective yields and account being taken of all those elements of doubt and uncertainty, interested and disinterested advice, fashion, convention and what else you will which affect the mind of the investor, they offer an equal apparent advantage to the marginal investor who is wavering between one kind of investment and another' (*ibid.*, 116–117). It is on the basis of these prices relative to the cost of newly produced assets that decisions are taken to produce new capital goods, *i.e.* the level of investment which *via* the multiplier produces the level of aggregate income (*cf.* Kregel, 1987).

As Townshend (1937) was quick to point out, Keynes' explanation of the role of prices in equating the advantages of holding money and other durables is an implicit criticism of traditional microeconomic theory: 'It would seem therefore, not to be the case that competition (even if perfect) would secure, even in the long run, an equality between selling-price and money-cost in new production at the margin...' ... 'Prices – even relative prices – are therefore not to be regarded as wholly *causally* determined by supply and demand at the margin of production' (*ibid.*, pp. 165, 168) but will rather be such to bring the prices of newly produced and existing assets into equality. This equality may be associated with either an excess or a deficiency of price and cost of production at the margin of production. 'Moreover, the compensating factors of supply and demand in new production never catch up with the continuous spontaneous variations in the liquidity-premiums attaching to the existing stocks. For production takes time; ... its effects on prices will not in general neutralise the instantaneous effects of the variations in the psychological preferences attaching to existing stocks' (*ibid.*, p. 168).

This point of view provides a new insight into the problem which first initiated the entire microfoundations debate: Keynes' claim to have derived a theory of unemployment equilibrium. Such a claim implied that it was possible to have equilibrium while one market was in disequilibrium in the sense that there was an excess supply of labour at the ruling real wage rate and this was in conflict with the general equilibrium configuration of traditional microeconomics. At the very least, the existence of excess supply in one market should be balanced by excess demand in some other market. Unemployment could thus still be explained by a disruption in the process of flexible price adjustment in either the labour or goods market.

But, Keynes' theory of nominal prices suggests that equilibrium should be identified not by equality of supply and demand as represented by cost of production equal to price, but rather by the equality of rates of return on all existing durable assets. If it is the spot prices of newly produced and existing assets which are equal in equilibrium then it will generally be the case that spot prices will not equal forward or supply prices representing the costs of producing new future supplies. This means that as new supplies come onto the market through new production, supply will diverge from demand and the spot prices of existing and newly produced assets will have to be brought into equality.[4]

As Sraffa first pointed out in his 1932 review of Hayek 'in equilibrium spot and forward prices coincide' but, 'if, for any reason, the supply and demand for a commodity are not in equilibrium (*i.e.* its market price exceeds or falls short of its cost of production), its spot and forward prices diverge' (1932, p. 50). In Chapter 17 of the *General Theory* Keynes elaborated on this conception and proposed that at every point in time, equilibrium in a monetary economy, given the state of confidence, would be characterised by the equality of spot prices for all existing and newly produced goods. It was then also possible to speak of a long-period stationary equilibrium for the economy in which the spot and forward prices of all durables had been brought into equality so that their rates of return in money were all equal (and prices equaled costs of production). The question that was then posed was the level of investment and the rates of return at which this state would occur.

It is in answering this question that the nexus of uncertainty, money and prices intersects, for Keynes argues that it is the liquidity premium as given by the state of confidence which sets the limit which the rates of return of all other durable assets must achieve. But since it is a rate which is determined by the 'rational spirits' of entrepreneurs it will be a psychological, or better, a conventional, variable influenced by factors independent of the level of output which primarily affect costs of production and thus the supply prices of other durables. It is in this sense that liquidity preference sets the equilibrium relative money prices at which the prices of existing assets and newly produced assets are brought into equality. It is thus not an imperfection in the operation of the flexible price mechanism in determining prices which is at the basis of Keynes 'unemployment equilibrium, it is rather the imperfection of agents' knowledge causing uncertainty over the propositions determining the return of investment projects. Neither is the absence of a sufficient microfoundation the cause of the macroeconomic result of unemployment equilibrium; it is rather due to a difference in the specification of equilibrium prices in terms of both spot and forward prices and the determination of one crucial price, the rate of interest, by conventional factors because of the existence of uncertain knowledge.

Notes

* Comments by L. Hoogduin are gratefully acknowledged. He is relieved from any responsibility for my impressionistic presentation of Keynes' views on probability.

1 I shall continue to use ergodic and non-ergodic in the sense in which they have come to be known although it is apparently quite easy (as a statistician in Göttingen pointed out to me on the back of an envelope some years ago) to produce non-ergodic systems that are predictable from their past behaviour.

2 Instead of contesting the meaning of 'rational' it might be better to adopt Pareto's (1963) terminology and define Keynes' treatment as relating to 'non-logical' actions, *i.e.* to cases where the objective end of an action differs from its subjective purpose; in particular Pareto's 'Genus 2' where objectively actions do not have logical ends and purposes while subjectively they do. Such a case might be described as one in which an objective probability distribution does not exist, while agents attempt to form a subjective distribution. These would be cases in which the fallacy of composition applies.

3 A fuller discussion of the problems of price determination can be found in Kregel (1984).

4 It is thus possible to explain why prices will in general diverge from long-period costs of production without having to rely directly on arguments concerning the impact of the degree of competition on prices and employment (which Keynes always resisted) or the necessity for descriptive realism of the model; it is also obvious that this is an additional element in the explanation of the divergence between prices and costs that has been the main objective of the post Keynesian microeconomic theories based on mark-up pricing cited above p. 223.

REFERENCES

Carabelli, A. (1985), 'Keynes on Cause, Chance and Possibility,' in: Lawson and Pesaran.

Davidson, P. (1978), *Money and the Real World*, London.

———. (1982–3), 'Rational Expectations: A Fallacious Foundation for Studying Crucial Decision Making Processes,' *Journal of Post Keynesian Economics*.

Dornbusch, R. and S. Fischer (1984), *Macroeconomics*, Third edition, New York.

Dow, A. and S. Dow (1985), 'Animal Spirits and Rationality,' in: Lawson and Pesaran.

Earl, P. (1983), *The Economic Imagination*, Brighton.

Eichner, A.S. (1976), *The Mega-Corp and Oligopoly*, Cambridge.

Hoogduin, L. (1987). 'On the Difference between the Keynesian, Knightian and the "Classical" Analysis of Uncertainty,' *De Economist*.

Keynes, J.M. (1921), *The Theory of Probability*, Vol. VIII of *The Collected Writings*, London, 1973.

———. (1936), *The General Theory of Employment, Interest and Money*, London.

———. (1973), The General Theory and After: Part II, Vol. XIV of *The Collected Writings*, London.

Kregel, J.A. (1976) 'Economic Methodology in the Face of Uncertainty,' *Economic Journal*.

———. (1984), 'Expectations and Rationality within a Capitalist Framework,' in: E.J. Nell (ed.), *Free Market Conservatism*, London.

———. (1987), 'The Multiplier and Liquidity Preference: Two Sides of the Theory of Effective Demand,' in: A. Barrère (ed.), *The Foundations of Keynesian Analysis*, London.

———. (1985), 'Sidney Weintraub's Macrofoundations of Microeconomics and the Theory of Distribution,' *Journal of Post Keynesian Economics*.

Lawson, T. (1985), 'Uncertainty and Economic Analysis,' *Economic Journal*.

Lawson, T. and H. Pesaran (eds.) (1985), *Keynes' Economics*, London.

Maital, S. (1982), *Minds, Markets and Money*, New York.

Marris, R. (1964), *The Economic Theory of 'Managerial' Capitalism*, London.

Pareto, V. (1963), *The Mind and Society: A Treatise on General Sociology*, Vol. I, Non-Logical Conduct, New York.

Shackle, G. (1949), *Expectation in Economics*, Cambridge.

———. (1974), 'Decision: The Human Predicament,' in: *The Annals of the American Academy of Political and Social Science*, Vol. 412.

Sraffa, P. (1932), 'Dr. Hayek on Money and Capital,' *Economic Journal*.

Townshend, H. (1937), 'Liquidity Premium and the Theory of Value,' *Economic.* Journal.

Weintraub, S. (1957), 'The Microfoundations of Aggregate Demand and Supply,' *Economic Journal*.

Wood, A. (1975), *A Theory of Profits*, Cambridge.

Chapter 19

THE THEORY OF VALUE, EXPECTATIONS AND CHAPTER 17 OF *THE GENERAL THEORY*(*)

INTRODUCTION

The first edition of this book was directed to my fellow economists. At that time it was reasonable to presume that they would be sufficiently familiar with my prior work that a few brief references would be sufficient to indicate the extent to which it was incorporated in the present book. With the passage of time this presumption is no longer true; indeed, despite precise indications in the text and in footnotes, few readers of the original edition seem to have recognized the genesis of certain important innovations, such as user costs, in my earlier *Treatise on Money* (1930a, b). This problem was particularly acute in Chapter 17, which built on the interest rate parity theorem first set out in my *Tract on Monetary Reform* (1923), and on an extension of what I had called the 'short-period' theory of prices in Volume II of the *Treatise on Money* (1930b).

Although I alerted readers of the first edition to what I considered to be the important differences with respect to the *Treatise on Money,* they could only be appreciated by those familiar with my earlier work, and I was perhaps remiss in failing to stress sufficiently the continuity that remained. For example, in the Preface (page vii) I noted that:

> The relation between this book and my *Treatise on Money* . . . is probably clearer to myself than it will be to others; and what in my own mind is a natural evolution in a line of thought which I have been pursuing for several years, may sometimes strike the reader as a confusing change of view.

I went on to summarize 'the general relationship between the two books', noting that in the first:

> I failed to deal thoroughly with the effects of *changes* in the level of output. My so-called 'fundamental equations' were an instantaneous picture, taken on the assumption of a given output. They attempted to show how, assuming given output, forces could develop which involved a profit-disequilibrium, and thus required a change in the level of output. But the dynamic development . . . was left incomplete and extremely confused. This book, on the other hand, has evolved into what is primarily a study of the forces which determine

> changes in the scale of output and employment as a whole. . . . A monetary economy . . . is essentially one in which changing views about the future are capable of influencing the quantity of employment and not merely its direction. But our method of analysing the economic behaviour of the present under the influence of changing ideas about the future is one which depends on the interaction of supply and demand, and is in this way linked up with our fundamental theory of value.

Although this seems a clear enough indication that my main purpose was a dynamic theory driven by the impact of the future upon present decisions, and that this impact was linked to the role played by money in the economy, most economists have chosen to interpret my theory in terms of a static equilibrium of the economy described in terms of real output and expenditure with little if any reference to the impact of the future on the present. For example, they seem to have overlooked statements such as 'to-day's employment can be correctly described as being governed by today's expectations taken in conjunction with today's capital equipment' (*G.T.*: 50) given that 'It is by reason of the existence of durable equipment that the economic future is linked to the present' (*G.T.*: 146) and that this linkage could be represented by 'the introduction of the concepts of user costs and the marginal efficiency of capital' (ibid.). Such a position requited a major change from my earlier analysis, which I noted as follows:

> Whilst liquidity-preference due to the speculative-motive corresponds to what in my *Treatise on Money* I called 'the state of bearishness', it is by no means the same thing. For 'bearishness' is there defined as the functional relationship, not between the rate of interest (or price of debts) and the quantity of money, but between the price of assets and debts, taken together, and the quantity of money. This treatment, however, involved a confusion between results due to a change in the rate of interest and those due to a change in the schedule of the marginal efficiency of capital . . .
>
> (G.T.: *173)*

Since I presumed that readers of the *Treatise on Money* would be familiar with the theory of bearishness, I also presumed it would be obvious that the basic change and innovation in the new book involved, first, the limitation of this theory to the explanation of the rate of interest (or the price of financial assets), thereby making the supply and demand for saving and investment redundant; but more importantly, the creation of a separate, independent theory to explain the return to capital assets, which I called the marginal efficiency of capital.

The first difference created the possibility of adopting Richard Kahn's multiplier analysis to explain the equality of savings and investment and served to reinforce the role of liquidity preference, or 'bearishness', in determining the rate of interest. The second was the result of carrying to its logical conclusions the realization that there was no general, theoretical basis for a relation between the physical output produced by physical capital assets and the return obtained by the entrepreneur operating the equipment and selling the output produced. Although this realization was not revolutionary – it had already appeared in Irving Fisher's rate of return over cost[1] and I was able to cite passages from Marshall's *Principles* which also make the point – other writers, aside from

Marx and a few ignored heretics, had failed to draw its full implications for economic theory.

My own position was based on prior work[2] which convinced me that Marx had been correct when he argued that the capitalist is only interested in his monetary return. The operation of capital goods could thus be profitable, even without being productive in the sense of producing a large amount of physical product. Of course, once one sees the point there is no more reason to believe that capital earns a return because it is productive than because of some other physical (or even metaphysical) attribute, such as being 'smelly'. The point was that there was no identifiable relationship between the difference between money costs and money receipts, and the physical conditions which characterize the production process.[3]

This rejection of a natural, or physically determined, rate of return such as Wicksell's natural rate, which had played a role in my *Treatise on Money* analysis of the relation between saving and investment, meant that the explanation of the investment decision and the role of 'bearishness' had to be reconsidered. But rejecting the natural rate of interest also meant that a single explanation could no longer explain both the rate of interest and the return on capital assets (or the prices of both assets and debts). I thus restricted 'bearishness' to the determination of the prices of financial assets in the form of liquidity preference', and developed the marginal efficiency of capital for capital goods. I subsequently discovered that this approach was similar to the theories of a number of earlier writers such as Veblen and Myrdal, as well as Schumpeter whom I had used as an authority for my analysis of investment in the *Treatise on Money*. I believe that the novelty of my own presentation of this line of thought lies in the introduction of the concept of user costs into supply prices, in particular of capital goods, and thus its inclusion in the calculation of the marginal efficiency of capital.

What I did not stress sufficiently was that my attempt to remedy my 'incomplete and confused' description of dynamics was built on the earlier attempt to enunciate a theory of short-period prices to complement what could be considered as the 'normal prices' which emerged from the 'fundamental equations' of the *Treatise on Money*. This was particularly true of the idea of user costs, which was meant to introduce the impact of future expectations into the dynamic structure of *The General Theory*.

THE GENESIS OF THE DYNAMICS OF *THE GENERAL THEORY* IN THE SHORT-PERIOD THEORY OF PRICES

Since most readers have failed to recognize both the continuity and the importance of user costs, I shall try to make this more explicit. It is useful to start with the fundamental equations of the *Treatise on Money*. They represented a departure from the quantity theory tradition by explaining the equilibrium (or normal) prices of 'available goods' by unit costs (primarily wages, but including 'normal' remuneration of entrepreneurs). They were equilibrium prices in the sense that no one had any incentive to change the contractual cost relations upon which they were based. This applies to quantities produced, as well as to prices and wages.

Any divergence from normal conditions was represented by windfall profits or losses; the divergence of prices from normal is an expression of aggregate disequilibrium between demand and supply for 'available output', or equivalently, between savings and investment representing demand and supply conditions for 'unavailable output'. This was represented in the second term of the fundamental equation. Windfall profits or losses would be reflected in undesired decreases or increases in stocks of unsold goods; any attempt to adjust production would then reveal deficient or excess productive capacity. In such conditions normal prices would no longer rule, and attempts would take place to renegotiate contracts concerning both prices and quantities to determine a new set of normal prices and quantities. It is in this sense that the theory dealt with a given level of output.

The most important question which was left unanswered was whether the price and quantity adjustments which would be set in motion by the disequilibrium would automatically eliminate the imbalance without changing the level of output and employment. It was clearly beyond the scope of the fundamental equations to predict the results of these changes and my discussion of these aspects of adjustment was contained in a short section on the 'short-period theory of prices' in Volume II. The idea was to indicate how disequilibrium in the form of excess (or deficient) stocks and productive capacity would influence the movement of prices and quantities with respect to the normal flow supply prices and quantities embodied in the 'fundamental equations'. Given the period in which the book was written, it was natural to deal with conditions of generalized excess supply, although the theory was not restricted to that case.

In simple terms, the idea is that excess stocks will cause prices to fall below their 'normal' levels; if this creates expectations of further reductions in prices, the actual behaviour of prices will shift from being determined by the 'fundamentals' of costs of production, to the short-period conditions of stock supplies in which production costs become irrelevant because supply is dominated by decisions to sell from existing stocks. This change in the factors determining prices is roughly similar to Marshall's distinction between market prices and long-period prices, but the distinction is not analytical or temporal, it is determined by actual supply conditions and expectations.

In conditions of excess stocks, prices will continue to fall as long as producers believe they can minimize losses by selling today at a higher price than they expect tomorrow. Thus prices will continue to fall until they reach a level which convinces entrepreneurs to reduce production and to hold existing stocks on the expectation that a competitive return may be made by selling them at a better price at a later date. The movement of short-period prices will then be determined by the relation between current prices and the expected future prices. For convenience I assumed that the expectation of future prices was of a recovery to the 'normal' prices given by the fundamental equations, so that 'a mere change in expectations is capable of producing an oscillation of the same kind as a cyclical movement . . . which I discussed in my *Treatise on Money*' (*G.T.*: 49).

Thus a fall in prices would only come to a halt when it was sufficient to convince a speculator that he could earn a competitive return by buying existing stocks at the reduced current, or spot, price and holding them for sale at the normal future or forward price. Crucial to the calculation of this return is the length of time expected to elapse until restoration of normal conditions, as well as the costs of holding the stocks, which would include warehousing, insurance and financing costs given by the rate of interest. Also, any changes in the rate of current production and consumption of output will change the expectation of the holding period. In general, I concluded that the higher is the rate of interest, or other components of carrying costs, the longer is the time to recovery, the larger is the size of stocks relative to normal demand, the lower is the reduction in production with respect to price and the lower is the expansion in demand in response to the fall in price, the greater is the fall in the current price which will be required to induce the expectation of a market rate of return from holding excess stocks. All this I set out in a neat little formula, $pq = xy$, where q is the proportionate reduction in normal output due to the fall in price, x is the cost of carry as a proportion of the expected normal price, y is the time period until the return to normal conditions, and p is the proportionate fall in the spot price relative to the expected future price. These are the factors which will determine both the depth and the length of the cyclical downturn, as well as the behaviour of prices. Of course, the cyclical evolution of prices may itself bring about changes in the factors which determine 'normal' prices and quantities; this is what I failed to work out fully. Nonetheless, for analytical purposes it is useful to start by keeping the two arguments separate by assuming given expectations and thus an expectation of a return to 'normal' conditions. This is what might be called static or stationary conditions, which stop short of the 'shifting' equilibrium which represents the dynamics of *The General Theory*.[4]

The idea of 'user costs' followed directly from this analysis. Since stocks which are being held are expected to yield a return equal to the difference between their current or 'spot' price and the expected normal, or 'forward', price, a decision to 'use' them, either as an input in production or by selling them at the current spot price, will lead to the loss of this expected future gain. The 'user cost' associated with using stocks today is thus the present value of the expected net future return which could be realized by waiting to sell at the expected normal price.

THE PRESENTATION OF EFFECTIVE DEMAND IN TERMS OF SPOT AND FORWARD PRICES

In my attempt to break away from the quantity theory of money in the *Treatise on Money* I shifted the focal point of the analysis to the effective decision-makers in the economy, to the 'effort of producers or to the expenditure of consumers' (1930a: 120). The realization that there was no theoretical relation between real returns and profitability thus led me to define the 'efforts of producers' as

> whether it is expected to *pay* a firm in possession of capital equipment to spend money on incurring variable costs: i.e. whether the result of spending money on employment and of selling the output is expected to result in a larger net sum of money at the end of the accounting period than if the money had been retained. Other criteria, such as the relation between the real output which a given employment will yield and the disutility or real cost of that employment, or the relation between the real wages of a given employment and the

> amount of its marginal output, are not appropriate to the actual nature of business decisions in a world in which prices are subject to change during an accounting period, such changes being themselves a function *inter alia* of the amount of investment during the period.
>
> *(C.W. XXIX: 66)*

But it was clearly insufficient to suggest that entrepreneurs would be satisfied simply by recovering their money sums committed; they would seek the highest possible returns available by committing their funds in any way, not only for production of output.

I put the idea in the last 1933 draft of *The General Theory* as follows:

> The employment of the factors of production to increase output involves the entrepreneur in the disbursement, not of product, but of money. The choice before him in deciding whether or not to offer employment is a choice between using money in this way or in some other way or not using it at all. . . . The only question before him is to choose . . . that way which will yield the largest profit in terms of money. It must be remembered that future prices, in so far as they are anticipated, are already reflected in current prices, after allowing for the various considerations of carrying costs and of opportunities of production in the meantime which relate the spot and forward prices of a given commodity.[5] Thus we must suppose that the spot and forward price structure has already brought into equilibrium the relative advantages, as estimated by the holder, of holding money and other existing forms of wealth. Thus if the advantage in terms of money of using money to start up a productive process increases, this will stimulate entrepreneurs to offer more employment. . . . For the entrepreneur is guided, not by the amount of product he will gain, but by the alternative opportunities for using money having regard to the spot and forward price structure taken as a whole.
>
> (C.W. *XXIX: 82–3)*

Now, define the per unit cost associated with producing output as the current supply price, or spot price, of that output, and the present value of the net sum received per unit of output as its demand or forward price. Then the 'actual nature of the business decision', which determines the 'effort of producers', will be described by the comparison of the spot and expected forward prices. If this is positive, and as a proportion of the initial expenditure represents a return greater than the interest promised by the 'alternative opportunities for using money' (or the costs of borrowing the money expended), then production will proceed, and output and employment will be created.

I extended this basic idea of comparing spot and forward prices for an individual commodity, derived from the short-period pricing formula, to the actual sums expended and the sums expected to be received by each entrepreneur relative to the amount of employment created. Given the number of entrepreneurs in the economy, it was thus possible to derive a similar relation for the economy as a whole, which became the 'Aggregate Supply Price' and 'Aggregate Demand Price' functions of Chapter 3 of *The General Theory*. The point at which the aggregate supply price and demand price functions intersect represents the equality of the rate of return from engaging in production and the 'alternative uses of money' represented by the rate of interest. Employment, and the output produced, could then be described as being determined at the 'point' of effective demand representing the intersection of the two functions.

The explanation that I attempted to give in Books III and IV[6] of the determinants of Aggregate Demand Prices in terms of the decision to consume and invest should then be understood as a discussion of the determinants of forward or futures prices. The formal presentation of the question of 'whether it is expected to *pay* a firm in possession of capital equipment to spend money on incurring variable costs' set out in Chapter 3 of *The General Theory* thus starts with the precise definition of the amount of money spent on 'the employment of a given volume of labour by an entrepreneur' as 'the amounts which he pays out to the factors of production for their current services' and 'the amounts he pays out to other entrepreneurs for what he has to purchase from them' plus 'the sacrifice which he incurs by employing the equipment instead of leaving it idle, which we shall call the user cost of the employment in question' (*G.T.*: 23). User cost thus plays a central role in determining variable costs. As a result, the difference between the expected states and the sum of costs paid to factors, plus user costs, is what it is expected to 'pay' a firm to operate the equipment: 'in a given situation of technique, resources and factor cost per unit of employment, the amount of employment, both in each individual firm and industry and in the aggregate, depends on the amount of proceeds which the entrepreneurs expect to receive from the corresponding output'.

The reason for these rather complicated definitions of aggregate or national income (which most readers have chosen to ignore) was to make clear the role of future expectations through user costs and aggregate demand prices. If A = aggregate sales proceeds, F = factor costs and U = user cost, then the sum of entrepreneurs' incomes will be the difference between gross receipts and costs of production: $A - (F + U)$. From this it follows that the total income for the economy, Y is composed of factor incomes, which are given by entrepreneurs' factor costs, F, plus entrepreneurs' income or $Y = F + [A - (F + U)] = A - U$. Defining A′ as entrepreneurs' acquisitions of output from other entrepreneurs, the value of consumption expenditures can be defined as $A - A'$, while investment will be $Y - (A - A')$ or $I = (A - U) - (A - A') = A' - U$. Entrepreneurs can only be expected to commit money to engage in production if they expect to recover their outlays. In the aggregate this is $F + A' - U = F + I$, which is defined as aggregate supply price.

Entrepreneurs will then have to determine whether the proceeds that they expect to receive from selling the output, or the aggregate demand price, meets or exceeds the aggregate supply price. The aggregate demand price will be composed of the sum of D_1, the proportion of the aggregate outlays (i.e. a proportion of $F + A' - U$) which entrepreneurs expect to earn from the public's expenditures on consumption, and D_2, the amount which entrepreneurs are expected to devote to new investment expenditures. Note that both amounts are net of user costs. Equality of aggregate supply and demand price, defined as the point of effective demand, is then where $F + I (= A' - U) = D_1 + D_2$. It will thus 'pay' entrepreneurs to increase expenditures of money to hire factors of production in order to increase output whenever 'demand price' is greater than 'supply price', for in such conditions current costs of production are below the expected future price (the price of the futures contract) so producers can 'go full steam ahead' on the expectation of selling their output to the future at a profit equal to the difference between the current spot or aggregate supply price and the expected futures or aggregate demand price.

This incentive will only be exhausted when the two prices have come into equality, which is the 'point of effective demand' and short-period equilibrium.

The determinants of this equality will depend on the proportion of F + A′ – U which consumers choose to spend as D_1 and determines firms' receipts from sales of consumption goods to the public. This proportion is given by what I called the 'propensity to consume'.[7] It will also depend on D_2, which is determined by the inducement to invest, and in particular on the second set of changes introduced in the book, the marginal efficiency of capital and user costs. In order for the equality between aggregate demand and aggregate supply price to occur at any particular level of employment, investment expenditures given by D_2 must make up for any divergence between income and consumption expenditures given by the difference between D_1 and F + A′ – U. If it does not automatically do so, the level of output and employment will change. Hence the enunciation of the factors leading to changes in the level of output.

It is important to notice that both aggregate supply and demand prices are net of user costs, so it might appear that they may be eliminated. However, this would not be appropriate for analysis of the decisions of individual producers, since user costs are the equivalent of carrying costs in the short-period price analysis. It would thus be possible to convert the difference between expected prices (aggregate or unit) and prime costs of production into a relation between the spot price of existing goods, flow supply prices and forward (or expected demand) prices. As long as the costs of production of new goods are less than the costs of carry of existing goods it will pay producers to sign contracts to supply goods at the expected future demand price and to go ahead and incur costs of using capital equipment to produce them. This is the condition which will allow entrepreneurs to end up with more 'money than they started with'. Note that expectations of future prices enter both the supply and the demand side, for they will determine the size of user costs, a component of marginal prime costs, and the expected future net receipts which are discounted to obtain demand prices. User costs will thus play a role in determining individual prices as well as the general price level.

Thus, the relation between spot and forward prices and the role of user costs in determining this relation based on the short-period pricing relation formed the basis for the presentation of effective demand on the aggregate level in Chapter 3. This is also the case for my 'new' explanation of the inducement to invest in Chapters 11 and 12, and the discussion of the rate of interest in Chapter 13 in relation to the estimation of D_2.

THE MARGINAL EFFICIENCY OF CAPITAL AND USER COSTS

Readers will recall that the *Treatise on Money* contained no 'fundamental equation' for the prices of capital goods. In discussions of the book I was criticized for this asymmetrical approach to the determination of the prices of available and non-available output by both Richard Kahn and Piero Sraffa. They suggested that since both are produced goods, consistency required that costs of production should determine both the prices of consumption and capital goods. While this may be the case for newly produced capital goods under normal conditions, they clearly differ from consumption goods in that they are long-lived and will survive into conditions which had not been foreseen, and thus may no longer be normal. From this point of view, the pricing of capital goods corresponds more closely to my short-period pricing theory, for since they are long-lived durable goods, old capital goods represent the equivalent of stocks which compete with newly produced goods.[8] As noted above: 'It is by reason of the existence of durable equipment that the economic future is linked to the present' (*G.T.*: 146).

Given the impact of the future on the present, current costs of production will no longer be relevant to the supply price of existing capital goods. The definition of effective demand given above requires the specification of the costs incurred by entrepreneurs in undertaking production. The costs incurred in the use of existing capital goods thus cannot be ignored. User costs provide the solution to this problem by defining the cost of using existing capital goods as the difference between the cost of holding them idle (i.e. the cost of keeping them in good productive condition plus interest charges) and the expected net return from using them to produce in the future. The rate of discount which equates the expected stream of future returns to the cost of producing new capital goods thus has to compete with the rate of discount which equates the expected stream of future returns to the supply prices of existing capital goods as determined by user costs. Just as in my short-period theory, if the prime cost of using existing capital is below the flow supply price for newly produced goods because their prices are expected to continue to fall, no one will demand new investment goods and investment expenditures included in A′ – U will be reduced.[9]

Thus my response to the criticisms of my *Treatise on Money* explanation of the prices of capital goods involved the introduction of future conditions for capital goods prices, which enter the supply prices of capital via user costs, and the expectations of conditions for output prices which determined expected future net receipts from operating the capital goods. As I noted, it is the correction of supply prices, rather than the specification of expected future profits, which represents the innovation. This explains why I wanted to emphasize the role of changes in marginal efficiency as being independent of the influence of liquidity preference and the rate of interest. For this reason Chapter 12 attempted to give 'full weight to the importance of the influence of short-period changes in the state of long-term expectations as distinct from changes in the rate of interest'.

Looked at from this perspective, the key to recovery is to produce conditions in which current spot prices stand in relation to future prices such that it again becomes more profitable to purchase newly produced goods rather than existing goods (i.e. 'backwardation' exists in the market). My short-period price analysis suggested that the easiest way to do this would be to reduce the rate of interest (to reduce the carrying costs) and to increase demand for existing stocks, i.e. by monetary expansion or by government expenditures.

There were two obstacles in the way of taking such action to promote recovery, the 'Treasury view', which opposed government expenditures, and the Bank of England's perceived unwillingness to reduce interest rates because of the fear of jeopardizing the foreign balance. My experience on the Macmillan Committee indicated to me that these two impediments were similar in nature. It there emerged that the 'Treasury view' was not, as commonly supposed, that government investment 'crowds out' private investment because investible resources, in the form of the supply of saving, are given;

but rather, that government investments are inefficient because they represent the use of resources in projects which earn returns that are lower than competitive market rates of return. In short, government investment to support demand was the equivalent of subsidizing investment and thus a distortion of the free market allocation of resources.

But there is a fallacy in this argument. Consider government investment in a project yielding a 4 percent return when the Bank rate is 6 percent. 'It is not true that the money going into the four per cent investment is going otherwise into a six per cent investment; for six per cent does not represent what an alternative investment is yielding, it represents the rate that has to be enforced by the banking system to prevent us from lending abroad more than we can finance by our trade balance' (*C.W.* XX: 146). In short, the alternative was not investment projects offering a 6 percent return, but the Bank of England offering that rate in order to stop capital flowing out of the country in an amount that exceeded the positive balance on current account. Further, since the current balance was primarily determined by relative wage costs, Bank rate did not even represent the returns which could be earned by investing abroad. Thus, far from the government subsidizing capital investment, it was the Bank of England that was subsidizing the purchase of financial assets. It was the Bank that was crowding out productive investment.

In this case, it was the requirements of foreign balance which produced a rate of interest that competed with domestic investment. But this explanation of the impediments to recovery by relaxing monetary policy was directly linked to the assumption of an open economy operating under the gold standard. In *The General Theory* I reconsidered this position, for it may have implied that a closed system, or even an open system with flexible exchange rates, might achieve full employment if the monetary authority set the rate of interest at the level at which investment took off full-employment saving.

In developing *The General Theory* I worked out the concept of a 'monetary economy' in which individual decisions concerning the disposition of liquid assets expressed in 'liquidity preference' could exercise an impact on interest rates which was as difficult to overcome as that represented by the necessity for the central bank to defend the foreign exchanges. This brought the formulation of the 'Monetary Production Economy' and the idea of effective demand formulated in terms of conditions of backwardation in the relation between spot and forward prices. In simple terms, not only would existing capital goods compete with new investment expenditures, financial assets would too. Since the return on existing capital goods was given by user costs, the supply price of financial assets would also be given by user costs, i.e. by a relation between spot and expected future prices.

I was thus able to avoid the contorted discussions of the determinants of the rate of interest found in the works of my contemporaries, and in logical conformity with the definition of aggregate demand and supply prices and the marginal efficiency of capital to define the rate of interest on money as 'nothing more than the percentage excess of a sum of money contracted for forward delivery, e.g. a year hence, over what we may call the "spot" or cash price of the sum thus contracted for forward delivery' (*G.T.*: 222). It is for this reason that I have on various occasions referred to the liquidity premium on money as its 'marginal efficiency' or of the rate of interest as measuring its 'user cost', for this is the return which is forgone by retaining wealth in liquid form. This then became the 'alternative employment' (rather than Bank rate) which competed against the use of the entrepreneur's money to produce output and offer employment.

CHAPTER 17 AS A 'GENERAL' THEORY OF SPOT AND FORWARD PRICES

As we have seen above, the specification of aggregate demand and supply was derived from the decisions of individual entrepreneurs to initiate production. Having applied this spot-forward price framework to the general decisions to purchase capital goods and non-liquid financial assets, it seemed reasonable to provide a general presentation, which I attempted in Chapter 17. I thought this would make it easier to see the role of money in producing the impact of future expectations on present decisions.[10] To do this I went back to my *Tract on Monetary Reform* and applied the interest rate parity theorem, substituting possible investment expenditures for the decisions to make investments denominated in the currencies of foreign countries. Just as an international investor must keep his accounts in one currency, and compare his returns from investments in foreign currencies to the rate of interest he earns on that currency, I argued that entrepreneurs would decide 'whether it is expected to *pay* . . . to spend money on incurring variable costs' to provide employment by keeping these accounts in terms of money. Thus the returns available on investments in other types of real or financial assets would have to compete with the return available on money.

In simple terms, if the relative prices of all alternative investments are expected to be stable, the equivalent of international interest rate parity is the equality between the liquidity premium attached to money as given by its marginal efficiency or rate of return, and the marginal efficiencies representing the rates of return available on the various possible investment alternatives. Just as international investors will adjust their portfolios of international currencies until there are no arbitrage gains to be made, investors will adjust their investments until they cannot increase their aggregate return by an alternative composition of investments.

Although I pointed out in Chapter 17 that any durable or producible good can be analysed by the method of spot and forward prices which I had already employed in the definition of the rate of interest on money and the rate of return to capital, so that it was formally the same as the analysis of the interest rate parity theorem, none of my readers seem to have taken these indications seriously. It is thus possible to envisage spot and forward prices for every durable commodity in the economy, including specific types of capital goods, which will determine its rate of return or marginal efficiency, as well as for every financial asset which will determine its rate of interest.

In an open economy under the gold standard the Bank of England was constrained to keep the rate of interest high enough to prevent capital outflows exceeding the current account balance, given British wages, productivity and prices. This was the rate of return which all other investments had to match. If the return on domestic investment is 4 percent, the return to investment abroad is 5 percent, and Bank rate is 6 percent, the Bank succeeds in limiting capital outflows, but only by redirecting entrepreneurs' funds into financial assets rather than capital investments, which causes a reduction in D^2. But if the level of interest rates required to bring balance on foreign account is sufficiently high, it may produce conditions of contango, the opposite of backwardation, and bring even the use of existing capital goods for production to a halt, producing a fall in F and a decline in D_1. At some proportionate fall in prices and restriction of output the expected rate of return from buying excess stocks and holding them until recovery will reach that available on financial assets so that prices stabilize. This would be what I defined in my Macmillan testimony as a 'spurious equilibrium', for although the rates of return on all alternative uses for entrepreneurs' funds are uniform, there is unused potential productive capacity which is not being used and there are idle workers available who would be willing to work for current levels of wages. In such conditions there is no incentive for entrepreneurs to commit new funds to produce additional output and provide employment, nor is there anything to stop an increase in national income and employment, except the level of the rate of interest.

It was thus British bank rate which set the standard that British investors had to meet in assessing the returns available on investments in diverse national currencies. In equilibrium the returns to be earned from holding any foreign asset denominated in foreign currency would be the same; yet this did not imply that the various national interest rates were identical. This difference was resolved by means of the adjustment of the premium or discount of the forward relative to the spot price of the various foreign currencies. Given one dominant international rate of interest, such as sterling Bank rate, the relative spot and forward prices will be determined so as to equalize the advantage of any individual currency, irrespective of its absolute rate of interest.

Chapter 17 thus follows my decision to separate liquidity preference and marginal efficiency by substituting the rate of return (or user cost or marginal efficiency) on money (or liquidity) for British bank rate, and by substituting the rate of return (or marginal efficiency) of every available durable good for the interest rates on foreign assets measured in terms of their own home currency. I called these latter rates their 'own-rates of own-return' because, just as with foreign interest rates, they were expressed in terms of themselves.[11]

This became the conceptual equivalent of what might be considered a 'real' or 'natural' rate of interest. For wheat, it would be the difference between the kernels of wheat planted and those harvested as a proportion of those planted. A 10 per cent 'own-rate of own-return' with reference to wheat was then eleven kernels of gross return for every ten advanced. This can equivalently be expressed as the forward or demand price of wheat relative to the spot or supply price, measured in terms of wheat.[12] Just as in the international system, equilibrium would occur when the relative advantages of all types of investment, in holding existing goods, in operating existing capital goods, in building new capital goods, in lending to businessmen and so forth, had reached equality.

However, the calculation of this equilibrium position, just as in the international case, has to be undertaken in terms of a single currency or durable good, which is money, so that while entrepreneurs would look at 'own-rates of own-return', they would only be interested in those which will 'yield the largest profit in terms of money' so that it could be compared to 'the alternative opportunities for using money having regard to the spot and forward price structure taken as a whole'.

Following my simple definition of the rate of interest, money takes a spot price equal to unity and an own-return given by the difference between its spot and forward price. For other durables, their return will be given by their own-rate of own-return, for example the wheat rate of interest, which has to be converted into a return comparable to money just as foreign investment returns have to be translated into a domestic return by the difference between spot and forward discounts or premiums in terms of money. The total return to holding wheat or any other investment will then be composed of two elements: the sum of the expected appreciation or depreciation of wheat in terms of money (the equivalent of the forward discount or premium) and the own-rate of own-return measured in terms of itself. I represented the first term by a, which may be defined as the forward money price of wheat less the spot money price of wheat as a proportion of the spot price. The 'own-rate of own-return', defined as the forward price of, for example, wheat in terms of wheat less the spot price as a proportion of the spot price, was presented in terms of three component characteristics: q, the real or natural return of productive goods; c, the carrying costs involved in investments which involve the holding of goods in the expectation of better future prices; and l, the user cost of liquidity or the liquidity premium.

> For money, just as for the domestic currency, the value of $a = 0$, since it always buys the same amount of itself. Its return is given by l, its liquidity premium, while it has no other carrying cost or 'real' return from increasing production since it cannot be produced. For capital goods, on the other hand, the primary return is given by q, while for commodities held on speculation they will have high values of c.

The equilibrium of the system is given by equality between the return on money, i, and the value of $a \pm (q - c + l)$ for every other activity in the economy (which may include consumption).[13] Just as it was the Bank of England that could determine the profitability of investing at home and abroad and in domestic assets (capital equipment) or debts (domestic Treasury bonds) because of its role in the international gold standard, in Chapter 17 it is the user cost of money as envisaged by households, firms and banks, relative to the decision of the central bank to create money, that determines the equilibrium which is produced. Aside from this formal generalization of the previous analysis of the book, the remainder of Chapter 17 explains why the rate of interest on money may behave differently from that of other assets and debts, and why this distinguishes the role of money assets from all others in setting the point of effective demand.

THE ROLE OF MONEY AND CHAPTER 17

I could have retained my Macmillan Committee analysis and explained the peculiarity of the behaviour of the money rate of interest by the necessity of the Bank of England to fix bank rate at the level which assured international equilibrium. However there are more fundamental factors in a monetary economy which will prevent market forces from automatically producing a rate of interest compatible with full employment equilibrium.

I again approached the problem as an extension of the short period pricing theory. The general thrust of that theory was to enquire as to the possibility for short-period changes in spot relative to forward prices to provide sufficient incentives in the form of expected returns to produce changes in demand or supply which would change output levels so as to bring returns on all available investment opportunities into equality.

It was thus natural to ask the same question with respect to money. Would changes in the demand for money produce changes in the forward price of money relative to the spot price which would increase the incentive to produce money? For an economy based on what I called 'Representative money' in the *Treatise on Money* (1930a: 6ff.), I concluded that the answer was no. Since representative money is not created by entrepreneurs deciding to produce it in relation to its relative rate of return, an increase in the demand for money will not automatically increase its supply, no matter how much its forward price and relative yield changes. This became one of the 'essential properties' of money, a low or negligible 'elasticity of production'.

But if it was possible for an increase in demand to drive up the return on money without generating an increase in supply, was it possible that some alternative source of liquidity might be produced which could substitute for money? Representative money differs from other durable assets in that it has a negligible cost of carry, c, and no q, so that its entire return comes from its liquidity premium. Alternative assets that might substitute for money in this respect will usually have carrying costs that are a positive function of the demand for them because of storage, insurance and financing costs, so their returns will eventually be driven below that on money. This became the 'essential property' of the low or negligible 'elasticity of substitution' for money and is linked to the fact that the carrying cost on money is negligible and independent of demand.[14] These two factors taken together suggested that there is no reason for the supply of money to respond automatically to demand and thus that its return may move independently of the level of demand and output. The result is that there will be no automatic tendency for the return on money to fall so as to increase the attractiveness of using money to initiate the production of new output and create employment.

I was thus able to conclude that it was not a malfunction in the operation of the price mechanism, but rather the nature of money in a monetary production economy which impeded the fall in the rate of interest to the level which produced full employment. Even if expansion occurred in other sectors, this would eventually run into the limit given by the liquidity premium on money.

This, however, left the question of whether active policy might not be able to expand the money supply sufficiently to bring about the rate of interest required to achieve full employment. However, if an increase in the supply of money simply caused a matching increase in the demand for money, this would prevent the decline in the rate of interest required to increase output to the full employment level. Indeed, I concluded that this might well occur if there is a generalized expectation that the prices of other assets will be lower in the future, such that individuals choose to sell assets in exchange for money.

The decision to hold money rather than to use it is determined by the relation between its liquidity premium and the returns available on other assets. If money is 'used' today to buy investment goods or consumption goods, or to buy financial assets (which includes bank lending to either households or entrepreneurs) in order to gain a return, this means that money cannot be 'used' at some future date. The 'user cost' of money will then be the present value of the potential future gain forgone by parting with money today. This will depend on the forward prices of investment goods, consumption goods and financial assets. With respect to other financial assets the user cost of money is the forgone gain that could have been achieved by waiting to purchase financial assets at lower prices and earning higher interest rates.

If 'using' money is defined as becoming 'illiquid', then the user cost of money measures the premium which is required to convince holders of money to become illiquid. Just as spot prices have to fall sufficiently relative to expected future prices to convince people to hold excess supplies rather than sell them, in the case of money, spot asset prices have to fall relative to expected future prices to convince them to hold financial assets rather than money.

However, if an expansion in the supply of money has driven current spot prices above expected future rates, then the user cost of money may rise above the current rate of interest and the demand for money will rise, offsetting the fall in rates. Indeed, the rise in prices may reach a position in which the increase in demand just offsets the expansion in supply, blocking any further reduction in the rate of interest. This will occur when the annual percentage decline in price given by the difference between the current spot price and the expected future price is equal to the square of the current rate of interest on consols. In this case the expected capital loss from holding the non-monetary financial asset offsets the year's interest return.[15] It is for this reason that the interest rate will be primarily determined by what people expect future asset prices (or interest rates) to be, and changes in the money supply may not have a direct impact on interest rates. This is the basis of Hick's and Robertson's criticism of my theory of interest as being held up by its own bootstraps.[16]

HOW THE NEW APPROACH CHANGED MY POLICY POSITIONS

Thus, even if the Bank of England could overcome the constraints of the gold standard (or structural changes in wages and productivity could be introduced which would reduce the required capital inflows), my own view was that 'it seems likely that the fluctuations in the market estimation of the marginal efficiency of different types of capital . . . will be too great to be offset by any practicable changes in the rate of interest' (*G.T.*: 164). This shows the importance of eliminating the 'confusion between results due to a change in the rate of interest and those due to a change in the schedule of the marginal efficiency of capital' (*G.T.*: 173). It also led me to the necessity of 'the State . . . taking an ever greater responsibility for directly organising investment' because I was 'sceptical of the success of a merely monetary policy directed towards influencing the rate of interest [in] continuously stimulating the appropriate volume of investment' (*G.T.*: 164).

Despite these very precise indications, presentations of my theory have continued to restrict discussion of marginal efficiency and investment to an inverse monotonic relation between investment expenditures and the rate of interest, and have restricted their concerns to the appropriate fine-tuning of monetary policy to influence investment through this channel.

It also shows the importance of the break between the rate of interest and the real return to capital. As soon as I could show that the return on money given by the liquidity premium (*l*) on money would be determined by different factors than the return to other assets (*q*, *c*) I could argue that the automatic operation of the competitive price mechanism could not guarantee that changes in relative prices of assets (representing, say, an adjustment of demand and supply which shifts the investor from a declining to an expanding sector, such as discussed by Pigou) would necessarily bring about an adjustment in their relative returns so as to produce a progressive shift in labour and capital resources among productive uses without changing the level of employment; for as long as money's return was independent of this process, any funds released from declining sectors would be committed to investment in money or other financial assets which would not provide an offsetting change in output or in employment. I could thus argue that a

> monetary economy . . . is essentially one in which changing views about the future are capable of influencing the quantity of employment and not merely its direction. But our method of analysing the economic behaviour of the present under the influence of changing ideas about the future is one which depends on the interaction of supply and demand, and is in this way linked up with our fundamental theory of value. (*G.T.*: vii)

Professor Pigou had argued that the operation of relative prices would bring about shifts in investment and employment across different industries (bring changes in the 'direction' of employment), but that the overall level of output and employment would remain unchanged. It was for this reason that I attempted to couch the entire theory in terms of the short-period theory of spot and forward prices determining the relative rates of return that direct expenditures to different types of investment. Those who have failed to grasp the importance of my approach to price theory and the role of user cost in providing a vehicle to introduce the influence of the future on the present have failed to grasp the basic shift in emphasis, not only with respect to my previous work, but with reference to all of what I called 'classical theory'.

Notes

* *Advertisement to the reader.* As this is a 'second edition' of *The General Theory*, I have composed this chapter as Keynes might have written it. It is *not* the result of another discovery in an attic at Tilton, and J.M. Keynes declines all responsibility for it. I have benefited from comments on numerous earlier versions from G.C. Harcourt, L.R. Wray, A.J. Cornford and the members of the MURST (40 per cent) Research Group directed by Mario Tonveronachi, all of whom also decline responsibility.

1 It is for this reason that I identified Fisher as my great grandparent (cf. 'Alternative Theories of the Rate of Interest', *C.W.* XIII: 202, n.2) antecedent to Hawtrey, in my treatment of money as a 'real' factor, rather than physical productivity, in determining the return to capital. It is to be hoped that this exposition will indicate that, despite divergences in other areas, there is no difference between Fisher and me on this point of definition.

2 For example, in 1914 I noted that the 'destruction of paper values' caused by the collapse of stock prices was independent of any change in the ability of capital goods to produce real output: 'With a . . . fall in the value of securities, we learn not, as with the destruction of Liège or Louvain, of a loss in the world's real wealth, but only of the financial worlds extreme urgency for money . . . We experience, therefore, a sudden and violent change in our relative valuation of present and future income' (*C.W.* VIII: 268).

3 I had included these points more explicitly in early drafts. Compare the last draft of 1933: 'An entrepreneur is interested, not in the amount of product, but in the amount of *money* which will fall to his share. He will increase his output if by doing so he expects to increase his money profit, even though this profit represents a smaller quantity of product than before' (*C.W.* XXIX: 82).

4 This approach also played an important role in the transition to the new book. During my university lectures in 1932 I used it to investigate the question of whether an automatic adjustment of the system to full employment might take place by means of such short-period adjustments of the prices of capital and labour in conditions of excess supply, noting that 'in the case of a machine, we assume that when it is in over supply those of its utility-giving powers which evaporate with time will accept anything rather than go to waste. Consequently its short-period supply price is equal to the discounted long-period price of those of its qualities which will "keep", and drops like a stone, as soon as it is in oversupply, from its long-period price to the equivalent of the extra depreciation involved in using it over not using it. . . . Now suppose that the short-period supply price of labour was just like that of a machine . . . Prime cost would be next door to zero. There could be much more violent changes in relative prices without affecting output . . . Thus if we assume that the short-period supply price of labour is determined on the same principles as that of machines under free competition and that prime cost (in terms of money) is next door to zero, it follows that there will be no unemployment in the short period any more than in the long. Indeed the short period will not be so very unlike the long. . . .' This would have been the explanation of traditional theory, in which price adjustments are sufficient to eliminate any excess of demand or supply. However, I believe that this represents an inappropriate assumption concerning the behaviour of labour, since 'We cannot assume that a labourer regards any reward as better than none, *or that he will be worked whenever the value of his service is greater than the excess of his "running cost" over his cost on a "care-and-maintenance" basis.* We have to remember, on the contrary, (a) that there is a disutility in work, and also (b) that, unlike a machine, he can often insist on a care-and-maintenance basis of cost, *even when his value if in work would be greater than the excess of his running cost over what he costs the community on a care-and-maintenance basis.* Accordingly whilst the short-period supply price of a machine is almost vertical, the short-period supply price of labour is nearly horizontal; – prime cost being arrived at by combining these two supply curves. . . . The net advantages of different employments of capital and labour will be unequal in the short period, whereas they will be equal in the long period. This will be the only important difference' (*C.W.* XXIX: 51–2, emphasis added).

5 Here I added a note directing the reader to the theory of short-period prices in Chapter 29 of the *Treatise on Money*.

6 This material had been Chapter 1: 'The Differential of Consumption and Capital Goods' of Book III: 'The Determination of Price' in the 1932 table of contents.

7 Since the decision to consume was determined primarily by the expectation of future income of households, it also reflected the impact of the future on the present. However, it was excessively difficult to present this relation in terms of current and expected prices and thus the decisions of entrepreneurs became the dominant of the two equal factors which had motivated equilibrium in the *Treatise on Money*.

8 Just as newly produced capital goods will have to compete with more technically efficient capital goods produced in the future.

9 This is the condition which I described as 'backwardation' in the *Treatise on Money* (and which has gained a place in the financial literature on futures prices). In normal conditions of balanced supply and demand this will occur when prices for future delivery are driven below current spot prices because long hedgers seeking cover dominate short hedgers and speculators. In conditions of slump this requires that the prime costs (user costs of operating) of existing equipment be greater than the prime cost of producing new capital goods so that, given the expectation of the recovery of prices, it is cheaper to order new capacity for future delivery than to buy existing capital goods to hold until future recovery. In the language of the futures market, flow supply prices are below futures prices which are below spot prices, so the most profitable action is to sell capital goods futures, hedging by producing them for sale at maturity rather than buying them spot.

10 Readers who followed the discussions of the book immediately after its publication will note that I myself found it easier to employ these terms in debating with my critics, Thus I used the framework of Chapter 17 either implicitly or explicitly in a series of *Economic Journal* exchanges in 1937, in my contribution to Irving Fisher's *Festschrift* and in my *Quarterly Journal of Economics* reply to Jacob Viner's review (all reprinted in *C. W.* XIV). Even I sometimes underestimated the implications of this approach, and it was Mr Hugh Townshend who astutely reminded me of some of the implications when I was backsliding into previous modes of thought (cf. some of his correspondence in *C. W.* XXIX: 236ff. and his article in the 1937 *Economic Journal*).

11 Although interest rates are pure numbers, and thus can be compared, a 10 per cent return on a dollar asset, compared to 10 per cent on sterling, yields US dollars, not sterling, and thus the two rates are not comparable. They thus express 'own' rates in that they give returns in terms of their own unit of account.

12 Piero Sraffa (1932a) had already employed the same concept under the name of commodity rates in his critique of Hayek's idea of neutral monetary policy. It is a straightforward application of techniques applied in futures markets for commodities and currencies in which we both were involved, so it is difficult to determine who was responsible for their application to questions of theory.

13 Recall that these relations can all be rewritten in terms of the appropriate spot and forward prices, e.g. $i = [F(t, T) - S(t))/S(t)$, where F and S are the forward and spot prices of money as in my formal definition of the rate of interest on money. Equivalently, $a = [F_{m,w}(l,T) - S_{m,w}(t) / S_{m,v}(t))$ representing the forward and spot prices of wheat in terms of money, and $q = \left[F_{m,w}(t,T) - S_{m,w}(t)\right] / S_{m,w}(t)$, representing the forward and spot prices of wheat in terms of wheat.

14 I had originally discussed these matters in rudimentary form in Part V of a draft of Chapter 2, entitled 'The Distinction Between a Co-operative and an Entrepreneur Economy', in the provisional table of contents for 1933 (cf. *C.W.* XXIX: 85–7).

15 This is the 'square rule' which I gave in Chapter 15 (*G.T.*: 202) and is the basis for the 'liquidity trap': 'For example, if the rate of interest on long-term debt is 4 percent., it is preferable to sacrifice liquidity unless on a balance of probabilities it is feared that the long-term rate of interest may rise by faster than by 4 per cent. of itself per annum, i.e. by an amount greater than 0.16 per cent. per annum.' If this were the case, then the capital loss on holding a consol would exceed the annual interest. Thus user costs (measuring the liquidity premium) of using money to buy assets at current prices, instead of waiting to buy at lower expected future prices, would be greater than the interest return earned from buying them today; a rational investor should thus hold any increase in money balances in liquid form. Although the reinvestment of future interest receipts at the higher expected future rates would eventually offset the expected capital loss (often called the duration point), the time required is longer the lower is the current rate of interest. It thus follows that the conditions associated with the liquidity trap are more likely the lower is the current rate of interest, although they can occur at virtually any level because the evaluation of user costs and, what is the same thing, the expected future value of interest rates will depend crucially on recent experience of the volatility of interest rates. The higher the volatility of interest rates, the higher the 'balance

of probabilities' that the rate of interest will rise by its square and thus the higher the level of rates at which the liquidity trap may become operative. (The experienced investor will note that the square relation holds precisely for consols (perpetual bonds) and approximately for finite maturities. He or she will also have noted the affinity with the concept of duration which has recently become popular as a measure of the volatility of bond prices.)

16 I believe these critics failed to understand the full implications of the fact that the forces determining physical productivity (reflected in q) have no direct role in determining the money returns earned from holding or operating assets. It is interesting to note that the interest rate parity theorem has never been criticized as relying on bootstraps.

Chapter 20

KEYNES AND THE NEW KEYNESIANS ON THE ROLE OF UNCERTAINTY AND INFORMATION

Competitive Markets: Failure or Inexistence? The Early Critics

A telling comment on the current state of confusion in economics is offered by the decision of the Swedish Academy to award this year's Nobel Prize to Ronald Coase, only a year after awarding the Prize jointly to Harry Markowitz, Merton Miller and William Sharpe for their analysis of financial markets based on the principle of perfectly competitive efficient markets. Amongst the many interpretations of Coase's ideas is one which says that the "auctioneer" of Walrasian theory cannot remain exogenous to the analysis of price formation. Real, live market makers, whether they be auctioneers or dealers, expect to be remunerated for their time and effort and to earn the market rate of return on capital employed. These are what are now referred to as "transactions" costs, and they lead to all sorts of anomalies when introduced into efficient, perfect market theories.

In perfectly competitive conditions, if the costs of maintaining the auctioneer exceed the benefits of exchange, then competitive equilibrium may not be reached by the free market; in competitive conditions new entrants should bring down transactions costs or new transactions technologies or organisational forms should be introduced in order to reduce transactions costs. As Coase suggests, one competing form of organisation is to internalise transactions within a central coordinating mechanism to replace the auctioneer and which is commonly called a firm. It is interesting that traditional theory has been no more prolific in analysing the firm than it has in analysing the life and habitat of the auctioneer.

If the excessive costs of using the market lead to replacing it with an internal organisation called the "firm", this will reduce market transactions and further increase transactions costs associated with the market, creating a vicious cycle in which eventually no transactions take place via the market. The introduction of the traditional competitive process into the analysis of the provision of the transactions services of the market leads to the paradox that without intermediaries markets cannot function, but when intermediaries are too costly, the market may not exist.

There is a more direct way of seeing the difficulty of combining perfect competition with the existence of intermediaries or market makers: where market makers use bid-ask spreads to earn their income, a price range exists within which prices may vary without provoking any impact on supply or demand, and two different prices may exist for the same good without generating any profitable arbitrage to eliminate the discrepancy, violating the basic conditions of perfect competition and the law of one price. However, if the wage or return given by the spread is above the market wage or return, new entry will drive down the spread; if it drives it down to zero, all market makers withdraw and the "market" disappears. The simple introduction of individuals who make markets, whether they be live auctioneers or intermediaries, threatens the existence of competitive equilibrium and the existence of the perfect market of neoclassical theory.

It is important to remember that Coase defined those forces (now defined as transactions costs) which produce the impetus to innovation in market organisation (such as firms) as arising from the "uncertainty" associated with using the free, competitive market to organise transactions. A similar argument was made by G.B. Richardson in a slightly different way in a 1959 *Economic Journal* article and a 1960 book. He argued that if prices in a competitive market were to produce signals leading to the appropriate allocation of resources, then they must reflect changes in prospective rates of return to investment across sectors. But, if a rise in the prospective return from one sector is signaled by a rise in the price of its output all other producers would be induced to shift resources. If everyone follows the price signal and shifts resources this will lead to excess supply and actual returns which are lower than those which were signaled by the initial rise in price.

Richardson argues that in order for producers to make rational resource allocation decisions the intentions of all other agents must be known. However, if prices reflect the future intended actions of agents, then they will not rise and no one will receive the signals necessary to produce the appropriate reallocation of resources. If all producers have perfect information, none of them will undertake investments for fear of loss, and the new equilibrium cannot be achieved; if prices are perfect predictors of future resource commitments in the sector, then they should not rise, for they should reflect the new flow of resources to the sector which will cause a rise in output which reduces prices. Thus the paradox: if prices do not change then no new investment will take place.

To resolve the paradox a market coordinator or auctioneer is required to provide the information that is necessary in order for the competitive process to operate; since it is not in the interest of any single producer to provide the information he possesses concerning his own intentions he cannot be relied to do so without remuneration; but, the information concerning his intended actions is only useful if no one else possesses it. The individual is thus naturally led to conceal his intentions.

It is interesting that both the Coase and Richardson arguments, which might be called competitive market "impossibility" theorems, have been well-known for some time[1]. It is also interesting that both rely on the idea that it is the operation of the competitive market mechanism itself which produces uncertainty in market transactions. This is what has been called endogenous, rather than exogenous, disequilibrium or instability. They are arguments of the "beauty contest" variety cited by Keynes in Chapter 12 of the *General Theory* and as such are compatible with what I would call the post-Keynesian approach to a monetary production economy which considers uncertainty as arising from the very operation of the perfectly competitive market in conditions of capitalistic production, conditions which make the use of money a response to that uncertainty, and in which money itself can then introduce endogenous elements of disturbance.

Competitive Markets: Incomplete or Inefficient or Just Lemons?

In response to the success of the market-clearing, perfectly competitive equilibrium assumptions of the Rational Expectations Hypothesis, there have been a number of attempts in the 1980s to formulate a criticism of the self-regulating nature of the competitive market economy which builds on the idea of incomplete information or incomplete markets produced by externality or moral hazard type problems.

This approach was initiated by George Akerlof's (1984) application of the "lemon principle" to used cars. Trying to answer the question of why the secondary market price of a new automobile is substantially lower than its primary market price, he noted that the price difference is not really between a new and a "used" car, but between buying in the primary market with a "high" probability of getting a "good" car, and buying in the secondary market where there was a "high" probability of getting a "bad" car or a "lemon". He argued that a car purchased in the secondary market (irrespective of the extent of its physical deterioration or "use") has a higher probability of being a lemon than a car purchased in the primary market.

Before proceeding, note that the analysis presumes that there are "good" and "bad" cars produced and sold in the primary market without quality control procedures being able to distinguish bad cars, and that there are objective probability distributions explicating the occurrence of each event which are equal to the subjective distributions held by agents.

Thus, we know that there are good and bad cars, although no one knows the category of the particular car he buys when it is acquired. Purchasing and operating (using) a car produces "inside" information, available only to the (user) owner. New and used cars are thus different products for a "used" car has more information attached to it, but that information is only accessible by the owner.

If both new and "very recently" new cars sold in the market at the same price, the buyer of a new car which had revealed itself to be a lemon as a result of use could resell it in the secondhand market and buy another new car until he succeeded in finding a "good" new car. His information would have been gained at the expense of buyers in the secondary market. In these conditions no one will pay the same price in the secondary market for a "used" car (here "used" no longer refer to physical use, but to the learning by using that has caused it to reveal its true identity as a lemon) as the primary market price for a new car[2].

Thus, even if a "liquidity trader", *i.e.* someone who has to sell in order to finance current expenditures rather than someone adjusting his portfolio as the result of a change in his evaluation of existing information concerning the fundamental value of the asset, has to sell a "good" car in the secondary market, the most it will fetch is the price of a "lemon". Thus two "different" goods sell at the same price, which in itself does not reflect the "fundamental" value of the car. No one should rationally sell "good" used cars, for they will not fetch a "fair" price. Akerlof notes that if there are degrees of "lemony-ness", then the above argument implies that one should not sell a better than average "lemon" because it would only receive the average lemon prices, and so forth. This leads to the limiting result that only the very worst cars (below average lemon quality) will be offered on the market and implies that there will be no buyers because everyone is certain that it is the worst of the worst lemons. Thus the secondary car market disappears.

Now, there is always a common-sense response to paradoxes of this sort. Might it not be possible for a technically competent auto mechanic to act as a middleman, offering to sell information on the lemony qualities of cars traded in the secondary market. Certainly there should be some space for intermediation and profitable arbitrage as a result of this specialised knowledge of car quality.

Incomplete Competitive Markets: Lemons and the New Keynesians

Stiglitz, and an increasingly diversified portfolio of co-authors, have adapted the Akerlof argument to markets in general, and to financial markets in particular, to deal with this very question. If there are people who know the value of used cars and, to be symmetric, people who don't know the value of anything but the price of everything, and who believe that quality is a positive function of price so that higher prices reflect better quality cars, then they will be attracted to cars with higher prices. Since "informed" traders can identify "good" cars without reference to relative prices, they can buy irrespective of price (this is an adaptation of Grossman & Stiglitz, 1980). By doing so they drive up prices of good cars, creating signals to other buyers. Since they buy before the price goes up, they can sell the cars for a profit.

If the uninformed notice that there is easy money to be made in becoming informed about car quality, more of them should decide to become experts. But, the increase in the number of experts increases competition for good cars and this reduces the benefits of buying first. Being informed is only valuable if you are in a minority.

If it is costly to become expert, the decreasing benefits of buying first may no longer offset them, for the number of people trying to be first is continually increasing; when everyone is informed it is no longer worthwhile, so everyone stops trying to evaluate lemon quality and the second-hand car market again risks disappearance. If everyone is perfectly informed about cars there is no benefit which offsets the costs of acquiring information, while if prices perfectly reflect information, then no one needs to seek information and it is impossible for prices to perfectly transmit information.

The similarity of this argument with the Coase paradox should be sufficiently clear not to require explanation. But, the differences should also be crystal dear, for this is a case in which all necessary information is available; it is simply costly, not impossible, to obtain: a little elbow grease and we have "learning by using" increasing the completeness of our information. The incompleteness of information is a state of nature, but it is not the result of the operation of the system. Note that there appears to be very little difference from Stigler's original analysis of the cost of information.

But, it was not enough to use lemons as stones to throw at the divine intervention of the invisible hand, they have recently been transmuted into apples which, as anyone knows, may be good or rotten, and the rotten ones may spoil the barrel, or produce involuntary unemployment or insufficient investment, not necessarily in that order. To see how Akerlof's original story can be extended to provide the New Keynesian explanation for unemployment and stable unemployment equilibrium, assume that there are "rotten-apple" workers, and there are employers who insist that it would be irrational to hire more labour when it is offered at a lower price, for certainly they will be all rotten apples, "shirkers" only willing to work for lower wages because once hired they have no intention of working as hard as other workers. Thus, there are fewer employed workers because good workers who are unemployed cannot manage to get themselves hired in place of the shirkers, not even by offering to work for lower wages, because employers can't know if they will be good workers.

The same type of story applies to the shortage of investment due to the unwillingness of bankers to lend to entrepreneurs (Stiglitz & Weiss, 1981). In the place of workers who want to work, we now have entrepreneurs who would like to invest, and are even willing to take lower rates of return on their own equity by paying higher than prevailing interest rates to the bankers, but can't convince the bankers that they are not "bad eggs" or "Ponzi" financiers. This is because the banker facing the entrepreneur reasons just as the entrepreneur facing the worker: if the entrepreneur is offering to pay over the odds for a loan it can only be because he has no intention of putting the money to work, but rather intends to misappropriate it.

Thus, an honest entrepreneur, who could make a profit on his investment project at the current interest rate, is denied funding while the bank ignores his request to borrow at higher rates (excess demand for funds) and refuses to raise interest rates to efficiently allocate credit because it believes that this will simply cause the quality of the loan portfolio to deteriorate, charge-offs to rise and the bank's return to fall. This is because, as interest rates rise to accommodate the "bad egg" borrowers, the honest borrowers with projects paying lower rates of return will repay their existing loans or withdraw their current loan applications, so the bank is left in the limit with only "bad eggs".

In this version of the story the level of investment is kept too low because the marginal efficiency of capital cannot fall to equality with the interest rate. (Of course, this difference could also be explained by means of a borrowing and lending spread which would prevent equality of the interest rate and the return to capital). This is the "New Keynesian" interpretation of Keynes: "Keynes analysis of investment was, however, basically a neoclassical analysis: it was failure of the real interest rate (the long-term bond rate) to fall sufficiently that was the source of the problem" (Greenwald, Stiglitz and Weiss, 1984, p. 194).

There are always some who are unconvinced by a "new" theory: What if the entrepreneur finds an investment banker who is unconcerned to ruin his reputation and advises him to issue shares to replace the absent bank lending? Now the lenders are not sceptical bankers, they are sceptical institutional portfolio managers (Greenwald, Stiglitz & Weiss, 1984). A new share issue dilutes the return on existing shares and prices fall (except in Japan where the opposite regularly occurs). A fall in prices represents an increase in the costs of borrowing to the firm, the equivalent of a rise in interest rates. The portfolio manager now asks himself, why is an entrepreneur willing to pay higher than market interest rates to borrow via an equity issue? Or they might also think that good managers will be more willing to undertake more risky bank borrowing (they don't know the New Keynesian economics and thus do not realise that it is precisely the good borrowers that the bankers do not lend to), so that any firm which is increasing equity must be a bad firm and share prices are will be appropriately reduced in price.

In another variant bankers consider that since managers should recognise that borrowing increases leverage and thus the manager's potential remuneration, while share issues give all the extra profit to shareholders so the managers should become shirkers as the debt/equity ratio falls (the managers apparently don't hold stock options nor do they set the dividend rate). On the other hand, it might be reasoned that higher debt/equity ratios have higher risk and a higher risk of bankruptcy and loss of employment for the managers: managers thus work harder with higher debt/equity ratios (again, no golden parachutes). There are enough reasons for bankers not to lend to firms which cannot borrow in debt markets, so that the effective constraint is the cost of bank borrowing and the constraint on the full employment level of investment is the failure of the rate of interest to come into equality with the real return on capital.

Note that in all these cases the "normal" laws of supply and demand are inoperative: wages do not fall when there is excess supply of labour (marginal productivity of labour is below the wage), interest rates do not rise when there is excess demand for loans (marginal productivity of capital is above the interest rate). This produces the conclusion of the New Keynesian economics that employment will settle at an equilibrium level in which there is excess supply (excess demand for capital) with perfect competition. We thus have the traditional fixed wage and fixed interest rate model, but now explained in terms of incomplete markets produced by imperfect information. If there were an omnipotent economist who could produce perfect information, the system would naturally produce full employment.

Competitive Markets: Incomplete and Risky or Inefficient and Uncertain?

I would not want to argue that these are not important insights into the operation of markets, but I believe they do not take into account the range of factors which led both Coase and Richardson to reject the traditional explanation of the operation of perfect competition. First, all the information in these models is known by someone—it is an information coordination problem. Second, the kind of information that is assumed to be known in general cannot be known: entrepreneurs know the mean and the distribution of the real marginal product of their investment projects, borrowers know their probability of paying off a loan, workers know the mean and distribution of their real marginal product. But we know from Coase and Richardson that in a market economy these values cannot be known, ex ante. We also know from the capital theory controversies that they cannot be unambiguously defined without assuming the type of operation of the perfectly competitive market that the New Keynesians are trying to argue cannot exist (the knowledge of the real marginal products which the theory requires can only exist on the basis of conditions which it shows cannot exist).

If we look at the simplest version of incomplete information in the bank debt market, it still remains true that the interest rate which is charged does not have any impact on the mean rate of return to the investment project, so that the separation theory of traditional theory which makes the behaviour of real variables independent of monetary variables still holds. Nor, in that model, does credit rationing have any role in explaining unemployment, since an increase in the rate of interest which reduces rationing also decreases the supply of loans, so that total investment falls as the interest rate rises, just as in traditional Keynesian theory. The New Keynesian credit rationing caused by incomplete information on borrowers turns out to be precisely equivalent to that which would have been imposed by the price mechanism. The argument then returns to the interest rate being "too high" relative to full employment marginal efficiency, and we still have to use the assumption of a fixed supply of money to explain why the interest rate is too high.

This leads to the final observation—these models are purely exogenous money models. No bank run by Basil Moore (*e.g.* 1988) would ever run into such conditions, for they would lend to all comers at the prevailing rate established by the central bank which would then have to come up with the reserves to support it—if there are dishonest borrowers the bankers can always get the central bank to lend to them as a last resort.

But, this is not the most disturbing factor about the approach. In the tradition of the Modigliani-Samuelson neoclassical synthesis, it excludes monetary factors from a role in generating instability. Although the New Keynesian tradition appears to be asking the right "Keynes-type" questions and producing "Keynes-type" answers, what does all this have to do with Keynes? My understanding of Keynes' argument, and the interpretation of Keynes' theory of monetary production which has been given by Doyen Barrère in all his writings (most recently 1985), is that even in the presence of a perfectly functioning competitive price mechanism, there was no necessity for full employment to result. A decrease in wages in the face of excess labour supply would not bring about full employment, and an increase in interest rates certainly could not, although a decrease might, depending on how expectations responded. It is the recognition of the monetary nature of production which produces the explanation for these natural but unsatisfactory results in any real economy. It is not that information is incomplete, but that the information that the market requires simply does not exist, could not be discovered, even by hiring a firm of consultants, nor by waiting or by "using" cars. Entrepreneurs have to form expectations about values of variables at future dates about which there is no currently existing "objective" information. As a result the economy would be prone to fluctuate as expectations fluctuate, although usually not violently, around a level of output below potential and below full employment. Since expectations are formed in part on the basis of the functioning of the economy and in part on the "imagination" of entrepreneurs, they will have both endogenous and exogenous elements.

Aside from any discussion of whether borrowers misrepresent the probability of successful outcomes or to the proportion of shirkers and slackers due to moral hazard, it is necessary to explain this expectations formation process and the uncertainty which makes it necessary. This is what Keynes attempted to do in the monetary theory of production, an aspect of Keynes' work that has gone unnoticed by most of the profession, but which Doyen Barrère has dedicated most of his writings. It would appear that the New Keynesians would have much to learn from a French Keynesian.

Notes

1 Richardson apparently gave up economics in despair of the lack of recognition of the implications of his work; Coase did not give up, but recently (1988) lamented the fact that no one has taken any notice of the implications of his work. It will be interesting to see his Nobel Lecture.

2 Note that normally primary issue market prices and secondary market prices for securities are uniform; what we learn about old securities reflects on the prices of new ones, the distinction between good and bad IBM shares seems implausible to the imagination.

References

Akerlof, G.A., *An Economic Theorist's Book of Tales* Cambridge University Press, 1984.

Barrère, A. *Keynes aujourd'hui*, Editions Economica, 1985.

Coase, R., *The Firm, the Market and the Law*, University of Chicago Press, 1988.

Greenwald, B., and J.E. Stiglitz, "Keynesian, New Keynesian and New Classical Economics", *Oxford Economic Papers*, 39, 1987.

Greenwald, B., J.E. Stiglitz, and A. Weiss. "Informational Imperfections in the Capital Market and Macroeconomic Fluctuations", *American Economic Review,* May 1984.

Grossmann, S.J. and J.E. Stiglitz, "On the Impossibility of Informationally Efficient Markets", *American Economic Review*, June, 1980.

Keynes, J.M., *A Treatise on Money*, Macmillan, 1930.

Keynes, J.M., *The General Theory of Employment, Interest and Money*, Macmillan, 1936.

Kregel, J.A., "Irving Fisher, Great Grandparent of the General Theory: Money, Rate of Return over Cost and Efficiency of Capital", *Cahiers d'Économie Politique,* Nos. 14–15, 1988.

Minsky, H.P., "Financial Instability —A Restatement", *in Can "It" Happen Again,* M.E. Sharpe, 1982.

Moore, B., *Horizontalists and Verticalists*, Cambridge University Press, 1988.

Richardson, G.B., "Equilibrium, Expectations and Information", *Economic Journal*, June, 1959.

Richardson, G.B. *Information and Investment*, Oxford University Press, 1960.

Stiglitz, J.E., "Credit Markets and the Control of Capital", *Journal of Money, Credit and Banking*, May, 1985.

Stiglitz, J.E. and Weiss, A., "Credit Rationing in Markets with Perfect Information", *American Economic Review*, June, 1981.

Part Four

UNCONVENTIONAL MONETARY POLICY, QUANTITATIVE EASING, YIELD CURVE TWISTING AND LIQUIDITY TRAPS

Chapter 21

KEYNESIAN STABILISATION POLICY AND POST WAR ECONOMIC PERFORMANCE(*)

1. Keynesian Stabilisation Policy and Deficit Spending

In conditions in which economic debate is dominated by the "New Keynesian" Economics and New Macroeconomics and governments claim that they can do nothing to remedy the enduring conditions of recession in the industrialised countries because of the excessive size of their budget deficits it seems pure folly to discuss the role of "Keynesian" policy to further economic growth. But, as the current recession persists, pressures build for something to be done, and as Dennis Robertson noted of highbrow opinion, if you stand in one place long enough it comes back round to you. It thus seems appropriate to recall a number of generally overlooked aspects of Keynes' approach to economic policy so that if like the hunted hare, opinion does come this way again, it might be diverted from past errors.

The first problem is to define Keynes' economic policy views. Even before Keynes published the *General Theory* proposals for public works financed by public debt to combat the depression were promoted by a wide range of economists of various political persuasion. Public spending as an anti-cyclical policy tool was part of the economic legacy of the Hoover administration, and Franklin Roosevelt's first presidential campaign was based on balancing the budget (providing Ronald Reagan with cutting quotations for the same purpose). Something more precise than deficit spending is required.

2. Offensive Policy to Cure an Existing Depression

Keynes supported those who proposed deficit spending, but made a sharp distinction between what I will call "defensive" and "offensive" economic policy. The latter relates to the policy to apply in depressed conditions, while the former is to be ever-present in order to provide a defence against depressions.

On the offence Keynes tried to shock received views by suggesting such schemes as burying jars filled with banknotes in order to dig them up again. Many critics did not notice that although this was "make-work", at least it was "work" and not an entitlement or a handout. They also failed to notice that Keynes quickly added that such schemes were rather foolish, and that the "make-work" should better be "real" work on things that might actually serve some useful purpose such as schools, hospitals and the like. Keynes' humorous sarcasm was not meant to be taken seriously. The holes in the ground were to make the point that productive labour power was being lost; it was not a practical proposal, Keynes also recommended that deficit spending policies supporting investment should be preferred to increasing consumption.

"Offensive" policies were considered temporary; they would eventually restore "normality" and could then be replaced by "defensive" policies. It was not blind faith in deficit spending that brought Keynes to this conclusion, but rather his theoretical[1] analysis of the disequilibrium operation of price adjustment in durables markets. It is often repeated (unfortunately by some of his closest collaborators) that he knew nothing about price theory, yet, the theoretical foundation for the success of offensive policy is based on his analysis of price determination in the *Treatise on Money*. The conditions of "normality" in price relations is what that book defines as "Normal Backwardation".

3. The Outline of Offensive Policy and the Short Period Price Equation

The buyer of a futures contract profits (loses) if the price of the commodity rises (falls) over the life of the contract. Since a futures contract represents the equivalent of spot delivery of the commodity at maturity, its price should not differ from the spot price when it reaches maturity. Thus, over its life, the price of a futures contract "converges" to the spot price. This means that in conditions of expectations of stable spot prices holders of long futures contracts will profit only if they buy futures when their prices are at a discount on spot prices.

If supply and demand of a durable commodity are currently in balance and expected to remain constant individuals should not pay a price for future delivery which is different from the current spot price. However, the seller of a futures contract who hedges his position will have to buy the commodity spot and hold it until delivery, incurring carrying costs composed of storage, insurance and wastage. Sellers will thus only be willing to enter a contract if the futures contract price is sufficiently above the current spot to provide a fall in price as the contract approaches maturity which yields a profit sufficient to offset the carrying costs. Buyers of futures contract would then be paying a price above the current spot price and suffer a loss equal to the fall in the price as the future converges to the spot price. They would only be willing to buy contracts if the loss on the contract is just equal to the carrying costs that they would have had to pay had they held the physical commodity.

But commodity markets are in general one-sided. Producers of commodities have a natural long position in commodities and will normally incur both carrying costs and the risk of changes in spot prices. If they want to hedge this risk by selling futures contracts they will have to offer speculators, who do not have an inherent demand for the commodity, a return equal to the risk-free rate plus a premium for the risk of a change in spot prices. Since the buyer of a contract can only profit if prices rise this means that long hedgers will have to offer to sell futures contracts to speculators at prices which are below the current spot price, guaranteeing speculators a profit as the futures price rises to converge to spot. Keynes argued that "backwardation",[2] future prices below spot prices, was the "normal" state of affairs in balanced market conditions dominated by long hedgers.[3]

On the other hand, if there is a shortage of existing output, the spot price may be driven above the futures price and produce backwardation.[4] But, as long as current costs of production are below the futures price, producers can sell their output forward and still make a profit equal to the futures discount. But, if there is an excess supply of commodities the spot price will be driven down and eventually create a position of "contango" in which it becomes profitable to buy commodities at the spot price and hold them for sale at the higher expected future spot price. When "speculation" on the expected return of holding existing output exceeds the return on producing new output, current production is halted and employment falls. How long will such conditions last?

Instead of asking what contango premium of future over spot prices will be necessary to produce equilibrium, Keynes instead starts his analysis from a given expected future equilibrium price and asks what fall in price relative to expected normal prices would be required to convince speculators to buy the redundant output and hold it until normal conditions are restored. From the above analysis, it is clear that it must cover carrying costs, which will depend on interest rates, storage and insurance, plus the length of time that the position has to be held until it can be unwound at a profit.

Let X represent the annual per unit interest, storage and insurance costs for holding an excess supply of commodity stocks given by S. Let A represent the expected number of years until the position can be unwound. Then the required decline in the current price, P_1, relative to the normal price P_2 must be such that $(P_1\text{-}P_2)S = AXS$ or, the expected gain from the rise in price is equal to the total costs of the position. The percent decline relative to the expected normal price, p, is then $(P_1\text{-}P_2)/P_2$ and will be equal to AX/P_2.

It remains to determine the value of A. If Q is normal annual output, and normal annual consumption is C, then if output falls to zero and consumption remains unchanged, the excess supply would be worked off in $y = S/C$ years. However, if current output remains positive then $A > y$ because the surplus will be reduced by only $C\text{-}(1\text{-}q)Q$ in each period, where q is the proportionate reduction in normal output actually being produced due to the fall in price below normal. This effect will be offset if at the same time annual consumption increases because of the fall in prices for then the surplus would be reduced by $(1+c)C - (1\text{-}q)Q$, where c is the proportionate increase in consumption due to the fall in prices. For y to be finite $(1+c)C > (1\text{-}q)Q$.

Assuming[5] that $Q = C$ and $q = c$ and substituting accordingly, $y = S/[(1+q)Q\text{-}(1\text{-}q)Q] = S/Q(1+q\text{-}1+q) = S/Q(2q)$. If P_1 rises smoothly to P_2 over time, then both q and c will be declining towards zero. At the beginning of the adjustment period the rate of reduction of stocks will be 2q and at the end zero; on average over the period it will be $2q/2$, so that A can be defined in terms of y and q as $A = y/(2q/2) = y/q$. The answer that Keynes gives is then found by rewriting $p = AX/P_2$ as $[(y/q)X]/P_2$ or $pq = xy$ where x is the cost of carry as a proportion of the expected normal price. This equation is what Keynes calls the overlooked theory of "short-period prices".[6]

From this relation it is clear that the required fall in prices will be higher the higher is x, determined by the rate of interest, insurance and storage costs; the higher is y, determined by the size of excess stocks relative to normal consumption and the lower is C, annual consumption, and the lower is q, the reduction in animal production relative to normal. The crisis will then be shorter the lower the costs of carry, the higher current consumption, and the lower current output.[7]

Keynes' price equation thus provides an indication of the action to be undertaken in an offensive strategy against the slump. It is clear that there is a trade off between the fall in production q, and the fall in prices, p. If prices are sticky, then the fall in production will have to be larger, and given multiplier considerations will have an impact on the excess of supplies of other goods as well. Recalling that $A = y/q$ there is also a trade off between the length, y, and the severity, q, of the slump. Finally, the higher are interest rates and the other factors entering into carrying costs, the larger the required decline in prices or the greater the reduction in output or the longer the slump. Thus, restrictive monetary and fiscal policies, which increase interest rates and reduce the normal levels of consumption will cause spot prices to be driven down further relative to expected future prices and increase the cost of carry, both of which will delay the return to "normal" conditions of backwardation.

There is no immediate way out of such a situation. But, there are ways to influence the variables in the equation in order to influence the way in which equilibrium is re-established. The value of x can be lowered by lowering interest rates, storage and insurance costs, thus decreasing the required p. Even y and q can be lowered by reducing the outstanding stocks - giving them away (burying them in the ground?) or better, by creating purchasing power which increases the rate of normal sales. Another alternative, which Keynes was to return to in the post second World War period was creation of an agency to "invest" in excess stocks and hold them until recovery; for commodities this means buffer stocks.

This is difficult when it comes to productive capacity: better to use it than to hold it idle (user costs come into the calculation of the cost of carry here). The only way to use it is to insure demand for its output, which requires increasing current expenditures, either on consumption or capital goods. Thus, government policy to expand demand for the output of productive capacity, or by directly increasing government demand for investment. Thus, either increasing consumption expenditures via policies to increase household incomes (burying banknotes) or by direct government investment projects. Keynes clearly preferred the latter.

It is thus possible to trace most of the "offensive" strategy to an attempt to influence short-period intertemporal prices, not by direct intervention on prices, as with tariffs and subsidies, but indirectly by operating on the rate of run off of existing stocks and on the costs of carry, The main concern was to get the system back to conditions of normal backwardation. Permanent intervention was not envisaged, for once normal conditions were restored, it was presumed that private investment would again become profitable and be resumed. Then the only question became the problem of liquidity preference, setting the rate of interest on alternative employments of capital at a rate which was higher than that on productive investment.

Since the alternative to holding positions in commodities or productive capacity was to hold money, a forward discount on commodities was a forward premium on money. This is precisely how Keynes was to define the rate of interest in the *General Theory*, the difference between the spot and forward price of money. If the forward premium on money was too high, investors would choose to hold positions in money, rather than in productive assets, leading to an insufficient level of investment. The defensive strategy against the slump was thus to make sure that liquidity preference was kept sufficiently low to ensure the full employment level of investment. This was not a question of deficit spending, but of keeping a high and stable level of income so as to make consumers and investors confident in their predictions of future conditions regarding their incomes and rates of return on investment respectively.

There were thus two points: one concerned the stability of prices, or better the stability of normal backwardation representing profitable conditions for new investment expenditure the other concerned the relation between the discount of future prices of investment goods and the premium on the future price of money. The latter is now better known as the relation between the rate of interest and the marginal efficiency of capital or between the demand price and supply price of capital. It involved the supply of money and expectations. The, former was subject to policy control, the latter could only be influenced indirectly by influencing general economic conditions.

4. From Offence to Defence

It was to be the role of "defensive" policy to ensure that general economic conditions do not get out of control. In this respect Keynes proposed that the government budget be divided, as any business budget, into a capital and current expenditure budget. Keynes envisaged that the current expenditure budget would be kept broadly in balance. He argued that this was necessary "to preserve sound accounting, to measure efficiency, to maintain economy and to keep the public properly aware of what things cost" (Keynes, 1980, pp. 224–5).

It will certainly come as a surprise to the denigrators of Keynes, but his "defensive" policy was to "aim at having a surplus on the ordinary Budget, which would be transferred to the capital Budget, thus gradually replacing dead-weight debt by productive or semi-productive debt. ... I should not aim at attempting to compensate cyclical fluctuations by means of the ordinary Budget, I should leave this to the capital Budget" (pp. 277–8). It was thus capital expenditures, which should be largely self-financing, which should deal with the problem of offensive policy. Over the long run, the government budget on both ordinary and capital account should be roughly in balance, although when demand fell off, the capital expenditures would increase, creating a temporary deficit which would be eliminated as the capital projects paid off in terms of higher tax receipts and surpluses on the ordinary budget.

I have tried to give a summary (Kregel, 1985) of Keynes' various pronouncements on "defensive" budgetary policy;

1. Long-term full employment in conditions of laissez-faire will require substantial government control of investment in order to make investment a more stable proportion of national output.
2. This process of government control should be undertaken through "semi-autonomous" public corporations and publicly owned joint stock corporations which are independent from direct government intervention.

3. In order to facilitate policy the government budget should be divided into a current and capital account budget. The current account budget should be in balance or run a surplus which is transferred to the capital budget which is to be used to offset exogenous cyclical changes in investment spending. The capital budget may exhibit deficits, but should be balanced over the long run.
4. The proportion of total investment which is subject to government control through the capital budget should be in the range of 7.5 percent to 20 percent of national income.
5. Investment spending on government capital budget account should be countercyclical relative to national income and vary inversely with cycles in private spending on plant and equipment.
6. The capital and current account budgets should both be balanced at the long-run target unemployment rate of between 3–5 per cent. If this is achieved, both outstanding debt and the deficit should become a declining proportion of national income.
7. Those services and transfers which are provided by the state should be "technically social", i.e. those which the private sector is unwilling and/or unable to provide in amounts and prices considered socially acceptable.
8. All state services should be furnished efficiently, which means that they should cover all costs, capital charges and should not include on or off-budget subsidies.

Most economists, as well as laymen, are so convinced that Keynes was a wild-eyed deficit spender bent on planning the minute details of the economy that this presentation will seem strange. It certainly falls awkwardly in the current professional debate between those who argue that no policy can improve the performance of the economic system and the New Keynesians who argue in terms of direct government intervention by means of tariffs, subsidies and all sorts of fine-tuning devices. There may be good reasons for such direct intervention in the economy, but they are not founded in Keynes' policy pronouncements. Since they usually deal with some sort of externality, they are perhaps closer to the views of Abba Lerner's "Functional Finance" approach, It is clear that Keynes was never a "fine-tuner", and it is somewhat paradoxical that current attempts to give modern justification to government intervention should resurrect this particularly inappropriate version of his views on government policy.

In addition to budget policy, Keynes had a long-standing position in favour of low interest rates, this predates both the *Treatise* and the *General Theory*. This is a position which he never relinquished and which was also developed on the basis of the short-period pricing equation given above. What did change was his early belief that money policy alone would be sufficient to offset recession and excessive liquidity preference. "It is not quite correct that I attach primary importance to the rate of interest ... I should regard state intervention to encourage investment as probably a more important factor than low rates of interest taken in isolation" (Keynes, 1980, p, 350). Keynes thus eventually concluded that operating on x might not be sufficient to offset changes in expectations concerning future normal prices so that direct intervention capable of influencing expectations would be necessary. But, this intervention is not of the kind that adjusts real relative prices by means of taxes, tariffs or price subsidies, but the kind which changes the overall level of investment through government spending, thus acting directly on the values of both y and q in hopes of limiting the decline in p or the fall in q, and thus placing a floor on expectations of future profits.

It is for this reason that Keynes stressed point 4 in the list given above: in order to place a floor under price and profit expectations. On the other hand, there was no question that these government agencies should operate on a profitable basis. Public investments provide public services which are operated through the ordinary budget, and this budget is presumed to charge economic prices for these services. Thus, much as a firm will have a rising proportion of debt when it engages in an active investment programme, which, if successful will generate profits which will repay interest and principal, government agencies were presumed to operate in the same way. The only difference was that they should increase their indebtedness in periods when private firms' investments were low and when the general economy appeared to be falling away from the desired levels of employment because of structural, demographic or external reasons.

As already mentioned, Keynes' views on the use of the government budget for stabilisation policy were formulated with the post-war reconstruction in view. It is also interesting to note that Keynes envisaged three phases in this process of reconstruction (cf. Guger and Walterskirchen, 1988):

1) A five-year transition period in which formal constraints would have to be placed on both consumption and investment spending;
2) A twenty-year phase in which government would be active in ensuring full employment - this is the period to which the proposals outlined above referred;
3) A third phase in which, after twenty years of investment at more than 20 percent of GNP, there was the possibility of saturation of investment and stagnation was a risk. Here offensive policies to discourage savings and increase consumption might become necessary, and Keynes accepted the possibility of permanent deficits: "I should expect for a long time to come that the government debt or government-guaranteed debt would be continually increasing in grand total" (1980, p. 278).

5. Has the Post War Period Been Offensive or Defensive?

All this is far from the simple idea of "deficit spending". If we ask the question, has any economy applied Keynes' policy in the post-war period, the answer must be no. No country has ever tried to separate its current and capital account budgets, although this has been suggested a number of times in the past[8] and is currently gaining a following as a way of surmounting the impasse created by the large deficits of the 1980's. Indeed, most governments have acted in precisely the opposite fashion, allowing their budget balances to develop more or less independently of underlying economic conditions, When growth in the government deficit appeared too large to be sustainable, the response was to cut capital expenditures to create more room for deficits caused by overspending for transfers on the ordinary budget. Table 1 shows the decline in overall government influenced spending on gross fixed capital formation, i.e. by all levels of government and by public-owned enterprises. The reversal in policy in the UK is clearly influenced by the privatisation of state enterprise; the reversal in Japanese policy is even more striking, but given the behaviour of the economy, explicable as a counter-cyclical activity.

However, the importance of government investment policies in the post-war period may be seen in tables 2 and 3(a) and 3(b), which deals with a wider sample of countries.

In general, high and stable ratios of government investment to output produced a more stable growth performance as measured by employment performance and growth variability.

Table 4 shows the extent to which social security transfer expenditures by government rose as a proportion of GDP as investment expenditures dropped, Only in Germany does the upward trend seem to be stopped, although not reversed. The increases in transfers are generally larger than the reductions in investment.

This has brought the increase in total government outlays noted in table 5, Even in the US, where the official policy was to decrease the role of government in the economy, the ratio rose in the 1980's, In the UK, similar policies have, however, stabilised the figure. It is still the US and Japan, however, which show similar, and substantially lower, proportions than those for the major European countries.

This rise in expenditures has not been matched either by cuts in spending or increases in taxation, leading to ever increasing borrowing by general government given in table 6. The UK is the sole exception, and much of this is explained by the policy of financing expenditure by the sale of public assets.

TABLE 1 General Government and Public Enterprises Gross Fixed Capital Formation as a Percent of GDP

	1962–72	*1973–9*	*1977–9*	*1980–9*
USA	3.50	2.81	2.83	2.48
Japan	8.78	9.46	9.85	7.69
UK	7.94	7.46	6.08	3.62

Source: OECD National Accounts, Detailed Tables, Vol. II, 1981, 1991.

TABLE 2 Ratio of General Government Gross Fixed Capital Formation to GDP (averages)

	1955–64	*1962–72*	*1973–9*
USA	3.25	2.75	2.83
Japan	9.78	4.62	5.63
Austria	5.45	4.84	5.11
France	2.75	3.91	3.28
Germany	3.80	4.07	3.50
Italy	2.53	2.88	3.14
Netherlands	4.63	4.76	3.65
UK	2.07	4.47	4.08

Source: OECD National Accounts, Detailed Tables, Vol. II, 1981, 1991.

TABLE 3(a) Ratio of Unemployment to Total Labour Force (averages)

	1962–72	*1973–79*	*1977–79*
USA	4.65	5.66	6.30
Japan	1.22	1.45	2.00
Austria	1.67	1.50	1.66
France	1.86	4.24	5.26
Germany	0.80	3.21	3.70
Italy	4.62	6.00	6.70
Netherlands	1.82	5.61	6.30
UK	3.08	4.61	5.60

Source: adapted from Maddison (1982), pp. 207–8.

TABLE 3(b) Variability of GNP and Unemployment: USA

	*Standard deviation of GNP Gap**	*Unemployment rate:*	
		mean	*standard deviation*
Period			
1920–41	12.99	11.52	7.59
1900–45	13.58	7.77	6.51
1946–76	3.56	4.95	1.34
1962–73	2.46	4.74	0.88
1966–76	2.26	5.25	1.66

* GNP Gap = (GNP/trend GNP)-1
Source: Bally (1978).

Looking at the employment experience, and recalling Keynes' projections of 3–5 per cent as the standard for full employment in the UK, there are a number of countries that have done substantially better than this. The UK clearly has paid for its budget reductions through rising unemployment, while the rising budget deficit does not seem to have had any positive impact on the US level of unemployment.

The other side of Keynes's argument concerns the control of liquidity preference and the impact of interest rates on carrying costs. Tables 8 and 9 give figures for the inflation corrected growth in M1 + quasi money. It is interesting that in all countries except the US the rate of increase has fallen throughout the period.

Accompanying the fall in the rate of growth of real money was a rise in real long-term interest rates, which in some countries was substantial.

The combination of high interest rates and rising budget deficits has, however, brought another change, the sharp increase in interest payments in government transfers. Table 10 shows the proportion of gross interest paid by general government to GDP and to general government expenditures. The first two columns should be read in comparison to the figures given in table 6 showing government borrowing requirements as a proportion of GDP. Most governments are now in classic conditions of what Minsky has called "Ponzi finance", i.e. they have to borrow in order to be able to pay interest on their outstanding debt. This is the major problem facing most governments,

TABLE 4 Social Security Transfers as a Proportion of GDP

	60–7	*68–73*	*74–9*	*80–9*	*60–89*
USA	5.4	7.7	10.3	11.1	8.7
Japan	4.2	4.8	8.4	7.3	
Austria	14.3	15.6	17.8	20.1	17.2
France	15.5	15.6	17.5	21.3	17.8
Germany	12.4	13.2	16.7	16.5	14.8
Italy	11.1	13	15.4	16.7	14.2
Netherlands	17.7	23.5	26.7	23.4	
UK	7.3	8.8	10.7	13.2	10.3

Source: OECD 1991 Table 6.4, p. 67.

TABLE 5 Ratio of Total Government Outlays to GDP

	60–7	*68–73*	*74–9*	*80–9*	*60–89*
USA	28.3	31.1	32.6	36	32.3
Japan	18.7	20.5	28.4		25.6
Austria	37.6	40.2	46.7	51	44.4
France	37.4	38.9	43.3	50.3	43.2
Germany	35.7	39.8	47.5	47.6	42.8
Italy	29.3	34.7	39.2	45	37.6
Netherlands	37.8	44.8	52.8	59.6	49.5
UK	34.7	39.5	44.4	44.9	41

Source: OECD, 1991 Table 6.5, p. 68.

TABLE 6 Government Borrowing Requirements as a Proportion of GDP

	60–7	*68–73*	*74–9*	*80–9*	*60–89*
USA	–0.6	–0.6	–1.4	–3.4	–1.7
Japan	1.0	0.9	–3.4	NA	–0.8
Austria	0.6	0.8	–2.1	–3	–1.1
France	0.5	0.5	–1.1	–2.1	–0.7
Germany	0.8	0.2	–3	–2.1	–1
Italy	–1.8	–4.8	–9.2	–11	–6.9
Netherlands	–0.7	–0.5	–2.3	–5.7	–2.7
UK	–1.1	–0.4	–4.1	–2.4	–2

Source: OECD, 1991 Table 6.7, p. 69.

and which is the obstacle to the use of expenditure policy, not the absolute value of the outstanding debt.

The difficulty can be remedied only by means of lower outstanding indebtedness or lower interest rates. The former requires net government surpluses which can be achieved by culling net expenditures, which in current conditions means a high probability of simply increasing deficits. The latter course is the only possibility.

TABLE 7 Standardised Unemployment Rates

	64–67	*68–73*	*74–9*	*80–9*	*60–89*
USA	4.2	4.6	6.7	7.2	6.0
Japan	1.2	1.2	1.9	2.5	1.9
Austria	2.0	2.5	6.3	10.8	6.5
France	1.7	2.6	4.5	9.0	5.4
Germany	0.6	1.0	3.2	5.9	3.3
Italy	5.1	5.7	6.6	9.5	7.3
Netherlands	0.8	1.5	4.9	9.7	5.3
UK	2.5	3.3	5.0	10	6.1

Source: OECD: 1991 Table 2.20, p. 45.

TABLE 8 Real Money Supply: M1 and Quasi Money (annual rate of growth)

	60–8	*68–73*	*73–9*	*80–9*	*60–89*
USA	5.8	4.5	2.5	3.6	4.1
Japan	11.9	12.4	3.6	7.4	8.7
Austria	9.5	8.4	9.3	4.1	7.4
France				2.4	
Germany	5.4	6.6	2.4	3.6	4.4
Italy	8.1	9.3	3	–0.1	4.4
Netherlands	3.5	4.6	2.7	5.5	4.2
UK			–2.3	8.2	

Source: OECD, 1991 Table 10.4 p. 103: M1+ Quasi money/GDP Implicit Price Index.

6. Keynes and Stabilisation Policy for the Current Recession

Might we apply Keynes' policy as a means of current policy? A positive impact could be achieved by reversing the trend towards increasing transfer payments and offsetting this with increased capital expenditures. The possible decline in defence expenditure should make this easier. This shift in the composition of expenditure would require the introduction of separate ordinary and capital budgeting. It is interesting to see that this idea is starting to be discussed in the United States (cf. Levy and Levy, 1992).

The current recession in the US may be explained by means of Keynes' short-period pricing equation presented above. During the 1980's peculiar legislation effectively reduced the financing costs of investment in commercial real estate and speculative purchase of publicly quoted companies to zero, or negative, despite high real rates of interest so that the US is experiencing conditions of excess supply of certain types of capital goods. The p in the equation given above has been driven down by the high values of x and y despite the fact that q has been reduced to near zero. The only way that y can be reduced is by increasing government capital expenditures. This seems paradoxical in the presence of excess capacity, but might be achieved by increasing expenditures on social overhead capital which does not create additional capacity in the areas of excess, but only increased incomes. The

TABLE 9 Real Long-Term Interest Rates

	68–73	*74–9*	*80–9*
USA	0.6	–0.6	5.5
Japan	0.5	0.1	4.8
Austria	2.3	2.6	4
France	1.6	–0.4	4.7
Germany		3	4.5
Italy	0.2	–4.2	2.7
UK	2	–2	3.4

Source: OECD, 1991. Table 10.10, p. 106.

TABLE 10 Gross Interest Payments of General Government in Proportion to GDP

	77–9	*80–9*	*77–9*	*80–9*
USA	2.63	4.51	8.17	12.4
Japan	2.23	4.01	7.19	12.12
Austria	2.13	3.38	4.39	6.61
France	1.30	3.50		
Germany	1.61	2.66	3.35	5.56
Italy		7.57		15.31
Netherlands	4.02	6.70	7.46	11.36
UK	4.30	4.54	10.08	10.16

Source: OECD, 1991 Vol II (Germany to 1988).

other factor is the reduction in interest rates, which continue to remain high despite the recent reductions and should be reduced further. With inflation now expected to settle around 3 per cent, long-term real rates are currently (June, 1992) above 5 per cent. Table 10 above shows that there is still a possibility of a 300 basis point (3 percentage points) fall in long rates. The current opinion is that long rates are being held up by the size of the rise in the expected borrowing requirement due to the continued recession and the level of long-term interest rates abroad, in particular in Germany. The increase in capital spending, by reducing the value of y/q brings recovery nearer and thus reduces the expected borrowing requirement. At the same time, the announcement that the government was proposing to split the ordinary budget from the capital budget and balance the former should have a positive impact on market expectations, A similar move in Germany, to cut transfer expenditures associated with unification, and to increase public investment expenditures in the former East German Länder, should have similar effect (it is interesting that the German government did not have a ready plan of public investment in the East at the moment of unification).

Thus the first priority is government expenditure switching, and the second the further decline in interest rates. Keynes's approach suggests that this can be achieved without a sustained depression, which is the only other alternative that has worked in the past, aside from massive destruction of human and fixed capital.

Notes

* The research underlying this paper has been supported by a MURST-University of Bologna (60%) grant.

1 As well as practical - recall that during the 1914–18 war Keynes virtually controlled the international commodity markets.

2 The source of these terms is the settlement procedure in the London Stock Exchange: backwardation representing the payment that a seller of a stock speculating on a fall in price which has not yet materialised has to pay the buyer for the right not to deliver (or to pay an owner of the stock to borrow it in order to make delivery) in order to wait for the expected fall, while contango is the payment the buyer expecting a rise in price which has not yet materialised makes to the seller to postpone receipt (or to someone short the stock to receive it in his place). If on balance speculators expecting a fall dominate those expecting a rise, the latter will pay the former to "carry over" settlement into the next account and vice versa. Thus the seller's effective price is lower than the actual price or spot price by the amount of the backwardation payment, If this were greater than his expectation of the fall in price he would not be willing to carry over the bargain. Backwardation thus represents a shortage in the spot market.

3 Keynes believed that producers would have less flexibility in changing production plans than consumers will have in changing their consumption plans; therefore the former will be more risk averse and dominate in seeking to hedge their positions-since producers are long and consumers are short of output, the sales of futures contracts will dominate the purchase, causing excess supply and pressure on future prices relative to spot.

4 These same relations are spelled out in Chapter 17 of the *General Theory;* I have argued in a number of articles (e.g., Kregel, 1982) that they may be considered as a general theory of pricing for Keynes's system.

5 Keynes, in a 1923 article in the *Manchester Guardian Supplement* (XII) suggests that production will fall off more quickly than consumption rises (or may even fall, although at a lower rate than production).

6 Had Keynes used the more normal notation of the futures market this would have required asking what rate of return could be expected from buying spot at P_1 and selling the future at P_2 for a return of $(P_2\text{-}P_1)P_1$ which would be established by borrowing P_1S for a cost of $(T/360)P_1S$ and earning $-c(T/360)P_1S$ over the holding period, T, and i is the borrowing rate on money and c the rate of carrying costs per unit. Thus $(P_2\text{-}P_1)S = P_1S\ [(1+i(T/360)) -(1-c(T/360))] = P_1S\ ((i+c)T/360)$ and $(P_2\text{-}P_1)/P_1 = (i+c)T/360$. In Keynes' terms: $x = i+c$ and $T = y/q$ and his equation could be written as $f = (i+c)T/360$ and P_2 is the expected future spot price which should be equal to the price paid for a future contract, Since $x > 0$, $P_2 = P_1(1 + x)$, $P_2 > P_1$ which is a contango.

7 The formula can also be applied to the production of investment goods and thus to investment expenditures by considering current costs of production relative to the discounted present value of the expected earnings of existing capital goods. Investment will be positive when it is profitable to hedge futures contracts for future delivery of capital goods by producing them, rather than buying existing goods and holding them for delivery. Thus, in a slump, the same argument made about excess stocks of commodities may be made about investment goods, with their spot prices falling below expected future prices by an amount determined by the cost of carry arid investment coming to a halt when the return on holding existing investment goods exceeds the return to producing new goods.

8 Sidney Weintraub (1981) proposed this in the early 1980's in response to the rhetoric of the new Reagan administration, but as far as I know it was without any knowledge of Keynes' post-war policy proposals.

References;

Baily, M.N. (1978), "Stabilization Policy and Private Economic Behavior", *Brookings Papers on Economic Activity*, No. 1.

Guger, A. and E. Walterskirchen (1988), *Fiscal and Monetary Policy in the Keynes-Kalecki Tradition*, in: J.A. Kregel, E. Matzner and A. Roncaglia (eds.), Macmillan, London.

Keynes, J.M. (1923), "Some Aspects of Commodity Markets", reprinted in: *Economic Articles and Correspondence: Investment and Editorial, Collected Writings of J.M. Keynes*, Vol. XII, Macmillan, London, for the Royal Economic Society, 1983.

———. (1930), *A Treatise on Money*, Macmillan, London.

———. (1980), *Activities 1940–46 shaping the Post-War World: Employment and Commodities, Collected Writings of J.M. Keynes*, Vol. XXVII, Macmillan, London, for the Royal Economic Society.

Kregel, J.A. (1982), "Money, Expectations and Relative Prices in Keynes' Monetary Equilibrium", *Economic Appliquée*, Vol. 36, No. 3.

———. (1985), "Budget Deficits, Stabilisation Policy and Liquidity Preference: Keynes's Post-War Policy Proposals", in: F. Vicarelli (ed.), *Keynes's Relevance Today*, Macmillan, London.

Lerner, A. (1943), "Functional Finance and the Federal Debt", *Social Research*, Vol. 10, February.

Levy, S. Jay and D. Levy (1992), *How to Restore Long-Term Prosperity in the United States and Overcome the Contained Depression of the 1990s?*, The Jerome Levy Economics Institute, Annandale-on-Hudson, New York.

Maddison, A. (1982), *Phases of Capitalist Development*, Oxford University Press, Oxford.

Minsky, H.P. (1986), *Stabilising an Unstable Economy*, Yale University Press, New Haven.

OECD (1981), *OECD National Accounts: Detailed Tables Volume II* 1962–1979, Paris.

———. (1991), *OECD National Accounts: Detailed Tables Volume II* 1977–1989, Paris.

———. (1991), *OECD Historical Statistics* 1960–1989, Paris.

Weintraub, S. (1981), "Where Red Ink Is a False Alarm", *The New York Times*, December.

Chapter 22

WAS KEYNES'S MONETARY POLICY, À *OUTRANCE* IN THE *TREATISE*, THE MODEL FOR ZIRP AND QE?

KEYNES'S CHALLENGE TO MONETARY AUTHORITIES IN 1930: INTRODUCE ZIRP AND QE

At the end of 1930, as the US stock market crash was starting to have a negative impact on the real economy in the form of falling commodity prices, falling output, and rising unemployment, John Maynard Keynes, in the concluding chapters of his *Treatise on Money*, launched a challenge to monetary authorities: take 'deliberate and vigorous action' to reduce interest rates and reverse the crisis. He argued that until 'extraordinary', 'unorthodox' monetary policy action 'has been taken along such lines as these and has failed, need we, in the light of the argument of this treatise, admit that the banking system can *not*, on this occasion, control the rate of investment, and, therefore, the level of prices' (Keynes 1930a: 387).[1] The 'unorthodox' policies that Keynes recommends are virtually identical to the Japanese central bank's experiment with zero interest rate policy (ZIRP) in the 1990s and the US Federal Reserve's experiment with ZIRP, accompanied by quantitative easing (QE1 and QE2), during the recent crisis. While too late to be considered a response to Keynes's challenge, these modern policy measures provide a clear test of Keynes's belief in the power of monetary policy to counter financial crisis. This modern response to Keynes's challenge would appear to be a clear admission of the inability of monetary policy to influence the rate of investment as a means of responding to the crisis. Indeed, Keynes himself seems to have modified his position as his thinking evolved towards the analysis of the *General Theory*.

THE OBJECTIVES OF MONETARY POLICY

In the penultimate chapter of volume 2 of the *Treatise*, Keynes raises 'the crux of the whole matter' of monetary policy: '[D]oes it lie within the power of a central bank in actual practice to pursue a policy which will have the effect of fixing the value of money at any prescribed level?' (Keynes 1930a: 339).[2]

Despite some residual doubts,[3] Keynes nonetheless answers his own question in the affirmative, urging central bankers to adopt 'extraordinary', 'unorthodox' measures to reduce interest rates to near zero in an attempt to counter the deepening recession.

THE *TREATISE* AND THE ALTERNATIVE DETERMINATION OF PRICES

Keynes's proposal is built on his explanation of price determination provided in the *Treatise*. His approach was based on the formulation of 'fundamental equations' for the prices of what he called 'available' and 'non-available' output. In simple terms, Keynes argued that prices would be determined by unit labour costs (efficiency wages) and the pressure of demand caused by a divergence of savings from investment driving profitability of production. The focus of recovery policy should thus be to increase investment in order to drive up the demand for output, absorbing excess production and encouraging entrepreneurs to again expand employment and output. Keynes points out that his approach is substantially different from that of the quantity theorists, in that there is no direct impact of money on prices; rather it is investment that is the crucial factor. Since Keynes believed that banks had the power to determine the terms of credit, they could influence the rate of investment, which would then determine the price level.

Although Keynes attributed 'to the banking system much greater power to *preserve* investment equilibrium than to force the prevailing rate of money incomes away from the existing level or from the level produced by spontaneous changes, to a new and changed level imposed by conditions abroad or by arbitrary decree at home' (Keynes 1930a: 352), he nonetheless urged central bankers to attempt to do so in response to the crisis.

SHORT-TERM RATES OF INTEREST AND LONG-TERM RATES

Keynes notes a major difficulty in his proposal that while 'the main direct influence of the banking system is over the short-term rate of interest', the control of the rate of investment will primarily depend on the long-term rate of interest. It is thus necessary to 'be sure that the long-term rate of interest will respond to the wishes of the currency authority which will be exerting its direct influence, as it must, mainly on the short-term rate' (Ibid.).

Keynes's 'experience shows that, as a rule, the influence of the short-term rate of interest on the long-term rate is much greater than anyone who argued on the above lines would have expected' (Ibid.: 353). In support of this position Keynes refers to statistical studies by the Federal Reserve Board (Riefler 1930) showing that 'all the important movements in short-term rates from 1919 to 1928 were reflected in bond yields' (Ibid.: 353). Keynes emphasizes that the surprising fact 'is not that bond yields are relatively stable in comparison with short-term rates, but rather that they have reflected fluctuations in short-term rates so strikingly and to such a considerable extent' (Ibid.: 355–6).[4]

In further support of this relationship Keynes raises an issue that would take on greater importance in The *General Theory*: the predominant impact of short-term realizations on long-term expectations.

> 'In truth,' he writes, 'we know almost nothing about the more remote future. … The ignorance of even the best-informed investor about the more remote future is much greater than his knowledge. … But if this is true of the best informed, the vast majority … know almost

nothing whatever about what they are doing. They do not possess even the rudiments of what is required for a valid judgment, and are the prey of hopes and fears easily aroused by transient events and as easily dispelled. This is one of the odd characteristics of the capitalist system under which we live, which, when we are dealing with the real world, is not to be overlooked' (Ibid.: 359–61).

SHORT-TERM MONEY: QUANTITY IS AS IMPORTANT AS PRICE

Having established the importance of the short term in formulating long-term expectations, and thus the possibility that short-term interest rates could be used to influence long-term capital investment decisions, Keynes goes on to admit:

> 'I do not believe … that the volume of investment either in working capital or in liquid capital is sensitive to changes in the short-term rate of interest by itself.… On the other hand, the direct effects of cheap money operating through changes, even small ones, in the bond market … on the volume of new investment is probably of more importance' (Ibid.: 364).

EXTRAORDINARY MEASURES: ZIRP AND QE

But Keynes goes on to note that these arguments apply to 'normal and orthodox methods by which a central bank can use its powers for easing (or stiffening) the credit situation to stimulate (or retard) the rate of new investment'. But, if the central bank has not acted peremptorily 'more extreme measures will have to be invoked'. (Ibid.: 369)

> 'These extreme measures involve the purchase of securities by the central bank until the long-term market rate of interest has been brought down … to any figure at which it is itself prepared to buy long-term securities.[5] …Thus I see small reason to doubt that the central bank can produce a large effect on the cost of raising new resources for long-term investment, if it is prepared to persist with its open-market policy far enough' (Ibid.: 371).

Thus, Keynes recommends not only pushing the rate of interest down towards zero, but also dealing in the long-term market to set long rates.

Keynes notes that there may be implementation difficulties. For example, many central banks have restrictions on the type of securities acceptable for purchase or discount, so that if the bank continues such purchases beyond a certain point, it may create an entirely artificial position in them relatively to other securities. 'It is to provide against the contingency of insufficient ammunition for the carrying on of open-market operations à outrance that I have suggested that the central bank should have power to vary within limits the reserve requirements of its member banks' (Ibid.: 369–72).

An alternative would be to vary the eligibility of the assets that the bank can acquire, which is precisely what the Federal Reserve did in invoking Section 13 (3) of the Federal Reserve Act to create special facilities for lending against alternative types of collateral and to nonmember institutions.

Keynes also notes that the central bank may be purchasing securities at rates 'far beyond what it considers to be the long-term norm', *and* that when the central bank reverses strategy it 'may show a serious financial loss'. But this should be accepted since the central bank, representing the public interest, should 'be ready to run the risks of the future prospects when private interest reckons these risks to be unusually high'.[6]

The conclusion for policy is that, 'if my diagnosis is correct, we cannot hope for a complete or lasting recovery until there has been a very great fall in the long-term market rate of interest throughout the world towards something nearer pre-war levels. Failing this, there will be a steady pressure towards profit deflation and a sagging price level' (Ibid.: 384). Without these extraordinary policies, 'the thing will never cure itself by the lack of borrowers forcing down the rate; for it absorbs just as much savings to finance losses as to finance investment' (Ibid.).

> 'The remedy should come, I suggest, from a general recognition that the rate of investment need not be beyond our control, if we are prepared to use our banking systems to effect a proper adjustment of the market rate of interest. It might be sufficient merely to produce a general belief in the long continuance of a very low rate of short-term interest. The change, once it has begun, will feed on itself' (Ibid.: 386).

Again, it is interesting to note that the Federal Reserve has made a public commitment to the preservation of the ZIRP for a sustained period.

It would appear that the Bank of Japan, by introducing a ZIRP, experimented with Keynes's recommendation that interest rates be set as low as possible, and that the Federal Reserve, through its programme of quantitative lending, has followed his recommendation in full by purchasing long-term securities to bring down the long-term rate of interest and satiate the desire to hold deposits. Keynes notes that these policies are not at all different from normal open-market policies, and that the central bank possesses the power to set any interest rate, short or long, at any level it desires. It also appears as if Keynes's expectation that the public would become willing buyers of government securities upon a sharp reduction in short rates, aiding the policy of lowering the long-term rate, was accurate. In addition, in response to Fed policy, there has been the recovery of stock prices that Keynes would have expected.

What has not been borne out in the current experiment is the expected impact on the rate of investment. Businesses have indeed increased their borrowing, particularly low-grade credits, and the spread between corporate junk bonds has fallen to near-historic lows as companies seek to borrow at historically low interest rates. However, these funds are not being used to finance new investment. Similarly, banks have accumulated record levels of excess reserve deposits at the Fed, earning the short-term interest rate, which is nearly zero. Thus, the policy has been successful in influencing the spectrum of interest rates in the way Keynes's predicted, but it has not had the impact on investment that he outlined in the *Treatise*.

SCEPTICISM BETWEEN THE *TREATISE* AND THE *GENERAL THEORY*

Keynes progressively modified his belief in the efficacy of monetary policy in the interim between the publication of the *Treatise* and the completion of The *General Theory*. The first indications came during a visit to the United States in 1931 in which he gave policy lectures at the New School for Social Research in New York and at the Harris Foundation in Chicago.

His lectures at the New School in mid-June were entitled 'Do We Want Prices to Rise?' and 'What Can We Do to Make Prices Rise?' There is some controversy over the exact content of the second lecture; contemporaneous press reports appear to contradict the truncated version that appears in the *Collected Writings* published under the auspices of the Royal Economic Society (see the discussion in Kent 2004). Kent surmises that Keynes changed his presentation from the prepared written version due to his discussions with policymakers in New York. He notes that in the version of the second lecture published in the *Collected Writings of John Maynard Keynes* (CWK), Keynes does not recommend government intervention and repeats his analysis of the *Treatise*: 'if…the rate of interest can be brought down sufficiently, I do feel confident that the demand for loans will in due course develop for buildings, for transport and for public utilities' (CWK XX: 553).

Kent cites local news reports that suggest in his oral presentation he added two new points: restoring confidence and direct government action. 'Recommending government action in the United States was a very significant change for Keynes [who] was an advocate of government intervention in Great Britain, but that was because of Great Britain's ability to reduce interest rates was restricted by concerns about the outflow of gold that it was thought would occur if this were done' (Kent 2004: 204). Keynes did not believe that the US was so constrained, suggesting a softening of his confidence in the willingness or the ability of central banks to produce interest rate reductions sufficient to generate recovery.

This interpretation finds support in Keynes's lectures to the Harris Foundation in Chicago at the beginning of July. In Lecture I Keynes identifies the 'leading characteristic' of the crisis as 'an extraordinary willingness to borrow money for the purposes of new real investment at very high rates of interest—rates of interest which were extravagantly high on pre-war standards, rates of interest which have never in the history of the world been earned, I should say, over a period of years over the average of enterprise as a whole' (CWK XIII: 345). As a result, Keynes says he can 'see no hope of a recovery except in a revival of the high level of investment'. He thus directs his analysis to the 'causes of the collapse of investment and the means of reviving investment' (Ibid.: 349). He concentrates on the 'variability of the rate of investment' since it is 'the element of the economic situation which is capable of sudden and violent change' (Ibid.: 354–5). In Lecture 3, 'The Road to Recovery', he notes that this is 'essentially a technical banking problem. The practical means by which investment can be increased is, or ought to be, the bankers' business, and pre-eminently the business of the central banker' (Ibid.: 363).

He then outlines three channels of attack, restoring confidence, government action, and a reduction in the rate of interest. Here he reiterates scepticism concerning the possibility of sufficient action on the interest rate:

> I am ready to believe that a small change in the rate of interest may not be sufficient. That, indeed, is why I am pessimistic as to an early return to normal prosperity. I am ready enough to admit that it may be extremely difficult both to restore confidence adequately and to reduce interest rates adequately. (Ibid.: 365).

He amplified this position in a Round Table following his presentation: 'I am in favour of an admixture of public works …I should use the public works program to fill in the interegnum (sic) while I was getting the interest rate down' (Harris Foundation 1931: 494). However, in the September 1932 issue of *The Economic Journal* he reaffirms his position: 'A reduction of the long-term rate of interest to a low level is probably the most necessary of all measures if we are to escape from the slump and secure a lasting revival of enterprise' (Keynes 1932: 415).

A SHIFT OF POSITION IN THE *GENERAL THEORY*?

However, Keynes's position changed with his development of *The General Theory*. Keynes tells his readers that one of the basic differences from the earlier book is the separation of the analysis of investment in financial assets and capital assets through the separation of their determinants via liquidity preference and the marginal efficiency of capital. While the *Treatise* made a distinction between industrial and financial circulation, the prices of both assets and liabilities were treated in a single fundamental price equation and financed by the financial circulation.

In his *General Theory* analysis, Keynes amplifies the explanation of determinants of investment, stating that 'current investment will depend … on what we shall call the inducement to invest; and the inducement to invest will be found to depend on the relation between the schedule of the marginal efficiency of capital and the complex of rates of interest on loans of various maturities and risks' (Keynes 1936: 27). 'The schedule of the marginal efficiency of capital may be said to govern the terms on which loanable funds are demanded for the purpose of new investment; whilst the rate of interest governs the terms on which funds are being currently supplied' (Ibid.: 165).

Another novel feature of *The General Theory* is its emphasis on the conditions of a monetary economy as 'one in which changing views about the future are capable of influencing the quantity of employment and not merely its direction' (Ibid.: vii). In particular, Keynes notes that the major determinant of the rate of interest will be 'largely governed by the prevailing view as to what its value is expected to be' (Ibid.: 203), while 'the schedule of the marginal efficiency of capital is of fundamental importance because it is mainly through this factor (much more than through the rate of interest) that the expectation of the future influences the present' (Ibid.: 145). The current long-term rate of interest is thus no longer the sole or direct determinant of investment.

Echoing his views in the *Treatise*, he writes:

> It would be foolish, in forming our expectations, to attach great weight to matters which are very uncertain. … For this reason the facts of the existing situation enter, in a sense disproportionately, into the formation of our long-term expectations; our usual practice being to take the existing situation and to project it into the future, modified only to the extent that we have more or less definite reasons for expecting a change. [Thus,] there is no clear evidence from experience that the investment policy which is socially advantageous coincides with that which is most profitable. It needs *more* intelligence to defeat the forces of time and our ignorance of the future than to beat the gun. Moreover, life is not long

> enough;—human nature desires quick results, there is a peculiar zest in making money quickly, and remoter gains are discounted by the average man at a very high rate. (Ibid.: 148–57)

As a result, Keynes modifies his prior belief in the positive impact of lower interest rates on the rate of investment. For example, an expectation of a future fall in the rate of interest will have the effect of *lowering* the schedule of the marginal efficiency of capital; since it means that the output from equipment produced to-day will have to compete during part of its life with the output from equipment which is content with a lower return. This expectation will have no great depressing effect, since the expectations, which are held concerning the complex of rates of interest for various terms which will rule in the future, will be partially reflected in the complex of rates of interest which rule to-day. Nevertheless there may be some depressing effect, since the output from equipment produced to-day, which will emerge towards the end of the life of this equipment, may have to compete with the output of much younger equipment which is content with a lower return because of the lower rate of interest which rules for periods subsequent to the end of the life of equipment produced to-day. (Ibid.: 143)

Keynes also modifies his position on the ability of the central bank to influence the lending practices of financial institutions through a reduction in interest rates:

> We must also take account of the other facet of the state of confidence, namely, the confidence of the lending institutions towards those who seek to borrow from them, sometimes described as the state of credit. A collapse in the price of equities, which has had disastrous reactions on the marginal efficiency of capital, may have been due to the weakening either of speculative confidence or of the state of credit. But whereas the weakening of either is enough to cause a collapse, recovery requires the revival of *both*. For whilst the weakening of credit is sufficient to bring about a collapse, its strengthening, though a necessary condition of recovery, is not a sufficient condition. (Ibid.: 158)

Further, Keynes argues that there may be difficulty in pushing interest rates down to extremely low levels due to extreme liquidity preference:

> We have seen … that *uncertainty* as to the future course of the rate of interest is the sole intelligible explanation of the type of liquidity preference … which leads to the holding of cash. … It follows that … what matters is not the *absolute* level of *r* but the degree of its divergence from what is considered a fairly *safe* level of *r*, having regard to those calculations of probability which are being relied on. (Ibid.: 201–2)

Keynes then goes on to give a precise definition of the liquidity trap:

> Every fall in *r* reduces the market rate relatively to the 'safe' rate and therefore increases the risk of illiquidity; and, in the second place, every fall in *r* reduces the current earnings from illiquidity, which are available as a sort of insurance premium to off set the risk of loss on capital account, by an amount equal to the difference between the *squares* of the old rate of interest and the new. … *This, indeed, is perhaps the chief obstacle to a fall in the rate of interest to a*

> *very low level.* Unless reasons are believed to exist why future experience will be very different from past experience, a long-term rate of interest of (say) 2 per cent leaves more to fear than to hope, and offers, at the same time, a running yield which is only sufficient to offset a very small measure of fear. (Ibid.) [emphasis added][7]

Although Keynes continues to maintain that the 'short-term rate of interest is easily controlled by the monetary authority, both because it is not difficult to produce a conviction that its policy will not greatly change in the very near future, and also because the possible loss is small compared with the running yield (unless it is approaching vanishing point)', he also observes that the long-term rate may be more recalcitrant when once it has fallen to a level which, on the basis of past experience and present expectations of *future* monetary policy, is considered 'unsafe' by representative opinion. For example, in a country linked to an international gold standard, a rate of interest lower than prevails elsewhere will be viewed with a justifiable lack of confidence; yet a domestic rate of interest dragged up to a parity with the *highest* rate (highest after allowing for risk) prevailing in any country belonging to the international system may be much higher than is consistent with domestic full employment. (Ibid.: 203)

Thus, the introduction of the influence of the marginal efficiency of capital on the rate of investment independent of the impact of the rate of interest and the introduction of expectations and liquidity preference as the independent determinant of the rate of interest leads Keynes to modify his *Treatise* analysis of the impact of 'extraordinary' monetary policy on the long-term rate of interest:

> A monetary policy which strikes public opinion as being experimental in character or easily liable to change may fail in its objective of greatly reducing the long-term rate of interest, because M_2 may tend to increase almost without limit in response to a reduction of r below a certain figure. The same policy, on the other hand, may prove easily successful if it appeals to public opinion as being reasonable and practicable and in the public interest, rooted in strong conviction, and promoted by an authority unlikely to be superseded. (Ibid.)

'FOR MY OWN PART I AM NOW SOMEWHAT SCEPTICAL'

Thus, in *The General Theory*, Keynes, 'after giving full weight to the importance of the influence of short-period changes in the state of long-term expectation as distinct from changes in the rate of interest', further modifies his belief in the efficacy of monetary policy to influence the rate of investment, noting that 'we are still entitled to return to the latter [i.e., the rate of interest] as exercising, at any rate, in normal circumstances, a great, though not a decisive, influence on the rate of investment. Only experience, however, can show how far management of the rate of interest is capable of continuously stimulating the appropriate volume of investment' (Ibid.: 164). He then goes on to state:

> For my own part I am now somewhat sceptical of the success of a merely monetary policy directed towards influencing the rate of interest. I expect to see the State, which is in a position to calculate the marginal efficiency of capital-goods on long views and on the basis of the general social advantage, taking an ever greater responsibility for directly organising

investment; since it seems likely that the fluctuations in the market estimation of the marginal efficiency of different types of capital, calculated on the principles I have described above, will be too great to be offset by any practicable changes in the rate of interest. (Ibid.)

* * *

While Keynes can be considered the true father of the 'unorthodox' monetary policies introduced by the Bank of Japan and the Federal Reserve, these policies also provide the test of their efficacy that Keynes called for. They suggest that Keynes's *Treatise* optimism was misplaced, and that his more nuanced, sceptical, position in *The General Theory* was more appropriate; in particular, his emphasis on the need to provide an external source of demand through government expenditure. Finally, in comparison with the current period, Keynes did not take into account the impact of capital loss on the inducement to invest and the propensity to consume, factors that in all likelihood would have led him to place even greater emphasis on the role of government spending in bringing about recovery.

Notes

1 Already in May 1930 Keynes expressed this view in an article in *The Nation* that reflects the conclusions of the *Treatise*:

> The fact is—a fact not yet recognized by the great public—that we are now in the depths of a very severe international slump, a slump which will take its place in history amongst the most acute ever experienced. It will require not merely passive movements of bank rates to lift us out of a depression of this order, but a very active and determined policy. (Keynes 1930b)

2 The question is considered in the context of a proposal to amend the Federal Reserve Act 'to lay upon the Federal Reserve Board the duty of using all the powers at its disposal to "promote a stable price level for commodities in general"' (Keynes 1930a: 340).

3 Raised by Congressional hearings on the proposal that surveyed the difficulties of using monetary policy to counter the impact of international conditions on commodity prices, and thus on domestic prices, and the difficulty of using monetary policy to counter declining prices in a depression.

4 Keynes does not, however, report Riefler's (1930: 123) caveat that this is more the result of the impact on the stock of existing long-terms bonds than on the prices of newly issued long-term securities.

5 If the central bank supplies the member banks with more funds than they can lend at short term, in the first place the short-term rate of interest will decline towards zero, and in the second place the member banks will soon begin, if only to maintain their profits, to second the efforts of the central bank by themselves buying securities. This means that the price of bonds will rise until there are many persons to be found who, as they see the prices of long-term bonds rising, prefer to sell them and hold the proceeds liquid at a very low rate of interest.

6 In Keynes (1932: 421–2) he notes that in the US 'the fear of the Member Banks lest they should be unable to cover their expenses' may have provided an 'obstacle to the adoption of a whole-hearted cheap money policy'.

7 Keynes also notes that the classical theory proposed an alternative method of lowering the rate of interest, by 'reducing wages, whilst leaving the quantity of money unchanged'. Just as a moderate increase in the quantity of money may exert an inadequate influence over the long-term rate of interest, whilst an immoderate increase may offset its other advantages by its disturbing effect on confidence; so a moderate reduction in money-wages may prove

inadequate, whilst an immoderate reduction might shatter confidence even if it were practicable. 'There is, therefore, no ground for the belief that a flexible wage policy is capable of maintaining a state of continuous full employment;—any more than for the belief that an open-market monetary policy is capable, unaided, of achieving this result. The economic system cannot be made self-adjusting along these lines' (Keynes 1936: 267).

REFERENCES

Harris Foundation. 1931. *Reports of Roundtables: Unemployment as a World Problem.* Chicago.

Kent, R.J. 2004. 'Keynes's Lectures at the New School for Social Research', *History of Political Economy*, 36(1): 195–206.

Keynes, J.M. 1930a. *A Treatise on Money. Vol. II: The Applied Theory of Money.* London: Macmillan.

———. 1930b. 'Monetary Policy Alone Will Not End Depression', *The Nation*, 10 May.

———. 1932. 'A Note on the Long-Term Rate of Interest in Relation to the Conversion Scheme', *The Economic Journal*, 42(167): 415–23.

———. 1936. *The General Theory of Employment, Interest and Money.* London: Macmillan.

———. 1971–89. *The Collected Writings of John Maynard Keynes* (CWK), edited by D.E. Moggridge, 30 vols. London: Macmillan; volumes are identified as CWK followed by volume number in Roman numerals.

CWK XIII. *The General Theory and After. Vol. 1: Preparation. C WK XX. Activities, 1929–31: Rethinking Employment and Unemployment Policies.*

Riefler, W.W. 1930. *Money Rates and Money Markets in the United States.* With an Introduction by E.A. Goldenweiser. New York and London: Harper & Brothers.

Chapter 23

KRUGMAN ON THE LIQUIDITY TRAP: WHY INFLATION WILL NOT BRING RECOVERY IN JAPAN(*)

1 Introduction

The failure of the Japanese economy to respond to aggressive monetary easing in the form of a zero bid rate on the Bank of Japan's overnight financing facility has reminded some economists of Hicks's rendition of Keynes's "liquidity trap". Those who use Hicks's IS-LM diagram to evaluate monetary policy will recall that the horizontal portion of the LM curve emanating from the vertical axis indicates the minimum below which the interest rate cannot fall. It is meant to represent the lack of influence of monetary policy on the rate of interest. The conclusion is that in the horizontal range it has no influence on the equilibrium level of output since a rightward shift of LM does not change its intersection with IS. If monetary policy has no impact on output, debt financed government expenditure remains the only policy capable of influencing output.

The explanation usually given of the failure of monetary policy is that interest rates are so low that they cannot be reduced further. Since Japanese policy rates are zero and cannot be reduced it is considered to be the first clear example of an economy facing a liquidity trap.[1]

Those who have studied Keynes's analysis of changes in the quantity of money on the level of output will recall that there "may be several slips between the cup and the lip" (JMK:VII, p. 173) and that his theory of liquidity preference, the foundation for the liquidity trap, challenged the mechanical relationship between money creation, the price level and the nominal level of output in the traditional quantity theory. It is paradoxical that the theoretical explanation of the recession in the Japanese economy should be founded on quantity theory models in which the rate of expansion of the quantity of money directly determines the rate of change in the price level. Indeed, in canonical quantity theory models money is neutral and has no impact on the long-run equilibrium of real output, irrespective of any reference to a liquidity trap, since money only affects nominal variables. The failure of a positive rate of change in the quantity of money to reverse the decline in the price level in these traditional quantity theory models is considered to be equivalent to the failure of expansionary money policy to reduce the rate of interest in Keynes's explanation of the liquidity trap.

This apparent contradiction is resolved once it is recognised that the liquidity trap in these neo-quantity theory models represents the failure of changes in the quantity of money to influence the "real" rate of return. Thus, with the nominal rate of interest bounded at zero, the real rate of interest can only be reduced if prices are rising. If prices are falling, then the real rate is rising, and if the Central Bank nonetheless increases the money supply and prices are not responding, then the real rate is not falling and the economy is said to be in a liquidity trap since monetary policy has no influence on the real rate.

The reason for the liquidity trap is then the failure of money growth to raise prices as postulated by the traditional quantity theory. This failure is not explained by any shortcoming in the theory, but failure of the Central Bank to make credible its intention to produce inflation. After decades of urging Central Banks to adopt independent policies and to create credibility in their pledge to keep prices stable by tying their hands and other sorts of sadistic practices, it is now argued that in Japan it is precisely this credibility that makes the attempt to create inflation incredible. Paradoxically, the current policy prescription for the Bank of Japan is to make its commitment to price stability incredible in order to convince market participants that it will produce a rate of inflation that is sufficient to reduce the real rate of interest to the level that causes domestic savings to fall to the near zero level of real domestic investment expenditures.

This modern explanation of liquidity preference is in fact based on Irving Fisher's version of the theory in which the nominal rate of interest is determined by the real rate of return adjusted for the rate of change in the price level. If instead of rising, the price level is falling then nominal rates will have to be below real rates of return and equilibrium may require negative nominal interest rates if the real rate is less than the deflation rate. But, if nominal rates are bounded at zero, then nominal interest rates cannot be adjusted downwards and the only way to restore savings-investment equilibrium is a policy of inflation. This is precisely the policy that Fisher urged on Franklin Roosevelt during the Great Depression in the United States. It was also the basis of the decision to devalue the dollar by raising the price of gold and the various measures to create US government agencies designed to put floors under domestic prices. The inflation policy that Paul Krugman is recommending for Japan is based on exactly the same principles as Irving Fisher's recommendations during the Great Depression.

2 Hicks's Horizontal LM Curve as Liquidity Trap

Hicks not only claimed to be "a convinced liquidity preference man" (JMK:XIV, p. 83), he also claimed that "Keynes accepted the IS-LM diagram as a fair statement of his position" (Hicks, 1977, p. 146) However, Keynes was not an uncritical reader of Hicks's exposition of his theory in the *Economic Journal* review of the *General Theory* and the subsequent derivation of the now famous IS-LL (as it was originally called) diagram. In particular, Keynes notes that Hicks inserted two illicit assumptions concerning the elasticity of supply of consumption goods and the income elasticity of the rate of interest in his discussion. Both were important to the derivation of the horizontal portion of the LM curve that represents the liquidity trap for most economists, but both were extraneous to Keynes's theory.

In his review Hicks notes that even if one accepts Keynes's multiplier proposition that an increase in investment will cause a rise in demand for consumption goods and thus a multiplied increase in aggregate income, the empirical magnitude of the increase in real output will be small if the elasticity of supply of consumption goods is low. Hicks thus concludes that Keynes must be implicitly assuming "a high elasticity of supply in the consumption goods industries ...; and if things do work out this way, it is perfectly intelligible that the increased demand for loans from the investment industries should encounter an increased supply, so that there is no reason for the rate of interest to rise" (Hicks, CEII, pp. 89–91) when investment and output increase. The idea is that the increased output of consumption goods will produce the increased savings necessary to fund the loans for the new investment expenditures.

Hicks also argues that if the supply of consumption goods is inelastic during the expansive phase of the cycle: 'Mr. Keynes's analysis of this case would evidently lead to the conclusion that there would be an indefinite rise in the prices of consumption goods ... but he would admit, on second thoughts, that this would lead to a more or less corresponding rise in the demand for money; and therefore that, unless the supply of money was indefinitely expanded, the rate of interest must rise ... I do not think that this differs essentially from what has been said by earlier writers [Hicks refers in a footnote to Hayek's *Prices and Production*]; they would, however, begin by assuming the supply of money not indefinitely expansible, and so proceed straight to the rise in the rate of interest. But they would admit, on their second thoughts, that if the supply of money were to be indefinitely expanded, the rate of interest could be kept down, and the inflation proceed without limit' (Hicks: CEII, pp. 93–4).

Thus, Hicks concludes that Keynes is assuming either a highly elastic supply of consumption goods or an infinitely elastic supply of money and that it is one or the other of these assumptions that allows Keynes's theory to differ from the traditional explanation of the response of the rate of interest to an increase in the level of activity. Thus, Hicks's explanation of the stability of the rate of interest in the face of an increase in investment and output, which becomes the horizontal range of the LM curve, is based on the assumption of either a high elasticity of supply of consumption goods (implicitly loanable funds) or of money.

Keynes, however, rejects any dependence of his theory on the elasticity of supply: "you argue ... that my argument depends on the assumption of a 'high elasticity of supply of consumption goods', but why high" ... "Towards the end you speak of the imperfect elasticity of supply of consumption goods in a trade cycle leading to a 'consequent hardening of interest rates'. I do not follow why the one is consequent on the other" (JMK:XIV, p. 71, 72).

In answer to this criticism Hicks agrees that the elasticity of supply need only be greater than zero and then goes on.

"Surely it is quite in accordance with your own theory to speak of the imperfect elasticity of supply of consumption goods in the trade cycle leading to a consequent hardening of interest rates. *As investment increases*, the prices of consumption goods rise; this raises the transaction demand for money, and if the supply of money is not perfectly elastic, *interest rates must rise too*. The same thing may indeed happen to some extent merely by increasing employment, even if the supply of consumption goods is perfectly elastic, but imperfect elasticity of supply intensifies it. Is not this orthodox?" (JMK:XIV, p. 73 italics added).

Keynes agrees that this is orthodox, but not his own theory, replying "I quite misunderstood what you meant ... I quite agree with what you say" (*ibid.*, p. 75).[2]

The reader will note that this discussion confuses two separate points. Hicks's initial statement concerned the low probability of a rise in the rate of interest increasing saving out of a given income in order to balance the failure of the consumption goods industries to expand in step with increased investment, the same effect being produced by an elastic supply of consumption goods keeping prices constant and allowing the required increase in the supply of saving. What Hicks had in mind was presumably the availability of stocks to allow the operation of the temporal multiplier process without raising prices.

The second argument, on the other hand, refers to the impact of higher consumption goods prices in increasing the demand for money and thus raising interest rates, even when the multiplier is able to proceed without encountering supply shortages. Thus it is the assumption of the infinitely elastic supply of money that is crucial to the presumed constant rate of interest. But this proposition Keynes clearly accepted as being consistent with classical theory, and as such was not a distinguishing feature of this own theory or of any relation to the liquidity trap as defined above.

Having agreed that in his theory, as in any other, an increase in investment would in general cause an increase in output and probably prices and, via an increase in transactions demands for money an increase in the rate of interest, irrespective of the value of the elasticity of supply above zero, Keynes must have been perplexed by Hicks's statement in the article that set out the IS-LL analysis, "Mr Keynes and the Classics", that Keynes's theory leads to the "startling conclusion, that an increase in the inducement to invest, or in the propensity to consume, *will not* tend to raise the rate of interest, but only to increase employment" (Hicks: CEII, p. 107, italics supplied) and that "*the most important thing* in Mr Keynes's book" is that "It is not only possible to show that a given supply of money determines a certain relation between Income and interest (which we have expressed here by the curve LL) it is also possible to say something about the shape of the curve. It will probably tend to be nearly horizontal on the left, and nearly vertical on the right" (*ibid.*, p. 109, italics supplied), implying that the rate of interest would not rise as investment and output expanded until full employment was reached. But, given the above discussion the horizontal behaviour of the LL curve "on the left" could only take place even in the presence of a perfectly elastic supply of money, while its behaviour "on the right" could only result from a less than perfectly elastic supply of money.

Keynes was quick to note his disagreement with Hicks's clearly ad hoc representation of the behaviour of the rate of interest as the 'most important thing' in Keynes's theory:

> From my point of view, it is important to insist that my remark is to the effect that an increase in the inducement to invest need not raise the rate of interest. I should agree that, unless the monetary policy is appropriate, it is quite likely to. In this respect I consider that the difference between myself and the classicals lies in the fact that they regard the rate of

interest as a non-monetary phenomenon, so that an increase in the inducement to invest would raise the rate of interest *irrespective of monetary policy*

(*JMK:XIV, p. 80, italics added*).

Thus Keynes rejects the argument that the difference between his theory and the Classics lies in the restrictions placed on the money supply function, in particular the existence of a horizontal portion usually known as the 'liquidity trap' or in any restriction on the elasticity of supply. Keynes clearly stated that liquidity trap conditions, while possible, had not yet been experienced; they thus could not serve as an explanation for the Great Depression.[3] Nonetheless, Hicks's formulation of liquidity preference led to a presentation of Keynes's theory which implicitly required either 1) the operation of the liquidity trap due to the elasticity of supply of money, or 2) the assumption of unchanging prices of consumption goods, for a horizontal LM curve represented stable prices in conditions of perfectly elastic supply of consumption goods. However, the IS-LM framework makes no reference to any supply conditions for money or consumption goods output, only the supply of savings. Even though this representation was never accepted by Keynes – Hicks's suggestions to the contrary – it has become the standard representation. Tobin, for example comments 'In terms of the Hicksian language ... I thought (and I still think) ... the main issue ... is the shape of the LM locus' (Tobin, 1972, p. 853). Indeed, both Friedman and Tobin accept a positive slope for the LM curve, rejecting a vertical or horizontal curve. But, as Hicks's article pointed out, here there is no difference between Keynes's and the 'ordinary method of economic theory'. Clearly, Hicks's explanation of the liquidity trap as the horizontal portion of the LM curve is consistent with traditional theory, as Keynes agreed. But it cannot be considered as an analytical foundation for the failure of the rate of interest to respond to policy changes in the amount of base money created by the central bank for it deals with the behaviour of rates when output is increasing with perfectly elastic money supply, not the behaviour of rates when the quantity of money is increasing with perfectly elastic supply of output.

3 The Modern Theory of the Liquidity Trap

Although Krugman considers Hicks's model as a 'very useful heuristic' (Krugman, p. 7) he notes that it is considered too ad hoc and thus not the best vehicle for presenting the traditional version of the liquidity trap. In his view 'A liquidity trap may be defined as a situation in which conventional monetary policies have become impotent, because nominal rates are at or near zero – so that injecting monetary base into the economy has no effect, because base and bonds are viewed by the private sector as perfect substitutes'.

He notes that an alternative 'way of stating the liquidity trap problem is to say that it occurs when the equilibrium real interest rate, the rate at which savings and investment would be equal at potential output, is negative' (*ibid.*, p. 16). As noted above, in traditional theory, if the nominal interest rate is determined by adjusting the real rate of return for depreciation in the monetary standard a rise in the inflation rate, given the nominal rate should cause the real rate to decline. If a rise in the growth of base money causes a rise in the rate of inflation, then it should be possible for monetary policy to achieve the required equilibrium real rate. This raises the question of, "how is the liquidity trap possible? The answer lies in a little-noticed escape clause in the standard argument for monetary neutrality: ... there is no ... argument that says that a rise in the money supply *that is not expected to be sustained* will raise prices equiproportionally – or indeed at all. In short, to approach the question from this level of abstraction already suggests that a liquidity trap involves a kind of credibility problem ... if monetary expansion does not work, if there is a liquidity trap, it must be because the public does not expect it to be sustained" (*ibid.* p. 7).

Although a one-shot increase in base money will lead to a once over increase in the price level, this should have no impact on the rate of inflation and leave the nominal rate of interest unchanged if the real rate of interest is unchanged. The liquidity trap thus occurs because the central bank cannot make individuals with rational expectations believe that it will keep money growing in perpetuum at the new higher rate so as to ensure a higher rate of inflation in perpetuum.

This looks just the opposite of Hicks's theory, which is based on stable prices of consumer goods and belief in the perfect elasticity of the money supply.

Krugman argues that investors do not believe that the money supply will be perfectly elastic, indeed the increases that occur in the present period will be reversed in future. Thus, monetary policy cannot influence the real rate of interest to make it adjust to the level that will lower private sector savings to equality with the voluntary investment decisions of the private sector. 'The easiest way to think about this is to say that there is an equilibrium *real* interest rate which the economy will deliver whatever the behaviour of nominal prices' (*ibid.*, p. 10). Thus, the liquidity trap occurs because the real rate cannot be influenced by monetary policy.

As already noted, this is a perfectly standard result within Fisher's version of the quantity theory and formed the basis for Keynes's belief that Hicks had not captured his essential difference from classical theory:

"Put shortly, the orthodox theory maintains that the forces which determine the common value of the marginal efficiency of various assets are independent of money, which has, so to speak, no autonomous influence; and that prices move until the marginal efficiency of money, i.e. the rate of interest, falls into line with the common value of the marginal efficiency of other assets as determined by other forces. My theory, on the other hand, maintains that this is a special case and that over a wide range of possible cases almost the opposite is true, namely, that the marginal efficiency of money is determined by forces partly appropriate to itself, and that prices move until the marginal efficiency of other assets fall into line with the rate of interest" (JMK:XIV, p. 101).

4 Liquidity Preference and the Liquidity Trap

Krugman notes that unlike Hicks's ad hoc version his explanation of the liquidity trap depends on the modern theory of intertemporal choice. But, it is precisely in the exposition of this intertemporal relation that Keynes differed from Fisher. Fisher's explanation – which is the one used by Krugman – of the determination of nominal interest rates is based on expectations of future goods prices relative to present goods prices as expressed in the expected rate of inflation or deflation of goods prices. The theory is based on a proposition presented in Irving Fisher's *The Theory of Interest* (1930) that on Fisher's own admission only applied to conditions in which "rational tendencies", based on "rational and empirical laws ... analogous to rational and empirical laws of physics and astronomy" (Fisher, 1930, p. 321). However, Fisher notes that where actuarial risk cannot be applied and "uncertain" conditions make the value of money unstable, "We must ... give up as a bad job any attempt to formulate completely the influences which really determine the rate of interest" (ibid.). These are precisely the conditions that Keynes believed to be normal and thus the basis for this theory.

Both Fisher and Keynes specify the rate of interest as an intertemporal relationship represented by a spot-forward swap, or by the excess of the forward price over the par or spot price. However, In Fisher's *time* preference approach the rate of interest is the discount of future over present income that makes their utility equal at the margin, while for Keynes *liquidity* preference represents the return that must be paid on illiquid assets to make investors indifferent to holding more liquid assets.

Since time preference is a relation between real income today and in the future, it would be disturbed by changes in relative prices, thus Fisher argues that the money rate of interest that allows individuals to transfer income from the present to the future, r, must be corrected for the rate of inflation, p, in order to leave the time transformation of income undisturbed: thus the Fisher relation:

$$(1+p)(1+r) = (1+i) \text{ and } i = [(1+r)(1+p)] - 1 = 1 + r + p + rp - 1$$

which is usually written

$$i = r + p$$

when rp is small and p is the rate of inflation, r the rate of increase in real income, and i the rate of interest on money.

In the case of Japan, the problem is not inflation, but deflation, and $p < 0$. Then if i is constrained to be non-negative, r must be positive and it is impossible for the competitive market system to achieve an equilibrium which requires r to be negative. In simple terms this is Krugman's version of the liquidity trap. In Krugman's simple monetary view, p should be determined by the rate of growth of base money; but if money growth is indeed positive and p remains negative this can only be explained by the expectation that money growth will not remain positive and the expansionary monetary policy will be reversed in the medium run. Thus the system is stuck in a liquidity trap with a real rate of interest that is too high, or a nominal rate of interest that is too high, because the rate of inflation is too low when nominal interest rates are fixed at zero. The reason can only be the failure of the central bank to convince the public that p will be permanently higher. Overcoming the liquidity trap thus requires permanent and perfectly anticipated inflation in the form of a positive value of p sufficient to allow r to be negative when i is constrained to be non-negative.

Keynes has a very simple objection to Fisher's relation between the rate of interest and the rate of inflation. First, *pace* Krugman's emphasis on the lack of central bank credibility, he objected because it relied on the assumption of perfect foresight over the path of future incomes and prices (see 1930, pp. 202–3 and JMK:VII pp. 142–3). Second, he objected because Fisher's argument that the money rate of interest should automatically reflect a perfectly foreseen rise or fall in the price level overlooks the impact of a rise or fall in interest rates on the capital value of existing stocks of financial assets. While it is true that if a rise in the price level for the coming year of 2 per cent is perfectly foreseen, interest rates must be 2 per cent higher to keep real returns for investors in one-year bills constant, the same would not be true for an investor holding fixed-interest assets of longer maturity in order to sell after one year, since there would be a positive or negative change in its capital value if interest rates change. Since market arbitrage should ensure that the one-year holding period rate of return should be the same for any instrument (even 30-year bonds sold one year after purchase) held for one year, longer-dated instruments should have a larger adjustment in their interest rates to offset the fall in capital value due to the rise in interest rates. A change in the rate of inflation should then have a differential impact on the rate of interest along the maturity spectrum, rising with time to maturity.[4]

Keynes noted that a rise in the rate of interest from 10 per cent to 12.2 per cent will cause the price of a £100 par value British consol paying a £10 coupon to fall from £100 to £81.96, a decline of 1.8 per cent and a capital loss of over £18. While the "variations in the rate of interest earned during the year in question are too small to make much difference" (e.g. the extra 2.2 per cent earned on the reinvestment of the £10 coupon) relative to the much more substantial capital loss since the benefit of being able to invest the future £10 interest coupon payments at the higher rate of 12.2 per cent will be swamped by the £18 decline in the capital value of the bond. The rise in the rate of interest equal to the rise in the rate of inflation could by no means be considered as sufficient to compensate for the loss in purchasing power. Thus, Keynes argues, Fisher's relation goes in the wrong direction for existing bondholders, since the higher yields required to preserve real yields cause capital losses that will more than offset the increased interest earnings.

What change in the rate of interest would be required to keep the capital position of the bond holder unchanged? Since the impact of the rate of interest will increase interest earned on reinvestment of coupon interest, while it changes capital values in the opposite direction, the breakeven condition for a perpetual bond will be $\Delta P\text{-}C=0$, where ΔP is the annual cumulative change in price, and C its annual coupon payment. The price, or present value, of a perpetual bond is C/i, where 'i' is its current yield to maturity and C the annual coupon. The change in price ΔP of a perpetual bond is given by the product of its market price, the change in the rate of interest, Δi, and the modified duration of the bond. For a perpetual bond duration is given by $D = (1+i)/i$, and modified duration by $D/(1+i)$, which simplifies to $1/r$. Thus $\Delta P = P * \Delta i * MD$, which can be expressed $\Delta P = (C/i) * \Delta i * (1/i) = \Delta i * (C/i^2)$. Substituting in $\Delta P\text{-}C=0$ gives $\Delta i * (C/i^2) - C = 0$ which simplifies to $\Delta i = i^2$ as the condition under which $\Delta P=C$ and is Keynes's square rule.

From (13.1) and (13.2) we obtain $i = i^2$ as the condition under which $P = C$ and is Keynes's square rule.[5] Thus, for increases in the rate of interest equal to the increase in the rate of inflation to leave capital values unchanged they must be equal to i^2. Thus, the Fisher relation will hold only for an increase in the rate of inflation $p = i^2$, but this only keeps capital values constant and does not provide any adjustment for inflation. For the Fisher relation to hold, interest rates must rise by more than this, but this means that capital value will fall further, etc., which illustrates Keynes's point that in general it is impossible for a simple adjustment in the interest rate to keep purchasing power unchanged once the impact of the interest rate on the value of existing stocks of assets is taken into account. There is thus no reason to expect the Fisher relation to hold, as has indeed turned out to be the case empirically.

But, Keynes's calculation also served another purpose. It can also be represented as the "breakeven" point for the two opposing forces working on the value of the bond, that is, the point at which the change in capital value is just offset by the opposite change in interest income from reinvesting coupon interest at the higher or lower interest rate over the remaining time to maturity of the bond. This point is called the "duration" of the bond in the finance literature. The lower the rate of interest, the higher the bond's "duration", and the longer it takes to recover the fall in capital values from the increased reinvestment earnings due to higher reinvestment interest rates. At a 3 per cent nominal interest rate, duration is 34.33 years, at 2 per cent to 51 years. At 1 percent it is 101 years. Keynes's explanation of the liquidity trap is based on this relation. If an investor has to wait 101 years to recover the capital loss due to a rise in the rate of interest equal to 1 per cent squared, which is only an absolute increase in rates from 1 per cent to 1.01 per cent, it seems rational for the investor to decide that it would be better not to hold bonds, but to hold money instead since the loss in holding money is only the interest rate, while the loss from holding the bond is the much larger decline in capital value. Thus, on Keynes's definition the liquidity trap will occur whenever investors expect interest rates to rise by more than the square of the current interest rate, for they will then prefer to hold money rather than bonds. Thus Keynes's statement that the lower the rate of interest, the more likely that liquidity trap will be sprung, since the longer it takes to recoup the capital loss through higher interest earnings and thus the higher the probability there will be a reversal in interest rates.

Since liquidity preference is a relative concept, it should be clear that the existence of a liquidity trap at high interest rates cannot be ruled out. At 8 per cent, duration is 13.5 years and modified duration, 12.5 years. A rise in the rate of interest to 0864 would produce a fall in the price of a par 8 per cent consol of 100*12.4*.0064 = €8 which is exactly the coupon value. An expectation of a rise in interest rates of more than 8 per cent then should lead to a decision to sell bonds for money. If this expectation is generally held by investors then there will be no buyers of bonds other than the monetary authority and it will be impossible to change interest rates by buying bonds from the public since there is perfectly elastic supply at prevailing interest rates. The expected percentage rise in interest is however, twice as high as in the case of 4 per cent rates. However, these should be judged relative to recent changes in bond prices. If 8 per cent lies within two standard deviations from the mean of rate changes over the recent past, then it would be just as rational to remain liquid at 8 per cent as it was at 4 per cent in similar conditions of volatility. It is clear that the liquidity trap depends on expectations of future bond prices, and that expectations will be based on recent volatility of rates.

In a volatile rate environment, it will become more difficult to use changes in interest rates to influence the demand for money since they will have to be larger in order to produce an impact.[6]

It is also important to remember, as noted above, Keynes's argument refers primarily to the impact on long rates, or more precisely on the range of rates of assets of different maturities as represented by the yield curve. Of course, the argument given above concerns the impact of changes in short rates on the prices of assets of all maturities. Thus, Keynes notes that "If the monetary authority deals only in short-term debts, we have to consider what influence the price, actual and prospective, of short-term debts exercises on debts of longer maturity" (JMK:VII, p. 206).

Thus, the existence of the Keynesian liquidity trap does not depend on the absolute level of the interest rate, but on the size of the value of the square of the interest rate relative to the historic volatility of the interest rate and the uniformity of expectations concerning increases in interest rates in excess of this rate. It is also clear that it does not depend on the lack of credibility of the central bank in producing inflation, for even if the central bank's pledge to raise the inflation rate were credible and believed by the public, it would also have to induce the credible belief that there would be no upward shift in the entire yield curve as a result. As a result, Keynes recommends "Perhaps a complex offer by the central bank to buy and sell at stated prices gilt-edged bonds of all maturities, in place of the single bank rate for short-term bills, is the most important practical improvement which can be made in the technique of monetary management" (ibid.) capable of overcoming the liquidity trap.

Although investors in Japanese securities may believe in the ability of the central bank to set the rate of growth of the money supply and/or its short-term policy rate, they certainly do not believe that the central bank can control the shape of the yield curve. This would be particularly improbable given the changes that have taken place in ten-year rates since the Japanese Central Bank adopted its zero rate policy. Thus, even if investors have perfect confidence in the Central Bank's ability to increase the rate of inflation, the existence of a zero bid rate means that there is a zero probability of a further fall in short rates, making the expected value of the change in short rates positive. As long as there is a uniform market expectation that interest rates would rise by more than the square of themselves, the expectation is that long rates will rise by more than this and the failure of the economy to respond to monetary policy will remain (although the actual existence of a liquidity trap could only be confirmed if the Central Bank did attempt to influence long rates).

From a Keynesian point of view, Krugman's policy cannot work for a credible central bank policy for inflation would have to create perfect certainty not only that short term interest rates would not rise, but that the yield curve would remain stationary. In current Japanese conditions it is extremely unlikely that such conditions could be created. Government bond issuance has increased dramatically along with the rising government expenditure packages that have been introduced in response to the slump. The largest proportion (around 40 per cent of existing stocks) of these bonds have gone into the portfolios of government agencies such as the Trust Fund Bureau (TFB). The next largest proportion went into bank portfolios (around a quarter). This shift was facilitated by what is called the "dual flight to quality" that has occurred in the post bubble period. in which the weakness of the banks caused households to shift from risky bank deposits to government guaranteed postal deposits (and the newly introduced ten-year compound interest bearing savings accounts) which provided the funds for the TFB which invests in government securities. The weakness in the corporate sector caused a sharp fall in bank lending to the private sector, and banks increased their holdings of government securities in their reduced balance sheets.

In the end of 1998 and early 1999 two important structural changes took place which are quite independent of the credibility of the Central bank's inflation policy. First, as part of Japan's financial liberalisation, banks will be required to mark their investment portfolios to market. The duration of a ten-year bond issued at a 1 per cent current yield is above 9.5 years. Any increase in long rates, such as the jump from around 1 per cent to 2.25 per cent that occurred during the last quarter of 1998 would produce a decline of around 12 per cent in the value of the 1 per cent par bonds in bank portfolios. For conditions prevailing in February 1999 it has been estimated that a 100 basis point rise in interest rates on long bonds would have produced a 15 trillion Yen capital loss for all financial holders of Japanese government bonds. It is thus likely that banks will be reducing their portfolio holdings of bonds, causing falling prices.

Further, the TFB announcement that it would reduce its purchases of securities from the 25 trillion Yen in fiscal 1998 to less than half (in January of 1999 it was only 5 trillion on an annual basis) because of maturing postal term deposits and the elimination of the requirement that postal deposits and pension contribution be held by the Bureau, concentrated the market's attention on the importance of public bond market management on supply conditions. It is quite clear that the continued financial liberalisation will reduce the holdings by government agencies, and that banks will reduce their portfolio holdings as the volatility of bond prices increases. Finally, banks will be given permission to raise funds through bond issues from the last half of fiscal 1999. All of these factors put a sustained upward pressure on term interest rates. This also means that banks will not only be unwilling to buy bonds, they will be hesitant to lend to finance private sector holdings of bonds or productive enterprise. In these conditions the market will suffer from continued fears of a steepening of the yield curve and the associated capital losses associated with holding long-term issues. Since there must be equivalence between short issues and long issues with short holding periods, this will mean continued upward pressure on short rates. Thus, the policy that the central bank would have to adopt in order to eliminate the risk of a rise in rates according to the square rule would be to peg long rates, much as was done in the US in the Second World War (see IBJ Securities, 1999). This, however, does not seem likely for a Central bank that was just granted its independence in the context of big bang liberalisation.

Clearly, in present conditions it is not the lack of a credible inflation policy, but a credible interest rate policy that is creating difficulty. As Keynes notes in relation to Fisher's recommendations of inflating out of the Great Depression:

'The stimulating effect of the expectation of higher prices is due, not to its raising the rate of interest (that would be a paradoxical way of stimulating output – in so far as the rate of interest rises, the stimulating effect is to that extent offset), but to its raising the marginal efficiency of a given stock of capital' (JMK:VII, p. 143).

That is, raising the expectation of returns on new investment relative to the rate of interest, and this requires a credible policy that interest rates will not rise along with the rate of inflation, which is to say that the Fisher relation and the quantity theory should not hold. But the failure of a higher rate of increase in the quantity of money to increase prices and the rate of interest is what Krugman calls the liquidity trap and he identifies as the cause of Japan's recession. In Japan even if the Bank of Japan could mount a credible inflation policy, there would be no guarantee of the stability of the yield curve. What is required is a credible policy to ensure increased higher rates of return on investment, which may or may not be accompanied by rising prices. In general in Japan it has not. This requires credible increases in aggregate demand. Traditionally in Japan this has come from exports. Given recent Yen strength and other structural changes in global markets this is now unlikely. What Japan needs is a credible policy of increasing the return on producing for domestic demand. From a Keynesian point of view it might be more appropriate to say that Japan is in an underemployment equilibrium with deficient aggregate demand than in a liquidity trap.

Notes

* I am grateful to Paul Davidson, Rogerio Studart, Mario Tonveronachi and Randy Wray for reactions to the argument presented here without implicating them in the final result.

1 Although it is interesting to note that interbank deposit bid rates were in fact less than zero during 1998.

2 See Joan Robinson's comment on this aspect of Hicks's Review (1937, p. 16): "There appears to be no warrant for Mr. Hicks' view... that an indefinitely great rise of prices will develop in a state where capacity is limited but available labour unemployed. It is true, as Mr. Hicks says, that when effective demand increases and the supply of money is constant, the rate of interest will rise if the supply of consumption goods is less than perfectly elastic, so that prices rise. But it will rise even if supply is perfectly elastic and prices are constant".

3 "I know of no example of it hitherto" (p. 207).

4 Keynes always notes that his argument refers to "the objective of reducing the long-term rate of interest" (p. 202) or "a determinate rate of interest or, more strictly, a determinate complex of rates of interest for debts of different maturities" (p. 205). He lists one of the reasons (in addition to the liquidity trap) why central banks have difficulty influencing the rate of interest as 'the monetary authority's own practices in limiting it willingness to deal to debts of a particular type' (p. 207), and that "owing to the unwillingness of most monetary authorities to deal boldly in debts of long term there has not been much opportunity for a test [of the liquidity trap]" (ibid.). It is thus the influence on the long-term rate of interest that is crucial, but we would now talk in terms of affecting the slope of the yield curve.

5 The duration of a par perpetual bond with a £4 coupon is 26 years. Modified duration, defined as $D/(1 + i)$, which measures the volatility of bond prices, is 25 years. The change in the price of the 4 per cent par consol is thus calculated by multiplying modified duration by the current price and the change in the bond's yield to maturity. In the case of a 16 basis point (4 basis points squared) rise in the yield from.04 to.0416, the value of the bond will fall over the year by 25*100*.0016 = £4, which is precisely the bond coupon. For any greater increase in interest rates, the fall in the bond's value will exceed the current coupon of the bond, producing net losses for the holder. If an investor expects interest rates to rise by more than the square of the current rate Keynes says the investor should prefer to hold cash rather than bonds. In such conditions, attempts to lower the rate of interest by increasing the purchase of

bonds will find ready sellers at the prevailing interest rate, and the attempts of the monetary authority to lower rates will be prevented by a "liquidity trap".

6 As rates rise, the square rule produces larger and larger absolute changes in the interest rate, and the use of modified duration to calculate the change in price becomes less and less accurate. The full calculation of the change in the bond price will require the calculation of convexity. It is interesting to note that Hicks (1939, p. 261, note 2) reproduces the square rule, and notes that it is very likely that returns will be negative, since the fall in capital values will be even greater if changes in risk are taken into account.

References

Hicks, J. (1939) *Value and Capital*, Oxford: Clarendon Press.

Hicks, J. (1965) *Capital and Growth*, Oxford: Clarendon Press.

Hicks, J. (1977) *Economic Perspectives*, Oxford: Clarendon Press.

Hicks, J. (CEII) *Collected Essays on Economic Theory, Volume II: Money, Interest and Wages*, Oxford: Blackwell, 1982.

IBJ Securities (1999), "The dual managed system of the moratorium period," IBJS Research & Reports, April/May.

Keynes, J.M. (1930) *A Treatise on Money*, Vol. II, London: Macmillan.

Keynes, J.M. (JMK:VII) *The General Theory of Employment, Interest and Money*, London: Macmillan for the Royal Economic Society, 1973.

Keynes, J.M. (JMK:XIV) *The Collected Writings of J. M. Keynes: The General Theory and After - Part II*, London: Macmillan for the Royal Economic Society, 1973.

Krugman, P. (1998), "It's baaack! Japan's slump and the return of the liquidity trap", at http://web.mit.edu/krugman/www/bpea_jp.pdf

Robinson, J. (1937) *Essays in the Theory of Employment*, London: Macmillan.

Tobin, J. (1972) "Friedman's theoretical framework", in R. Gordon (ed.), *Milton Friedman's Monetary Framework*, Chicago: University of Chicago Press.

PUBLICATION HISTORY

The editor and Anthem Press would like to kindly acknowledge the original publishers of the following essays. Permission has been sought for their inclusion in the present volume.

1. "Economic Methodology in the Face of Uncertainty: The Modelling Methods of Keynes and the Post- Keynesians," *Economic Journal,* 86, June, 1976, pp. 209–25.
2. "Post Keynesian Theory: An Overview," *Journal of Economic Education*, 14:4, Fall, 1983, pp. 32–3. 3.
3. "Evolution versus Equilibrium," *Journal of Economic Issues*, XLV:2, June, 2011, pp. 269–75.
4. "Shylock and Hamlet: Are There Bulls and Bears in the Circuit?" *Economies et Societés*, serie MP 3, 1986, pp. 11–22.
5. "The Theoretical Consequences of Economic Methodology: Samuelson's Foundations," *Metroeconomica,* 32, February, 1980, pp. 25–38.
6. "Effective Demand: Origins and Development of the Notion," in *Distribution, Effective Demand, and International Economic Relations*, ed. J.A. Kregel, London: Macmillan, 1983, pp. 50–68.
7. "Effective Demand," in *The New Palgrave: A Dictionary of Economics*, London: Macmillan, 1987, pp. 99–102.
8. "The Changing Place of Money in Keynes' Theory from the Treatise to the General Theory," in *Keynesian Theory, Planning Models and Quantitative Economics: Essays in Memory of V. Maramma*, Vol. I, eds. G. Gandolfo and F. Marzano, Milan: A. Giuffrè, 1987, pp. 97–114.
9. "The Multiplier and Liquidity Preference: Two Sides of the Theory of Effective Demand," in *The Foundations of Keynesian Analysis*, ed. A. Barrère, London: Macmillan, 1988, pp. 231–50.
10. "Money, Expectations and Relative Prices in Keynes' Monetary Equilibrium," *Economie Appliquée,* 36:3, 1982, pp. 449–65.
11. "Irving Fisher, Great-grandparent of the General Theory," *Cahiers d'Economie Politique,* 14–15, 1988, pp. 59–68.
12. "Capital and Income in the Theory of Investment and Output: Irving Fisher and John Maynard Keynes," in *The Economics of Irving Fisher: Reviewing the Scientific Work of a Great Economist*, eds. Hans-E. Loef and Hans G. Monissen, E. Elgar: Cheltenham, 1999, pp. 271–83.

13. "Queries about Coincidences and Correlations Between Fisher and Keynes, the Gibson Paradox and the Idea of Duration," Paper Presented at the '(Dis)occupazione e Moneta: variazioni su temi Keynesiani a sessant'anni dale General Theory' Seminar, Turino, Fondazione Einaudi, 6–7 December, 1996.
14. "Fisher's Relation Purchasing Power Parity and the Interest Rate Parity Theorem," UMKC Financial Macro Class Handout, 1999.
15. "Aspects of a Post Keynesian Theory of Finance," *Journal of Post Keynesian Economics*, 21:1, Fall, 1998, pp. 113–37.
16. "Keynes's Influence on Modern Economics: Some Overlooked Contributions of Keynes's Theory of Finance and Economic Policy," in *The Return to Keynes*, eds. B. Bateman, T. Hirai, and M. C. Marcuzzo, Cambridge, MA: Harvard University Press, 2010.
17. "Instability, Volatility and the Process of Capital Accumulation," in *Economic Theory and Social Justice*, eds. G. Gandolfo and F. Marzano, London: Macmillan, 1998, pp. 149–67.
18 "Rational Spirits and the Post Keynesian Macrotheory of Microeconomics," *de Economist*, 135:4, 1987, pp. 519–31.
19. "The Theory of Value, Expectations and Chapter 17 of the General Theory," in *A Second Edition of the General Theory*, eds. G. C. Harcourt and P. Riach, London: Routledge, 1996, pp. 251–72.
20. "Keynes and the New Keynesians on the Role of Uncertainty and Information," in *Nouvelles Perspectives de la Macroéconomie, Mélange en l'honneur du Doyen Alain Barrère*, ed. G. Grellet, Paris: Publications de la Sorbonne, 1995, pp. 209–20.
21. "Keynesian Stabilisation Policy and Post-War Economic Performance," in *Explaining Economic Growth Essays in Honour of Angus Maddison*, eds. E. Szirmai, B. van Ark, and D. Pilat, Amsterdam: Elsevier, 1993, pp. 429–45.
22. "Was Keynes's Monetary Policy, à outrance in the Treatise, the Model for ZIRP and QE?" in *Keynesian Reflections: Effective Demand, Money, Finance, and Policies in the Crisis*, eds. T. Hirai, M. C. Marcuzzo, and P. Mehrling, New York: Oxford University Press, 2013.
23. "Krugman on the Liquidity Trap: Why Inflation Won't Bring Recovery in Japan," *Economia*, 1:1, Rio de Janeiro, 2000, reprinted *Essays in Honour of Augusto Graziani*, eds. Richard Arena and Neri Salvadori, Aldershot, England: Ashgate Publishing, 2004, pp. 225–38.

INDEX

Page numbers in **bold** refer to tables and figures in **exhibit**.

www.ingramcontent.com/pod-product-compliance
Ingram Content Group UK Ltd.
Pitfield, Milton Keynes, MK11 3LW, UK
UKHW041830100926
8556IPUK00002B/105

9 781839 990335